The Liberatio

Berg French Studies

General Editor: John E. Flower

ISSN: 1354-3636

The Liberation of France

Image and Event

Edited by

H. R. Kedward and Nancy Wood

BERG PUBLISHERS

Oxford / Washington, D.C.

First published in 1995 by
Berg Publishers Limited
Editorial offices:
150 Cowley Road, Oxford, OX4 1JJ, UK
13590 Park Center Road, Herndon, VA 22071, USA

Library of Congress Cataloging-in-Publication Data

A catalogue record for this book is available from the Library of Congress.

British Library Cataloguing-in-Publication Data

A catalogue record for this book is available from the British Library.

Cover Design based on a poster produced by Katy Bignell
Original photographs from BDIC.

ISBN 1 85973 082 5 (Cloth)
1 85973 087 6 (Paper)

Printed in the United Kingdom by WBC Book Manufacturers, Bridgend,
Mid-Glamorgan.

Contents

Contents

Contents

Editors' Preface

It could well be argued that the identity of contemporary France is rooted in the history of Vichy and the Resistance in the same way that nineteenth century France was rooted in the Revolution of 1789. If that seems too bold a claim it must at least be granted that French republicanism today could not be defined without detailed reference to the Resistance, and that controversy about Vichy and collaboration has grown and not diminished with time. In both respects the Liberation of France in 1944 is a pivotal image and event.

To explore the complexities of the Liberation, and to commemorate the year of its fiftieth anniversary, an interdisciplinary conference was held at the University of Sussex in April 1994. The aim was to present new research by scholars writing in English and there was a deliberate mix of age and attitudes as well as approach. This book grew out of the conference and retains the same diversity, and also the same commitment of historians, literary experts and media specialists to open the subject of the Liberation to close conceptual analysis. What did the Liberation represent? How has it been constructed in French public memory? How can its conflictual images best be interrogated? Is there a need to demythologize the event? Whatever the most probing question may be, the result of so many different approaches is to expose the inadequacy of any one history, image or interpretation of the Liberation.

Plurality there must be, but not just any multiplicity of images. The structure of the book is designed to raise fundamental questions about historiography, representation and memory. In parts 1 to 4 we argue that local and specific Resistance narratives, questions of gender, an open confrontation with the problems of the *épuration* (purges), and neglected perspectives of France overseas, must all be interwoven if an understanding of the Liberation is to be achieved. In the process a large number of rival images, meanings and memories are evoked. In part 5 this contestation and ambiguity, which has been evident throughout, is made explicit.

The experiences of the Occupation and the Liberation constitute a past which is permanently present in post-War France and their legacy functions more than ever as a site of intense social contestation. Nowhere is this more evident than in scholarly activity and debate itself. If the Liberation currently occupies pride of place in a re-imagined past whose contradictions continue to impact on the present, then the question arises as to how best to represent them in any scholarly enterprise. How can the force of such contradictions be investigated and articulated, all the while resisting the neutralizing and relativising thrust which a multiplicity of perspectives seems to entail?

One key premise of this book is that the Liberation established a dual primacy of assertiveness and doubt – a tension which found expression in a diversity of political, cultural and social arenas. Yet while all our contributors recognize the Liberation's manifold dimensions and ambivalent status, there is no unanimity of critical perspective or uniformity of methodologies. This is evident, for example, in the contrast between authors who are concerned to strengthen or improve what might be called a Resistance perspective and those who wish to register their critical distance from it. The volume has welcomed this open – and sometimes covert – clash of opinions as one which can best stimulate research and discussion. Moreover, many chapters often and unexpectedly resonate with each other, demonstrating the overlapping dimensions of the Liberation as event and image, and the attendant value and necessity of interdisciplinary studies of this period.

Today, there is a constant stream of publications subjecting Vichy, the Resistance and the Liberation to new and ever more detailed scrutiny. Many of the most interesting 'commemorations' of the Liberation have emerged as this book was being written and edited, and their insights are therefore insufficiently acknowledged. Of all recent research, we would like to mention two scholars in particular: the historian Henry Rousso, whose groundbreaking work in *Le Syndrome de Vichy* (1987) inaugurated French 'memory studies' of this period, and the philosopher Alain Brossat, whose recent books *Les Tondues, Un carnaval moche* (1992) and *Libération, fête folle* (published in 1994 after this book had been written), have opened up the possibility of a 'semiotics' of the Liberation, especially receptive to interdisciplinary perspectives. We are well aware that these two approaches by no means coexist comfortably or unproblematically, but we believe that together they have helped to map out the main contours of the field and to highlight the key stakes of contemporary debate.

We are delighted also to acknowledge the research time and skills given by all the contributors to both the conference and the book, and we wish to thank them for their generosity. As a collective venture it could not have been achieved without their enthusiasm for interaction and the sharing of insights and discoveries. We were fortunate, too, to have financial backing from the University of Sussex through the School of European Studies and a much-appreciated subsidy from the Association for the Study of Modern and Contemporary France. Finally, family, friends and colleagues always contribute more than they know and we are sure that all the authors represented here would echo our individual thanks. The book is dedicated to you all.

Roderick Kedward and Nancy Wood

Illustrations

List of Abbreviations

AAOF	Archives de l'Afrique Occidentale Française
AD	Archives Départementales
AEF	Afrique Équatoriale Française
AMGOT	Allied Military Government of Occupied Territory
AML	Amis du Manifeste et de la Liberté
AN	Archives Nationales
ANSOM	Archives Nationales, Section Outre-Mer, Aix-en-Provence
AOF	Afrique Occidentale Française
BDIC	Bibliothèque de Documentation Internationale Contemporaine
CDJC	Centre de Documentation Juive Contemporaine
CDLR	Ceux de la Résistance
CFLN	Comité Français de la Libération Nationale
CGT	Confédération Générale du Travail
CHRD	Centre d'Histoire de la Résistance et de la Déportation, Lyon
CLCF	Comité de Libération du Cinéma Français
CNE	Comité National des Écrivains
CNR	Conseil National de la Résistance
CPL	Comité Parisien de Libération
CRS	Compagnies Républicaines de Sécurité
FFI	Forces Françaises de l'Intérieur
FFL	Forces Françaises Libres
FLN	Front de Libération Nationale
FTP(F)	Francs-Tireurs et Partisans Français
GMR	Groupes Mobiles de Réserve
IMT	International Military Tribunal, Nuremberg
JO	*Journal Officiel*
LDH	Ligue des Droits de l'Homme
LICP	Ligue Internationale des Combattants de la Paix
LVF	Légion des Volontaires Français contre le Bolchevisme

MM	Musée Mémorial, Caen
MOI	Main d'Œuvre Immigrée
MRP	Mouvement Républicain Populaire
MUR	Mouvements Unis de la Résistance
NRF	*Nouvelle Revue Française*
OAS	Organisation Armée Secrète
OCM	Organisation Civile et Militaire
OS	Organisation Spéciale
OSE	Œuvre (or Organisation) de Secours aux Enfants
PCA	Parti Communiste Algérien
PCF	Parti Communiste Français
PPA	Parti Populaire Algérien
PRL	Parti Républicain de la Liberté
RDA	Rassemblement Démocratique Africain
SD	Sicherheitsdienst
SFIO	Section Française de l'Internationale Ouvrière
SiPo	Sicherheitspolizei
STO	Service du Travail Obligatoire
UFF	Union des Femmes Françaises
UJC	Union des Jeunesses Communistes
UJRE	Union des Juifs pour la Résistance et l'Entraide
WRI	War Resisters' International

Introduction: 'Ici commence la France libre'

H.R. Kedward

Mont Mouchet, which rises at the northern end of the Margeride, due west from Le Puy, has none of the dramatic scenery associated with the Maquis citadels of Les Glières and the Vercors. Densely clad with pines, and beech woods fringing the base, it has an extensive rounded summit with rolling views over the Auvergne. In early summer there are clumps of huge dark violets, and carpets of wild narcissi. It was here that almost 3,000 *maquisards* were mobilized at the end of May 1944. Unlike the Alpine plateaux there were easy routes for dispersal. Many who came from the urban centre of Clermont-Ferrand remarked on the stillness and beauty of the Margeride, but within days they were exchanging machine-gun fire with a German unit which attacked their position early on 2 June. After several hours of fighting, a small but well-armed Maquis relief-group surprised the German forces from the rear, close to the village of Paulhac, and towards five o'clock in the afternoon the Germans retreated into their lorries and took the route towards Mende. Shortly afterwards the *maquisards* descended into Paulhac, and the villagers returned from their hiding places in the woods. A celebratory banner was hastily prepared and erected at the entrance to the village. It read: 'Ici commence la France libre.' It was four days before the Normandy landings, but it might have been forty; no one was confidently predicting the date of an Allied 'débarquement' which seemed never to come. Eight days later the Germans returned in force to take Mont Mouchet and exact reprisals on the surrounding villages.[1]

There are other examples of premature, or abortive, liberations in the months from June to August 1944, but the Paulhac banner was a potent signifier for the whole Liberation of France, whatever the setbacks that followed. '*Ici* commence...' indicates a specific place, an encounter, a boundary, a crossing, a spatial beginning. The Liberation of France is first and foremost about territory, specific territory. It is about the fight for territory, and the reclaiming of territory. On 2 June 1944 this territory begins at Paulhac-en-Margeride. On 6 June 1944 it begins on the Normandy beaches; on 8 June, momentarily and tragically, it begins at Tulle in the Corrèze; on 15 August on the rugged coastline of Provence. It had already begun earlier, in November 1942 in Algeria, and in October 1943 in Corsica.

The banner at Paulhac images the liberated territory in national terms. It is not 'Ici commence l'Auvergne libre' but '...*la France* libre', though there is a certain zonal echo in the sense that it triumphantly displaced notices which had proclaimed 'zone libre' at the crossing points of the demarcation line. It signified a new frontier, the crossing into a France that was genuinely free. It is true that the return of the Germans soon made it ironic, but by contrast 'zone libre' had been fraudulent from the start. It is also true that the image of 'la France libre' encodes a specific and selective identity. Detailed Resistance accounts of the Liberation show that the hopes and disappointments, the successes and the failures, reinforced the sense that a minority of French men and women were carrying the onus of liberation on their own shoulders. Those who had chosen to become Resisters embodied selective aspects of French history; they were disaggregated; they have often remained anonymous in the national history. They have their own specificities of motivation and organization. And yet they claimed to stand for the whole. At Annonay, in the Ardèche, the scene of another premature liberation, four days after Paulhac, the local Resistance ran off two editions of a broadsheet which they entitled *Gazette du Comité de la libération nationale*.[2] It was the same universalizing claim. Was this small paper-making town really the epicentre of the national struggle? Relatively speaking, yes: so too was Paulhac, Lyon, Vassieux-en-Vercors, Paris, Albertville, and every other location of Resistance activity. In terms of events, each Resistance locality had its own liberation (sometimes twice); each Resistance group its own liberational struggle. In terms of image, each local liberation proclaimed the 'libération nationale'. Liberation of French territory in 1944 is therefore pluralistic but unitary; its relative chronology, as a series of local events, is symbolically represented as the Liberation of France. However atomized or localized, the Resistance never really imaged itself in any other way.

The unitary image does not foreclose research, or preempt controversy. Studies of the Liberation are complicated and sustained by the unending arguments about agency. These are due not only to rivalry between different strands within the Resistance narrative but also to the pivotal role of the allied *débarquements*. Tears welled up in the eyes of Pierre Boyer, a grain merchant in Saint-Affrique in the Aveyron, when he described the rows of American, British and Canadian graves in Normandy. He had been a *maquisard* at the liberation of Montpellier, but in 1991 he stated unequivocally that the French only participated in the national liberation. Ultimately, he said, they owed everything to the invading Allies.[3] And what of the debts, less often recognized, to the troops from Algeria, Morocco, West and Equatorial Africa, and more distant French colonies, who fought in the liberating armies? The overwhelming case that France could only be liberated by invasion has never seriously been contested, and it is certainly not the intention of this book to do so, though the huge cost in French civilian lives, as well as Allied military lives, has to be confronted.

The people of France had been expecting the Allies ever since the liberation of Corsica in October 1943. There is a great deal of evidence from the letters intercepted by Vichy's 'Contrôle postal' that many French people imaged the Liberation quite simply as the Allies arriving one day and driving out the Occupiers, and careful use of this admittedly flawed source would suggest that a majority who expressed an opinion favoured such a liberation from outside over one dependent on a period of armed conflict within.[4] 'Liberation by whom?' is not just a post-War controversy about the relative merits of Allied invasion, on the one hand, and arming the Maquis, on the other; it was an issue which occupied people's minds long before the summer of 1944. The arguments live on, and show no signs of abating. This is necessarily so. The Resistance narrative must surely be enriched by researching a plurality of agencies. Through such research it becomes multilinear, and this is much closer to the evidence on the ground. What cannot be lost, because it was manifest throughout, is the image of a unitary 'libération nationale' with all the promises of a new beginning.

In his celebrated, but Delphic, message to the internal Resistance in June 1942, General de Gaulle claimed that 'le peuple français' had condemned both the pre-War Republic and the Vichy regime, and he added, 'Tandis qu'il s'unit pour la victoire, il s'assemble pour une révolution.'[5] Wresting the concept and promise of revolutionary change away from Vichy's 'Révolution nationale' was one of the major recuperative aims of Resistance writing and action, inside and outside France. The term 'libération' remained a stronger mobilizing concept than the term 'révolution', but the two shared many column inches in the clandestine press as if they were synonymous. Liberation was to be a new dawn: 'Ici *commence…*'

Fifty years on, with the discourse of revolution under continuous deconstruction, and revolutionary studies diverted from the mainstream of academic enterprise, there are few, if any, new works on 1944 as a revolutionary situation. And yet, paradoxically, the criteria for judging the liberational potential of 1944 are wider than ever. Revolutionary studies are flanked and even challenged by the growth of resistance and liberational studies. Common ground is being discovered across historical time, geographical space and intellectual disciplines, in which previously discreet patterns of resistance and liberation can be conceptualized together. These include: the struggle against any form of repressive rule; day-to-day strategies of peasant refusal, named by James C. Scott 'weapons of the weak';[6] gender, sexual and racial liberation movements; working-class industrial action, and the politics of the dispossessed. This is the soil in which theories of radical opposition and change currently take root. It signals the return to a more Utopian understanding of revolutionary forces, and one freed from the energizing, but constraining certainties of historical necessity.

The sheer extension of resistance studies accentuates the demands made on any particular liberational event and multiplies the potential images of liberation, both prospective and retrospective. Is liberation divisible? How radical is a new beginning? Did the Liberation of France radically change the lives of women, colonial subjects, or ethnic minorities? Or, are the expectations implicit in these questions anachronistic? In what sense was the *épuration* liberational? The Liberation, one of the pre-eminent 'lieux de mémoire' within the landscape of French history, and one where the two revolutionary traditions of the 'Marseillaise' and the 'Internationale' appear to conjoin, is justifiably a site of celebration.[7] The Resistance narratives present it as a triumphal climax; and so it was, but on closer scrutiny the thrust of this narrative history, however multilinear, is dislocated by the ambiguities created by the expectations of the liberational period, by the spontaneous acts of insurgency, and by the moral issues of the *épuration*. There is a tendency in oral and written memoirs to become over-defensive at this point, or factional and accusatory.

The only Resistance narrative that seems to thrive on the events of the liberational period is the Gaullist one, a narrative of steadily evolving authority and national representation, in which the carefully chosen Resistance authorities are seen to establish control and re-establish order in the name of the provisional government and national reconciliation. Most other Resistance accounts admit to considerable problems in dealing, firstly with the turbulence and *épuration* that occurred, and secondly with the collapse of so many Resistance ideals, not least the virtual disappearance of the radical charter of the Conseil

National de la Résistance (CNR). Descriptions of power in the streets, and of threats and vengeance, which suggested anarchy in orderly minds, almost all return to the question of agency, of who was responsible: the Maquis? the urban Francs-Tireurs et Partisans (FTP)? the Communists? the *milices patriotiques*? the thirteenth-hour resisters? nameless 'voyous'? named individuals? Establishing, or in many cases denying, agency continues to be the aim of the narratives. But it remains deeply unsatisfactory, and suggests an embarrassed exculpation. Equally problematic is the longer-term search for those responsible for the collapse of radical hopes and ideals. Ambiguity and ambivalence dominate in both these domains, frustrating linear causality and explanation.

It is at this point that the growing theorization of resistance and liberational studies can offer an approach which de-centres linear, even multilinear, narratives and embraces a process of analysis in the manner of Foucault. In *The Archaeology of Knowledge* (1969) Foucault sought to replace conventional intellectual history with a process which he (stipulatively) calls 'archaeology'. He states that such a process 'labours to untie all those knots that historians have patiently tied: it increases differences, blurs lines of communication and tries to make it more difficult to pass from one thing to another'. This enables differences and discontinuities to emerge, and emphasizes non-identities, internal fractures and ambiguities. He was seeking mainly to transform the treatment of discursive formations, such as texts, sets of ideas, intellectual positions and arguments, all of which have been treated by historians as documents to be unravelled, with the stress on authorship and agency. Archaeology, he claims, would treat them as monuments, separating them from the question of agency. The archaeologist, he says, digs in all directions, in spaces liberated from the constraints of agency, in sites, each with its own specificity, unearthing identities which clash and overlap.[8]

Foucault's concepts, liberational in themselves, have run into problems of over-extensive use, but his process is ideally suited for the period of the Liberation, not least because it allows an exploration of carnival theory, one of the central theoretical constructs of resistance and liberational studies. Carnival is more and more seen as an archetypal and recurrent pattern of public behaviour, ritualized in the Middle Ages and acted out as ritual ever since, but going back well beyond Christian festivals to patterns of controlled, or permitted, inversion in Greek and Roman times. Rendered colloquially as 'the world turned upside down', it has been rigorously conceptualized, notably by Mikhail Bakhtin, so that its most prominent elements can be generalized across a diversity of historical situations.[9] It entails: a transient overturning of power relationships; generational inversion; social inversion; transgressive behaviour; the displacement of high by low culture; a world of disguised or indeterminate identities; animalism; sensuousness, and violent male sexuality. Equally important is the act of closure, the end of carnival and a rejection of disequilibrium, followed by a return to what is held to be order, normality and balance.

The sense that carnival theory makes of the liberational period in France is persuasive. It is not a new approach, but it is only in the last few years that historians have seriously begun to explore its relevance. One such, who cannot quite bring himself to use the word, is Jean-Marie Guillon, whose work on the liberation of the Var is a rich evocation of liberation ambiguities, with more than a hint of ritualized euphoria and violence. He describes the Liberation in the department as 'une révolution de quelques jours', an enactment of collective exaltation, excess, transgression and inversion of the social order. 'La Libération,' he says, 'est une fête', in which youth is omnipresent, inverting the hierarchy of age, and exerting the kind of pressure of numbers which give young *maquisards* or young *milices patriotiques* the characteristics of the nineteenth century 'classe dangereuse'.[10] Much of his evidence can be used to draw attention to an aspect of carnival which figures constantly in Daniel Fabre's classic analysis of *La Fête en Languedoc*: the merging of identities, the coming together and intermingling of roles, which traditionally is achieved by masks, and at the Liberation was the product of overflowing crowds, the parades of known and unknown liberators, and the bewildering new emblems of authority.[11] Confusions of identity at the Liberation were widely reported to have been both exhilarating and disturbing.[12]

Alain Brossat has no difficulty is using the concept of carnival for his study of 'les femmes tondues' and his subtitle 'un carnaval moche' signals not only his own contempt for the acts of the 'tondeurs' but also the element of barbarism within 'fêtes populaires' which has traditionally ritualized violence against women. He follows Henry Rousso in seeking explanations of the 'tontes' by, to quote Foucault, 'digging in all directions', in cultural history, philosophy, anthropology and psychology, and in one highly perceptive footnote he places the 'tontes' in 'the ambiguous space which exists between war and peace...in a "non-lieu"'.[13] This is just the kind of discontinuity privileged by Foucault, and indeed the experience of the Liberation as a kind of unreality, a vacuum in time, a highly charged present without past or future, a period of dislocation or hyperaction, occurs repeatedly in both written and oral memoirs. All the ambiguities that are found in carnival *and* in the period of the Liberation would be revealed by Foucault's process of 'archaeology'. It would not matter that the festivities and the *épuration* took different, or similar, forms in different places, nor that the shaving of women's heads occurred in some towns and not others. The essence is to move away from the search for specific agents and to place the events outside the resistance narrative. Carnival theory re-sites the liberational 'liesse' and 'débordement' within the *longue durée* of cultural ambiguities and ritual behaviour, not least in the field of gender relations. Such a re-siting does not replace the resistance accounts, but it sits provocatively alongside. It is an irritant, and provokes indignant responses. It is difficult, to quote Foucault once more, to pass from one to the other, still more to make them mutually inclusive.

Using the insights of carnival theory enables the historian to put the questions of agency into a perspective which the archives largely confirm. Any licensed turbulence implicates the authorities as well as the revellers. The way is open to investigate a much wider social complicity than many embarrassed resistance accounts are prepared to consider. Guillon, referring to the few examples of 'femmes tondues' in the Var, concludes that the acts were another expression of the kind of licensed violence evident in the nineteenth century charivari of youth. Did the Resistance authorities, whom he calls 'les politiques', disapprove of these acts? 'They say so today', he writes, 'but in fact it was a reality which did not shock many people at the time.' He can find no trace of disapproval in the local documents of the period, though such disapproval can be found elsewhere.[14]

As for the collapse of revolutionary hopes, and the perceived failures of the Liberation to effect the transformations in politics and society that the Resistance appeared to have promised, there seems a *prima facie* case for talking about the end of carnival. The re-emergence of old social élites, the reassertion of patriarchal values, the return to old political rivalries, the reaffirmation of empire, all point to the resilience of ideas of 'normality' at the very time when inversion and transgression established their temporary rule. There has rarely been, even in times of actual carnival, so much public investment in *both* celebration *and* measures to limit its effects. The satirists, in fiction and in cinema, feast on the discomfiture of the resistance narrative in explaining these contradictory pressures. Revisionist historians pounce on what they see as evidence of Resistance hypocrisy. A combination of Foucault and carnival theory may seem too detached for some, and too determinist for others, but it avoids satire, cynicism and revisionism, and opens up the study of the Liberation to the ambiguities of the time.

Unsurprisingly in four years (1940–44) of dramatic reversals of fortune and inversions of power, the theory of carnival cannot be confined to the Liberation. Louis Malle and Patrick Modiano stumbled on a different carnival scenario in their film of *Lacombe Lucien* (1974): the carnival of collaboration. Lucien, the young peasant outsider, is first an onlooker, then a participant in the cynical revelry of the French *gestapistes*. His world is turned upside down, through drink, the flattering attention of Betty, the instant sex with Marie, and the delinquency of his licensed power. He becomes a strutting 'roi du carnaval', theatrically dressed in comic clothes (*pantalon golf*), brandishing his gun and the magical words 'police allemande'. Social transgression is there throughout: he has the bourgeois and stuffy Monsieur Horn to taunt and dominate, and his cultivated daughter France to assault and seduce in a mix of brutality and tenderness which can be seen in the end to excite her own sexuality; there is derision for the dignified image of Pétain, used as target practice; the destruction of the life and property of the country doctor, and the humiliation by Lucien of Monsieur Horn's hypocritical landlord.[15]

Local accounts of the strutting and bravado of collaborators, both male and female, make Malle and Modiano's portrait almost a documentary. Collaboration was a protean phenomenon, and Resisters were not unaware of its diversity. But from 1942 onwards they developed a single response: collaborators would be punished. In this perspective the Liberation, well before the return to so-called normality, was a closure. It ended the Occupation; it ended the inversionary world of a Lacombe Lucien; it extinguished the collaborationist vitality of a Brasillach and the opportunism of a Luchaire; it closed down the torture chambers of the Milice; it brought an end to the 'New Order', to the 'New Europe', and to the 'Révolution nationale'. The mentality of closure was widespread and needs far more analysis. Against the collaborators the insistence on closure was fiercely judgemental, and the extent of people's anger at the perceived insufficiency of the *épuration* still has to be fully researched. The *épuration* cannot simply be seen as negative: it was widely stated in the liberation press that a positive new beginning could only be made if the purging of collaboration was complete. The Liberation Committee of the Hérault, for example, which was far from revolutionary and had opposed all acts of unregulated vengeance, was hostile to any softening of the *épuration*. On 31 October 1945, over a year after the Liberation, it expressed horror at the government's proposal to close all the remaining 'camps de concentration' within France, and declared that it would lead to the release of hundreds of *miliciens* and traitors.[16] It was in the face of such unswerving moral severity that certain young, and not so young, right-

wing intellectuals promoted a vogue for satire and iconoclasm after
the first enthusiasms of the Liberation were over.

The Liberation was a complex amalgam of opening and closure. It
looked backwards as well as forwards, and felt it necessary to do so.
In the private sphere, scores of Resisters, particularly women, but
many men also, closed a chapter in their own lives at the moment of
liberation. Despite all the evidence of a Resistance bandwagon onto
which people climbed, in many localities the notion of using acts of
resistance as a personal *point de départ* was equated with unseemly
careerism.[17] People, once more, went back home. The return to what
many saw as 'normality' was not just a closure of the euphoria and
inversions of the heady days of liberation, it was, before that, and
alongside it, a closure of 'les années noires'. The right that the
Liberation gave to people to see 1944 as an end as well as a beginning
must surely be more fully explored beyond the topic of *épuration*, in
order to explain the relative conservatism of the outcome within
France and the myopic reactions to stirrings of liberation within the
empire.

To call it a 'libération manquée', which it clearly was in the wider
spheres of liberational possibilities, runs the risk of underestimating the
human immensity of the struggle to close the door firmly on Nazism
and to proclaim 'Ici commence la France libre.' On 22 October 1944,
an article in the Languedoc paper *Le Volontaire* struck one of the
recurrent notes of melancholy which accompanied the refrains of
jubilation: 'For us, the civilian population of the Lozère, the war is
over...and on Sunday Mende staged its official celebration of the
liberation of the département. But some of us are sad...sad to see the
reality of the struggle so quickly forgotten.'[18] The Resistance narrative
will rightly be protective of the Liberation as a culminating event, and
wary of any image which betrays signs of forgetting. But one aim of
research must be to achieve a narrative which recognizes its
explanatory limitations. This need not be either threatening to the
memory of Resistance or a denial that the Liberation of France should
remain a privileged 'lieu de mémoire'. The act of stepping outside the
narrative, like the process of analogy and allusion, and even
contestation, allows the event to be creatively re-sited. This can
ultimately threaten only those who operate the mechanism of closure,
not within liberation, but against it.

Notes

Unless stated otherwise, the place of publication is Paris.

1. Gilles Lévy and Francis Cordet, *A nous Auvergne*, Presses de la Cité, 1981, pp.222–65.
2. The dates of the broadsheet were 10 and 17 June. Bibliothèque Nationale, Réserve G.1470 (622).
3. H.R. Kedward, *In Search of the Maquis*, Oxford, Oxford University Press, 1993, p.256.
4. Archives Départementales, Aude, M2 656, SCT synthèse, 25 December 1943.
5. Charles de Gaulle, *Mémoires de Guerre. L'Appel 1940–1942*, Plon, 1954, p.678.
6. James C. Scott, *Weapons of the Weak. Everyday forms of Peasant Resistance*, New Haven, Yale University Press, 1985. See also Ranajit Guha, *Elementary Aspects of Peasant Insurgency in Colonial India*, Delhi, Oxford University Press, 1983; and H.R. Kedward, 'La Résistance 1940–42: quelques domaines de la théorie', in *La Résistance et les Français*, Toulouse, Université de Toulouse-le Mirail, 1993, pp.43–69.
7. Pierre Nora (ed.), *Les Lieux de mémoire*, vols.1 and 2, Gallimard, 1984–86. See also Nancy Wood, 'Memory's remains: *Les Lieux de mémoire*', *History and Memory*, vol.6, no.1, 1994, pp.123–49.
8. Michel Foucault, *The Archaeology of Knowledge*, trans. by A.M. Sheridan Smith, London, Tavistock, 1972, pp.162–70.
9. Mikhail Bakhtin, *Rabelais and his World*, trans. by H. Iswolsky, Cambridge, Mass., M.I.T., 1968.
10. Jean-Marie Guillon, 'La Libération du Var: résistance et nouveaux pouvoirs', *Les Cahiers de l'IHTP*, no.15, June 1990.
11. Daniel Fabre and Charles Camberoque, *La Fête en Languedoc*, Toulouse, Privat, 1977.
12. Guillon, 'La Libération du Var', pp.11, 15–18.
13. Alain Brossat, *Les Tondues. Un carnaval moche*, Manya, 1992, p.21. Another work by Brossat, equally imaginative, has been published since the writing of this introduction and the editing of this book. It is unquestionably the best exploration of the theme of carnival and the Liberation: Alain Brossat, *Libération, fête folle, 6 juin 1944 – 8 mai 1945: mythes et rites, ou le grand théâtre des passions populaires*, Autrement, Série Mémoires, 1994.
14. Guillon, 'La Libération du Var', p.13. For evidence of contemporary Resistance disapproval of the 'tontes', see Kedward, *In Search of the Maquis*, p.221.

15. *Lacombe Lucien*, 1974. The script by Patrick Modiano and Louis Malle was published by Gallimard in the same year. The final, enigmatic sequence of the film, in the depth of the countryside, with Lucien's arrest and execution announced on the screen at the very end, recall the dénouement of the carnival at Lagrasse (Aude) in 1946. Daniel Fabre's account ends, 'The group who organized the carnival let it be known that an unknown "person" was prowling in the Corbières: a hunted milicien or a maquisard unaware that the war was over...This unknown prowler...was captured after a hunt at Labastide-d'Anjou, and the effigy judged and burnt. The king-prisoner had ruled for three days.' At Vinassan (Aude) it was an effigy of Hitler that was burnt, a common occurrence at the Liberation, e.g. in the place du Martroi, Orléans. See Fabre and Camberoque, *La Fête en Languedoc*, pp.136–7, and *Le Journal de la France, les Années 40*, no.82, 1972, p.2272.
16. Séances du Comité départemental de Libération, 1945. Archives Départementales, Hérault, 138W18.
17. See, for example, the testimony of Michel Bancilhon from Aubenas (Ardèche) in Kedward, *In Search of the Maquis*, p.249.
18. *Le Volontaire*, no.3, 22 October 1944. Archives Départementales, Hérault, Journaux divers, no.397.

Part I

Resistance Narratives

– 1 –

La Bataille du rail: Unconventional Form, Conventional Image?

Martin O'Shaughnessy

When it was released at the beginning of 1946, René Clément's *Bataille du rail* received almost unanimous critical acclaim. It was not by any means the first film about the Resistance, but it seemed to be the one that people (or at least critics) had been waiting for. Raymond Jarry, writing in *Dimanche*, says 'finally we have a film which dishonours neither the Resistance nor the cinema'.[1] Denis Marion, the film critic for *Combat* tells us, '[the Resistance's story] has finally been told with the required dignity and talent.'[2] Michel Duran welcomes the film with relief: 'Finally! Here is a film about the Resistance. A real one, a worthy one.'[3] What image of resistance did the critics wish to see? Why did this particular film satisfy them? Answers begin to emerge when we examine the circumstances surrounding the making of the film.

The Comité de libération du cinéma français (CLCF), whose first venture was to organize the filming of the Paris insurrection, decided, in conjunction with the Commission militaire of the Conseil National de la Résistance (CNR) to commission several films on the Resistance.[4] One of the film makers they turned to was René Clément, then a fledgling director known for documentaries. The project was born while the war still continued. Clément and Colette Audry, his co-writer, then interviewed railway workers from across France about their resistance activities. Their initial intention was to make a purely documentary *court-métrage* but the project was expanded to become a feature-length film. The film was produced by the CLCF-sponsored Coopérative Générale du Cinéma Français, a resolutely participatory, democratic and profit-sharing body. The film's premiere took place at Chaillot on 11 January 1946 and was presided over by General de Gaulle. It toured the circuit accompanied by a travelling exhibition organized by Résistance-fer and was an overwhelming popular success, topping the box office in towns such as Lyon, Strasbourg, Nancy and Limoges. The film went on to become a national standard-bearer at a range of festivals before triumphing at Cannes. With Resistance, critical and public approval, it was a film that the French wanted to see, a film they wanted to be seen.

Yet in many ways it was an unlikely candidate, a strange hybrid, half documentary, half feature film. It has no star actors, indeed no rounded characters, and offers no romance. Its narrative is disjointed, episodic. The first section of the film has no clear chronology and a confusing geography. A large number of the cast were in fact not actors but *cheminots*. The film, unconventionally for its day, was shot entirely on location. A voice-over is sometimes heard in the early sequences and then goes silent.

The title sequence opens with dramatic music and shots of dark smoke that are enough to tell us that we are to see an action film. The actors' names are listed without prominence, in alphabetical order, followed by, in larger capitals, LES CHEMINOTS DE FRANCE. We are reminded of the film's sponsors and producers and told that 'ce film...retrace des scènes authentiques de la Résistance.' The public is immediately aware that the film is different, official, authentic. A brief text ensues that will shape our reaction to all that follows. Accompanied at first by slow mournful music, it reads:

> En juin 1940, brisant l'unité du pays, séparant les familles, les amis, bloquant derrière la ligne de démarcation l'outillage et le ravitaillement, les Allemands coupent la France en deux: d'un côté la zone occupée, de l'autre, la zone prétendue libre. Entre ces deux zones un lien encore solide mais que l'ennemi contrôle étroitement, les CHEMINS DE FER. La France doit maintenir à tout prix son unité intérieure et ses relations avec l'extérieur. Il faut que la barrière dressée par l'ennemi soit franchie par le courrier comme par les hommes. Les chemins de fer s'y emploient, première forme de leur résistance, puis ils s'enhardissent et, peu à peu, sous la terreur, au cours d'une lutte de quatre ans [at this point a muted but recognizable Marseillaise takes over], ils forgent une arme redoutable. Le jour du débarquement elle contribuera puissamment à la désorganisation des transports, à la défaite allemande, dans la bataille de la LIBERATION.

The text focusses on geographical France to the exclusion of the political, institutional or social, thus eliminating at a stroke all internal divisions. The German-imposed demarcation line is what divides France. By crossing the line the French can maintain their unity. France is present as a moral being ('la France doit...'). The *cheminots*, by subverting German control, are obeying France's imperatives. In an action film that withholds all information about individual motives, this national imperative becomes *the* motive for action, the explanation for all individual deeds that thus creates collective unity of purpose. This purpose ('forger une arme') has been constant for four years. Change in scope or scale is further smoothed over by the use of the unchanging and all-embracing 'les chemins de fer'.

The film proper commences. The first sequence confirms and reinforces the message of the preceding text; Germany is responsible for the division of France. German guards line a railway platform on the demarcation line. Recognizably Nazi music (the Horst Wessel song) accompanies these shots and, following on from the 'Marseillaise', confirms the Franco-German nature of the struggle. The next shot places us among a group of French civilians looking out from a train in silence – the crowded framing and the crossed bars on the window create a feeling of claustrophobia, imprisonment. A Frenchman looks anxiously at the approaching Germans. A girl is pulled away from the window by her mother. The papers of the nervous Frenchman are inspected. In the next shot, the passengers, crowded together, again look out the window of the train in silence as a different woman and her daughter are led away. The passengers disappear from the film without having spoken, yet much has been conveyed. The French have been constituted as an oppressed *group*. The spectator has been invited to see events not from any individual position (there are no individual point-of-view shots) but from a shared, national perspective. At the same time individual mini-dramas have been used to inject emotion (tension, fear, relief, compassion) and to draw the spectator into the film, to invite participation.

The sequence which immediately follows has no apparent relation to its predecessor. The characters are different. But we are once again on the demarcation line. A single German soldier jumps on to a train and calls for it to stop. The driver looks down at him and orders him to dismount, saying 'reste ici' (note the disrespectful *tu* form of the verb). The next shot shows the locomotive pulling to a halt in the country. A group of men (fleeing soldiers?) dismount and run off. Montage has achieved what the French army failed to do. German dominance has immediately been reversed. France has rediscovered its voice. The sequence is largely seen in long shot, sometimes from a high angle. We are apparently positioned outside the action as privileged observers, not as vicarious participators, but, due to the preceding sequences, we are able to perceive events both as a reversal of humiliation and as part of a struggle for national unity. At the same time the film reclaims its documentary credentials.

Clearer documentary form is in evidence soon after in a scene which takes place in the *poste de commandement* at the (same?) station. We hear the voice-over for the first time: 'Les cheminots...veillaient sur les TCO [trains en cours d'opération] avec une sollicitude toute particulière et ne négligeaient rien pour leur affliger des retards considérables.' The movement of a single tracking and panning camera clearly draws attention to itself as the voice-over explains how the Germans are hoodwinked: 'Ce graphique établit par avance le parcours de tous les trains prévus. Ça, c'est la théorie. La réalité, c'est cet autre graphique' (with a hint of a laugh on *réalité*). On the one hand, we seem to be watching classic documentary footage: the voice-over reminds us we are watching a film and pulls us back from over-involvement; camera movements and cutting are clearly motivated by the voice, by the need to inform. Yet on the other hand, we are invited into an intimate, conspiratorial circle which encompasses resisting rail workers, narrator and spectator but excludes the Germans, the butt of the joke. At the same time, something very important has happened which shapes our perception of all that we see. The imperfect tense has been used ('veillaient...négligeaient'). Events are released from a specific time and place and given a general focus. What we are seeing on the *ligne de démarcation* is in fact valid for the whole of France.

If we turn to one of the key sequences of the film, the one which shows the execution of the French hostages, we can gain further insight into the effect of the film's apparent avoidance of cinematic effects. The voice-over tells us, 'ici s'efface le pouvoir des mots,' before disappearing from the film. We are shown a side-on shot of the line of hostages. The last man is in close-up. His face is impassive. The film will constantly cut back to this shot as the line shrinks. The first man falls. The last man does not blink. He watches a spider. The spider, the builder of webs, of networks and thus symbol of the Resistance, drops. Another man falls. The shootings are punctuated by shrill, metallic noises from the yard. The man's eyes blink. A watching driver blows his whistle. Other drivers follow suit. As the whistling continues the camera pans to take in the whole yard. Two men remain. They link hands. The younger man falls. The last man's eyes close and blink rapidly. The sequence is without dialogue and music, yet it raises intense and complex emotions. Firstly, the use of repeated close-ups and point-of-view shots in a film which uses both exceptionally sparingly gives a special intensity to our identification with the last man as he hears his comrades fall. Secondly, the very minimalism of the sequence gives any slight gesture great power. Thirdly, the engine whistles, combined with the long panning shot of the yard, unite the entire workforce in a community of protest, a protest whose unanimity is made possible by the avoidance of words. Moreover, here as often, we see a French audience within the film itself, in this case constituted by the watching workers, which strongly cues cinema audience response. As the sequence fades to black, faint music is heard which carries the mood of mourning forward into the next shot of a Frenchman gathering information. The struggle resumes immediately despite the losses.

It is now possible to see how the film's mixed aesthetic works. The documentary features (the use of 'real' events, people and locations, voice-over, the desire to inform and instruct, the overview offered by the imperfect tense) and its avoidance of the more obvious forms of cinematic emotional manipulation, seem to offer reassurance of objectivity. Yet at the same time, the full range of techniques available to the feature film director – from camera movement to close-up and from *mise en scène* to montage – are used to draw us in emotionally and shape our reaction.

In terms of narrative structure, the film can be divided into three sections: the period of occupation, the battle after the Normandy landings, and the experience of the Liberation.

The first section of the film has no precise chronological markers although it does suggest a clear progression. Nor is it clear where events are supposed to take place, although there are strong indications that they are all located at Chalon-sur-Saône on the demarcation line. We see a series of episodes which often uses completely unfamiliar characters. The first cluster shows people and objects being smuggled across the line. The second shows various acts of sabotage. There is then a series of meetings. Finally, we see more acts of sabotage leading to threats and to the climax of this first section, the hostage scene. Progression occurs from passivity to activity, from isolation to organization, from small groups to large and from non-violent to violent action. Despite their episodic qualities, all events are linked by an implied, underlying motivation, established in the key introductory sequence; the defence of French national unity. At the same time, the German response progresses from the polite officer in the first sequence, through threats, to repression.

The second section begins with news of the Allied landings and focusses on a convoy bringing German reinforcements towards the battlefield and on French efforts to stop it. Events are now situated chronologically and geographically. Urgency is conveyed through temporal references – dates, clocks, delays, deadlines – and montage. Loose juxtaposition of episodes gives way to cross-cutting between opposing forces as tension builds. Previous shared general purpose now focusses into coordinated action towards a specific goal as the *poste de commandement* directs a range of French groups in their common task. The action continues to broaden in its scope. The railway workers are joined by the Maquis. Major battle scenes occur: first when a German *train blindé* inflicts defeat on a Maquis group; secondly when a German train laden with tanks is derailed; and thirdly when the Resistance immobilizes the rest of the German convoy which is then bombed by the Allies.

The third section is less dramatically focussed, although it continues the process of broadening, as the French general public is now reintroduced at the moment of liberation. The *poste de commandement* becomes a centre for processing a stream of information about German disintegration as we are invited to perceive events through the eyes (or rather ears) of the jubilant railway controllers. A reversal of roles occurs when the former outlaws and saboteurs try (successfully) to prevent the Germans from destroying railway equipment and when the task of rebuilding begins.

The final sequence of the film, showing the first 'liberated' train, reverses the situation we found in the very first sequence where the French were confined in claustrophobic silence under German domination. The little rural town of Saint-André – encapsulation of *la France profonde* – has been liberated by the French themselves, by the Maquis. The town is unanimous in its joy; 'Ecoutez, le premier train va partir...Il y a des drapeaux à *toutes* les portières ... *Toute* la ville est sur le quai de la gare' (my emphasis). As the news comes through, the large group round the loudspeaker in the *poste de commandement* break into smiles. Close-ups of one or two faces inject further emotion into the scene. The train is bedecked with flags. *Maquisards* hang from the sides. The train, shot from a low angle, is shown against the sky, suggesting freedom and openness. Railway workers set to repair the track. The three major groups (railwaymen, *maquisards*, the public) are brought together in one shot, as national community is fully restored. Choral music suggests a nation singing with one voice.

Although the film can be divided into different sections, each with its own shape and focus and beyond that into numerous small episodes, there are certain recurring narrative features that should be considered. Firstly, the film unfailingly foregrounds the German presence and the Franco-German nature of the struggle. The long section devoted to the German convoy, for example, starts with a shot of the Resistance leader looking at a map, cuts to the German command looking at another map, cuts to the *Transport Kommandantur*, where two German officers consider a railway map and then fades to the same map, but this time being studied by two Frenchmen. The montage and continuities of content clearly establish an equivalence between the German and French leaderships. This equivalence will be underscored by subsequent cross-cutting between the two commands.

Although the film shows several French reversals, they are always followed by an act of defiance or by a French victory. Moreover, the Germans are repeatedly hoodwinked, be it by French sabotage, trickery, disrespect or bluff. Although they occasionally use their greater force to chilling effect, they are more often than not reduced to stereotypical but ineffectual ranting. The film's moulding of essentially factual information into this image of repeated French triumph and German humiliation relies primarily on ellipsis, montage and, in the early stages, indeterminate chronology.[5] Defeat can be avenged immediately when events can be selected and juxtaposed at will. Montage and ellipsis can turn a patchy, hesitant and discontinuous struggle into a seamless growth of national revolt.

The film also repeatedly broadens the scope of resistance by a series of outward slippages. It spreads geographically by mobilizing the staff in sleepy Saint-André. To the industrial-looking yard at Chalon is added this rural world, embodying *la France profonde*. Elsewhere resistance takes on unknown dimensions as workers discover that colleagues, unbeknown to them, are *résistants*. The *cheminots* are joined by the Maquis, but also by retired railwaymen. Even those who do not actually belong to the Resistance proper are seen to participate: the passing railway worker who stops to help derail a train; the woman who sees a hidden fugitive but turns a blind eye; another woman who refuses to share a compartment with a German. The spirit of resistance motivates the French publics that are created within the film – the railway yard witnessing the executions, the *poste de commandement* hearing of liberation, the public riding the first train to freedom. Moreover, by its very structure, its mobilization of numerous anonymous characters, its temporal and – at times – spatial indeterminacy, the film allows the network of resistance to spread ever wider, while still apparently being rooted in a documented reality authenticated by the presence of the *cheminots*. Finally and perhaps most importantly, the story of the railwaymen can be seen as largely homologous with a broader national story of resistance which it thus both authenticates and is authenticated by. The steady growth from 1940, the *filières d'évasion*, the *réseaux*, the increasing coordination, the first German killed, execution of hostages, the Maquis, their heroic defeat when faced with overwhelming force, Liberation of the French by the French. All the major elements are there.

These slippages outwards are accompanied by the expected silences

– or near silences. Vichy is never mentioned although 'la zone dite libre' is evoked in the introductory sequence. This is strange, to say the least, as the action takes place on the demarcation line. People smuggled over the line disappear into a non-space. Anti-Semitism is evoked only fleetingly. More serious engagement with the problem might have required the film to explain why the Resistance's apparent ability to disrupt any train at will did not seem to have prevented trains departing for the death camps. Moreover, reference to oppression of the Jews is through a German sign where the French appears underneath as a translation. Anti-Semitism is apparently imposed from outside. The Service du Travail Obligatoire (STO) makes a brief appearance as forced labour working directly under German guns. French involvement is thus again absent. Collaboration is invoked only twice. The first time, when a sabotage is planned, one railwayman advises another to be careful of a third. The second case is more interesting. The network leader, expecting criticism for delays, remarks to his superior: 'C'est une histoire regrettable...une série de malchances et d'interventions de terroristes.' The superior, true to form, is also in the Resistance, but, perhaps unwittingly, the film has admitted the existence, as late as July 1944, of an alternative French official discourse that breaks the mood of national consensus. The above-mentioned seamless growth of resistance, allied to the silence over individual motivations, draws a veil over other non-consensual aspects of the past such as different reasons and times for joining the struggle. The film accords little or no time to the Allies while tacitly admitting their preponderant role. The one train the French derail was, famously, filmed by fourteen different cameras while the eleven remaining trains bombed by the Allies are given a few seconds of film. The final silence or near silence concerns the contribution of women to the film's action. The one word of dialogue, 'rien,' accorded to the token female Maquis member sums this up well.

We have now seen how the film creates a vision of a united French nation freeing itself from the oppressive dominance of an external enemy. Integrated with this national myth, we also find a specifically left-wing vision. The German officer class, for example, is portrayed in caricature, and combines the stereotypes of the arrogant Prussian and the ranting Nazi, while the ordinary Germans are shown in an almost favourable light. One scene shows them by the track, sunbathing, writing letters home and cooking, while an accordion plays decidedly unmilitaristic music. Furthermore, *Bataille du rail* is devoted to 'les Cheminots de France' who are present in the film as workers, not merely as Frenchmen. All their acts of sabotage depend on their skill and their knowledge of the railways. When the hostages are led away to be shot, the camera lingers on their abandoned tools, be they spanners or pens.[6] The film strictly avoids individual heroism. Only a collective effort achieves liberation. This is illustrated in a striking, visual manner on several occasions. When a water tender needs to be filled, the workers form a human chain to fulfil their task. When a rail needs to be removed, only teamwork can achieve this. Similarly, in meetings, strength comes from the collective.

This implicit collectivist and class message seems to be endorsed most fully in the final sequence. The victory train becomes a metaphor for the French nation emerging from war and heading for a future of liberation and rebuilding. It passes the spot where a railwayman sacrificed himself for the cause, and the wreck of a German train derailed by the Maquis, before finally saluting a group of *cheminots* bending together to begin reconstruction. A hammer and sickle can clearly be made out on the side of the train. The ideological message seems clear. The French people owe their salvation to the sacrifice of working people and to the internal Resistance and they will rebuild by espousing collectivist values.

Blended with this celebration of collective strength we find a more diffuse, popular Frenchness: the *réseau* leaders playing *belote* in a café; the *chef de gare* from Saint-André with his *litre de rouge* on the table; the old *cheminots* pausing to swig from a large jug of *rouge* as they work on the train; the railwayman translating a German's threats as 'on vous cassera la gueule' while wiping his nose with the back of his sleeve. Specific proletarian identity merges into a more general, popular identity as the film spreads to embrace the national community. The collectivism implied in the final sequence is similarly integrated into the broader national unity of the Marseillaise-singing public.

We could of course seek to account for the ideological complexity of the film by looking at the multiple potential influences on it (Clément and Audry, their sources, the *cheminot* performers, the CNR, the CLCF). But what it undoubtedly shows is that, in the heady days and months following the Liberation, a left-wing, collectivist discourse and a populist, nationalist one could sit easily together. Testimony to this can be provided by a reading of contemporary critics. Few of those I have examined even felt the need to comment on the film's politics.[7] None took exception to its marriage of a collectivist and a nationalist discourse. Most simply applauded the film for finally providing an authentic picture of the Resistance.

Surveying critical response, Bertin-Maghit says: 'The theme of authenticity is taken up by all the cinema critics of the period.'[8] There were a few isolated voices expressing doubts. Alain Spenlé says, '[I]t is always the same side which wins. One feels that the Germans let themselves be fooled too easily.'[9] Jean Fayard makes a more specific criticism: '[W]e do not see how the spirit of resistance evolves... Yet everybody knows that in 1941 the Resistance had a skeleton organization and recruitment was often very difficult. Everything seems too easy.'[10] These criticisms are essentially about accuracy and do not explicitly attack the underlying myth of the nation resisting in its spirit. First signs of more serious criticism of the mythical quality of the film appear, as far as I can tell, in 1969. The critic from *La Croix* reports on a *Dossiers de l'écran* screening which talked of the late *ralliement* of the Communist party and of collaboration by the official railworkers' federation.[11]

The vast bulk of comment finds a variety of reasons for praising the film's realism and authenticity. The use of real locations is mentioned by some, the authentic sources and the documentary value of the film by others. The presence of real *cheminots* clearly lent weight to the film.[12] However, its sheer unconventionality, the fact that it is not *du cinéma*, is the reason most often cited. Two examples will give the flavour:

> No stars, no big-budget style, no sentimental pathos, just the truth, straight from the heart and the guts of hard men, a film that needed to be made.[13]

> No need to fictionalize such a subject: authenticity was all that was needed to move us.[14]

A certain simplicity was also required. Georges Aubert in *Front National* finds in the film 'the simplicity that good taste and historical truth demanded'.[15] Michel Duran writes in *Minerve*: '[T]he resistance members are not heroes... When they die, it is without any phrase of Déroulède on their lips, with enormous regret, but without weakness.'[16] It would seem that at least part of what made an acceptable, 'authentic' image of resistance was a question of tone; the avoidance of melodrama, of 'cinema', the adoption of a low-key, quiet heroism that avoided phraseology.

One crucial question related to authenticity is the scope the critics read into the vision of resistance in the film. This is a hard question to answer. Because of the film's many slippages, we cannot be sure whether those who praise it for its authenticity are seeing it narrowly as a true reflection of the *cheminots'* struggle or more broadly as a reliable image of a nation at war. Evidence for the latter reading is provided by the number of critics who suggest that the image of France in the film is the one that should be shown to the world:

Without doubt France owed it to itself to leave this document to the world.[17]

If the authorities... knew what was in their own interests, this film would be shown on all the screens in the world.[18]

Here, finally, is a good French film. It would be good French propaganda to show it as much as possible abroad.[19]

The critics were doubtless swayed by aesthetic considerations, but propaganda is clearly a major factor. Interestingly, the new enemy is the United States:

Hollywood has never made anything as realistic.[20]

The cinematography is masterly and the Americans, who specialize in this genre, could not do better.[21]

Unsurprisingly perhaps, the French wanted a film that could act as a national standard-bearer. They had suffered humiliation at the hands of the Germans and had faced a potential loss of independence at the hands of the Americans, followed by a dramatic influx of American films after the war.

La Bataille du rail is then a classic early example of Resistance narrative. It illustrates perfectly how, through slippage and silence, document drifts into myth. Its merging of left-wing collectivism and populist nationalism seemed so natural at the time that most critics felt no need to comment upon it. The film's appeal came partly from its non-conventionality, its mixing of documentary and feature film form in a way which guaranteed authenticity while allowing emotional involvement. The appeal can also be explained by the (re-)vision of the recent past offered, in which we see a Resistance movement that had begun immediately, had grown smoothly and was actively or passively supported by a united population. The critics were not only influenced by the content of the film but also by the tone. They wanted to see quiet, low-key heroism. But what of the public? What vision of Resistance did they want to see? Occasional comments by critics suggest that they were volubly appreciative. (One critic, for example, refers to his experience 'listening to the audience stamp their feet or applaud at the exploits of the conscientious pointsman or the cautious stationmaster').[22] It might seem that the public too was seduced by the left-wing vision of resistance in this hybrid film, but then we must consider that they likewise flocked to see Clément's *Le*

Père Tranquille, a studio-shot star-vehicle with a good helping of romance, and, if anything, an underlying Gaullist message.[23] We could accuse the public of fickleness, but it could also be that the rival myths of Resistance were far less radically separate immediately after the war than in later years.

Notes

Unless stated otherwise, the place of publication is Paris.

1. Raymond Jarry in *Dimanche*, 17 March 1946. Unless otherwise specified *contemporary* film reviews were found in the file devoted to *Bataille du rail* in the Bibliothèque de l'Arsenal. Dates of publication and sometimes authors' names were handwritten. All translations are my own.
2. Denis Marion in *Combat*, 28 February 1946.
3. Michel Duran in *Minerve*, 8 March 1946.
4. A wealth of detail about the film's production is given by Jean-Pierre Bertin-Maghit in '*La Bataille du rail*; de l'authenticité à la chanson de geste', in *Revue d'histoire moderne et contemporaine*, vol.33, April–June 1986, pp.280–300.
5. Interestingly the film uses real Germans, apparently played by POWs ('The Germans were generally chosen from among prisoners' [Alain Spenlé, '*Bataille du rail*', in *Revue du Cinéma*, no.1, October 1946, p.74]). The French public is given the opportunity to see symbolic humiliation of representatives of their real enemies.
6. By using the same sequence of shots for the manual and clerical workers the film establishes the equivalence of the two types of workers, their common condition.
7. Several critics refer to the collective efforts of the *cheminots*, the *travail d'équipe* but without any specific ideological slant. A few are more explicit. Eugénie Helisse, for example, expresses her approval of the cooperative that produced the film 'for the benefit of the whole profession and not to make some financier or another richer' (in *Arts*, 27 February 1946).
8. Bertin-Maghit, '*La Bataille du rail*; de l'authenticité à la chanson de geste', p. 282.
9. Spenlé, '*Bataille du rail*', p.73 .
10. Jean Fayard in *Opéra*, 6 March 1946.
11. R.-R. in *La Croix*, 21 March 1969.
12. Bonzo, for example, commented: '[T]he good faces of the

cheminots... just as they were, I tell you', *Enseignements*, (9 March 1946).
13. Georges Drouet in *Juin*, 5 March 1946.
14. Pierre Lagarde in *Résistance*, 10–11 March 1946.
15. Georges Aubert in *Front National*, 1 February 1946.
16. Michel Duran in *Minerve*, 8 March 1946.
17. Jean Néry in *Le Monde*, 5 March 1946.
18. Bonzo in *Enseignements*, 9 March 1946.
19. Eugénie Helisse in *Arts*, 22 February 1946.
20. Ibid.
21. Georges Zevaco in *Mondes*, 19 March 1946.
22. Drouet in *Juin*, 5 March 1946.
23. In the film the entire community seems to participate in the spirit of resistance. There is an older, leader figure. Images of workers' collective strength are absent. As the war ends, unanimity gives way to division as political parties resume their activity.

– 2 –

Immigrant Fighters for the Liberation of France: a Local Profile of Carmagnole-Liberté in Lyon

J.C. Simmonds

Communist-led movements of the French Resistance struggled to grow out of the ideological and organizational chaos caused by the German-Soviet pact, the declaration of war in September 1939, the banning of the Communist party and the French defeat. But whilst they built a clandestine existence in the period before the 'release' of the German invasion of the Soviet Union in June 1941, conditions were difficult. The armed Communist Resistance emerged from similar chaos under the umbrella title of the Francs-Tireurs et Partisans Français (FTPF, often shortened to FTP) in early 1942. In the provinces, individual Communist immigrant resisters belonging to the Main-d'Œuvre immigrée (MOI) had already joined many groups, including the Jeunesse Communiste (UJC), the Organisation Spéciale (OS), the Union des Juifs pour la Résistance et l'Entraide (UJRE), the Groupes Francs, and Union des Jeunes Juifs. From these disorganized beginnings, an early Organisation Spéciale activist, Kutin, on instructions from a southern zone FTPF leader, Ravine, set about the establishment of an effective direct action group in Lyon. As a result, the FTP-MOI group Carmagnole was founded on 6 June 1942 at 55,

The research for this paper has been greatly aided by the advice of Professeur Claude Collin of the Université de Grenoble III, whose book *L'Insurrection de Villeurbanne a-t-elle eu lieu?* was published by Presses Universitaires de Grenoble in June 1994. Clarity and passion have been provided by members of Carmagnole-Liberté whom I interviewed in 1992: Leon Landini, Jean Ottavi, Paul Mossovic, Ezer Najman, Henri Krischer, Natalie Krischer, André Schmer and Christine Boico. See also the video testimony of former members in R. Requena and R. Trempé, *'Mémoires de Résistance: FTP-MOI'*, videotape, Université de Toulouse-Le Mirail, Centre Audio-Visuel, 1992.

Boulevard de la Croix Rousse, by eight Communist militants: Kutin, Kugler, Ravine, Fred, Fryd, Schapochnik, Tancerman and Teper. Kugler took over the leadership of the group after Kutin was arrested; both men being immigrant veterans of the International Brigades in Spain. When numbers began to expand in 1943, some members of the Lyon group went to join individuals of the FTP-MOI in Grenoble to form the group Liberté. (Sometimes known in Grenoble as the 5th Battalion of the FTP-MOI.) Together, Carmagnole and Liberté formed the Inter-Region HI4 of the FTP-MOI (H=Rhône, I=Isère, 4=MOI). The Regions had their own leadership, as did the Inter-Region, (after May 1944, Georges Grunfeld, 'Lefort', for HI4) who were supposed to maintain liaison with the national FTP-MOI leadership.[1] This national leadership had little effect upon the actions of the provincial FTP-MOI groups in the crucial months leading up to the Liberation of France, but the groups nevertheless intervened dramatically in many areas; none more so than in Lyon, where some of the 'local' movements – so characteristic of the Liberation story in provincial France – were anything but local. The FTP-MOI Carmagnole, in particular, demonstrated that immigrant left-wing solidarity was a significant force in the fight against the occupier.

In the summer of 1944, with a large influx of recruits, the FTP-MOI group Carmagnole began 'patrolling' the streets of Lyon and seized large amounts of arms in raids on barracks and police posts. By 20 August it was clear that the Germans were retreating as fast as they could northward through Lyon and the idea of an insurrection was common currency, especially among the armed Resistance groups. A more immediate concern of the FTP-MOI Carmagnole in August 1944 was the fate of fellow Resisters arrested and incarcerated during the 'rafles' of the previous months. There was evidence that the retreating Germans were emptying the prisons in some towns and executing the inmates *en masse*. On 22 August a small group liberated three FTP-MOI members (along with ten others) from the St Paul prison.

On 24 August some forty FTP-MOI Carmagnole members set out to do the same thing at the St Paul and St Joseph prisons, behind the Perrache railway station in the centre of town. They met at the Municipal Garage in the rue Son Tay near the Parc de la Tête d'Or, wearing their newly-made ' FFI ' armbands, only to discover that the prisoners had already been released. About to be dismissed around 9 o'clock, they were spotted and fired at by German troops on a train passing over a viaduct which ran very close to the garage. The Regional FTP-MOI commander Filip (Lefort) divided them into four groups and ordered a retreat. The detachment of Henri Krischer

(Lamiral) moved towards the working class area of Villeurbanne in the northeastern suburbs of Lyon. The strikers and crowds of Villeurbanne, who were already on the streets and had been alerted by the gunfire, acclaimed them as 'liberators'. Krischer tried to disperse the crowd and retreat further to the east, but the crowd, filling a traditional meeting place outside the town hall, would not let the battalion leave. The traditional barricades of revolutionary France sprang up to defend the town hall and spread out across the commune.[2]

There were clashes throughout 25 August as the cautious Germans tested the strength of the barricades and the size of FTPF forces. The commune remained liberated until 26 August when the Germans returned with heavy arms to reoccupy the main buildings as a means of securing their retreat. The emotional excitement of the population suddenly evaporated in the face of real firepower and the crowd dissolved, leaving the armed Resisters to man barricades and tall buildings. Three FTPF detachments had been sent to Monchat, Monplaisir, and Vénissieux to extend the uprising, but each of the efforts failed against superior German arms and civilian hesitancy. To complete the confusion, Radio Geneva ironically announced a successful insurrection in Villeurbanne on 26 August, and conflated the code names of Filip and Krischer into a mythical leader called 'L'Amiral Lefort'. The insurrection in Villeurbanne was too early for Allied intervention and was soon out-gunned by the Germans. Units withdrew eastward to join up with those Maquis advancing on Lyon, and the liberation of the town was delayed until the first week of September. The insurrection failed, but it was a spontaneous response of French citizens to the example set by immigrant-led Resisters. It was an episode, but in military terms it was a serious disruption of the German withdrawal and resulted in a significant recruitment of numbers to the fight for Liberation.

Motivation

Joining the Resistance, or at least hiding, was quite a natural option for immigrants with no citizenship, and an even more pressing imperative for anti-fascist refugees in France. Many appreciated from an early date that it was a choice between disappearing into French and German camps, or taking up some form of clandestine existence. But joining an armed assault group and facing the enemy in the streets was an entirely different undertaking. The motivation of young people who joined the FTP-MOI Carmagnole-Liberté has been seen in simple idealistic terms: 'It was France, her fate, her freedoms that were threatened. All of their homelands, be it Poland, Spain, Rumania, Belgium, Hungary or Italy had been embodied in the interests of France which was why the majority of immigrants in the Lyon region answered the call of the F.T.P.'[3]

Many youngsters on the edge of the FTPF had already taken dramatic resistance actions and were readily integrated into the battalion. Ottavi, for example, had already assassinated a leading member of the Italian security police in Antibes. Landini had killed officers of Italian occupation forces in Nice, and Krischer was a member of a Jewish Groupe Franc in Lyon. Their motivation for joining the FTP-MOI was to find the best opportunity for direct action. Anti-fascism was a common drive. In the case of Landini, he had been brought up by his Italian Communist refugee father to hate fascism and intolerance and to see the only way forward as struggle with the Communist movement: 'My whole family and all our friends were militant Communists, I learnt Marxism at my father's knee...I learnt to hate Mussolini and to hate all oppression. It was quite natural to fight. I remained "legal", in my family and at school, but it did not stop me going to kill the occupiers.'[4] 'The war simply continued for these people; their parents had fought in Spain, they went on in this struggle.'[5]

In August 1944, the FTP 'Bataillon Bayard', located near Lyon, published a pamphlet entitled *Pourquoi nous luttons*. With reference to the FTP-MOI it made two international proletarian points: '[T]he immigrants fight because they love their adopted country, because they have the same interests as French workers', and, 'The FTP, issuing from the people, fights for a better future, where the sun will shine, but not only for some privileged people, the war profiteers and a few capitalists.'[6]

Such class-based, egalitarian sentiments can be found as a motivation among many members, not couched in clearly Marxist or Communist terms, but seeing a 'new society', not simply political freedom, as the long-term goal of their commitment. Some former members described it as the desire for 'justice' and 'freedom from oppression'; age-old desires of persecuted minorities.

Membership

The membership of Carmagnole-Liberté was very fluid; many were transitory and exchanged places within the FTP-MOI to avoid the French police and the Gestapo. At the beginning of 1944, for example, it was reinforced by the addition of Michel Fey and Joseph Francesconi. Both were experienced Resisters – Fey from Marseille and Francesconi from Grenoble – and on the run from the Gestapo. Following the general line taken by the FTP at that time, Francesconi went off to fight in northern Italy in June 1944, and Fey was arrested by the Gestapo and tortured to death in July 1944. Henri Krischer ('André', 'Lamiral'), the leader of the Bataillon Carmagnole at the Liberation, and the historian Collin both refer to a list of its members and their origins established at the Liberation and then corrected in the 1970s by members of l'Amicale du Bataillon Carmagnole Liberté, FTPF-MOI. Poles were the largest group with 34 per cent, followed by the French (17 per cent), Spanish (15 per cent), Italians (10 per cent), Hungarians (7 per cent), Austrians (5 per cent), Romanians (5 per cent), Germans (4 per cent) and Belgians (3 per cent). Twenty-three per cent of the members were Jewish, most were between eighteen and twenty-five years old and a very high proportion of them were political refugees.[7] The numbers of FTP-MOI in Lyon (Carmagnole) were about thirty-two in early 1944,[8] although some members put the general numbers in 1943–44 at only around twenty-four to twenty-five.[9] Ninety-six members of Carmagnole were killed over the period from June 1942 to September 1944, not all of them in or around Lyon and Grenoble.

But at the Liberation there were one hundred and forty-four survivors of Carmagnole and related groups, as recruitment in the last days had been very rapid. The Maquis du Croix de Ban, established by Carmagnole in December 1943 and reinforced in June 1944, had 220 men by August 1944. This contributed to fluidity as men were sent to recuperate in the maquis or hide, and then returned later with different papers. The wide variety of nationalities and the fluidity of membership obscures the fact that Jews from Poland made up the bulk of the long-term members, and were prominent in its establishment and in its actions.

Collin, using figures from Konigsberg and the Amicale, compared the nationalities of those killed before the clashes of the Liberation (forty-nine) and the total killed (ninety-six) for the whole period of Carmagnole. He notes that at the level of the HI4 Inter-Region, there were in effect two FTP-MOI organizations, corresponding to two time periods and two different situations. The original, 'historic' organization, started armed struggle with only a few fighters and it specialised in urban guerrilla warfare. It was certainly well developed, but its composition always fundamentally relied upon Jewish immigrants from Eastern Europe. And then there was the organization of the last few weeks, which was equipped with a Maquis and which grew considerably by integrating numerous 'legal' Italians into its ranks, welcoming Polish miners and also a good number of French citizens.[10]

Annette Wieviorka has suggested that there were three generations of Jewish Resisters. The 'old' generation of Jewish Communist militants went into the Resistance because they were politically committed. The next group, and the largest in number, was the generation of the 'rafles' of Jews – especially that of the Vélodrome d'Hiver in July 1942 – who were previously apolitical but were shocked into militancy by this treatment. Then thirdly there was the generation of younger men, who might have belonged to a left-wing youth organization or some other association within the Jewish community, who first expressed their commitment in the youthful radicalism of armed resistance.[11] In the FTP-MOI Carmagnole-Liberté all these three generations were represented. But the additional fourth group were Polish Jews who were miners or were working in the fur trade, millinery, tailoring, leather and finishing. The Polish miners either worked in small mining communities near Lyon, or had fled the German advance from their homes in the Nord and Pas-de-Calais. The few miners still in work were a good source of explosives, but all had skills which were valuable in the Resistance. Over and above this, most of the early Carmagnole-Liberté group were also refugees from European fascism and thus committed ideologically on a broad front, whatever their age. Many were also illegal entrants, who had worked illegally and been ruthlessly exploited in dreadful conditions, but who were all dismissed at the beginning of the war when their employers, fearing police checks and accusations of harbouring 'fifth columnists', sacked them, thereby taking away their only shred of personal security. This specific group of immigrants, and in particular the Jews, were therefore on the margins of society before the war and were thrust into a kind of clandestinity as soon as it was declared. After the defeat, Vichy laws made life tenuous in the extreme for all Jews and immigrants. Outsiders by virtue of these characteristics, they often spoke French with strong accents and poor grammar. Driven from their homelands and having suffered extremes of poverty, they were toughened to living *in extremis*.[12]

Of the survivors, thirty-one were women. They were essential in assuring the liaison between leaders and groups and between the different levels of the hierarchy. They also maintained contact between Lyon and Grenoble. Young women circulating in towns on bicycles were numerous and inconspicuous, whereas the male members of Carmagnole-Liberté were all of military age and would be constantly stopped to see why they had not joined a Vichyite organization, gone on the Relève or been conscripted into forced labour (STO) for Germany. Many women in Carmagnole-Liberté were also engaged in bomb-making, the distribution of food, clothes and money and intelligence-gathering. In the last activity there was no one with the stature of Mme Boico of the FTP-MOI in Paris, but several women in Carmagnole played an important part.[13] Some women fought in the direct action attacks and a number were involved in industrial sabotage, placing the bombs and incendiary devices that they had concocted. The most celebrated of these was Janine Sonntag, who was captured, tortured and executed after a failed attack on a German garage on 3 July 1944.[14]

Immigrants and others who wanted to join the FTP-MOI – and especially its fighting groups – were carefully selected and screened for character and loyalty. Recruitment was via the existing networks of MOI groups, the Communist party, Jewish and immigrant organizations. The recruits were almost all young men who were strangers to Lyon. Most of them had already lived for a long time in clandestinity, adopted false identities or lived on the margins of society. They were recruited initially through contact with one man, who set them simple, relatively safe tasks. Their reaction to these tasks would determine whether they were invited to join 'les Sportifs', a vague, familiar title which covered the other members of any team they met, until they were included in the FTP-MOI. Some applicants were experienced Resisters, but even in these cases there were tests before they would be taken into Carmagnole. The level of experience in the Carmagnole-Liberté group, even in its early days, was very high. For example, Georges Grunfeld (Lefort) – sometimes known as Filip – was already a well-known activist in Combat when he joined in late 1942 and soon rose to lead the Inter-Region organization. The members were placed in a 'safe house' if they could not find anywhere to live, and were told to have as little contact with the owners and neighbours as possible and to live as solitary a life as they could manage. They were not allowed to write to their families, socialize with other members of the group or contact anyone except their 'chef'. Rent was paid for them; they were given 2,500 francs a month in three instalments for living costs, which relieved them of the need for employment, and all their papers were provided by the support groups of the MOI who undertook other types of normal Resistance activities, including the production of large numbers of tracts.[15] It was these people, sometimes called the 'politicals', who also provided the money, clothes and other essentials. Bank raids were a frequent source of cash, together with money from the FTPF and other Communist organizations.[16]

'Les Sportifs' were discouraged from moving about unnecessarily and they rarely met the other members of their group, although occasional group meals were arranged in safe restaurants. These were draconian measures, which were sometimes ignored, and recruitment towards the end of the Occupation was less cautious, but it was their skill in clandestinity which protected the many survivors of Carmagnole-Liberté. Such a life took a terrible psychological toll on men and women, who were young and constantly in fear. Their lack of social contacts and conversations, even within their group or the wider MOI and FTP, meant an isolation which was profound and only punctuated with moments of intense action and terror. Part of the reason for the establishment of their own Maquis at La Croix du Ban, was to provide a rest and recuperation centre for the most exhausted of the group. Naturally, these militants found it difficult to adapt at and after the Liberation. Part of the reason for the relatively minor role they played in the eventual liberation of Lyon and its aftermath, was the professional deformation which deep clandestinity had brought about. They were not used to raising and organizing large groups, nor converting to political and social action. They were unskilled in normal communication and they had no contacts with larger groups such as the Liberation Committees; even the smallest local committees in the suburbs of Lyon had never heard of them.

Direct Action

Direct action resistance in France was, by 1943, to be found in both rural and urban areas. But of all the occupied countries, France had perhaps the most highly developed urban Resistance movement. Lyon – 'capital of the Resistance' – was a model of this phenomenon, with dozens of movements active in all types of resistance. There were other notable direct action groups in Lyon – the Groupes Francs of Combat (later the MUR), the Union des Juifs pour la Résistance et l'Entraide (UJRE), the *groupes d'action* of the Union des Jeunes Juifs – but the FTP-MOI was a uniquely active, urban guerrilla group. Direct attacks upon the occupier were a way of continuing the war and at the same time encouraging the local population by example. The overall aim of the group was to make the occupiers and the French authorities feel insecure, and to provoke an intemperate reaction or at least an extension of the curfew. Occasionally this resulted in a specific response by 'les Sportifs' to action by the authorities. When Carmagnole suffered the arrest, trial and execution of Emile Bertrand and Simon Fryd, they countered by killing the

French judge of the Section Spéciale court, Faure-Pinguely, who had condemned Fryd to death. Effecting an entrance to his home, disguised as members of the German security forces, they killed him in his own study. It was an 'outrage' that the collaborationist press could not ignore, but in reporting the event, they compounded the existing sense of insecurity. As Landini later said, the battalions tried 'to make our towns inhospitable to today's victors, preparing, through action, the conditions for a distant Liberation'.[17]

Actions by the FTP-MOI Carmagnole-Liberté were often spectacular and always newsworthy. Their methods were not unique, but they were remarkable for their nerve and determination. In the early days the 'military leader' would contact the members of his team individually and fix a rendezvous in town. The 'technician' would bring the arms needed for the attack – often only two or three handguns – and distribute them at the meeting place. If the group were to attack a known German or collaborator in the street, his movements would have been studied beforehand by the intelligence gatherers of the support units. On the appointed day, the group would then walk along the pavement towards the advancing target, with one look-out ahead, one man on the opposite side of the road and one man behind. The killer would be in the middle of this triangular pattern. The target would be shot at close range from the front, any guns and ammunition would be taken, and the team would all walk quietly away by separate routes to where the 'technician' waited to collect up their arms. All would then again disperse in different directions. Towards the end of the occupation such teams consisted of six or eight members, with extra look-outs and backup for security, but there was still the need for the killer to fire from close quarters.

Of the two hundred and forty-one 'confirmed' actions by Carmagnole in Lyon,[18] thirty-four were attacks on Germans in broad daylight, counting the events of 24–26 August in Villeurbanne as one action. Germans were attacked in the street, in trams, and in hotels, restaurants and cinemas that were reserved for their use, and while they waited for transport at bus and train stations. There were also attacks by grenade against marching groups. Orders came to the leaders of battalions and detachments in early June 1944 (presumably from the regional command, but there is uncertainty about this) to begin 'patrolling' in town and to attack any German or Vichyite groups they came across, and these attacks intensified as the Liberation came closer. Collaborators were attacked with increasing frequency and in June, July and August 1944 some fifteen 'traitors, Gestapo agents and Miliciens' were 'executed'.

In July, however, another order came to the battalions urging them to stop and disarm policemen, Milice, GMR and Germans, but to avoid killing them if possible. The idea behind this was that the surprise random attacks of June had prompted the victims to fight back, whereas 'stop and disarm' actions might promote the idea among potential victims that they did not need to react. It was therefore hoped that by the time of the Liberation, clashes between the Resistance and their enemies might be reduced in number and more armed Frenchmen of all kinds (police etc.) persuaded to join the Resistance. The patrols and 'executions' by Carmagnole ceased immediately the battles of the Liberation began and few were carried out after the Liberation. The battalions were used to ambushes and covert actions, not open street battles, and they lost large numbers as a result. Attacks on transport, on administrative offices and factories working for the Germans, together with actions celebrating national holidays and famous dates, completed their direct resistance, but armed assaults were their most significant missions.

The Insurrection that Was Not a Liberation

The recent historiography of the FTP-MOI has been colourful and combative,[19] because the position of the French Communist party in post-War France has been so contradictory and contentious. The specific topics of armed assault and insurrection have received less attention and the case of Lyon is no exception to this.

Charles Tillon, the national leader of the FTP, declared that the uprising in Villeurbanne demonstrated a popular insurrection was possible in the Lyon agglomeration and that had it not been for Gaullist agents, 'attentiste' FFI leaders and French Communist party 'Stalinists', the town could have liberated itself.[20] General works on the Resistance in Lyon and the liberation of the town, on the other hand, have tended to underestimate the impact of the insurrection. Amoretti dismissed it as 'premature', whilst Rude devoted eight pages to the event, but saw it as nothing more than the automatic outcome of generalized calls for an uprising. In his memoirs, Alban-Vistel, regional commander of the FFI, called it a 'more or less spontaneous attempt at insurrection', and Ruby was more interested in command squabbles, than what happened in the streets, calling it 'a limited action with little outcome'.[21] One way of measuring its importance might be to assess its effect on other events in Lyon. It clearly made the Germans abandon a number of strong points and caused them to divert vital troops to 'street-clearing' operations. More than that, Leon Landini, a Carmagnole member, who was in the Fort Montluc prison at the time, insists that the insurrection in Villeurbanne caused the Germans to abandon the nearby fort, which led to the release of 190 prisoners. Ruby, amongst others, declares that it was the threats by Farge, the pleading of Cardinal Gerlier and the intervention of the FFI Groupes Franc who persuaded the governor, Boesche, to open the jail. Landini, who was there, insists that it was a by-product of Carmagnole's insurrection.

The French Communist party, which might have been expected to laud the actions of internationally-minded comrades in the Resistance, has only recently given them the publicity and support they deserve.[22] But any country's popular history lives to some extent on its heroic episodes and the real irony of Villeurbanne is that a patriotic uprising of the French against their oppressors was provoked and led by left-wing immigrants, many of whom were women and even more of whom were Jewish.

Notes

Unless stated otherwise, the place of publication is Paris.

1. 'Le rôle des FTP-MOI dans la libération de Lyon', p.2. Archives of Henri Krischer in the Musée de la Résistance et de la Déportation, la Citadelle, Besançon. Folder 3 (hereafter referred to as the 'Krischer Archives').
2. Interview with Henri Krischer, 14 September 1992.
3. Letter from Leon Landini (President of the Amicale du Bataillon Carmagnole-Liberté) to M J.P. Vittori, 7 June 1989.
4. Interview with Leon Landini, 16 September 1992.
5. Interview with Jean Ottavi, 9 September 1992.
6. Krischer Archives, Folder 3. II.
7. Krischer Archives, Folder 3.
8. Letter from Leon Landini to M J.P. Vittori, 7 June 1989.
9. Ezer Najman (Gilles), in M. Ruby, *Résistance Civile et Militaire*, L'Hermès, 1974, and Ezer Najman, interview with the author, 13 September 1992.
10. Claude Collin, '"Ces étrangers d'ici qui choisirent le feu" Francs-Tireurs et Partisans de la Main d'Œuvre Immigrée: le cas des unités "Carmagnole" (Lyon) et "Liberté" (Grenoble)', *Cahiers d'Histoire* (Lyon), vol.37, no.1, 1992, pp.51–2.
11. Annette Wieviorka, *Ils etaient juifs, résistants, communistes*, Denoël, 1986. See also David Diamant, *Les Juifs dans la Résistance française, 1940–1944. Avec armes ou sans armes*, Le Pavillon/Roger Mania,

1971; J. Ravine, *La résistance organisée des Juifs en France, 1940–1944*, Julliard, 1973, and RHICOJ, *Les Juifs dans la Résistance et la Libération. Histoire, témoignages, débats*, Le Scribe, 1985.

12. Interview with M Paul Mossovic, 16 September 1992.

13. See the citation for the FTPF Resister certificate for Mira Kugler (4 September 1944) in Krischer Archives, Folder 5.

14. Claude Collin, 'La Jeanne d'Arc de la FTP-MOI; Janine Sonntag', unpublished article.

15. M.-C. Rifkiss, *Les Juifs Communistes Résistants à Lyon, 1940–1944,* unpublished master's dissertation, Université de Lyon II, 1986, p.5, in Centre d'Histoire de la Résistance et de la Déportation (CHRD), Lyon.

16. Krischer Archives, Folder 11.

17. Landini, Letter to Vittori.

18. For a list of the actions undertaken by Carmagnole-Liberté in Lyon (which probably does not include every incident) see: B. and S. Konigsberg, *Carmagnole-Liberté: FTP de la MOI*, L'Amicale du Bataillon de Carmagnole-Liberté, 1981. This list was established at the end of the war from 'action reports' made by the teams at the time of the actions, and from reports made to the FTP-MOI Zone Sud leadership. Some of these are to be found in the 'FTP-MOI Zone Sud Communiqués Militaires, Sept.1943 à Sept.1944' in the Archives of the CHRD, Lyon, 432.8, FTP. Collin told the present author that he had checked many of them against contemporary newspaper reports and if anything the published list was an underestimate.

19. The historical struggle over relations between the PCF and the FTP-MOI during the war and over the party's treatment of the movement in the post-War period can be studied through the following: [anonymous], *Lettres des fusillés*, France d'Abord, 1946; R. Bourderon, 'le PCF, les FTP, la MOI, automne-hiver 1943–1944', (Présentation de textes), *Cahiers d'histoire de l'Institut de Recherche Marxiste*, no.22, 1985; S. Courtois, *Le PCF dans la guerre*, Ramsay, 1980; S. Courtois, D. Peschanski and A. Rayski, *Le sang de l'étranger. Les immigrés de la MOI dans la Résistance*, Fayard, 1989; H. Elek, *Mémoires d'Hélène*, Maspero, 1977; P. Garnier-Raymond, *L'Affiche rouge*, Fayard,1975; B. Holman, *Testament*, Calmann-Lévy, 1989; J. Jerome, *La Part des hommes*, Acropole, 1983; *Les Clandestins*, Acropole, 1986; A. Lecœur, 'L'affaire Manouchian. Les combattants FTP de la MOI, les responsabilités du PCF et la "double direction"', *Est et Ouest*, July–August, 1985; M. Manouchian, *Manouchian*, Les Editeurs Français Réunis,1974; A. Ouzoulias, *Les Bataillons de la jeunesse*, Editions Sociales, 1967;

A. Rayski, *Nos illusions perdues*, Balland, 1985; P. Robrieux, *Histoire intérieure du PCF*, vol.4, Fayard, 1984; Tchakarian, *Les Francs-Tireurs de l'affiche rouge*, Messidor, 1986; C. Tillon, *Les FTP*, Julliard, 1962; *Les FTP, soldats sans uniforme*, Rennes, Editions Ouest France, 1991.
On immigrants in the French Resistance see: Karel Bartosek *et al.* (eds), *De l'exile à la Résistance. Réfugiés et immigrés d'Europe centrale en France, 1933–45*, Presses Universitaires de Vincennes,1989; P. Joutard and F. Marcot (eds), *Les étrangers dans la Résistance en France*, Besançon, Musée de la Résistance et de la Déportation, 1992, and G. Laroche, *On les nommait des étrangers; les immigrés dans la Résistance*, Editeurs Français Réunis, 1965.

20. Tillon, *Les FTP, soldats sans uniforme*.
21. H. Amoretti, *Lyon Capitale: 1940–1944*, France Empire, 1964; Alban-Vistel, *La Nuit sans ombre*, Hachette, 1974; F. Rude, *La Libération de Lyon et sa région*, Hachette, 1974; M. Ruby, *La Résistance à Lyon*, L'Hermès, 1979. Note also the standard narrative in G. Chauvy, *Lyon des années bleues. Libération, Epuration*, Plon, 1987, pp.240–1.
22. See the caustic comments in G. Filip (Lefort), 'Mes souvenirs des combats de la libération de Lyon', typescript, Bibliothèque de Documentation Internationale Contemporaine (BDIC), p.26.

– 3 –

The Police in the Liberation of Paris

Simon Kitson

By the middle of 1943 most sources acknowledged widespread Gaullist sympathies amongst police personnel in Paris, even if they generally distinguished the base from a hugely compromised hierarchy and singled out certain branches as centres of collaboration.[1] The acceptance of these loyalties is seen as much in tracts addressed to the 'forces of order', such as the one sent to the Montreuil *commissariat* (police station) on 15 July 1943 claiming that 'in a large proportion, you approve the efforts of the patriots',[2] as in the more general Gaullist attitude to the police. Far from telling police officers to resign from the administration, the Resistance was instructing them to stay in their posts: 'So long as you assure policing, it will be a security for yourselves, at the same time as for the people of Paris',[3] although this did imply a responsibility to 'disobey orders intelligently'.[4] No one, and least of all the Germans, expected the police to defend German interests directly during an insurrection, as Dr Knochen, head of the SiPo-SD in France, acknowledged in August 1943: 'Today, less than ever, should we count on the French Police to intervene to whatever extent for the defence of German interests'.[5]

Some Resistance sources doubted policemen's level of engagement: policemen 'sympathize with the Gaullists but carry out instructions concerning the terrorists and the Jews philosophically, whilst recognizing they are doing an unpleasant job',[6] claimed one report on police opinion. The Communists were the most critical in this respect. They stigmatized the *attentisme* of the police which allowed Vichy's machine to function, despite a lack of enthusiasm on the part of its agents.[7] Nevertheless, even they were to be pleasantly surprised during the demonstrations on 14 July 1944 when 'the demonstrators shouted:

This paper could not have been written without the help and encouragement of Cécile Hochard. Thanks are also due to Mark Ledbury for a number of useful suggestions.

"the police are on our side!'"[8]

Overall, it was the possibility of turning these Gaullist sympathies into an active engagement *en masse*, which gained the upper hand in Resistance circles in the summer of 1944. The proof of this is that the Parisian police were included in the Gaullist insurrection plans. That they should be used to occupy public buildings in the name of General de Gaulle was the result of a compromise deal between the Conseil National de la Résistance (CNR) and the Comité Parisien de Libération (CPL), the former wanting the Police and Gendarmerie to be 100 per cent responsible for such operations, the latter preferring this responsibility to be passed to 'non-government' elements of the Forces Françaises de l'Intérieur (FFI) but finally agreeing that the 'forces of order' should be responsible for 75 per cent of these occupations.[9]

There still remained the question of whether the police would be in a position to carry out this role. It is here that a major problem of planning becomes obvious, because, despite all the preparation devoted to it, the insurrection would still have to leave plenty of scope for improvisation. It was not certain that the 'forces of order' who were being designated to take over certain buildings would have the freedom to do so. 'It is probable that after the start of military operations on the continent, the armed civil servants, whose attitude is known to the enemy, will be the first targets of internment measures', concluded the Comité Parisien de Libération in its discussion of the problems of the insurrection.[10] In a communication, dated 2 July 1944, Roland Pré, right-hand man to Alexandre Parodi, de Gaulle's delegate in Paris, had expressed his belief that the Police Municipale 'will certainly be disarmed and perhaps interned' by the Germans.[11] Thus, the possibility that the 'forces of order' would not be in a position to carry out the responsibilities allocated to them was thought to be serious. Such a threat seemed to be in the process of realization when the Gestapo, following some minor incidents, carried out the disarming of the commissariats of Saint-Denis and Asnières and interned their personnel on the morning of Sunday 13 August.

This disarming was to highlight an essential question of the whole Occupation period, namely, whether the Resistance or Vichy could best defend the interests of the French population or any given category of it, in this case the police. Vichy responded rapidly to the affront to its 'forces of order', ordering the police to abandon their posts, leaving arms and uniform behind them, so as to protect its personnel from further arrest. In a matter of hours, however, this order was retracted, when, following negotiations with the Germans, the Director of the Police Municipale received the assurance that the

Gestapo had acted on a misunderstanding. The police returned to work in the early afternoon, but the reaction of the Vichy authorities had unwittingly given official confirmation to a Gestapo action that might otherwise have been passed off as rumour.[12]

At about the same time, the meeting of the leaders of the Communist-inspired movement Front National de la Police was interrupted by news of this disarming. Serge Lefranc, in charge of this committee, reacted without hesitation: 'We cannot accept such an humiliation! We must give the order for a general strike of the Parisian Police immediately.'[13] The possibilities of including the police in the series of strikes that the Front National was organizing had already been examined, but it had been decided to maintain a more working-class base for these movements.[14] Now, however, the opportunity seemed too good to miss. Such an action, it was believed, would have a profound effect on public opinion. The strike of railway workers, begun on 10 August, had been important strategically, but it had not enormously affected the population, who had already been unable to use the trains for several weeks. Moreover, a police strike would provide the chance to test police reaction, as well as that of the Germans. Thus, the strike was approved unanimously by the fourteen members of this committee and set for Tuesday 15 August.

However, the Front National de la Police, although the largest of the clandestine police organizations, could not act alone in this affair, and neither did it want to do so. It consulted the Socialist-influenced Police et Patrie and the Gaullist Honneur de la Police to ensure the success of such a manœuvre,[15] but the response from these movements was initially less than favourable.[16] They both objected to the tone of tracts drawn up by the Front National, which threatened that any police officers who broke the strike would be shot dead.[17] Moreover, they believed that the presence of the words 'general strike' on these tracts was unlikely to mobilize the police. But their opposition was much more profound than a simple question of vocabulary. They considered this move premature, fearing vicious reprisals, of which the Germans were still capable. It was on Monday 14 August, at the first joint meeting of the three movements, that it was decided to give the strike the go-ahead. Police et Patrie and Honneur de la Police had been won over by an intervention from regional FFI leader, Rol-Tanguy. It is highly probable that the desire not to be overtaken by the Front National acting alone,[18] and the wish to be able to project a united image of the Resistance were fundamental in their change of position. The tracts calling for the walk-out were modified. They now featured a message from the FFI on one side and a call from the police movements on the other, whose vocabulary had been altered to say that anyone who showed up for work would be considered a traitor and treated as such.

These tracts and accompanying instructions were distributed by Resisters of all three networks who travelled by bicycle or motorcycle around the various commissariats of Paris. Others learnt about the action by word of mouth. Overall, news of the strike would seem to have been well received by the personnel. There are a few accounts of individual hesitations, but these were quickly overcome by 'persuasion' from colleagues.[19] On 15 August, the organizers were pleased to report a 99.7 per cent success rate, with the initial strike of uniformed officers encouraging other branches to associate themselves, until a total paralysis of police services was achieved.[20] Unlike the previous Vichy-organized walk-out, this time the *gardiens de la paix* (uniformed police officers) responded directly to a call for an insurrectionary strike. Taking their arms with them and wearing civilian clothes they began picketing their workplaces. German reaction was tame, probably because they hoped the police could still be persuaded to return to work and thereby to maintain a public order that indirectly served them well. The tameness of this reaction should not be allowed to disguise the fact that there was a risk in the action. The Resistance was offering the police the chance to be assertive, to play a part in the insurrectionary movement, and more importantly, to face any threats collectively and in solidarity with the wider initiative developing.

The strike was thus seen by many Resisters as a useful launching pad for a more offensive campaign. Others, and notably the Gaullist leaders in Paris, feared that the action would cause a premature and spontaneous combustion of the insurrection. This was implicit in Alexandre Parodi's cable to London on 18 August requesting 'General Kœnig to hasten the [Allied] occupation of Paris by reason of the situation created by the strike of the Police and the public services'.[21] Although the first three days of the police action passed in a relative calm, the very day that Parodi sent this cable was marked by the first major attack of the insurrection – the taking of the town hall in Montreuil by a group of Franc-Tireurs et Partisans (FTP). That night the walls of Paris were covered by posters signed by 'elected Communists, both living and dead' calling for the uprising.[22] Thus, when the Préfecture de Police was occupied by police Resisters on the morning of Saturday 19 August, it was not the first act of the Paris uprising, but, given the central geographical position of the building, it was the most visible.

The nature of the insurrectionary seizure of buildings synthesized a number of influences. It mirrored the late 1930s practice of occupying the workplace as part of the strike movement, a tactic used widely in factories by the Milices Patriotiques in August 1944.[23] It was also a question of 'securing a local objective'[24] as a microcosm of national liberation. This became all the more important in the case of buildings such as the Préfecture de Police that had a symbolic significance nationally as well as locally. It represented an important display of strength, legitimizing the Resistance, filling the void left by the departure of Laval two days before and turning the tables on the occupiers. Both Rol-Tanguy and Parodi have since denied prior knowledge of this police attack on their Préfecture.[25] It would seem, therefore, that the police organizations acted independently of the Resistance high command in Paris in the timing of their action. However, the taking of this particular building was not entirely spontaneous. Lamboley of Police et Patrie claimed to have presented an occupation plan as early as 1 August.[26] Moreover, written instructions on just such a take-over were being exchanged between London and Algiers on 11 August,[27] although in neither the plan put forward by Lomboley nor the communication of 11 August had the date of the operation been fixed. Some historians have suggested that, in the context, the occupation of the building was triggered by the Gaullist Honneur de la Police to outwit the Communist-controlled Front National who had taken the initiative in the strike movement,[28] but in fact all three police movements were actively involved in the venture and leaders of all three have since claimed to have participated in a joint preparatory meeting on Friday 18 August.

This meeting had taken place against a background of increasing impatience on the part of police strikers. It is therefore not surprising that once a joint decision was reached by the police organizations, it led the way to a fever of activity amongst the rank and file. The police world was being turned upside down. As one of those involved put it: 'In our Administration a veritable revolution took place.'[29] Policemen enjoyed turning the tables on the authoritarian bosses who had humiliated their institution. Everywhere, *brigadiers* or even *gardiens de la paix* designated by the Resistance replaced the *commissaires* compromised by Vichy.

Everywhere, those who had shown too much zeal in ordering or carrying out arrests were now finding themselves the object of internment. Thus, for example, in the sixth *arrondissement*, a *commissaire*, three *brigadiers* and four *gardiens de la paix* were arrested.[30] In the Préfecture de Police, whose courtyard immediately changed its name from the *cour de Jean Chiappe* to become the *cour du 19 août*,[31] the arrested Prefect was reduced to answering the telephone to deceive the Germans while the defence of the building was prepared.[32]

So keen were the police insurgents to assert their national identity that even before completing this defence, they had hoisted the tricolour on the flagpole of their Préfecture.[33] It was the raising of this flag that caught the attention of de Gaulle's delegate, Alexandre Parodi. He was later to claim that this was one of the most important factors influencing his decision to agree to the immediate launching of the insurrection, despite contrary advice from his military advisor, Jacques Chaban-Delmas. At the same time, from the *cour du 19 août* a vibrant 'Marseillaise' was heard, which attracted the attention of the FFI leader, Henri Rol-Tanguy, who happened to be in the area of the building that morning. He hurried back to his headquarters to instruct his General Staff to accelerate the insurrection. Thus, like elsewhere, Paris saw an inversion of the positions of Vichy and the Resistance in the pre-liberation stage, but in the capital there was an inversion within this inversion: the police, who had for a long time been considered *attentiste*, had taken an important initiative that had accelerated the beginning of the whole movement.[34]

It could be argued, however, that this police action was only a temporary accelerator to the insurrection. The seizure of public buildings was a premature move away from the mobile tactics of the Resistance. By gathering so many insurgents in one place,[35] by creating a static 'centre', it became a sitting target. When the Germans attacked the Préfecture in the early afternoon of Saturday 19 August, the rebels were panic-stricken:[36] having no anti-tank weapons and little ammunition for the few light weapons at their disposal, they saw little hope of holding out past five o'clock the next morning.[37] Parodi sent orders to evacuate, but this was not thought feasible by those trapped in the building.[38] They were fortunate, however, because German resolve was weak. Demoralized by months of Resistance harassment, military set-backs and the knowledge of impending defeat, the Germans were quick to accept negotiated compromises. Thus, on 19 August they agreed to a limited truce (*la petite trève*), concerning only the police building. This led directly to the *grande trève* which began on the morning of 20 August. This truce was never fully respected by either the Germans or the Resisters. Because it threatened to shatter the unity of the Resistance, even many of its proponents abandoned it on 21 August.[39]

There is a tendency amongst historians to see the seizure of the Préfecture de Police as the sum total of police participation in the insurrection and hence to consider their role as finished after the negotiation of the truce which consolidated this position. This ignores several facts. To begin with, the police occupation of buildings was not restricted to the Préfecture, but extended to the *commissariats*

d'arrondissement on 19 August,[40] as well as to a minor involvement in
the taking of buildings such as the Hôtel de Ville on the following day.
They also participated in two other major areas of insurrectionary
action. Firstly, they took part in the armed raids, beginning on 19
August. Thus for example an attack was launched by a mixed group
of *gardiens de la paix* and FTP against a garage in the rue des Morillons
on 20 August (in mid-truce).[41] Secondly, the police played a limited
role in the construction and manning of the 600 barricades[42] which
were to prove so successful from 22 August in immobilizing the
enemy's Panzer and Tiger tanks. Few barricades contained only
policemen, although the one organized by *Inspecteurs* of the Police
Judiciaire in front of their buildings on the Quai des Orfèvres was an
exception.[43] Others contained mixed groups such as a barricade in the
Place St-Michel which served as an advanced defence for the
Préfecture de Police. Here, besides police officers there were
representatives of various classes and political opinions behind a barrier
whose components included overturned German trucks covered with
paving stones and cemented before being topped with a tricolour
flag.[44]

The historical bias in stressing the importance of the take-over of
the Préfecture de Police may therefore be faulted as a complete
representation of police involvement in the insurrection. However,
the occupation of the building always did have greater symbolic than
military significance, and this might be seen to justify the exaggerated
place given to it by historians. Such significance was recognized during
the insurrection by both the population and the Allies. If Parisians
presented themselves at commissariats asking to join the ranks of the
police insurgents in the final days of the city's insurrection,[45] it was
due less to police resistance throughout the city, which had been
carried out in civilian clothing and was therefore professionally
anonymous, than to the sight of the tricolour flying above the
Préfecture not only on the Saturday but throughout the insurrection.
The fact that in reality this was due to a negotiated compromise was
irrelevant because although the public had knowledge of the truce,
they did not know that it had originated in the Préfecture. The Allies,
for their part, confirmed the importance of the building in two ways.
Firstly, when they wanted to inform the Parisian insurgents of the
imminence of the long-awaited arrival of the Leclerc division, it was
to the Préfecture de Police that the now famous note saying, 'hold
firm, we're coming', was addressed.[46] Secondly, once they had
consecrated the insurgents' victory and sealed the Liberation by their
arrival on 25 August, it was to the police building that they first
brought the captured German commander, Dietrich von Choltitz.[47]

The liberation of Paris encouraged a strong optimism amongst the people of the city. Widespread aspirations for a better society were at least partially engendered by the fact that the eternal quest for the *union des Français* seemed to have been largely achieved. The possibility had certainly been reinforced by the Parisian police action. Georges Bidault announced on 24 August that 'for the first time [...] the Police and the insurgents had marched together' and asked whether 'this reconciliation was not the magnificent proof of the union of the French around General de Gaulle'.[48] *L'Humanité* expressed a similar sentiment of unity (without, however, referring to de Gaulle): 'May the men of the people and the agents of the public forces always find themselves on the same side of the barricade.'[49] Buoyed up by this 'fraternity of arms', the 'forces of order' were 'wreathed in a glory which the Paris police had never known.'[50] Their action was recognized and legitimized by all. De Gaulle, who undoubtedly found police popularity useful for the reinforcement of state authority, pinned the cross of the *Légion d'Honneur* to the new flag of the Préfecture. He accompanied this ceremony with the citation: 'Braving the occupant from the 15 August, starting the fight from the 19th and continuing it until the 26th, the courageous "gardiens" of the Parisian Police gave a fine example of patriotism and solidarity to the whole nation which was one of the main factors in the success of the battles for the liberation of the capital.'[51] The CNR issued a statement calling the attention of the country to the 'magnificent courage of the defenders of the Préfecture de Police'.[52] Georges Cogniot wrote in *l'Humanité*: 'The people of Paris know that they can count on the Municipal Police. The Police fought well during the glorious days.'[53]

The emphasis in most of this praise was on the so-called 'armed' resistance of the Paris police. In some cases, their military prowess gained almost mythical proportions. Thus, *l'Humanité* recounted a quite unbelievable anecdote of an unarmed *gardien de la paix* in the eighth *arrondissement* who was said to have single-handedly captured forty German prisoners.[54] Given the proximity of the battle of Paris, this emphasis should come as no surprise. Moreover, stressing the spectacular side of resistance activity was by no means limited to the coverage of the police experience. It was consistently to the courage of the FFI that the liberation press paid tribute. When the French football team was beaten 5–0 by England soon after the deliverance of Paris, it was regretted that rather than playing with the spirit of the FFI they had played with that of the French Amateur Football Association. The glorification of the armed Resisters often ignored, or at least underplayed, the role of support communities, such as those who had provided shelter for Resisters on the run, though when it came to recognizing wider forms of resistance activity the Paris police did at least have an advantage over its provincial counterparts. When, for example, the newspaper *Libération* of 15 September published an article concerning the fabrication of false identity cards in Paris during the Occupation, at the Ecole Pratique des Gardiens de la Paix, the newly-found prestige of the Paris police meant that there was a reasonable chance that such activity would be taken seriously. Provincial police forces, despite widespread individual rallying to the national insurrection, did not produce the almost unanimous adhesion of their Parisian counterparts, and hence did not have enough credibility to assure that similar claims would be recognized in their case.

Although it was claimed that 'nearly all'[55] Paris police officers had participated in the Liberation, and it was acknowledged that a purge of their ranks had been carried out during the uprising, there was nevertheless a fear that such a purge was incomplete. 'The Police still contains some men who are camouflaged enemies of the people,' read *l'Humanité* on 30 August 1944. The purge was not, as Pierre Taittinger has suggested, designed to create vacancies for extreme left-wingers to occupy:[56] the police had had considerable difficulty recruiting under Vichy, thereby leaving ample room for anyone now wishing to pursue a police career. It was rather that the insurrection, like the French Revolution, was thought to have left a legacy, and vigilance was needed for its conservation. The police force with whom there was a 'new camaraderie, so frank and so striking'[57] was not to be allowed to incorporate those who did not recognize this legacy. This obviously did have a political aspect by excluding those who were too tainted politically: 'It is an absolute necessity that the uniform of these respected and esteemed *gardiens de la paix* should not be usurped by nazi agents.'[58] But it went far beyond direct political questions to a more general philosophy of a police 'in the service of the people', which eventually tried to exclude those police officers who, before the war, had conceived their role as being 'the defenders of the trusts'.[59] There were calls for the purge to be as thorough as possible: 'It is clear that the Brigades Spéciales, a disgrace to our civilization, must be exterminated first, but it is also necessary to purge the Municipal Police.'[60] Thus, even those who had participated in the battle did not escape scrutiny.

The forgotten question of the Occupation and Liberation is that concerning the deportation of 76,000 Jews from France. In Paris, the silence surrounding this issue was not the result of a desire to preserve police popularity at all costs. After all, this subject was no more addressed in those provincial cities where police image was poor.

Moreover, the popularity of the Paris police had not prevented calls for a thorough purge of those who had been particularly active in the tracking down of Resisters. The silence about the racial deportations was rather the result of two factors: firstly, the absence of the victims, because survivors of the concentration camps did not start returning until the middle of 1945; secondly, the fact that few, even in the Resistance, felt themselves to have good enough credentials on this question to raise it in public. A clear distinction should, of course, be made between the relative inactivity of the Resistance concerning this question and the active complicity of those who ordered or carried out the arrests. Serge Klarsfeld and Robert Paxton, amongst others, have clearly established Vichy's responsibility in these deportations. There is no doubt that the police had been put in a difficult position by Vichy's policy. Considerable divergences in police reaction to orders to arrest Jews are discernible, some expressing shock or disbelief at the measures, others seeing them as a chance to steal from their victims, exercise violence or power games or even to rid the country of what they saw as a 'pest'.[61] But for the most part there was a convergence in their response to these instructions: most policemen carried out such orders, even after obedience to Vichy had ceased to be automatic, thereby raising the question of their ideological choice. That the French police had arrested five hundred foreign Jews in Paris as late as July 1944[62] was not a question which the liberation authorities particularly wished to confront.

In the immediate post-Liberation period, it was not the reemergence of questions of wartime repression or persecution against any particular group which was to decide the end of the honeymoon period for the police, although political repression did come back into the limelight with the trials of wartime police chiefs such as David, Bussière and Hennequin. It was rather that this police popularity, although real, was nonetheless fragile. It rested on an almost unanimous rallying to the Resistance during ten days in August 1944. There was always a relativity in this position, as there was in the delicate unity of the Resistance. The post-Liberation period may be seen as a gradual return to normal.[63] A desire to see an end to the exceptional circumstances, which included high crime rates and a legacy of hatred, caused conservative solutions to be preferred to some of the more radical options proposed, and led to many of the hopes of a better society engendered in the Resistance to be disappointed. The police returned to their normal functions and saw their Resistance prestige gradually undermined. On 18 June 1945, as the trumpets and fanfares of a Gaullist march sounded through the streets of Paris, the *gardien de la paix*, Charles Chambon, of undoubted Resistance credentials, asked a colleague whether they should not join the march, but immediately answered his own question with the bitter words 'what's the point, we count for nothing now'.[64] At 12.30 that day he lifted a gun to his chest and pulled the trigger. The separation of the police from the Resistance was nearing completion. The French are still waiting for a 'police in the service of the people'.

Notes

Unless stated otherwise, the place of publication is Paris.

1. This distinction between the hierarchy and the base is particularly in evidence in Resistance documents concerning police attitudes, e.g. Archives nationales (hereafter AN) F1A 3729, *Note pour monsieur Boris*, London, 28 October 1943.
2. AN F7 14888 [tracts 1943]. Tract signed by the Comité de la France Combattante and addressed to the *gardiens de la paix* of the Montreuil station, 15 July 1943.
3. Ibid.
4. AN F7 14888 [tracts 1943]. Undated tract entitled *La voix de la France*.
5. AN F1A 3843. This quotation is taken from a note from Dr Knochen, intercepted by the Resistance.
6. AN F1A 3767. Resistance document entitled *Mesures de contrôle policier*, 2 March 1943.
7. AN F7 14888 [tracts 1943]. Undated tract entitled *Lettre ouverte aux fonctionnaires, conseillers municipaux, conseillers généraux, magistrats, policiers nommés par le gouvernement usurpateur Hitléro-Vichyssois* and signed by the Front National de Lutte pour la Liberté et l'Indépendance de la France.
8. André Tollet (a Communist member of the Comité Parisien de Libération) in Francis Crémieux, *La vérité sur la Libération de Paris*, P. Belfond, 1971, p.23.
9. René Hostache, *Le Conseil National de la Résistance*, P.U.F., 1958, p.441.
10. Henri Denis, *Le Comité Parisien de Libération*, P.U.F., 1963, p.179.
11. AN 72AJ 1902 [dossier 17]. Roland Pré to d'Astier and Comidac, 2 July 1944.
12. F. Dupuy, *La Libération de Paris vue d'un commissariat de Police*, Imprimeries Réunies, 1945, p.4; see also Association des Anciens Résistants et Combattants du Ministére de l'Intérieur, *Pages d'Histoire, 1939–1945, les Policiers français dans la Résistance*, 1975,

p.115.

13. Letter from Serge Lefranc (25 July 1964) in Association des Anciens Résistants, *Pages d'Histoire*, p.121.
14. Adrien Dansette, *Histoire de la Libération de Paris*, Fayard, 67th edition, 1966, p.122.
15. For information on these movements see AN boxes 72AJ 57, 72AJ 58 and 72AJ 71.
16. Evidence from Roger Pellevoizin of the movement Police et Patrie in AN 72AJ 71.
17. Oral evidence from Serge Lefranc, André Tollet and André Carrel of Front National, Paris, 10 December 1992.
18. Letter from Serge Lefranc (25 July 1964) in Association des Anciens Résistants, *Pages d'Histoire*, p.123.
19. AN 72AJ 71. Evidence from M Le Rousès of Police et Patrie.
20. Dupuy, *La Libération de Paris*, p.8.
21. AN 72AJ 514. War Department Special Staff Historical Division, *The Liberation of Paris*, Historical Manuscript File, no.8–3 Fr (vol. VII), p. 1244.
22. Association Nationale des Anciens Combattants de la Résistance, *La Libération de Paris*, 1964, p.61.
23. André Tollet in F.Crémieux, *La vérité*, pp.21–7.
24. H.R. Kedward, *In Search of the Maquis*, Oxford, Oxford University Press, 1993, p.162.
25. Henri Rol-Tanguy in Crémieux, *La vérité*, pp.36–7; Alexandre Parodi in *Le Figaro*, 19 August 1964, p.5.
26. AN 72AJ 71. Evidence from Joseph Lomboley of Police et Patrie.
27. AN 72AJ 1902. Telegram to M d'Astier, 11 August 1944.
28. See Henri Noguères and Marcel Degliame-Fouché, *Histoire de la Résistance en France de 1940 à 1945*, Laffont, vol.5, 1981, pp.473–4.
29. Dupuy, *La Libération de Paris*, p.11.
30. Ibid, p.12.
31. Jean Chiappe was a former Prefect of Police noted for his extreme right-wing sympathies.
32. Denis, *Le Comité Parisien de Libération*, p.100.
33. *Liaisons*, no.210, June–July 1974, p.7.
34. Evidence from Roger Gallois-Cocteau in Marie Granet, *'Ceux de la Résistance'*, *1940–44*, Editions de Minuit, 1964, p.357.
35. Estimates of the exact number of those who took over and occupied this building have varied, largely because their number was not static. The occupation was carried out in stages. Thus, at about 5.00 a.m., several commandos, each consisting of roughly ten men, presented themselves at the Préfecture. They gained

entry to the building by telling the *Gardes de Paris* assigned to its protection that they were *gardiens de la paix* returning to work. Once inside, they began to prepare the ground for the main body of their colleagues, which most estimates put at about 2,000 who arrived soon after 7.30 a.m.. An undetermined number, but probably approaching a thousand of these were then despatched in groups of ten to occupy other police buildings around Paris. Thus, somewhere in the region of a thousand police officers were left defending the building.

36. Association des Anciens Résistants, *Pages d'Histoire*, p.116.
37. Noguères and Degliame-Fouché, *Histoire de la Résistance*, pp.476–8.
38. Ibid.
39. Alexandre Parodi in Crémieux, *La Vérité*, pp.78–86.
40. Jacques Debû-Bridel in Association des Résistants, *La Libération de Paris*, p.66.
41. Association des Anciens Résistants, *Pages d'Histoire*, p.118.
42. Number of barricades taken from Henri Michel, *La Libération de Paris*, Editions Complexe, 1980, p.71.
43. *Liaisons*, p.7.
44. Michel, *La Libération de Paris*, p.71.
45. Dupuy, *La Liberation de Paris*, pp.15–16.
46. Maurice Toesca, *Cinq ans de patience (1939–1945)*, Emile Paul, 1975, p.332.
47. Michel, *La Libération de Paris*, p.86.
48. *Combat*, 24 August 1944, p.2.
49. Marcel Cachin, 'L'épopée de Paris', in *l'Humanité*, 30 August 1944, p.1.
50. Communiqué from the Comité de Libération de la Police Parisienne, quoted in Dupuy, *La Libération de Paris*, pp.33–4.
51. *Liaisons*, p.38.
52. *l'Humanité*, 24 August 1944, p.1.
53. Georges Cogniot, 'Pour l'Ordre Public', *l'Humanité*, 30 August 1944, p.1.
54. Ibid.
55. Denis, *Le Comité Parisien de Libération*, appendix XXXI, report of M Marrane to CPL, 4 September 1944, p.238.
56. Pierre Taittinger, *Et Paris ne fut pas détruit*, Nouvelles Editions Latines, 1956, pp.182–3.
57. Cogniot, 'Pour l'Ordre Public', p.1.
58. Ibid.
59. Ibid.
60. Ibid.

61. For police reactions to the arrest and deportation of the Jews, see for example the diary of Pasteur Manen in J. Grandjonc and T. Grundtner, *Zones d'Ombres*, Aix-en-Provence, 1990, Alinéa, pp.353–75. See also the following documents in the Centre de Documentation Juive Contemporaine (CDJC): CV 67; IV 117; XLIVa 19; XXVb 73/ 74/ 87; XXVc 170/ 188/ 205/ 207/ 213/ 219/ 228/ 232/ 233/ 238.

62. Serge Klarsfeld, *Vichy-Auschwitz*, 1985, Fayard, vol. 2, p.389.

63. Jean C., *gardien de la paix* in the fifth *arrondissement* claimed that 'during a certain time the police were seen favourably [but] at the end of a year police officers had returned to their normal functions.' Dossier d'interviews. Institut des Hautes Etudes de la Sécurité Intérieure.

64. Henri Longuechaud, *Conformément à l'ordre de nos chefs, le drame des forces de l'ordre sous l'occupation*, Plon, 1985, pp.307–8.

– 4 –

Plus ça change...? Propaganda Fiction for Children, 1940–1945

Judith K. Proud

From the worthy tracts aimed at the young people of the *chantiers* to cheap editions of the Maréchal's *Appels*, the *Etat français* sought to instill its ideology into the youth of Vichy France through the printed word – it even produced an alphabet primer to impress the idea of Pétain into the youngest minds alongside the very first elements of literacy.[1] Beyond such overt attempts at indoctrination, however, lay a less formalized, and therefore potentially more insidious form of written propaganda: children's fiction. A medium long-exploited for its socializing and integrationalist potential, children's stories provided a variety of settings in which the triple dogma of *Travail, Famille, Patrie* could be shown in action, and where the younger inhabitants of the New France could learn to love their new allies and despise their common enemies under the alias of a series of entertaining characters.

Covering a limited range of genres, the propaganda stories of the Vichy régime exhibit a number of recurring motifs in their choice of thematic and structural paradigms and lexical and syntactic range. At a material level, production of such literature is limited to a relatively small number of individuals (authors, illustrators), and companies (publishers and printers). While researching children's fiction propaganda produced under the *Etat français*, I came upon a number of similar texts written and published at the time of the Liberation or shortly afterwards. Without claiming to provide a comprehensive survey, this study presents this small corpus of Liberation texts with the aim of comparing a number of examples of works produced in the two periods in order to pinpoint elements of continuity in choice of form, theme, expression and authorship/production.

The kind of propaganda fiction available to children under Pétain[2] may essentially be divided into two categories – comic books, and short stories, although this division is not always clear cut. Comic books usually themselves contained short stories (as well as short documentary-style articles) while most story books were quite lavishly illustrated. In the story-book category, one should also include what might ostensibly appear to be works of non-fiction, that is, biographical accounts of the life of Pétain, although titles such as *Il était une fois un Maréchal de France*[3] give some clue as to the actual treatment of such material. This fairy tale presentation of reality is indeed one of the most notable features of a great deal of the propaganda fiction in short story form produced under Vichy, both through the adoption of recognized folk tales (*Little Red Riding Hood, Bluebeard*) and through an idyllic representation of a former Golden Age which France must seek to recapture.[4] If such tales might appear somewhat tame (although nothing could be more bloody than a classic fairy tale), adventure of a different sort is not lacking in the comic books of the period, where a host of clean-limbed heroes do battle with a variety of evil individuals. Here again, fantasy plays an important role, with many story-boards containing a strong element of science fiction, or of other temporal/geographical distancing.[5]

The first of the Liberation texts to be discussed, *La Belle aventure de Disque Rouge*,[6] by its title alone clearly falls into the 'adventure story' category. Set at the beginning of the German Occupation, this is the tale of a young lad whose father is taken away by the 'boches' when they arrive in the middle of the night at the little cottage where his father has charge of the level crossing. The boy escapes before he is spotted by the Germans, and he takes to the hills with the intention of joining the local Maquis. After a long journey, and a number of adventures en route, Disque Rouge (nicknamed after the large red discs used as signals on the railway line) finally links up with the Maquis, who are persuaded to take him under their wing when he tells them of a treacherous plot he has uncovered to betray their whereabouts to the Germans. Together the young lad and his new friends foil the German attack in a cunning ambush, the collaborator who betrayed them also meeting a violent death. From this time, Disque Rouge becomes an important member of the group, acting as go-between, able to spy unnoticed on German movements in the surrounding villages. In the course of these forays, he gets to know some of the local children, and is soon a very different boy from the solitary and introspective child who used to play alone by the railway tracks. His new young acquaintances finally stand him in good stead, for when the Maquis is attacked, the youngsters are able to save the day by drawing the Germans' fire away from the main camp. The tale closes as the children join the young men of the Resistance around their camp fire on Christmas eve to celebrate their recent victory and the birth of 'une nouvelle France'.

It is a notable feature of the literature of the Vichy period that the war itself (hostilities, Armistice, Occupation) is not used as the subject or setting for classic adventure stories of the type outlined above. This is in direct contrast with the First World War, when war stories provided the mainstay of the majority of children's publishing houses. Evidently there is nothing surprising in this discrepancy, given the defeat of 1940, the Occupation and the policy of collaboration embarked upon by Vichy. Contemporary events in many of the pro-Pétain stories published under Vichy are evoked only in very general terms and under guise of allegory in the form of the Golden Age idyll, where an ideal country is laid to waste by a great storm, and then rebuilt under the benevolent guidance of a noble patriarch...[7] Not only is there never any hint in these stories of an identification of the Germans as the destructive force, but it is actively stressed that the disaster is natural, ineluctable, and, if anything, largely brought on by the degeneracy and misguided behaviour of the native population itself. In some cases it is suggested that the people have been misled by the advice and subtle influence of 'strangers' or 'foreigners' and illustrations indicate that these foreigners are clearly of Semitic origin. Not only, then, do the Germans appear to be exonerated of any blame in the fall of France, but another section of the population, the Jews (and by extension Freemasons and Bolsheviks)[8] are designated as the real enemy. A very similar phenomenon can be noted in many comic books of the period (*Lisette, Robinson, Le Téméraire* etc.) where, in realistic and fantasy settings alike, heroes tend to be of marked Aryan extraction, while their adversaries are notable for their dark colouring, hooked noses and grasping claw-like fingers. Anti-Semitism is made explicit in a clever parody of the story of Little Red Riding Hood, in which 'Doulce France' encounters the evil 'Grojuif', and has to be rescued by 'un des fils de la Nouvelle France' (a *légionnaire* according to the accompanying illustration).[9]

After the British attack on the French fleet in the harbour of Mers-el-Kébir, the English, particularly the distinctive figure of Winston Churchill, became another favourite subject of caricature, such political satire touching the young audience through a 'dual function' publication entitled *Abécédaire à l'usage des petits enfants qui apprennent à lire et des grandes personnes qui ne comprennent pas encore le français...*[10] The fairy tale pastiche was also used to attack the Russians, whose leader Stalin became the eponymous hero of the Bluebeard parody, *L'Homme aux mains rouges.*[11]

Such works may appear to be a long way from the explicit anti-

German message of the Liberation tale of Disque Rouge, but what is perhaps essential is that at the root of all such stories there is the designation and vilification of a common enemy as a scapegoat on whom frustration, anger and guilt may be vented. The expiation of guilt is perhaps one of the most important functions of such creations in the context of the two periods under consideration here.

The Golden Age fantasy texts of the Vichy period were one way of presenting and coming to terms with the circumstances leading up to and including the Armistice. They also served to map out the future of the nation as it was envisaged by those close to the Maréchal at the time. The story of Disque Rouge is doing exactly the same thing, although this propaganda objective may be obscured for the modern reader by the fact that the story portrays, albeit in highly fictionalized form, what is today an accepted version of events occurring during the war. For the reader in 1945, however, the Resistance was still essentially an unknown force, but one which hoped to play a major role in the new order of things. It was of paramount importance, therefore, that the correct image of the movement should be portrayed, counteracting the propaganda previously put out by the French and German authorities, and compensating for the reprisals carried out against civilian populations as a result of Resistance activities. A similar public relations objective can be seen in creations such as the comic-strip serial 'Fifi, gars du Maquis' (*Vaillant*, from 1 June 1945), and a unique publication, *Le Corbeau déchaîné*, the 'official' comic book of the Auvergne Resistance movement, drawn by Marijac and produced in 1944.

As the events of the Liberation heralded the defeat of the armies of the Third Reich, the Germans could now be portrayed in their hereditary role of enemies to the French nation by the use of the term 'boche', as in *Disque Rouge*. The propaganda value of the Germans, however, was limited, for although their excellent credentials as a traditional foe gave the efforts of the Resistance added credibility and value, the threat they offered was effectively ended by the Liberation itself. Following a lead already taken by the *Corbeau déchaîné*, *Disque Rouge* gives a clue to the new enemy who was to give the Resistance continued meaning after 1944, the ideal scapegoat for past defeats, who would serve as a focus for national opprobrium and thus as a catalyst for national unity – the collaborator.

One of the most surprising points of similarity between *Disque Rouge* and the children's literature of the *Etat français* arises not out of the story itself, but from the material production of the book. Very little has been written about the publication of children's literature during the war years, and few details are available about authors, illustrators, publishers and printers.[12] Many company records for the period have been destroyed, and, not surprisingly, those active on behalf of the Vichy régime have usually remained silent about their wartime publications. It is worth noting, however, that *Disque Rouge* was printed by the Curial-Archereau company, a printing house that was quite prolific on behalf of the Maréchal during the Vichy period, as well as producing some less highly-politicized children's books. One can only assume that the company was able to satisfy the post-War authorities about its wartime activities, the production of a Resistance story perhaps being one of the first steps in a rehabilitation that also included a sixty-two-page illustrated book about de Gaulle.[13] The company was not alone in such acts of expiation – two comic books that survived the war unscathed (*Ames vaillantes* and *Jumbo*) both dedicated special numbers to the Resistance in the wake of the Liberation.

If the careful construction of an authorized version of recent history, and the designation of a common enemy are two standard techniques used by the propagandist in an attempt to foster national unity and to consolidate a new régime,[14] so too is the cult of the individual and the designation of a saviour-figure. This technique was heavily relied on by the Vichy régime whose authority largely depended on the figure of Pétain himself. Textual material, like the visual arts, concentrated, above all, on a number of distinctive physical attributes of the Maréchal (clear look, white moustache, cane/baton etc.) all of which, in the hands of the propaganda writer, became the symbols of a wide store of almost god-like virtues.

While Pétain featured in a number of the 'Golden Age' tales in the role of Wise Patriarch and Saviour of the Nation, the most blatantly hagiographic texts to appear consisted in a number of 'enhanced' biographies of the great man.[15] In such accounts, the facts of his life have not been tampered with in any way, but the terms in which he is portrayed – a mixture of fairy-tale fantasy and religious veneration – serve to elevate Pétain above the ordinary mortal to the ranks of the superheroes and saints of French history (Vercingétorix, Bayard, Jeanne d'Arc), with whom he is frequently compared.[16]

A similar approach appears to have been envisaged in a text celebrating General de Gaulle, published in 1945, entitled *La Merveilleuse aventure du Général de Gaulle racontée aux petits Français*.[17] Here, the title, like the biographies of Pétain, immediately suggests a fairy-tale element to de Gaulle's life, although this idea is not exploited in the text as it is in the stories about the Maréchal. Less well known to the people of France than his illustrious predecessor, de Gaulle offered his biographer fewer opportunities to capitalize on physical attributes, although his height is mentioned on a number of occasions. The 'adventurous' nature of his exploits is clearly designed to appeal to the energetic young audience, a deliberate contrast, perhaps, with the image of venerable old age that was inevitably associated with Pétain, and which was actively played upon in many of the Vichy texts for children.

Ironically, it is in the recounting of de Gaulle's rise to power, and particularly in the account of his early military career, that this tale most resembles the biographies of Pétain. Apart from the obvious fact that they both attended the military academy of St Cyr, other elements in their lives, more significant in the building of a superhero myth, bear comparison. Both men, for example, apparently showed a precocious and visionary grasp of military tactics, a form of genius that was not appreciated by the higher echelons of the military, and led to a certain amount of discrimination against them in their careers. Despite such setbacks, both men showed unwavering fidelity to their countries, responding unhesitatingly to the Nation's appeal in the dark days of both world wars (and during a number of other conflicts in between). Finally, just as the biographies of Pétain highlight the fact that his early promise and devotion to his country were vindicated at Verdun, so the Liberation appears as a first vital step in de Gaulle's vindication[18] – a confirmation of past endeavours and a guarantee for the future.

Among the most interesting Liberation texts is a two-volume comic strip entitled *La Bête est morte. La guerre mondiale chez les animaux*,[19] a presentation of the history of the war in which, as the title suggests, animals replace the human protagonists. As the two volumes themselves proclaim, the work was conceived and written during the Occupation, and printed only a few months after the Liberation, of which it is a celebration. The elements that link this text with a number of works of Vichy propaganda are particularly striking, not least the fact that its author, Victor Dancette, was also the author of a text entitled *Il était une fois un pays heureux*, published in 1943, only a few months, presumably, before the creation of *La Bête est morte*. As the title indicates, *Il était une fois un pays heureux* is the very epitomy of the Golden Age idyll, its clear support of Pétain and his régime being demonstrated not only by the story itself, but also by the terms of its production. The book was published by a company called La Générale Publicité on behalf of 'le Bureau de Documentation du Chef d'Etat', the Maréchal's personal propaganda machine, and fifty special copies of the edition were destined for Pétain himself.

Dancette himself is not the only link to be found between two such ostensibly contradictory narratives; *La Bête est morte* was also published by La Générale Publicité. In fact, the world of the comic strip seems to have abounded in 'résistants de la dernière heure', particularly where their illustrators are concerned. Many famous names apparently worked for both régimes with no obvious hiatus. André Liquois of the very right-wing *Téméraire* (15 January 1943 – 1 August 1944) subsequently worked on the Communist *Jeune Patriote*, which, having become the *Vaillant* in June 1945, featured his serial 'Fifi gars du Maquis' already referred to above. Raymond Poïvet also made the transition from *Le Téméraire* without difficulty, working on the pro-Resistance *Le Coq hardi* (founded 20 November 1944) in company with Liquois and Marijac. Marijac himself, the man behind the Resistance comic *Le Corbeau déchaîné* (1944), had only the previous year been working on the Vichy-orientated *Cœurs vaillants* and *Siroco*. Calvo, the talented illustrator of *La Bête est morte* worked on the Paris-based comic *Junior*, until this publication, like the majority of other comics produced in Occupied France, was forced to close down (5 March 1942). During this period he contributed to the profusion of stories for children that celebrated the valorous deeds of past French heroes, a genre particularly beloved of the Vichy regime, with a tale featuring d'Artagnan.

In terms of form, clearly *La Bête est morte* continues the very popular tradition of comic books for young children that had established itself in France long before the outbreak of war. The right-wing and the Catholic printing houses in France (Bonne Presse, Fleurus etc.) had effectively hijacked the comic industry during the 1930s in an attempt to counteract what they perceived as the pernicious imperialist Yankee propaganda put out by Walt Disney. From there it was but a small step to *Le Téméraire* (or as Ory terms it the 'Petit Nazi illustré')[20] whose first issue appeared in January 1943. Also an established convention, but in a tradition dating back much further, is the use of animals as the protagonists in a story. As the most famous examples – the fables of Aesop and La Fontaine – demonstrate, this is a method that has long been favoured by authors seeking to disguise their didactic aim behind an agreeable veil of allegory. The natural world was clearly seen as a promising means of reaching the young children of Vichy France by an author like Yvonne Estienne, who published, in 1942, a tale entitled *La Belle histoire d'un chêne*, a highly anthropomorphic tale about a great oak (Pétain) protecting all the flora and fauna in the forest against the ravages of the inevitable Great Storm. In *La Bête est morte*, Dancette combines this great tradition with another established convention of children's literature, the 'tale within the tale', a convention also used by a Vichy writer such as Jean Nohain (Jaboune) in his *Bonjour la France!*.[21] When *La Bête est morte* opens, Grandfather

Rabbit is surrounded by his young grandsons who entreat him to tell them the story of how he lost his leg in the war.

For anyone familiar with the Golden Age idyll so frequently used by children's writers under Vichy France, the tale that Grandfather Rabbit proceeds to recount has an uncannily familiar ring to it. The story tells of the ideal world of 'Fleury-la-Forêt' (in *Bonjour la France!* it was 'Coucy-les-Bois'), the enchanted woodland space of fairy tales where anything can happen. As in all the best fairy tales (and Vichy propaganda), nature is both abundant and perfect in this magic world (see figure 2, p.66), an image enhanced by the explicit use of the vocabulary of enchantment ('marvellous', 'enchanting' etc.), references to 'purity', and a high proportion of hyperbolic adjectives ('in the shade of enormous mushrooms' etc.). The very same technique had been used by Dancette only a year earlier in *Il était une fois un pays heureux*, to portray the land of milk and honey that Pétain was called upon to restore. Grandfather Rabbit even goes so far as to mention the Great Storm that, unbeknown to the happy inhabitants of the forest, was slowly gathering above their heads...

The philosophy of life in Fleury-la-forêt is also remarkably familiar. The work ethic of the bees is highly praised, and the importance of the building industry, particularly the building of family homes, is stressed (see figure 2, p.66). The fruits of the land are seen as one of the country's greatest riches, as are the hard-working peasants who reap nature's rich harvest. In conjunction with this very Pétainist insistence on the importance of the land ('La terre, elle, ne ment pas') and the twin imperatives of 'Travail' and 'Famille', also comes 'Patrie', although it takes the catastrophe of the war to remind the nation of its national identity: 'Il aura fallu ce cataclysme pour nous rendre notre âme nationale.' Compare this with *Il était une fois un pays heureux* in which the people of that happy land also find their collective soul in the midst of suffering: 'Et ce peuple, qui dans les souffrances avait retrouvé son âme.'

Not surprisingly, it is in its explanation of France's defeat that *La Bête est morte* appears to differ most from its Vichy counterparts. As we have noted already in the case of *Disque Rouge*, the propagandist was now free to indict the Germans for their part in the conflict; this they do, although the animal parallel is retained in the most entertaining manner. Hence, Hitler is portrayed as a permanently enraged wolf, with swastika armbands and a distinctive lock of dark hair falling over one eyebrow (see figure 1, p.65), Goering becomes a fat buffoon of a pig, and Goebbels, in a particularly virulent caricature, becomes 'a runt of a polecat, belligerent and deformed, a real gasbag'.

Figure 1. The title page of *La Bête est morte* (vol.1) showing details of illustrator and publisher and a caricature of Hitler as the leader of the Wolves. © Editions G.P., Paris.

Figure 2. Images of the idyllic Fleury-la-Forêt before the invasion of the Wolves (*La Bête est morte*, vol.1). © Editions G.P., Paris.

Figure 3. Caricatures of Winston Churchill (leader of the Bulldogs); Russia/Stalin (leader of the Polar Bears) – note the hammer and sickle (*La Bête est morte*, vol.1); Roosevelt (leader of the Bisons) in conference with de Gaulle (leader of the Storks) on the lawns of the White House (vol.2). © Editions G.P., Paris.

Figure 4. The massive military power of the Wolves (*La Bête est morte*, vol.1). © Editions G.P., Paris.

> • Cette déroute évidente des Loups devant les forces bisontines avait poussé au paroxysme l'impatience des citadins de notre capitale qui brûlaient du désir de secouer eux-mêmes le joug barbare si péniblement enduré pendant un lustre. Et brusquement, sans qu'on sache exactement de qui serait l'ordre, ce fut l'explosion ! Explosion de tout un peuple d'animaux pacifiques que l'imminence de la libération galvanisait et qui voulait montrer au monde que l'apparente soumission de quatre années d'esclavage n'avait rien changé à sa foi, à son courage, à son patriotisme.
> • Nos rues se couvrirent soudain de barricades où le pistolet du Lapin futé de la zone côtoyait comiquement l'arquebuse du Lapin cossu des quartiers bourgeois, car le soulèvement faisait l'unanimité chez nous et il n'était plus question de tribus, de castes ou de naissances. Tous les poils vibraient à l'unisson.
> • Je ne pense pas que dans l'Histoire notre capitale ait jamais connu pareilles journées d'universelle exaltation ! Les drapeaux, frémissant d'impatience depuis quatre ans dans un coin du terrier, avaient été sortis dès la première heure et palpitaient aux fenêtres alors que les Loups défendaient encore la chaussée. Déchaîné, un vent de résistance soulevait la capitale et, de quartier en quartier, balayait sur son passage tout ce qui sentait le Barbare.

Figure 5. The uprising of the people of Paris (after Delacroix). Note the image of the Sacré-Cœur in the top left-hand corner, and the date (1944) and the publisher's initials (GP) inscribed on the barrel, centre right (*La Bête est morte*, vol.2). © Editions G.P., Paris.

While the post-Liberation explanation of France's defeat at the hands of the Great Wolf's hordes appears not only quite different from the Vichy storm analogy, but also more akin to historical events, the fine detail of the account actually demonstrates a very similar capacity for self-delusion. According to Grandfather Rabbit, the sole cause of France's defeat at Germany's hands is the enormous technical superiority of the German weaponry, and the great numbers of tanks and aeroplanes ranged against them (see figure 4, p.68). This was also an argument used by Pétain himself in a number of his *Appels* (see for example his speeches of 20, 23 and 25 June 1940). Military experts today agree that the French forces were as well equipped as the Germans in terms of tank and aeroplane numbers, and that some of their heavy weaponry was indeed technically superior.[22] In portraying the great 'avalanche of material' by which the inhabitants of Fleury-la-Forêt are 'inevitably' ('fatalement') overcome, therefore, the Liberation propagandists are as guilty as their predecessors of glossing over the issue of French military incompetence, and of doing so in the kind of terms that come dangerously close to the Vichy 'storm' analogy.

One obvious change in detail to differentiate the Vichy and Liberation accounts of the history of the War, is the attitude shown towards the British and the Russians – evil traitors and dangerous foes for the collaborators of the *Etat français*, valorous saviours for liberated France. Ironically, however, the very same stereotypes and caricatures are used to portray these nations and their representatives in both sets of literature. Winston Churchill leader of the British bulldogs is unmistakeable, and the Russian bear, who featured prominently in a number of the illustrations in *L'Homme aux mains rouges* returns in *La Bête est morte,* this time as a far more genial polar bear (see figure 3, p.67), in one picture actually sporting the distinctive moustache worn by Stalin and his literary alter ego, the Man with Red Hands.

Recounting the events of the war is one matter; analysing and apportioning credit for the actual Liberation is another, for this is where the fine line is drawn between rationalization of past events, and justification of a current/future régime. All of the contenders for political power in post-War France are mentioned in the final pages of the second volume of *La Bête est morte*, but it is difficult to pinpoint any particular affiliation on the part of the author. The Allies, the Resistance and General Leclerc are all acknowledged for their contributions to the Liberation, and de Gaulle, going under the unlikely alias of 'our national stork' ('notre cigogne nationale') is depicted in America engaging in last-minute discussions with President Roosevelt, or 'le chef des Bisons' (see figure 3, p.67). Of the national participants in the Liberation, it is the people of Paris who receive the greatest accolade for their spontaneous uprising against the rapidly disintegrating German forces, the description of their valiant efforts being lavishly illustrated by a modern reworking of Delacroix's *La Liberté guidant le peuple* (see figure 5, p.69).[23] Even here, however, it is stressed that military equipment supplied by the Americans was needed to finish mopping up German resistance in the capital.

If the narrative fails to designate a single redemptive figure in the true propagandist style, and in marked contrast with the Vichy narratives, it nevertheless concludes, if a little clumsily, with a clear message to its readers, which in effect places it in the camp of Gaullist propaganda. One of the points stressed throughout this account of the war is the importance of military hardware, not just in the defeat of France, as we have noted above, but also in the Liberation. Courage and great leadership aside, it is the combined force of tanks and aeroplanes that is seen as the Allies greatest strength, a point of view that is highlighted in both text and illustrations. The final message of the story, encapsulated in a quotation, unattributed but unmistakeably Gaullist in tone, is that France should support and encourage the development of a strong, well-armed, modern army, the very basis of de Gaulle's military policy.

Rationalizing the past, self-justification, and mapping out the future; these are common propaganda objectives, and show clear elements of continuity between the politicized children's fiction of Vichy France and that of the Liberation writers. However, the points of resemblance linking the propaganda of the two periods go much deeper than this, touching every aspect of these texts, from creative conception and execution, to material production. And over-arching all these similarities is the common purpose of influencing the nation's youth through the established channels of traditional literary forms. This testifies firstly to a continuing belief that children can be influenced in this manner, and secondly to the adaptability of children's literature and its in-built capacity for didacticism. It is well documented that children were an intrinsic part of the political and social ethos of Vichy France. If the post-Liberation era was less regimented and idealistic in its approach to youth, the evidence of these few texts suggests that the younger reader continued to be perceived as a viable target in the campaign to establish the foundations of the new régime, even if some elements of these foundations had yet to be fully defined.

Notes

Unless stated otherwise, the place of publication is Paris.

1. [Anonymous], *Abécédaire*, Bureau de Documentation du Chef de l'Etat, Imprimerie Draeger, 1943.
2. Further details about publishing for children in the *Etat français* are available in a forthcoming monograph by the present author entitled *Children and Propaganda*, Intellect, Oxford, 1995.
3. A. Paluel-Marmont, *Il était une fois un Maréchal de France*, illustrations by Pierre Rousseau [and Germaine Bouret], 'Edité par Fanfan la tulipe, journal pour enfants', Editions et Publications Françaises, Imprimerie Curial-Archereau, [1941].
4. This is the particular theme of the monograph referred to in note 2.
5. For further details about comic books during the Second World War, see: P. Ory, *Le Petit Nazi illustré. Le Téméraire (1943–1944)*, Editions Albatros, 1979; and L. Gervereau and D. Peschanski (eds), *La Propagande sous Vichy 1940–44*, Collection Publications de la BDIC, 1990, pp.180–7.
6. P. Vincent, *La Belle aventure du Disque Rouge*, illustrations by Gad, Imprimerie Curial-Archereau, 1945.
7. See, for example, A. Paluel-Marmont, *Six petits enfants et treize étoiles*, illustrations by Lucien Boucher, Editions et Publications Françaises, 1942, and V. Dancette, *Il était une fois un pays heureux*, illustrations by P. Baudier, Editions de la Générale Publicité, 'Pour le Bureau de Documentation du Chef de l'Etat', [1943].
8. This link is discussed in detail in works such as H. Coston, *Les Corrupteurs de la jeunesse. La main-mise Judéo-maçonnique sur la presse enfantine*, Bulletin d'information anti-maçonnique, Centre d'Action et de Documentation Anti-maçonnique, n.d., and J. Bertrand, [Henry Babize] and C. Wacogne, *La Fausse éducation nationale. L'Emprise judéo-maçonnique sur l'école française*, Centre d'Action et de Documentation Anti-maçonnique, n.d.
9. [Anonymous], *Il était une fois (Histoire de Doulce France et Grojuif)*, illustrations by JB, NEF, [1942].
10. [Anonymous], *Abécédaire à l'usage des petits enfants qui apprennent à lire et des grandes personnes qui ne comprennent pas encore le français...*, G. Mazeyrie, n.d.
11. [Anonymous], *L'Homme aux mains rouges*, n.d.
12. Although a text like P. Fouché, *L'Edition française sous l'Occupation*, 2 vols, Paris 7, 1987, provides a useful guide to publishing in general in this period, it does not deal with children's publishing

at all, except for a very short section on school books in the first volume.

13. [Anonymous], *Le Général de Gaulle*, Hachette, 1945.
14. See J. Ellul, *Propaganda. The Formation of Men's Attitudes*, New York, Vintage Books, 1973, and R. Girardet, *Mythes et mythologies politiques*, Seuil, 1986.
15. R. Descouens, *La Vie du Maréchal Pétain racontée aux enfants de France*, illustrations by Mario Simon and Francis Dujardin, Editions de la Vraie France, Imprimerie de 'l'Eclaireur de Nice', [1940]; P. Hérault, *La Vie d'honneur du maréchal Pétain racontée et illustrée pour les jeunes français*, illustrations also by Hérault, Farré et Freulon, [1940]; A. Paluel-Marmont, *Il était une fois un Maréchal de France*.
16. This is also the aim of a number of history books in the form of 'exemplary lives' such as [anonymous], *Vercingétorix, la belle histoire de la France*, illustrations by Pierre Luc, Editions Artistiques et Littéraires, Imprimerie E. Desfossés, 1943.
17. H. Chandet, *La Merveilleuse aventure du Général de Gaulle racontée aux petits Français suivie de l'aventure du Général de Lattre de Tassigny et du Général Leclerc*, illustrations by Michel Haguenauer, [Lyon], [1945].
18. Ibid. Having voiced his doubts over the efficacy of the Maginot line, de Gaulle's worst fears are confirmed by the German invasion of France (p.4). His unswerving belief in the importance of superior tank and air cover is then vindicated once again (as the text is at pains to point out), as is his determination to continue the war from England, when the Allies finally crush the German army (p.6).
19. V. Dancette and J. Zimmermann (vol.1), V. Dancette (vol.2), *La Bête est morte. La guerre mondiale chez les animaux*, illustrations by Calvo, artistic direction by Williams Péra, Editions de la Générale Publicité, vol.1 (27 pp.) 'printed in the third month of the Liberation', vol.2 (48 pp.) printed in June 1945.
20. Ory, *Le Petit Nazi illustré*.
21. Jaboune [Jean Nohain], *Bonjour la France!* poems by Christian Schwaebel, illustrations by Emmanuel Cocard, Collection Tobby l'Eléphant, Lyon, Société d'Edition façonnage et impression, Presses Giraud-Rivoire, n.d.
22. According to John Keegan (*The Second World War*, London, Arrow Books, 1989, p.60) France had some 3,000 tanks compared with the Germans' 2,400, and the French Somua S35 tank was technically superior to its German equivalent.
23. Even here, however, the message is equivocal; Notre-Dame, the

'church of the people' that featured in the original painting has been replaced by the basilica of the Sacré-Cœur, the church more traditionally associated with the French Right...I am indebted to Dr Bill Kidd of the University of Stirling, who has made a study of modern reworkings of this painting, for his views on the transposition of these churches.

Part II

Gender

– 5 –

No Words to Say It? Women and the Expectation of Liberation

Karen Adler

'Strangely, the war for me was a great chance for liberation and permissiveness, which otherwise I would perhaps not have known.' (Nicole Clarence)

'I personally saw the extraordinary evolution of women between 1940 and 1945. And how they understood, at the price of a terrible experience, that public affairs are also their affair.' (Yvonne Dumont)

(Quoted in Marie-Louise Coudert, *Elles, la Résistance*, Messidor,1983, pp.47, 64)

When former Resisters equate their experience with liberation and learning, and portray the Resistance period as a time of personal, as well as national, struggle and growth, it is perhaps more indicative of the period in, rather than of, which they speak. Such sentiments finally came to be valued in the 1970s and 1980s when they were recorded, in a way that had been impossible in the previous thirty years. Political identifications based on gender were necessarily of a very different order in the 1940s, yet the moment was consciously conceived and constructed as 'historical' even as it happened, making its literature piquant and fertile. This chapter sets out to establish women's self-conception in the struggle against occupation and in the building of a 'new' France. It attempts to identify the routes women took into public life and the limitations which prevailed upon them. Were they 'neutralized' by the 'dominant culture', 'endorsing' images of themselves 'which were not their own'[1] or did they consciously invert

The author thanks Penelope Hamm, Margaretta Jolly and Lucy Noakes for their comments on earlier versions of this article.

the roles laid down in French tradition and remanufactured by Vichy? Was the idea of 'home' really taken out on to the streets so that women, while remaining wives and mothers, engaged in a radical redefinition of what wifehood and motherhood had previously meant? The following examination of the clandestine resistance press aimed at women hopes to offer an answer that lies somewhere between the two. Taking a cue from Marie-France Brive, the analysis centres on the resistance press in general, regardless of the zone in which it was produced, as geography seems to have had no discernible effect on the representations of women.

It has become almost a watchword in feminist histories of this period to move from a critique of the enfranchisement of women in 1944 as a supposed reward by General de Gaulle for their part in the Resistance, to the observation that, given the contradictory limitations which prevailed on them after the war, the accession to full citizenship really affected women very little.[2] Apart from fervent calls issued by the marginal Trotskyist Left for equality for the entire French population (which would include women and Jews),[3] this was scarcely a preoccupation among most Resistance women according to demands in their press. Suffice at this point to say that enfranchisement did not lead to an equal involvement of women in mainstream post-War politics, or even to involvement in similar proportions to those in which women had operated alongside men in the Resistance.[4] A similar pattern emerges on the social level as, it has been argued, despite the dramatic changes in women's wartime lives, the Second World War overall did not presage great breaks with the past,[5] although it was another matter for those close to the tens of thousands of Jews and political deportees who failed to return from the killing centres and concentration camps respectively.[6] This continuity is not disputed here but approached in terms of expectations and hopes developed during the Occupation that the challenges to and by women would be recognized by significant structural change afterwards. Women cannot, of course, be considered homogeneously; in particular, the active anti-Semitism of the French State produced fatal divisions between Jews and non-Jews, even resistant ones. In addition to taking account of the representations of Jewish women in the clandestine press, the self-representations of a single Jewish woman – both Resister and part of the editorial team of a clandestine newspaper – may provide clues to the limitations prevailing on her within a milieu of restricted and dangerous discourse and legislation.

The clandestine press itself (of which 1,106 titles have been preserved at the Bibliothèque Nationale), often a single stencilled sheet which appeared for one or more issues, could cover, for example, an occupation (metal workers, teachers, intellectuals), an aspect of the struggle (antiracism), a social group (Spanish immigrants) or, as is most frequent for those journals aimed at women, a small geographical area (such as a Paris *arrondissement*). Common to each example of the genre is the necessity for its secret production and distribution and readers were urged to pass the few copies around.[7] About 6 per cent of the press, sixty-eight titles, was overtly aimed at women.[8] Its agitational efforts far outstrip information or detailed political argument. A reading of this press confirms its 'limited repertoire', which can be thematically grouped under the headings *patriotic motherhood, sacrifice* and *daring*.

At first glance, the type of femininity addressed by the papers seems wholly traditional and emphatically heterosexual; readers are interpellated as mothers (or, frequently, 'mums'), housewives, nurses, godmothers, and concerned in general with the welfare of their families whose existence seemed to be in no doubt.[9] Virtually all demand that women take action by claiming increased rations, particularly of bread, butter, milk and coal, though regional and chronological variations sometimes add wine and meat to the shopping list. The limitations of these claims, precious though they were to a population whose health was seriously affected by the lack of calories, fats and dietary variety, are such that 'feminine interest' and the fight for food become utterly collapsed. Clearly, though, there was some dispute about this. The women's grouping within the French Communist Party, the Union des Femmes Françaises (UFF), described itself as 'not a political organization of women [but] a feminine patriotic movement'.[10] 'Some women,' it said stoutly in its internal bulletin, 'wrongly believe that "the battle for beef" is a fight without glamour, without glory, without interest or immediate result. What a mistake...'[11] By 1944, the UFF had become an organization 'for the defence of the family and the liberation of France', translating patriotic pride into family devotion. The readers of the many journals produced under its auspices and those of the local 'feminine committees' which grouped together in 1944 to produce the union, are addressed in a language which emphasizes their simultaneous role as carers of the nation and of the family, forming an inextricable link for women between 'la France' and 'la Famille' missing from the general clandestine literature, but mirroring the process undertaken by Vichy propaganda. In Vichy France, many of whose men were absent, the facile gendered division between loyalty to the public nation (for men) and devotion to the private home (for women) is disturbed, obscuring prior assumptions about the visible occupants of public and private space. We might argue that in the face of fragmentation imposed by war, occupying forces and the ideological and material structures of the Vichy State which regard only one sort of family as worthy (one which is Catholic, Pétainist, etc.), for some women to concentrate on keeping another sort of family or community intact (by taking in refugees or meeting together as political activists) necessitates a direct challenge to the prevailing order. Women who become mothers to hidden Jewish children, godmothers to groups of partisans or single mothers in sole charge of family decisions, practise their role in public to a far greater extent than previously. Motherhood itself takes on new meanings: 'for the defence of the family and the liberation of France' becomes a matter not of one private (family) and one public (France) entity, but of two public ones.[12] But it is not entirely so. Women, by and large, remained on the spot rather than take to the maquis; and the family, while the site of subversion, remains their traditional place, at once repressive and liberating. New versions of the part may have been invented, but the uniform is not shed. Demanding women's public political allegiance while wishing them to remain within their metaphorical and literal walls, the UFF's vacillation and uncertainty indicates its inability to shed its vision of women as subjects ruled more by gender than by politics, and reflects its vision of home in all its nuclear sanctity as their rightful place.

In a milieu of hardship, military occupation and frequent male absence, informed by traditional gender values where urban women spent many hours each week queuing for increasingly scarce food, we cannot be surprised to find a culture of sacrifice. Virtually every paper recommends that women agitate, often by forming delegations to the town hall to demand better rations, but this is most often expressed in terms of acquiring supplies for old people and children. Women themselves are not told of the need to feed or warm themselves better but always to act on behalf of others. Sometimes, though, sacrificial duty comes into conflict with familial responsibility. In an article on Resistance heroine Berty Albrecht, the weight of sacrifice is tempered with the paradox that in order to achieve full glory as a French woman, Albrecht had to give up her duties as a mother. 'After a profound moral drama,' *Femmes Françaises* tells us, 'about which only those closest to her knew how torn she was, she sacrificed her family, left her job in order to enter the underground.'[13] Only the shift into 'true' patriotism permits the relinquishment of family duty but for this, Berty Albrecht crucially made the ultimate sacrifice, for France, of her own life. More usual is a down-to-earth version of sacrifice, such as the notion that the godmothers of freedom fighters give up all for their team of 'soldiers without uniform'. The godmothers raised funds, supplied food, clothing and ration cards, did the partisans' washing and mending, hid them, and so on – essential tasks, but limited to a devoted, motherly role. The supporters of the 'Victor Hugo detachment' in Paris even sacrificed their pride: 'We, women of Paris, we admire the valiant FTP, sons of France, bearers of our hopes and of the future of our country. They are our pride.'[14]

Sacrifice for glory is echoed in parts of the Jewish press. While many non-Jewish, urban, women were experiencing hunger and separation (although this was mitigated by a never-previously experienced autonomy in running a home, earning a living and making decisions), for Jewish women, everyday life threatened constant danger. *La Voix de la Femme Juive* instructs its readers to

> be proud of your sisters in the Warsaw Ghetto who took up arms to fight proudly for the defence of their existence and the right to life for themselves and their children, for the honour of their people. Urge your husbands, fiancés, brothers to join the fight against fascism. Give the most valiant to our glorious Jewish freedom-fighters and partisans.[15]

Sacrifice here is coupled with an easy gender transfer that demands direct identification with the female Warsaw Ghetto fighters at the same time as remaining within the rigidity of roles at play in France. Where it exists, press representation of the Jewish woman adheres firmly to standard notions of womanhood. *Notre Voix* ('organ of the union of Jews against oppressive fascism') appeared in the southern zone for more than seventy issues from 1942 to 1944, and exhibits a propensity towards relatively complex political analyses. As a Jewish paper which was well, and early, informed regarding the likely outcome for deported Jews, its content differs radically from that of most other journals which equate deportation with the transfer of forced labour to Germany and which scarcely refer to anti-Semitism in any form. By February 1943 it could announce, 'DEPORTATION IS A CERTAIN DEATH, A TERRIBLE DEATH',[16] yet where women are concerned, the tone melts into something far more familiar and banal. The article, 'Women! Let's take our place in the fight which will liberate France!' takes as its starting point International Women's Day (8 March): 'On this 8 March 1943, Jewish women suffer cruelly in servile France. Their husbands, their sons, their parents, their sisters have been deported to the East where the Nazis assassinate them at the same time as the unfortunate Jews of Poland, in their thousands.' The emphasis on others almost implies that women themselves are not in danger. And to combat the threat against their families, women are encouraged not to arm themselves or go into hiding, but to 'go to the town hall, demand that bread and milk be given to their children instead of it going to the *Boches*'.[17] Unable to retreat from the image of woman as nurturer, such stock representation of women's struggle by *Notre Voix* almost indicates that there are no acceptable ways to describe women, whether housewives and mothers or not, who are yet themselves endangered. The essential feminine separation of the self from others and in the service of others obliterates all else, so that even at a time when to be Jewish was recognised as implying death, the fact of gender becomes all-encompassing and overriding.

The foregoing may suggest that women were entirely subject to a repressive social construction, but a strong element of *daring* to move beyond the boundaries of gender appears in the many references to women in the Soviet Union. Impossible to speak directly for the self, they act as a vehicle for the transference of desire. These projected hopes were, we may suggest, the way in which the wishes of French Resistance women for a recognized place in the active struggle were translated. Unable to express this overtly, the alleged strength and equality of Soviet women, constantly underlined, provides a clue to a potential vision of French women without actually saying so. It is, of course, no surprise to find in Communist party literature esteem for the Soviet Union as exemplar of hope for the future. But beyond the rhetoric of glory and reverence for Stalin's army can be glimpsed a more expansive vision of women's capacities. Early during the Occupation, *Jeunes Filles de France* alludes to the disruption of feminine roles: '[M]ore than 40,000 young [Soviet] women have completed their training as tractor drivers. Now scorn for women and their own lack of confidence in their strength which were formerly so much part of village life have long since been relegated to the past.'[18] Here is solid recognition that belief in women's physical weakness and in the need for them to undertake different tasks from men is ideologically produced (along with oblique reference to women's own rural place beyond the Pétainist 'retour à la terre'). It is not yet possible to make the same demands for French women; the article argues that while young French women want work which guarantees them independence, their real dream of the future is represented by a happy home, a dream turned nightmare by Vichy. Fifteen months later, the paper notes that not only have Soviet women replaced men in heavy industry and agriculture, but some have gone into armed combat where, 'knowing neither weakness nor fatigue and moved by sublime courage, they remain proud.'[19] The superhuman quality attributed to these fighters notwithstanding, there is more than a hint that women's capabilities lie far beyond the call that they participate in the liberationist movement by claiming bigger milk rations.[20]

It is only at the very end of the Occupation that articles dare be more direct. It is true that this reflects the urgent need for fire-power and fighters and responds to the call from the Francs-Tireurs et Partisans (FTP) and the Communist party that all, women included, join its active units. But in the stirring recruitment pleas, can we not detect an almost undisciplined straining beyond the party line, that women's part in the visible struggle be admitted? No longer content with an earlier desire 'to be those who prepare the powder and cast the bullets of her [France's] soldiers', expressed only six months previously, we find a revelatory vigour:

> FRENCH WOMEN PARTISANS, the call which the FTPF has made to women to join up answers exactly the deep sentiments of French women, to which they responded immediately. They have joined the auxiliary services... but they have shown their desire to participate even more actively in the struggle.
> *WE WANT TO GO INTO ARMED COMBAT!*
> ... All our dead demand to be avenged. Communist women, our first gesture, right now, is to take up arms and to promise only to lay them down again on the day of Victory... The whole of France will salute the first actions of the Women-Soldiers, the courageous French women partisans.[21]

Such a self-conscious jostling for historical place might also reveal a prophetic awareness of the unlikelihood of any permanent recognition in the liberation period and beyond.

In the world beyond the rhetoric of the Resistance press, activists negotiated their roles in a way that still gave primacy to gender.[22] But given the special threats to Jewish women, the ways they may have dislocated themselves from the limitations which have been noted above is worthy of consideration. When the Occupation began, Denise Baumann was a young, conformist, Alsatian Jew. It is no accident that for the bourgeois Jews of the Alsace, given their fierce loyalty to the French State and firm attachment to bourgeois French culture, the conformist and tribally specific appellation 'israélite' was favoured over 'juif/juive'. Many, along with their compatriots, supported Pétain's armistice. Those Jews in France who did not, envisaged their identificatory possibilities along a scale of acculturation and integration. It is true that Jews were marked, literally, by anti-Semitic legislation and *forced* into an identification as 'Jew' which, it has been noted with a certain tragic irony, gave some a political consciousness.[23] Yet it has been suggested that many, particularly those whose families had been French for generations (those of 'vieille souche'), did not assume a specifically Jewish identity and, indeed, may have deliberately rejected it in their absolute allegiance to a 'true' France. As most overtly Jewish political organizations were made up of immigrants, becoming a patriot who fought for France necessitated, for some, dissociation from the ghetto (even if it has been euphemistically termed an 'intellectual ghetto'[24]) and its implications of foreignness and non-integration.[25]

The delineation of difference between 'French' (even second generation) and 'immigrant' Jew had its awful consequences. The counterpoising of the two sets of communities against each other by the German and collaborationist authorities was vigorously protested by the Jewish resistance press as soon as the major round-ups had started in the summer of 1942:

> At a time when our bloodthirsty enemies are seeking our extermination, all Jews, regardless of social origin or religious adherence, must forge unity in their ranks. FRENCH JEWS! We who have lived in France for centuries, we must not heed false prophets, who have always instructed us to separate ourselves from our immigrant brothers, lulling us into the dangerous illusion that in this way we can avoid being beaten by the wrath of antisemitism.[26]

Apart from being subject to specific anti-Semitic legislation, immigrant Jews were easier to find. Poorer and with fewer outlets to secure hiding places (no relatives outside large towns, no contacts from country holidays taken in less threatening times), their poverty and foreign accents exposed them; they formed the majority of those deported to the killing centres.

Denise Baumann, however, took another tack. Battling against her own internal will to conform, she joined the resistance group, Œuvre de secours aux enfants (OSE)[27] before joining the Mouvement National contre le Racisme and the editorial team of the Jewish clandestine journal *Droit et liberté*. Of her entry into the Resistance she said, 'for the first time, I heard Yiddish spoken and discovered an unknown culture... Then I understood the stupidity of fighting my identity: I was no longer "Israelite" but Jewish... My "*juiverie*" was part of myself, like my French culture. It gave me deep roots and extra strength.'[28] 'Juiverie,' she remarks, is a translation of 'Yiddishkeit' (Jewishness),[29] a concept of Jewishness encompassing a total Jewish identity which includes history, culture, food, and so on and which, for secular Ashkenazi Jews, is far more serviceable than the religious connotations of 'Judaism'. Many Jews of the Alsace, conscious of their proximity to high culture, would have rejected the idea of *Yiddishkeit* and its associations with poorer East European Jews. And while

Baumann accommodates without remark her 'French culture' as though it operated on an unbroken continuum, the implication is surely that it too has undergone intense change via the inversion of her identification with the French State and her participation in subversive activities hitherto regarded as unimaginable. Her family, on the other hand, resting secure in their French status, continued to find their treatment incomprehensible; comforting themselves that they would be treated differently because they were both well-behaved and French had no effect on their future and all were to perish. Nazi policy deliberately played on these suppositions across Europe to give the Holocaust added impetus since, as Zygmunt Bauman has convincingly argued, people who regard themselves and their world as rational expect their leaders to treat them 'rationally' and, even in the face of clear evidence to the contrary, that expectation overrides experience.[30]

Frenchness and Jewishness came suddenly into an unforeseen conflict for Denise Baumann. Her retrospective perception suggests that a French Jewish woman's background has made her certain of both these aspects of her identity, but by the action of history, they are transformed: she continues to be French and Jewish (and patriotically so), but her relationship to each and the tension between them is no longer certain and static. Identity cannot be adopted or shed at will: for someone like Denise Baumann, her alteration of outlook, the acquisition of that 'extra strength', meant deep loss, signalled for us by the actual loss of members of her family and the culture they represented. This transformation may also be significant in terms of gender in that the male Jewish resisters cited by Renée Poznanski as having taken on an emphatically French patriotism[31] may have more easily located themselves in a nation which, before the Vichy enactment of anti-Semitic statutes, regarded them as fully French citizens in a way that it did not accept women.

Still, throughout France, women engaged. Sidelined into stereotypical concerns, the dangers threatening them going unrecognized, they still shouldered a patriotic mantle. In this context, it is worth noting briefly how an internalized patriotism developed in the post-Liberation effort to imagine a 'real' France. Before the war, Communist women had organized in the internationalist Comité mondial des Femmes contre la Guerre et le Fascisme; this was abandoned after 1944, by the Union des Femmes Françaises, in favour of a more restricted nationalism,[32] which came hard on the heels of a war fought in part around the terrible impact of ideologies of nation and race. Echoed across the liberationist spectrum, the retreat into nationalism meant, for example, that Jews who returned from the killing centres often felt they could find no place in the very organizations which, given their anti-fascist allegiances, should have welcomed them.[33] It was also a context in which entitlement to certain welfare benefits was dependent on deportees' returning to their geographical origins, regardless of the displacement of other surviving members of their community.[34] This scandalous policy, ineffective in practice and resisted on all levels, gives some clue to the place envisaged for former deportees in a reborn France. Denied any right to a home, deportees had been shipped to their deaths and, returning against all odds, forced back to those places of denial. For Jews in France, who had confronted a more intensely contested notion of Frenchness than ever, the policy is suggestive in relation to what Salman Rushdie has called 'imaginary homelands',[35] those spaces of real geographical location which yet exist as evocative communal fantasies, commingling partial memory with the potential for an historical return.

Such limitations are mirrored in the Resistance press. The most striking difference between that aimed at women and the more general literature is the former's compelling necessity to focus on the immediate and its forceful attachment to everyday concerns. Its effect is to diminish the contemporary reader's sights: not for her the wider political context within which she was queuing for hours each day for her meagre ration of bread and fat; easily comprehensible sloganeering was provided in place of political contextualization. Such concerns situate women in both the nation and in time. History, with a capital 'H', so self-consciously written in the fervently literary months of the Liberation, is traditionally concerned with grand questions of wide significance and is not bothered about whether classrooms were too chilly for children to be comfortable or whether old people were freezing for lack of coal. Whether history ought to reflect the minutiae is not at issue here: by addressing the woman reader *only* in such an immediate way without offering her a more extended vision of either her place in the new France to come or of what that France would entail denies her own centrality in history itself.

Notes

Unless stated otherwise, the place of publication is Paris.

1. Marie-France Brive, 'L'Image des Femmes à la Libération', in Rolande Trempé (ed.), *La Libération dans le Midi de la France*, Toulouse, Editions Eché: UTM, 1986, pp.390, 397.

2. See, e.g., Jane Jenson, 'The Liberation and New Rights for FrenchWomen', in M.R. Higonnet *et al.* (eds), *Behind the Lines: Gender and the Two World Wars*, New Haven, Yale UP, 1987, p.273; Claire Duchen, *Women's Rights and Women's Lives in France 1944–1968*, London, Routledge, 1994. See Gilberte Brossolette in Laure Adler, *Les Femmes Politiques*, Seuil, 1993, p.135 and *passim* for continued subscription to the belief that women deserved the vote for Resistance work.

3. See, e.g., *La Lutte de Classes*, no.9, 5 February 1943.

4. Though see Hilary Footitt, 'The First Women *Députés*: "les 33 Glorieuses"?' in this volume.

5. See e.g., Gail Braybon and Penny Summerfield, *Out of the Cage: Women's Experiences in Two World Wars*, London, Pandora, 1987; Hanna Diamond, 'Women's Experience during and after World War Two in the Toulouse Area 1939–1948', doctoral dissertation, University of Sussex, 1992.

6. Deportations from France were as follows: Jews – 75,721 (31,157 women); 'political' deportations – 63,085; Gypsies – still unknown. Percentage of returning deportees: Jews – 3 per cent (2.4 per cent for women); political deportees – 59 per cent. See Annette Wieviorka, *Déportation et Génocide. Entre la Mémoire et l'Oubli*, Plon, 1992, pp.20–1. The term 'killing centre' is Raul Hilberg's: see *The Destruction of the European Jews*, 2nd edition, New York, Holmes and Meier, 1985.

7. Larger journals such as *Combat* covered wider regions, were more extensive and professionally produced. Very little of the women's press was typeset.

8. Brive, incidentally, refers to only fifty-nine titles.

9. Only *Jeunes Filles de France* speaks directly to unmarried women. It is arguable that calling on women as godmothers and nurses, while resting on their caring qualities, opens the way to those whose commitment to heterosexuality may have been more questionable.

10. *Union des Femmes Françaises Pour la Défense de la Famille et la Libération de la France Bulletin d'Information des Comités*, no.1, 1944.

11. Ibid., no.9, July 1944.

12. Thanks to Jolande Withuis for drawing this out in the case of Dutch women.

13. *Femmes Françaises*, no.1, January 1944.

14. *Quatre-Vingt-Treize*, no.3, January 1944.

15. *La Voix de la Femme Juive*, 15 August 1943.

16. *Notre Voix*, 15 February 1943. Emphasis and capitalization in original; this applies to all Resistance press quoted.

17. Ibid., 15 March 1943.
18. *Jeunes Filles de France*, no.1, October 1940.
19. Ibid., no.12, January 1942.
20. Other papers which refer to Soviet women's role in the armed forces include: *La Clamartoise* (no date); *Femmes Françaises*, no.1, January 1944; *Femmes Patriotes*, no.1, February 1944; *l'Humanité* (édition spéciale féminine), March 1943; and *Jeanne la Lorraine*, no.3, January 1944.
21. *L'Humanité* (édition spéciale féminine), January 1944, June 1944.
22. See Paula Schwartz, '*Partisanes* and Gender Politics in Vichy France', *French Historical Studies*, vol.16, no.1, Spring 1989.
23. See, e.g., anonymous interview recorded by Jewish Women in London Oral History Project, 1985.
24. Léo Hamon, *Vivre ses choix*, R. Laffont, 1991, p.104. Cited in Léo Hamon and Renée Poznanski, 'Avant les Premières Grandes Rafles. Les Juifs à Paris sous l'Occupation (juin 1940–avril 1941)', *Cahiers de l'IHTP*, no.22, December 1992, p.10.
25. See Jacques Adler, *The Jews of Paris and the Final Solution. Communal Response and Internal Conflicts, 1940–1944*, Oxford, Oxford University Press, 1987, especially chapter 4, for criticism of the disdainful attitude towards immigrants by conservative French Jewry.
26. *Notre Voix*, September 1942.
27. Sometimes called 'Organisation de secours aux enfants'.
28. Denise Baumann, *Une famille comme les autres*, Société d'Edition "Droit et liberté", 1973, p.180.
29. She says it is 'more all-encompassing than "judéité"'. Denise Baumann quoted in Adam Rayski, *Le Choix des Juifs sous Vichy. Entre soumission et Résistance*, La Découverte, 1992, p.288n.
30. Zygmunt Bauman, *Modernity and the Holocaust*, Cambridge, Polity, 1991, p.203. Use of the term 'Holocaust' is not unproblematic and is currently subject to sharp conflict; in the absence of a more acceptable term, I continue to use it here.
31. Hamon and Poznanski, 'Avant les Premières Grandes Rafles'.
32. See Renée Rousseau, *Les Femmes rouges. Chronique des années Vermeersch*, Albin Michel, 1983, for a critique (though not in terms of national identification) of the UFF's rejection of the Comité mondial.
33. See *témoignages* in Sylvie Lalario, 'Retours en France et Réadaptations à la Société française de Femmes Juives Déportées', master's dissertation, University of Paris VII, 1992–93, pp.222–3.
34. Frédérique Boucher, 'Abriter vaille que vaille, se loger coûte que coûte', in 'Images, Discours et Enjeux de la Reconstruction des

Villes françaises après 1945', *Cahiers de l'IHTP*, no.5, June 1987, p.128.

35. Salman Rushdie, 'Imaginary Homelands', in idem, *Imaginary Homelands. Essays and Criticism 1981–1991*, London, Granta, 1991, pp.9–21.

– 6 –

Women's Aspirations, 1943–47: an Oral Enquiry in Toulouse

Hanna Diamond

When discussing the aspirations of women at the Liberation, the historian should not make too many assumptions. It is certain that the nature of the sources used here, interviews in which women recount their experiences, can enable the historian to gain some considerable insights. But, it also has to be remembered that people are not always able to assimilate the events or their interpretation of events very clearly at the time. As one oral historian, Marie-France Brive, put it, 'What women say should not be taken literally, what they say today is not always what they thought then – they did not formulate everything there and then.'[1]

In the same way, the time lapse between the events and their telling has given informants time to interpret and give meaning to events such that they can take on a retrospective significance that they did not have at the time. One informant expressed this fact quite clearly:

> We suffered, we lived day by day impatient for it to be finished, but we were not sure how. I don't know if we expected much from the Liberation. Here, people carried on without really questioning things. It's only afterwards, in retrospect, that we realized the importance of the changes. When you're in the thick of it you can't really see it.[2]

Yet, despite this, my sources indicate that experiences of the War did bring some women, at, or after the Liberation, to reassess certain aspects of their lives:

> We hoped that after the War women would have more opportunities – before the war women stayed at home, they only thought about their personal appearance and were very tied to the kitchen. But during the War,

they had such different and intense experiences, and there were many who were not part of the Resistance, but who evolved a great deal during this war.[3]

As elsewhere, the War and the Occupation of Toulouse brought considerable disruption and change to households. Women were forced to reorganize the home to cope with the difficulties of wartime daily life. They tended to be affected differently according to whether they were married or single, or whether their husbands were present or absent. In the latter case, where husbands and fathers were absent as prisoners of war or because of their involvement in the Resistance, wives were obliged to take on extensive new responsibilities becoming *chef de famille*.[4] The absence of the men often also meant the loss of the main wage earner in the household; wives soon found that the state *allocations* were inadequate to sustain a family and were forced to go out to work and thereby take over financial responsibility for the home.[5] Women in this situation returned to jobs they had left before the War or before marrying if they could, but for a large number of women this was their first experience of the workplace. Fortunately, the conditions of the War, in Toulouse in any case, made it possible for most women to find a job if they wanted to, although these tended to be menial and unskilled. This was particularly true from early 1943 onwards, when the Germans reorganized the munitions and aviation factories of the area to work for their war effort. Labour was in short supply, so many women were employed.[6]

The problems of daily life were exacerbated by the conditions of the War and the Occupation.[7] The scarcity of foodstuffs, rationing, the need to queue for food and household goods, the dependence on the goodwill of the shopkeeper all added to the burdens of the housewife. Oral sources repeatedly described the search for the basic essentials as being a full-time (pre)occupation which normally fell to the female members of the household. This was generally experienced as one of the most trying aspects of the Occupation, although it has to be said that those in the Toulouse region did not suffer as much as in some other areas of France.[8]

Life appears to have been especially hard for women who lived in rural areas and who found themselves in charge of running the farms. Although it was often easier for them to acquire the basic foodstuffs, wives of farmers were confronted with an increased workload with responsibility for the harvests and the livestock at a time when agricultural labour was hard to come by. It cannot be denied that most of these women simply longed for the War to be over and for everything to return to normal as soon as possible. As Mme Gineste expressed poignantly: 'All we hoped for from the Liberation was to live normally again.'[9]

It is quite clear that the only hope or expectation that such women had of the Liberation was that the War should come to an end as soon as possible, that the Germans should depart, that their men should return and that life should be easier and get back to normal. Indeed it would seem that after the Liberation, these women were more than happy to embrace their pre-War roles: 'For me, the Liberation brought no changes. We took our lives up as we had left them before and I was very happy to do so.'[10] In fact everyday conditions did not improve for some time after the war and many women expressed disappointment at the amount of time it took for food supplies to return to normal.

However, not all women wanted to pick up their lives as they had been before the War. Some were deeply changed by their wartime experiences. Working was seen as a particularly important part of this experience and subsequently women often expressed the feeling that they wanted to continue working after the War:

> As a result of the fact that women had gained some access to the world of work during the War, they did not want to allow themselves to be manipulated afterwards. After the War they hoped to be able to work if they wanted to, to have the right to defend their right to work, and the right to discuss their working conditions.[11]

The return of the prisoner husbands also served to make women realize that they had come to hope for something different from their lives. These women who had taken on a new role and adapted the household to the circumstances of the War had to reintegrate men who had sometimes been away for as long as five years.

> The return of the husbands created enormous problems. Women did not want to give up the rights they had acquired by obligation in 1940. These women who during the War got used to dealing with the problems that had been left by their husbands did not accept that all of a sudden they should again become a negligible element in the couple.[12]

Some couples were able to renegotiate the terms of their relationship, but a significant number of women found that their lives had so much changed for the better that they were not prepared to take up the pattern of their old marital lives. In this context it is understandable that many marriages broke down and the post-War divorce figures bear witness to this both on a local and on a national level.[13]

However, it was, perhaps unsurprisingly, the category of women who became involved in the activities of the Resistance, who tended to envisage greater changes in their lives. For some this took the form of simply recognizing that there was no reason why they should not do what the men could do:

> First there were our male friends who went to join the Maquis. Between us women we asked ourselves – why them and not us? It's because we are women that they don't want us. It's over that issue that we fought to be on an equal footing with the men. With such success that I went to join the Maquis on 6 June, I had the impression that I had gained a certain equality with the men.[14]

Admittedly, this is a rather exceptional example because there were not many women who joined the Maquis. Nevertheless, it demonstrates how the departure of their male friends to the Maquis brought some women to assert themselves and to realize that they had equal talents to contribute to the Resistance.

Other women seem to have gained a new sense of their own self-worth from their Resistance experiences:

> Before the War, women were in the home. It was believed that a woman's place was to have children, to love and adore her husband and family, and to do the cleaning and cooking. A woman who worked was even quite badly thought of. But after everything I experienced of life during the War, the fact that I had fought – I said to myself – I want to be someone in my own right. This impression I had that you can be a mother but at the same time you don't have any status annoyed me. And I think this was the case for many women who were involved in the Resistance, they wanted their value to be recognised after the War.[15]

Such feelings and experiences led in turn to changed expectations and hopes that the Liberation, when it came, might be a time of increased opportunities for women, both in terms of their private and their professional lives, as Mme Rivals testifies:

> From my commitment to the Resistance I have kept a sort of intellectual independence which I have recognized in other women. We had become conscious of the roles we could play. After this period, young women who were between twenty-one and twenty-four years old at the Liberation, wanted to have the lives of independent women.[16]

The last two quotations demonstrate two themes that recur again and again in accounts that women give of their wartime experiences. The first is this idea of 'value', of women wanting their true worth to be recognized, and the second, this fact of becoming more self-aware, '*d'avoir pris conscience*' of their resources and capabilities.

For more politicized women it was the gaining of the right to vote which was to be the major breakthrough for women within the context of the 'new' France which was envisaged after the Liberation. Mme Dopazo describes her feelings thus: 'I thought about the woman's right to vote during the War. I expected something marvellous from France. All these movements which were forming, newspapers, a real democracy, a real freedom for men *and women*.'[17] An equally telling example comes from Mme Cazou: 'During the War, with my girlfriend we discussed women during the War. We thought that at the Liberation, with the right to vote of course, we would be able to take a full and proper place in society.'[18]

Certain political groups and most notably the Union des Femmes Françaises (UFF), which made tremendous efforts to mobilize and politicize women, were anxious to take advantage of these feelings of hope and the wish for things to change:[19]

> At the heart of the Union of French Women we felt that women had experienced something different during the War. Before the War women were considered to be less than nothing, we couldn't vote, no one listened to us. But with the right to vote we became citizens, something we had never been before. We became aware that we were individuals, an awareness that we did not have before all these events.[20]

In her recent book, *Les Femmes sous l'Occupation*, Célia Bertin summarizes her feelings of hope when speaking of herself and her Resistance colleagues: 'It seems to me that we all desperately wanted to help create a more just society. I hardly dare to write it down, the dream seems so naïve today. But we did have this dream and a large number of women were disappointed.'[21] It seems essential to bear in mind that, like Celia Bertin, women had not necessarily formulated exactly what they hoped from the peace in a very coherent way. But it is this pervading sense of disappointment which highlights the fact that women did have aspirations and that for many women they were not met.[22]

Initially things looked quite promising; women were awarded the vote and this seemed to herald a new political involvement. Furthermore, the events of the Liberation represented a time of intense political activity and women were very much a part of this.

As M Carovis, the former President of the Comité Départemental de Libération (CDL) of Toulouse describes it: '[W]omen who had participated in the Resistance were also involved in the organizations which were politically active at the Liberation.'[23] Indeed, a number of women were invited to sit on committees and to take on a public role for the first time; there were at least two women at every meeting of the CDL of the Haute-Garonne, representing the UFF and Action Féminine. Women were also present on the local liberation committees across the department and on the comités which were established in the factories.[24] Women were present on lists for local and municipal elections and women candidates were fielded for national parliamentary election.[25] Women were involved in party political meetings and most parties organized women's sections.[26] Generally speaking, this activity would seem to be quite representative of the national picture.[27]

However, women did not find this public role very easy to sustain. Once the men started to return and things appeared to be getting back to normal the vast majority of these women withdrew from the public scene. Reestablishing the home and starting a family seemed to take precedence over everything. Why? Célia Bertin explains:

> After the Liberation, things were immediately so different from what we had hoped for. And how were we to make ourselves heard? It seemed as if no one wanted to listen to us any more. It just did not occur to us to get together to challenge this attitude towards us [...]
> Women allowed themselves to slip back into their old habits, brought up to conform by so many centuries of Judeo-Christian morality. They accepted the old norms of past society, without even appearing to notice it. [...] Most of them returned to being the second-class citizens they had been before the War both within their families and in society.[28]

Many were reluctant to associate their commitment during the War with the political groups that emerged at the Liberation. Women who had been part of the Resistance battle against the Germans saw their role as finishing. They found it difficult to sustain their interest and involvement in politics. As we know, in 1946 the number of women elected as deputies was about 5 per cent and the number of senators – 4 per cent, figures which almost immediately declined and which have only recently reached similar levels.[29] Mme Ramos was particularly concerned about this:

> After the War, in the first governments, there were lots of women in parliament. Nowadays, there are fewer. Just after the War they still felt

motivated, and that's where their politicization came from. Suddenly they were free to express their thoughts. But an involvement in post-War politics was a difficult commitment for a woman to make. In spite of everything women have the children – the husband can only be a help because the larger burden always falls to us women.[30]

The structure of party politics was not very conducive to women's involvement – meetings often took place in the evenings when married women were tied to the house looking after children. Furthermore the political parties failed to relate to women's issues or at least did not address issues that women felt concerned them directly in the same way as they had felt implicated by the Nazi threat. 'Politics', in the words of one woman, 'remained men's business.'[31] Lucie Aubrac makes a clear analysis of this:

– Yes, at the Liberation the Assemblies included a large number of women, this number diminished rapidly. The return to pre-War political structures, the fastidious games of a formal and often fawning parliamentarism, and – why not – the masculine atavism which returned to ways of thinking, distanced women from becoming representatives of the country.[32]

In fact the gaining of the vote which had seemed to mark the beginning of something new and different for women brought them very little change. To the contrary, women promptly used their vote one year later to help a right-wing government into power which, with its strong religious input, had as traditional a conception of women's role as any past French government. De Gaulle's call for 'four million beautiful babies' after the elections would seem to demonstrate this.

As for women in the work place, in Toulouse, after the Liberation, women were expected to clear the way so that jobs would be available for the returning prisoners of war. In cases where they were no longer the wage earner of the family they were asked to leave.[33] The traditional picture of a massive return of women into the home seems to have held some truth in Toulouse. Nationally speaking, some progress was made in terms of legislation. Important measures were passed giving women access to a number of professions, culminating in the 1946 Constitution, in which it was written that 'the law guarantees women equal rights with men in all domains'. There were changes but they were only slowly put into practice. Trade unions continued to call for the right to work for women in the post-War years as did the UFF. At the first Congress of the UFF in 1945, it was affirmed that it was necessary to 'give women the means to enable them to work at the same time as having children' and the right to work was proclaimed for both married and unmarried women.[34]

Nevertheless, women were still excluded from a number of career possibilities, particularly from the better-paid jobs. The difference in salaries remained flagrant despite legislation. A report published in 1946 pointed out that there was a significant difference in the wages paid to men and women for the same work.[35] It was not until July 1956 that the Minister of the Interior passed the law which was designed to apply the principle 'equal pay for equal work', but even this was rarely put into practice.

In this context it is understandable that many *Toulousaines* abandoned their wartime aspirations when they had hoped for a new independent lifestyle and a career, or a job at the very least. However, certain individuals continued to fight for them to be realized throughout the post-War years, like, for example, Marcelle Rumeau, who as Deputy for the Haute-Garonne was the first woman from the region to take political office.[36] Some other women also succeeded in pursuing successful careers, reaching positions of importance in administration at the Préfecture or in the commercial life of the town as a result of openings they had during the war .

Since no similar studies have yet been carried out in other areas of France, it is difficult to assess the extent to which the experiences of the *Toulousaines* described here are representative of French women generally. An oral enquiry of this kind does have a number of drawbacks, not the least of which is that it is a lengthy and time-consuming process. But the value of this research is that it gives the historian access to how individuals experience major events on an everyday and individual level and it highlights elements that would otherwise be overlooked. In this context it is of particular value to historians of women's history in their quest to discover how women experience history differently from men. It is certainly true that for many French people, both men and women, the post-Liberation years were often a time of disappointment and disillusionment. But this study shows that despite the suffering caused by the War there were also positive sides for women. Women emerged from the War with new and important rights and most significantly with an increased awareness of their own potential even if French society has been slow to allow them to realize it.

Notes

Unless stated otherwise, the place of publication is Paris.

1. In the course of discussion after presentation of my research paper at the University of Toulouse–Mirail in 1990.
2. Mme Maux, 10 April 1987. The following excerpts come from interviews as research for my doctoral thesis. For more information about the informants and how the interviews were carried out see: Hanna Diamond, 'Women's Experience during and after World War Two in the Toulouse Area 1939–48: choices and constraints,' doctoral dissertation, University of Sussex, 1992.
3. Mme Ramos, 19 October 1987.
4. A situation which was recognized by the Vichy government.
5. Diamond, 'Women's Experience during and after World War Two', chapter 2.
6. Ibid. Chapter 3 – the *poudrerie*, the *cartoucherie*, and the *azote* factories.
7. This is now quite extensively documented. See, for example, Dominique Veillon, 'Culture matérielle et Modes de Vie: La vie quotidienne des femmes', in *Le Régime de Vichy et les Français*, IHTP-CNRS, 1991.
8. Toulouse was privileged in being a polycultural region; monocultural areas like those further south near Carcassonne had a much more difficult time.
9. Mme Gineste, 6 March 1986.
10. Mme Deleysses, 25 June 1986.
11. Mme Mazet, 28 October 1987. Another example: 'I became conscious of my potential through my wartime experiences and that is why I wanted to continue working,' Mme Bruno, 28 September 1987.
12. Mme Augot, 12 November 1986.
13. Diamond, 'Women's Experience during and after World War Two,' p.225; Christophe Lewin, *Le Retour des Prisonniers de Guerre Français*, Publications de la Sorbonne, 1986, p.71; Sarah Fishman, *We Will Wait. The Wives of Prisoners of War, 1940–45*, New Haven and London, Yale University Press, 1991.
14. Mme Dou, 8 May 1987.
15. Mme Lambert, 23 March 1987.
16. Mme Rivals, 13 October 1987. Another Resistance woman reiterated this: 'Women in the Resistance became conscious of the roles they could play. They did not want to be submissive to

their husbands as they had been in the past,' Mme Metzger, 19 March 1986.

17. Mme Dopazo, 19 March 1986.
18. Mme Cazou, 19 May 1987.
19. Diamond, 'Women's Experience during and after World War Two', chapters 5 and 8.
20. Mme Fontanier, 15 July 1987.
21. Célia Bertin, *Les Femmes sous l'Occupation*, Stock, 1993, p.217.
22. This sense of disappointment is present in much of the literature of women's Resistance. See, for example, Frances Hamelin, 'Femmes, fantassins de la Résistance', *Les Femmes dans la Résistance*, Union des Femmes Françaises, Editions du Rocher, 1977, p. 248: 'The "new world", this more fraternal world that we dreamt about at the time of the Resistance, and for which so many of our nearest and dearest died, remains to be built. I am convinced that there can be no new men without new women and until such a time, no new world can exist.' There were also, of course, men who had been in the Resistance who were very bitter and disappointed by the realities of post-Liberation France, but this is not my concern here.
23. M Carovis, President of the CDL de Toulouse, 5 January 1987.
24. There were two women on the local council of Toulouse which was established by Vichy; so this was not strictly the first time that women in Toulouse appeared in a public or representative capacity. See Diamond, 'Women's Experience during and after World War Two, chapters 6 and 8 for more on women's political involvement during and after the Liberation.
25. The Communists were particularly successful at putting women forward for election.
26. Claire Duchen, *Women's Rights and Women's Lives in France 1944–1968*, London, Routledge, 1994.
27. Camille Tauber makes considerable claims about the presence of women on CDL and CLL. See 'Evolution de la participation des femmes à la vie civique, telle qu'elle apparaît à la Libération', in *Les Femmes dans la Résistance*, pp.286–7. See also Charles-Louis Foulon in 'Les femmes dans les comités départementaux de Libération', *Les Femmes dans la Résistance*, p.273. According to him women were present on CDLs in many parts of the country.
28. Bertin, *Les Femmes sous l'Occupation*, p.218.
29. Denise Breton, 'La Résistance, étape importante dans l'évolution de la condition féminine', in *Les Femmes dans la Résistance*, p.231.
30. Mme Ramos, 19 October 1987.
31. Mme Fontes, 12 December 1987.

32. Lucie Aubrac, 'Présence des femmes dans toutes les activités de la Résistance', in *Les Femmes dans la Résistance*, p.21.
33. See Diamond, 'Women's Experience during and after World War Two', p. 229 onwards. This was certainly the case at the *poudrerie de Toulouse* and seems to have been a widespread policy.
34. Minutes of the Congress of the UFF, 1945.
35. Geneviève Vaillaud, *Le Travail des Femmes*, Les Documents Jeune Patron, 1947, p.20.
36. Marcelle Rumeau came to politics during the Occupation when she founded the Toulouse section of the UFF and was subsequently put forward as a parliamentary candidate by the Communist party. See Diamond, 'Women's Experience during and after World War Two, pp.180–2.

Now You Don't: Women, Cinema and (the) Liberation

Carrie Tarr

This chapter addresses the representation of women in French cinema in the three years following the Liberation. It does so, first, through a brief survey of the three women-authored films produced at this time, namely, Jacqueline Audry's *Les Malheurs de Sophie* (1945), Andrée Feix's *Il suffit d'une fois* (1946) and *Capitaine Blomet* (1947); then, through an analysis of two war narratives of the period, *Boule de suif* (Christian-Jaque, 1945) and *Le Diable au corps* (Claude Autant-Lara, 1946), both of which star Micheline Presle, one of France's most popular young actresses. Film narratives, whatever their ostensible subject matter, rework themes in ways which bear a relationship with their moment of production, and woman-authored films and/or films centred on a woman's story are most likely to focus on hopes and fears about women's changing and contradictory roles at this turbulent time. Through an analysis of these films, I aim to assess the extent to which the destabilizing of gender roles under the Occupation, and women's opportunities for change at the Liberation, are or are not recognized in post-Liberation French cinema.[1] The argument will be that they both are *and* are not – now you see it, now you don't.

French cinema has a reputation for privileging male stars and male-centred narratives. As Michèle Lagny, Marie-Claire Ropars and Pierre Sorlin have noted in their study of French films of the 1930s, 'Even when the cinema of the 1930s tells love stories, it only really gives roles to male actors.'[2] However, as I suggest elsewhere,[3] it is arguable that, during the Occupation, French cinema unwittingly opened up a space for more complex and positive representations of women. Certainly, the banning of Anglo-American films and the German policy of promoting a relatively autonomous French national cinema allowed the industry to thrive.[4] At the same time, censorship worked to evacuate contemporary, realist genres, by favouring moralizing melodramas and escapist genres like the costume drama which tend to privilege female-centred narratives and female viewing pleasures. Even if, as Bertin-Maghit has argued,[5] Occupation films generally sustained patriarchal representations of women in line with Vichy ideology, the period gave French actresses a volume and range of roles which they could not have hoped to sustain in peacetime. Indeed, a significant number of these films construct wilfully transgressive women alongside male figures who are either corrupt and impotent or weak and ineffectual: Odette Joyeux in *Douce* (Autant-Lara, 1942) defies her effete, hypocritical bourgeois family; Marie Déa in *Les Visiteurs du soir* (Carné, 1942) defies the devil himself; while in the remarkable *Le Ciel est à vous* (Grémillon, 1944) Madeleine Renaud defies normative concepts of what it means to be a wife and mother by becoming a long-distance flying champion, aided and abetted by her husband.[6]

With the return of peace, and in the face of renewed competition from Hollywood imports, post-Liberation French cinema might have undergone a radical transformation. However, film historians are generally agreed on the remarkable continuity it shows with the past. Institutionally, the structures put in place during the Occupation formed the basis of the post-War French cinema industry. Aesthetically, only a handful of films aiming to document the war years, such as *La Bataille du rail* (1946) directed by newcomer René Clément,[7] showed any desire for greater realism and immediacy in the cinema on the Italian neo-realist model. On the whole, the industry chose to turn away from the perhaps still too harrowing prospect of tackling sensitive contemporary issues directly, opting rather for popular genres such as comedies, *noir* poetic realism and literary adaptations in the quality tradition which had already become a hallmark of many Occupation films.[8] Film-makers who had made their mark in the 1930s or during the Occupation were to carry on virtually unchallenged until the New Wave of the late 1950s, and there was little opportunity or incentive for new film-makers to enter the profession. Even the stars of French cinema were largely the same as before the War. A 1946 survey in *Ecran français* lists the most popular female stars, in order of preference, as Danielle Darrieux, Gaby Morlay, Edwige Feuillère, Viviane Romance and Micheline Presle.[9] Of these five, only Micheline Presle owes her career to the war years. The others were well established before 1939.

The question, therefore, is whether, in a climate of consolidation rather than experimentation, when male-centred genres like the war film could return to claim an even larger share of screen time for male-centred stories, the cinema of the post-Liberation period was able to sustain the tentative exploration of female autonomy and women's changing roles discernible in a range of Occupation films. Could it even embrace more radical possibilities and represent the 'new woman' to be glimpsed in the pages of the more radical women's press?[10] The films made by Jacqueline Audry and Andrée Feix and the war narratives starring Micheline Presle constitute an initial corpus of films around which to build an answer.

Women Directors

During the Occupation, there were no feature films directed by a woman (Marie Epstein's last film, *Le Feu de paille*, co-directed with Jean Benoît-Lévy, was made in 1939). Women continued to be employed in the film industry, predominantly as actresses, but also as editors and continuity girls, in makeup and wardrobe. There were a few women producers and a handful of women who wrote screenplays, the most notable being Françoise Giroud and Solange Térac. But it was not until the end of the war that Jacqueline Audry and Andrée Feix were able to direct their first feature films, each having served long apprenticeships in the industry.[11] Audry had also made a short film, *Les Chevaux du Vercors* (1943), under the auspices of the Centre Artistique et Technique des Jeunes du Cinéma in Nice (precursor of the IDHEC, now the FEMIS). Arguably, then, it was the Liberation which opened up new opportunities for women to make their mark on French cinema as directors, just as the newly-decreed rights to vote and to stand for election seemed to offer women the chance to make their mark on the political landscape.

Nevertheless, these new women directors inevitably faced prejudice within the industry. Audry was expected to choose a suitably 'feminine' topic for her first feature film, and *Les Malheurs de Sophie* seemed to fit the bill as a period piece based on the popular *Bibliothèque rose* novel by the Comtesse de Ségur. However, throughout her film-making career Audry showed a keen interest in exploring women's struggles, and *Les Malheurs de Sophie* is no exception. She develops the story of the misadventures of naughty little Sophie by having her heroine grow up and actively rebel against the hypocrisy and boredom of upper-class family life: Sophie joins her cousin Paul on the barricades of 1851 before eloping with him to England. Despite the limitations of the nineteenth-century setting and romance scenario, the screenplay suggests a subversive story of female rebellion set against the liberating effects of revolutionary struggle. Indeed, according to Paul Léglise the film was subjected to censorship of 'all the riot scenes

Gender

and scenes judged to be politically inappropriate in the current climate.'[12] Arguably, it was not just revolutionary struggle *per se*, but women's participation in revolutionary struggle which was the object of censorship. Unfortunately, however, no copy of the film can now be located and an assessment of its significance as a model of female struggle for equality and autonomy in post-War France can therefore only be tentative.

Audry found it difficult to get financial backing for a second project after *Les Malheurs de Sophie*, and was forced to wait three years and accept a commission to make *Sombre dimanche* (1948). However, her subsequent collaboration with writer Colette and actress Danièle Delorme led to three highly successful period pieces – *Gigi* (1948), *Minne ou l'Ingénue libertine* (1950) and *Mitsou* (1956) – which enabled her to explore female sexuality from a woman's point of view, despite the fact that the genre could be (and was) dismissed by critics as 'feminine'. Her adaptation of Dorothy Bussy's semi-autobiographical period novel *Olivia* (1950) has become a lesbian cult classic.[13] Audry made sixteen feature films and two major television serials before her death in 1977 and her work constitutes an important, potentially subversive element within mainstream French quality cinema which has so far gone largely unrecognized. Jacques Siclier noted in 1957, 'Without exception her films have met with either polite interest, offhand condescension or outright scorn.'[14]

Andrée Feix's first film, *Il suffit d'une fois*, made (according to the press) under the supervision of Henri Ducoin, attempts to repeat the success of the Occupation hit, *L'Honorable Catherine* (L'Herbier, 1943), a screwball comedy. Feix draws on the same female team of screenwriter Solange Térac and actress Edwige Feuillère, and the film stars Feuillère as Christine, a successful sculptress with a double life, working on massive public 'masculine' statues in her Paris studio and on delicate private 'feminine' statuettes in the privacy of her country retreat in Chantilly. The narrative follows the pattern of the screwball comedy in which the independent female is finally contained through marriage. In *L'Honorable Catherine*, the exuberant eponymous heroine, an irrepressible blackmailer, constantly outmanoeuvres her charming male sparring partner, Raymond Rouleau, and the film's closure is very awkwardly contrived. However, in *Il suffit d'une fois*, Christine too rapidly abandons her glamorous independence and it is difficult to identify with her choice of love and life in Patagonia with Fernand Gravey, given that the object of her desire is a jealous, antisocial adventurer who constantly seeks to impose his version of events on hers, and who refuses to believe her when she tells the truth. The film was not as successful as *L'Honorable Catherine*, despite a build-up of excitement about it as a woman's film in the women's press.[15]

Feix's second film, *Capitaine Blomet*, shifts genres to a costume drama adapted from a play by Emile Bergerat. It centres on a jealous widower who seeks revenge on his dead wife's former lovers by successfully challenging them to a duel and then claiming the right to sleep with their wives, but who ends up by falling in love with one of his intended victims. Both films can be read as working through post-War anxieties in their conciliatory message that the errors of the past, be it female independence or female adultery, should be forgiven and forgotten in favour of the formation of the conventional heterosexual couple. In both films, however, the endings are formulaic and unconvincing. Feix subsequently chose to carry on working in the industry in the less demanding roles of editor or assistant director.

After the Liberation, then, there was a brief moment in which two women were able to make their first feature films, and which launched Jacqueline Audry on her career. However, both women were hidebound by the constraints of a fundamentally conservative, male-dominated industry and, as in so many films of the Occupation period, were able to put women's roles on the agenda only through the use of traditional genres such as the costume drama or the screwball comedy. By the end of the 1940s, a number of women were making shorts, documentaries and montage films (including Yannick Bellon, Nicole Védrès and Denise Tual), but no other woman made a feature film in France until Solange Térac's *Koenigsmark* in 1952, and it was left to Agnès Varda to become the first post-War woman film director in France to problematise the question of the modern heterosexual couple in a recognizably contemporary setting in her innovative first feature, *La pointe courte*, in 1954.

Micheline Presle

If Audry's Sophie depicts female rebellion, Feix's Christine rather uncomfortably suggests that the independent woman will readily embrace patriarchal subjugation. An analysis of the two roles played by Micheline Presle in the immediate post-War period provides a way of assessing whether such contradictions are also to be found in the 'prestige' productions of male-authored French cinema.

The Occupation had established Micheline Presle's star image as that of the modern, independent young woman. According to Françoise Audé,

She was the most popular actress of the dark years, because her vitality, energy and gaiety combined with her sudden pathos and gravity were antidotes to the sadness and weariness of the rest of the world: Micheline Presle represented truth for those who refused to be asphyxiated. She was alive. She was young. She was responsible.[16]

For Françoise Ducout,

She foreshadowed transformations which were not just those of an adolescent, but rather of a woman who, beneath her carefree exterior, was aware that the times were changing radically and that, to survive in a future which would not always smile on everyone, you had to be alert, and learn new ways of behaving, a new language, a new way of thinking.[17]

In her last film of the Occupation, *Falbalas* (Becker, 1944), Presle plays a young woman who rejects two conventional women's roles. On the one hand, she refuses marriage with a solid, companionable silk-manufacturer, a friend and fiancé whom she does not love. On the other hand, she refuses the love of a seductive but feckless couturier who is incapable of treating her as an equal. Presle's role in *Falbalas* leaves open the question of alternative roles for 'the new woman', but the film as a whole works to critique male idealization and exploitation of women at the same time as it foregrounds images of a community of women at work and independent women in positions of authority.[18]

Falbalas is a significant film in its challenging representations of relations between the sexes, made as it was just as the Liberation was about to take place. It is interesting, therefore, to see what becomes of Presle's star image immediately after the Liberation. In terms of her ability to sell a picture, she moves from taking second place to Raymond Rouleau in *Falbalas*, to heading the credits for *Boule de suif*, and, in *Le Diable au corps*, one of the resounding critical and commercial successes of 1947, her name takes precedence over Gérard Philipe, whom she had insisted on as her co-star, in his first major (award-winning) screen role. So the Liberation brought Presle both star billing and a measure of control over the films she was to make. Her success was to lead her to Hollywood.

However, in terms of the representation of women, it is not so clear that these films mark any sort of progression. Whereas *Falbalas* is a contemporary melodrama based on an original screenplay by Maurice Aubergé and Jacques Becker, both *Boule de suif* and *Le Diable au corps* are period literary adaptations, the one of two short stories by Guy de Maupassant, 'Boule de suif' and 'Mademoiselle Fifi',[19] the other of the novel by Raymond Radiguet.[20] Both displace contemporary concerns, *Boule de suif* onto the Prussian invasion of 1870 and *Le Diable au corps* onto the end of the First World War. Post-War French cinema did not provide Micheline Presle with a strong contemporary woman's role until 1954, when she played the doctor who has to choose between her lover and her job in Grémillon's *L'amour d'une femme* (she chooses the job, but the film was not a success).

Nevertheless, both *Boule de suif* and *Le Diable au corps* deal directly with the topic of women's roles during wartime, and can therefore be read retrospectively as narratives about the recent Occupation period. Contemporary 'realist' films about the Occupation, such as *La Bataille du rail* and *Jéricho* (Calef, 1945), unproblematically celebrate male heroism and marginalize female roles. To what extent does the combination of war narrative and costume drama allow for the exploration of non-normative gender roles? And to what extent do these narratives open up the possibility of the construction of 'a new woman' when war is over? An analysis of the narrative and visual strategies deployed by these texts suggests that however much they may gesture towards the recognition of change, ultimately any radical reevaluation of women's roles is quickly closed over.

Boule de suif

As film critic André Bazin signalled, *Boule de suif* is actually the first French feature film about the Occupation.[21] Its focus on a heroic female protagonist is all the more gratifying. Christian-Jaque's film welds together two Maupassant stories, casting Micheline Presle (against type) as the heroine of both. 'Boule de suif' recounts the tale of a stagecoach transporting various representatives of French society across Normandy in the hope of escaping the effects of the Prussian invasion. Among them is Elisabeth Rousset, nicknamed 'Boule de suif', a well-known prostitute. The travellers overcome their disdain for her in order to share her food, but when their departure from the inn depends on Boule de suif's agreeing to sleep with a Prussian officer, they shamelessly put pressure on her to do so. To her chagrin, they then refuse to speak to her or share their food on the next stage of the journey. 'Mademoiselle Fifi' is the story of a group of sadistic Prussian officers, occupying a château in Normandy, who send out for prostitutes and get their come-uppance when one of them, Rachel, stabs the vicious lieutenant nicknamed 'Mademoiselle Fifi', and escapes, protected by the local curé. In the film, Prussian soldiers hijack the stagecoach and capture Boule de suif and her fellow female travellers for the pleasure of their officers, and it is Boule de suif

(Micheline Presle) who murders Mademoiselle Fifi (Louis Salou).

The film's opening sequence establishes Boule de suif as a resister rather than as a prostitute, as her boudoir provides the setting for helping a French soldier escape from the advancing Prussians. The closing sequence shows her ringing the bells for Fifi's funeral, turning the death knell into a joyful celebration of victory. Throughout the narrative, she is the only character to respond to the Prussians with indignation and pride, showing up the cowardice and egoism of her compatriots and earning the respect of Cornudet, the democrat (and, by extension, the spectator). Despite her problematic sexual status, she is motivated primarily by patriotism and generosity towards her fellow citizens, pursuing neither personal gain nor sexual desire. However humiliated she may be in the first half of the film, there is no gainsaying her heroism in the second half when she stands up to Fifi's mockery and sexual advances and then knifes him to death. What is more, this is a murder which generates no remorse and goes unpunished. In effect, then, this film gives a female figure an exemplary role as an active, articulate and effective figure of resistance, a woman capable of sacrificing her pride by sleeping with the enemy if she thinks it will advance the cause of her fellow citizens, but also of getting her revenge through a resourceful act of physical violence.

In contrast, the two male characters who support her actions, Cornudet and the curé, are comparatively ineffectual: Cornudet gets shot in the leg when he tries to come to her assistance, while the curé, though he has resisted the Prussians by refusing to ring the church bells, is unable to persuade them not to shoot their civilian prisoners. However, Boule de suif's role serves primarily to underscore the hypocrisy of the upper- and middle-class characters, and it is notable that it is the female characters who are disproportionately punished for their egoism and their willingness to collaborate, mistaken for prostitutes and thereby humiliated in a way that their obnoxious male spouses are not. There is a misogynist side to the film, even if it takes care to include a fleeting but striking silhouette of a woman among the partisans glimpsed by the roadside.

The need to contain such a potentially threatening figure as Boule de suif is evident from the film's ending, for her heroism is rewarded by more than just getting to ring the bells. The end title informs us that 'Shortly afterwards, a patriot fell in love with her for her glorious action, married her and made a lady of her, worth many others.' War may bring out the best in a fallen woman like Boule de suif, and what better reward than having a man save her from prostitution by making her his wife? The active female Resistance heroine is to be put in her rightful place at the end of the War, in the domestic rather than the public sphere.

Presle's central role in the film is further limited or even undermined by a number of devices. She is absent from long sections of the narrative, especially the opening sequences which establish the characters of her fellow travellers and the Prussians occupying the Château d'Uville, and which allow her to reappear only when the coach journey is under way. Arguably, it is the coach, featured visually as the backdrop to the opening credits, which is the collective subject of the film, rather than Boule de suif. For example, her initial refusal to sleep with the Prussian captain at the inn is an obstacle to the development of the narrative, marked by the recurring image of the unhitched and stationary stagecoach. Narrative, coach and spectator all depend on her sexual submission to continue, and when she finally gives in, the camera invites the spectator to identify with the other passengers, pruriently listening to the noises from the floor above.

Furthermore, Boule de suif is regularly caught up within the male gaze, even in the opening and closing scenes of the film. She is first seen through the eyes of the fleeing soldier, and she is last seen through the eyes of Cornudet, as she tolls the bells. Even though the camera may show her in close-up as she delivers a stirring patriotic speech, or faces up to the Prussians, her role as subject is undermined by nods and winks from characters whose narrative knowledge is greater than hers. In fact, it is hard to take Boule de suif seriously when the Prussians and her fellow passengers are such wonderfully grotesque, comic caricatures.

The first French film about the Occupation, then, though safely distanced from the period through its 1871 setting, is wryly critical, not just of the Germans, but also of French collaborators. Rather than privileging images of general heroic resistance, it shows a nation thoroughly divided by class. It is significant, therefore, that it should select and mythologize the clichéd image of the idealized prostitute with the heart of gold as the patriotic figure of resistance, rather than a more realistic female figure with whom contemporary audiences could more easily identify. *Boule de suif* shows a world which is upside down. But it doesn't fail to point out that when order is restored, the isolated exceptional woman will know her place.

Le Diable au corps

Le Diable au corps also narrates a story which needs the framework of a war to be told at all because it constructs sympathetic young characters who openly flout conventional moral codes. The making of the film was beset by difficulties due to producer Paul Graetz's (justified) fear of scandal, and an opening disclaimer attempts to modify the impact of the film: 'The characters who bring this film to life with their impetuous and occasionally cynical youth express the feelings of a few young people who lost their heads in the worldwide upheaval of 1914–1918.' Certainly, the story contains a number of potentially shocking elements. The love affair between Marthe (Micheline Presle) and François (Gérard Philipe) is trebly transgressive. Not only does Marthe commit adultery, but she does so with a schoolboy (aged fifteen in the novel, but seventeen in the film, given that Gérard Philippe was actually twenty-four) whilst her husband, Jacques, is away at the Front, fighting for his country. The young couple thus rebel against family, church and patriotic duty, values which the film embodies in the figure of Marthe's mother (Denise Grey).

This film, then, sees Presle in the role of a young and attractive suburban middle-class girl caught between two men, or rather, a man and a boy, one representing security and convention, the other representing passion and risk. However, the narrative is focalized as a male-centred story, firmly constructed through a series of flashbacks from François's point-of-view. In the present time of the diegesis, Marthe is dead, and the news of the Armistice ending the First World War breaks through to coincide with her funeral. As the crowd in the street celebrates peace, the lonely figure of François is seen, first revisiting the flat in which their love affair had taken place, then witnessing the funeral, visually and spatially isolated from the legitimate mourners, and finally stepping out into the outside world, where the church verger cannot wait to hang out the flags for peace. The film thus firmly, even excessively, secures the link between Marthe's death and the end of the war and marks out the young man as the lone survivor.

François's story is evoked in three long flashbacks, accompanied on the soundtrack by the slowing down of the sound of the churchbells, a sign of the disorder of the past represented by Marthe, which returns to normal when the film returns the spectator to the present moment. Marthe first appears as an image in the mirror, taking the place of François's reflection, contained therefore within his subjective point-of-view. Nevertheless, the narrative does grant Marthe a limited independent existence outside the scope of François's focalization, allowing her to make choices which propel the narrative forward. The first flashback opens with her entering the Red Cross hospital where she fails to play the role she is expected to play of voluntary nurse and dutiful daughter: she faints when she first sees a wounded soldier. It ends on a shot of Marthe when François fails to meet her by the river, and the spectator subsequently realizes that it is at this point that she makes the decision to marry Jacques. In the second flashback, when François and Marthe meet again, it is Marthe who initiates their passionate love affair, and Marthe who finally realizes that she cannot rely on François and will have to make her husband believe that he is the father of her unborn child. The flashback ends this time on a shot of François left behind on the riverside, but taken from Marthe's point-of-view on the departing boat.

The final flashback opens with François's discovery that Marthe is leaving to have her baby in Brittany and ends with Marthe's collapse that same evening in a bar in Paris on the eve of the Armistice, followed by her death in a scene from which François is absent, although every element recalls his presence. Marthe calls out his name and the camera tracks round the back of the bed, focussing on Jacques's clenched fist and then on the fire going out in the fireplace, in a shot echoing the one following the couple's first night of love for which Marthe is now paying the price. Marthe's narrative thus exceeds the images produced by the flashback structure of François' memories. Nevertheless, some crucial emotional or decision-making moments are simply left to the spectator's imagination – her marriage to Jacques, for example, or the birth of her baby – and other moments are not shown from her perspective. When during their first night together Gérard Philipe strips off his wet clothes, an obvious object of desire, instead of providing Marthe's subjective point of view, the camera coyly retreats to a position behind the fireplace. The potential for identification with Marthe is thus repeatedly limited or frustrated.

Whereas François's motivation in this film is complex and ambivalent, Marthe's motivation is so straightforward as to be shocking. She acts in a completely pragmatic, self-centred and amoral way, refusing the bourgeois hypocrisy demonstrated by her mother. Unmoved by the war, her obligations to her mother or her duty as a married woman, she does exactly what she wants (or what François wants her to do) and feels no guilt or remorse. She loves François, and the most poignant scenes of the film are those in which she gives full expression to that love, regardless of the consequences: seducing him with a hot toddy, taking him boating in broad daylight, dancing to the gramophone with the curtains open during a black-out. But even in the midst of her pleasures, she remains aware of the reality of the situation, and makes the pragmatic choice of staying with Jacques for the sake of her unborn child. Her behaviour illustrates one of the options available to women during the Occupation period: making the most of life with the men who are left behind. As such, she also represents the ultimate in male fears: a woman who escapes from patriarchal control and provokes uncertainty over paternity.

Le Diable au corps works over a very different set of preoccupations from Boule de suif. Instead of characters who are good or bad, cowards or heroes, the film constructs characters who are simply indifferent to war and the call of duty, and does so in a way which invites spectators to feel sympathy for them. As François points out, normally neither of them would have any rights – he as a minor, she as a married woman. Only the disorder brought about by war allows such a relationship to carry on unchecked and the arrival of peace sets up the dilemma of how the story should end, a dilemma which they discuss during their farewell dinner. Marthe has reluctantly decided to rejoin her husband, but the spectator knows she would rather stay with Francois if they could only find a way. However, François accepts her decision and speculates instead on whether the appropriate ending for his role would be suicide, leading Marthe to wonder what would have happened if she had jumped into the river when François first failed to come to the rendezvous with her. However, as the spectator already knows, the story actually ends by having Marthe conveniently die, punishing the wilfully transgressive woman for the sins of the couple. So the narrative begins and ends with images of death; there is to be no liberation for women at the end of the war. Rather, as the church verger says, quite explicitly, in the final sequence on the church steps, 'This is the first funeral of the peace. Time for women to die now. Everyone in their turn.' At the end of Boule de suif, the transgressive woman tolls the bells to celebrate the death of the enemy, but here the bells toll simultaneously for victory and peace and the death of the woman.

Jacqueline Audry's first feature (as far as one can judge) and the war narratives starring Micheline Presle constitute a cluster of films in the period 1945–47 which address, if obliquely, the tension between women's aspirations towards autonomy and the reimposition of conventional patriarchal social structures. Made shortly after the Liberation, Les Malheurs de Sophie and Boule de suif allow for active, resistant female protagonists, even if they are distanced through period reconstruction and ultimately contained within a patriarchal scenario. These woman-centred films confirm the thesis that war destabilizes gender roles (unlike male-centred war films of the period), but also work towards restabilizing those roles at the end of the narrative, which coincides with the end of war. Both Boule de suif and the later Le Diable au corps attempt to close off women's wartime roles, be it active Resistance heroism or sexual transgression, as exceptional and past. Closure is most complete, to the point of excess, in Le Diable au *corps*. However, even in this film order is not completely restored, for the death of Marthe leaves behind a dysfunctional family and a distraught youth. In fact, if the films of the mid-1940s discussed here fail to construct satisfying representations of 'a new woman', neither do they successfully impose the normative order of post-War domesticity. Whatever the limitations of the representations of female characters in these films, patriarchal dominance is not easily or totally secured.

Notes

Unless stated otherwise, the place of publication is Paris.

1. See Hanna Diamond, 'Women's Aspirations, 1943–47: an Oral Enquiry in Toulouse', in this volume, pp.91–101, and Claire Duchen, *Women's Rights and Women's Lives in France 1944–1968*, London, Routledge, 1994, for a discussion of the issues affecting women at the time of the Liberation.
2. Michèle Lagny, Marie-Claire Ropars and Pierre Sorlin, *Générique des années trente*, Presses universitaires de Vincennes, 1986, p.195.
3. Carrie Tarr, 'Wilful Women in French Cinema under the German Occupation', *Women Teaching French Papers*, no.3, University of Nottingham, 1995.
4. See Evelyn Erlich, *Cinema of Paradox: French Filmmaking under the German Occupation*, New York, Columbia University Press, 1985.
5. Jean-Pierre Bertin-Maghit, *Le Cinéma français sous Vichy. Les films français de 1940 à 1944*, Albatros, 1980; also, idem, *Le cinéma sous l'occupation: le monde du cinéma français de 1940 à 1946*, Olivier Orban, 1989.
6. See Jeanie Semple, 'Ambiguities in the film *Le Ciel est à vous*,' in R. Kedward and R. Austin (eds), *Vichy France and the Resistance: culture and ideology*, London, Croom Helm, 1985, pp.123–32.
7. See Martin O'Shaughnessy, '*La Bataille du rail*: Unconventional Form, Conventional Image?' in this volume, pp.15–27.
8. 'The Tradition of Quality', famously attacked by François Truffaut in his article 'A Certain Tendency of the French Cinema' (*Cahiers du cinéma*, no.31, January 1954) refers to increasingly formulaic studio-made films, based on expertly tailored adaptations of preexisting literary works by professional scriptwriters, often using star performers with a background in the theatre, and paying more attention to the surface detail of their period settings than to the relevance of their stories to the contemporary world. The style was

to dominate French film production in the late 1940s and early 1950s.

9. 'Votre vedette préférée...' *Ecran français*, no.29, 16 January 1946.
10. For example, Brigitte Chevance, in *Femmes Françaises*, 21 September 1944, speaks of 'the emergence of a new woman whose complex face will not be liked by misogynists'.
11. See Paule Lejeune, *Le Cinéma des femmes*, Editions Atlas, 1987, for filmographies of Audry and Feix.
12. Paul Eglise, *Histoire de la politique du cinéma français*, Filméditions, quoted in Emile Breton, *Femmes d'images*, Messidor, 1984, p.46.
13. See Carrie Tarr, 'Ambivalent desires in Jacqueline Audry's *Olivia*', *French Cinema: Nottingham French Studies*, vol.32, no.1, Spring 1993, pp.32–42.
14. Jacques Siclier, *La Femme dans le cinéma français*, Editions du cerf, 1957, p.133.
15. For example, a report in *Elle*, no.31, June 1946, states: 'For the first time, there are eleven women in a film crew, doing the most important jobs. The director, the writer and nine female members of the crew surround Edwige Feuillère and Fernand Gravey under the watchful eye of Henri Ducoin who is supervising the making of *Il suffit d'une fois*, screenplay by Solange Térac.'
16. Françoise Audé, 'Filmographie de Micheline Presle', press release, Festival International de Films de Femmes de Créteil et du Val de Marne, 1987.
17. Françoise Ducout, *Séductrices du cinéma français 1936–1956*, Henri Veyrier, 1978, p.120.
18. For an analysis of *Falbalas,* see Michèle Lagny, 'Les Français en focalisation interne', *Iris*, vol.2, no.2, 1984, pp.85–98.
19. Guy de Maupassant, *Boule de suif*, Gallimard, 1973 (first published 1880); and idem, *Mademoiselle Fifi*, Gallimard, 1977 (first published 1882).
20. Raymond Radiguet, *Le Diable au corps*, Livre de poche, 1962 (first published Grasset, 1923).
21. André Bazin, '*Boule de suif* de Christian-Jaque', in *Le cinéma de l'occupation et de la résistance*, Union générale d'édition, 1975.

— 8 —

The Reconstruction of Masculinity at the Liberation

Michael Kelly

In her book, *X Y de l'identité masculine*, Elisabeth Badinter speaks of manhood as 'a task which must be carried out'.[1] The rocky road to manhood is marked by duties, ordeals and the repeated necessity to prove oneself a man. Badinter focusses on the individual, from the struggle of the XY-chromosomes to survive, through the trauma of separation from the mother, to the often brutal rites of passage and initiations into the world of manhood. But her perception of manhood as a task also illuminates the collective construction of masculinity as a social and cultural identity. And it has a particular pertinence at the Liberation period, when masculine identity was one of the many devastated reaches of French life which had to be reconstructed.

The failures and reverses of France during the war compose a familiar and bitter catalogue of humiliations. Politically, France lost part of its territory and all of its independence with the German Occupation and the puppet regime of Vichy. Economically, the direct payments, the requisitions, and the restructuring of industry constituted a super-exploitation geared to supporting the German war effort. Militarily, the defeat of 1940 was ignominious, while liberation was largely the work of foreign armies, however important the contribution of the Resistance and Free French. Physically, France was drained by mass deportations, labour conscription, arbitrary arrests, torture, executions, and the casualties of heavy fighting.

Much of the suffering is expressed in Paul Colin's remarkable poster

I should like to acknowledge the contributions of the Leverhulme Trust and the British Academy for funding the work on which this paper is based, particularly the CARAFE multimedia database.

'La Libération',[2] which was distributed around Paris at the moment of the insurrection and eventual liberation of the capital. Dated 17 August 1944, two days before the uprising began, it depicts Marianne, symbol of the Republic in her Phrygian bonnet, standing and shielding her eyes as she looks into the distance. She may be shielding her eyes from the heat of a blazing building or from the rays of the sunrise. Printed in colours which recall the French *tricolore*, she wears a tunic patterned in a way that suggests the shells of ruined buildings, and her hands are scarred with the stigmata of Christ crucified. The blue stripe behind her may also be an execution post. Colin's fellow *affichiste* Raymond Gid summarizes it as: '[A] tricolour image, in the blue of a cloudless sky, where France, with her hands crucified only yesterday, lifts her gaze beyond her own ruins towards the future.'[3]

Here, as almost always, France is represented as gendered and female. The conjunction of Marianne with Christ is unusual, not least because of the traditional enmity between the Roman Catholic Church and the secular Republic. However, these were heady days of reconciliation and Colin's poster conceivably helped to encourage the process. The implicit transgression of gender distinctions is not wholly unprecedented, and Jeanne d'Arc is an obvious association, but the tradition of women exhibiting Christ's stigmata is rather specific to Catholic spiritualism. Whereas Marianne may initially appear as France crucified, there are therefore residual echoes of her merely reproducing the signs of the Passion. At all events, the suffering visited on the female body of France raises the question of what might be, or have been, the role of the male gender in the events: co-sufferers, perpetrators, or absentees?

The spirit of Colin's poster is echoed in a prose poem by Gabriel Audiovisio which describes the same week of Liberation:

O Week stupefied by too many hopes so long contained. Assumption, in the summer, of wild expectations. Assumption, Virgin of Paris, in the sky at last illuminating the sun which rediscovered its birth in the first days of the world for the new men all astonished to feel that they would soon be alive.

It is you, week as disturbing as the changes at puberty; it is you, week already stirred by the blood which will well up with its future of fertility, but which first emptied you, purged you of a long infection; it is you, week already cracking with the surge of bunting reaching urgently for the light of day, which waited in hands and in hearts, with its flags rolled into hard balls but ready to blossom hugely like the multicolored scarves leaping from a magician's palm; it is you I wish first to sing.[4]

The theme of the Assumption recalls the mid-August Catholic festival, celebrating the reception of the Virgin Mary into heaven. This powerful mother-figure presides over the gestation and birth of the new men, who are astonished at the prospect of their own emergence. Liberation week is also characterized as a pubertal awakening, but the flowing of blood marks it as a female puberty. The only other male figure here is the conjuror pulling many-coloured scarves or flags from the palm of his hand. Without attempting to exhaust the possible meanings of the poem, it amply confirms the depiction of national identity based on an active female principle.

Perhaps the most strikingly gendered event of the Liberation is the wave of wildcat shearings of women as the liberating armies advanced through France. These are amply commented on elsewhere in this volume. Ostensibly punishing women for sexual relations with German soldiers or for passing information to them, the shearings took a carnivalesque public revenge on the bodies of women, revealing in the process that what they symbolically exorcized was experienced and constructed as male humiliation.

The maleness of the humiliation was a result, and confirmation, of the social gendering of the public domains in which the defeat and occupation had occurred, especially the political, military and economic domains. Since women could neither vote nor stand for election until 1944, politics was almost exclusively a man's world. Failure and shame attached themselves to the men of the Third Republic and of Vichy. Military defeat affected in the first instance the armed forces, which were a traditional male preserve. The 1.8 million prisoners of war were male, and, though 44,000 women are estimated to have been drafted for work in Germany, there were fifteen or twenty times more French men in the conscript labour force there.[5] Conversely, women and children formed a substantial proportion of those deported to concentration camps, from which few returned. The factories, transport and infrastructure in France were dominated by male workers, many of whom were therefore working directly or indirectly for Germany. They were largely deprived of their own means of organization and expression, particularly the trade unions which were predominantly institutions of male solidarity.

Hence the problem of masculine identity in France in 1944 was twofold: that French men had been humiliated in the activities which they most valued, notably work and war, and that they had conspicuously failed to protect their country, identified as feminine, or their womenfolk. The fact that women had played a significant role in both economic activity and in the Resistance movements compounded the problem more than it alleviated it, fuelling the instinctive reluctance of many men to give women access to political life. Having failed to achieve his major tasks during the War, French manhood's identity was plunged into crisis. However, the dialectics of task-oriented identity are infinitely recursive, in that identity is generated from pursuing a task rather than from completing it. A task is always required, and the greater the task the stronger the identity which it generates. As Camus famously pointed out: '[T]he very struggle towards the summits is enough to fill a man's heart. We must imagine Sisyphus happy.'[6] So paradoxically, the reconstruction of France appeared as a quintessentially male task, a Sisyphean labour offering a golden opportunity to reassert male identity. But before that could occur, two substantial difficulties had to be overcome. First was the crippling legacy of humiliation weighing on manhood, which could potentially hamper his rehabilitation. And second was the assertion of a female participation in the task, which would vitiate its effect on male identity. In the event, a simple strategy presented itself, which enabled men to have their cake and eat it: the humanist turn.

The discourse of humanism operated by framing male achievements and catastrophes as human ones, while retaining the male form as a convenient shorthand. Georges Rouault's well-known painting depicting a man hanging from a gibbet, *Homo homini lupus* (1944),[7] exemplifies 'man's inhumanity to man'. David Rousset's moving account of his experience in a concentration camp offered a similar perspective. Describing a ragged and emaciated inmate, he recounts that: 'He told me he was a lawyer in Toulouse, and I had all the difficulty in the world not to burst out laughing. The fact was that the social representation of lawyer simply did not fit this poor wretch. Putting the two together had an irresistible comic power. And it was the same for all of us. Man was slowly coming apart among the concentration camp inmates.'[8] The inhumanity is real and concrete, and it is the destruction of social relations which is felt as the most dehumanizing effect of the camps, leading ultimately to 'a complete collapse of man'.[9]

While this conception of man emerged from the experience of a group of (male) prisoners, a similar suggestion of the predominant maleness of humanity is to be found in Raymond Gid's poster, *Retour à la France, retour à la vie*,[10] which depicts a stylized naked figure emerging from the barbed wire of a camp. Though in appearance it could conceivably be male or female, the tricolour heart confirms its masculinity by reference to the familiar Catholic iconography of the Sacred Heart of Jesus. Georges Bernanos adopted a similar idea, identifying the recent conflict as Hitler's war against mankind and arguing that: 'The Great Germany of 1932 deliberately wagered against Man, and if you prefer me to put it in terms which come more naturally to me, I will say that it is quite the most considerable assault which has ever been mounted against Redemption, that is, against human nature justified and sanctified by Christ.'[11] Couching the point in two idioms, one secular and one religious, Bernanos confirms the ideological charge with which the notion of Man was invested.

Maurice Merleau-Ponty made the same point in more mythological terms, suggesting that 'the hero of our contemporaries is not Lucifer, nor even Prometheus, it is man.'[12] The philosophy of humanism was also urged by a fellow existentialist:

> One of the domains in which the intrusion of philosophy is the most intensely rejected is that of politics: political realism, so they say, should not be encumbered by abstract considerations. But if you look more closely, you quickly perceive that political and moral problems are indissolubly linked: in any case it is a matter of making human history, of making man, and since man is to be made, man is in question, and this is the question which is at the origin both of action and of its truth.[13]

Like her colleagues, Simone de Beauvoir in this and many similar analyses adopted the discourse of man, without apparently noticing or objecting to its ethos of masculinity. The task of reconstructing male identity could therefore be subsumed under the generic task of rebuilding human identity: 'refaire l'homme'. Something like Barthes's *tourniquet* then operated: a 'turnstile' effect which enabled the stigma of wartime humiliation to be occluded, as a generalized condition no longer attaching specifically to the male, while at the same time the fruits of post-War reconstruction, though also generalized, were associated with firmly masculine connotations.

A hyperinflation of humanism raged in the immediate aftermath of the Liberation, sweeping all before it. For perhaps six weeks after the Liberation of Paris, the new press and broadcast media felt their way towards an idiom appropriate to the time, but by the end of October 1944 the humanist consensus was firmly entrenched. Some impression of its impact can be gained from the two dozen or so books published in 1944–46 with explicitly humanist titles.[14] The list is all the more striking in view of the acute shortages in printing materials during this eighteen-month period. A listing of articles with similar titles published in newspapers and reviews would be many times longer, and the momentum was maintained for three or four years. The ecumenical nature of the humanist consensus is immediately clear from the recension. Politically, it included Communists, Socialists, Christian-Democrats and Gaullists; ideologically it included Marxists, liberals, existentialists and Catholics.

The assent of Beauvoir to this operation may appear surprising, but that of Bernanos was no less so, as his double discourse suggests. There were other surprising contributors. Sartre's assertion that existentialism was a humanism contrasted sharply with his earlier attack on humanists in *La Nausée* (1938). Lubac's initial attack on humanism as atheistic gave way to a subsequent championing of non-atheistic forms of humanism. And the PCF's espousal of humanist Marxism would have dismayed Paul Nizan and Georges Politzer, who had once denounced it. Within this consensus there were many differences and disagreements, reflecting the diversity of its proponents. But the existence and strength of the consensus was nonetheless remarkable. Clearly it was not powered only by the requirements of masculine identity.

I have argued elsewhere that the other driving force behind the humanist bandwagon was the urgent need to reconstruct national unity and a unified state.[15] Initially, the internal urgency arose from the state of virtual civil war from which France was attempting to emerge, while the external urgency arose from the desire to avoid the imposition of an Allied military administration (AMGOT), favoured by the United States, and to restore France's international influence. In the face of these imperatives, humanism offered a convenient ideological cement. It provided a common discourse and shared values at the most general level, and was tolerant of tactical silences and unresolved ambiguities. The pervasive presence of religious language and images in the humanist frame was emblematic of the weakness of both the State and the Church in the aftermath of the Occupation. The State was unable to sustain a self-sufficient secular republican authority, while the Church was unable to provide independent spiritual leadership. Pooling their ideological and symbolic resources, they undertook a combined holding operation to reconstitute the State and its ideological apparatuses.

The undeniable success of the humanist operation was achieved through the highly convergent pressures it exerted on all social identities in France, suppressing a wide range of differences, not only in national identity but also in class and gender identity. In particular, it produced a one-sex model of gender which Beauvoir, writing in 1945, articulates unambiguously: 'Man is one, the world he lives in is one, and in the action which he deploys throughout the world he commits himself in his totality.'[16] The unity of humanity, so forcefully propounded by the existentialists, carried with it the implicit assumption that the male was the norm. The point is vividly exemplified in the inaugural editorial for *Les Temps modernes*. Expounding the human situation, Sartre declares:

For us, what men have in common is not a nature, it is a metaphysical condition [...] they constitute undecomposable totalities, whose ideas, moods and acts are secondary, dependent structures, and whose essential character is to be *situated*, and they differ from each other just as their situations differ. The unity of these meaningful wholes is the meaning that they manifest. Whether he writes or works on a production line, whether he chooses a wife or a necktie, man is always manifesting: he manifests his occupational background, his family, his class and, ultimately, since he is situated in relation to the whole world, it is the world that he manifests. A man is the whole world. He is present everywhere, he acts everywhere, he is responsible for everything and his destiny is played out in all places: in Paris, in Potsdam and in Vladivostok.[17]

The totalizing ambition of what Sartre called his synthetic anthropology is centred on a vision of the human being as someone who works on a production line, chooses a wife or a tie, and takes responsibility for world affairs. A more masculine vision would be difficult to imagine, and its very vigour in conflating man and humanity was no doubt partly responsible for the awakening which led Simone de Beauvoir to blow the whistle on it:

A man never begins by presenting himself as an individual of a particular sex: the fact that he is a man goes without saying. It is in only in a formal context, in marriage registers and in declarations of identification that the two categories: masculine and feminine appear as symmetrical. The relations between the two sexes are not like those between the two electrical charges, which have two poles: man represents both the positive and the neutral to the point that in French we use 'men' ['les hommes'] to designate human beings. The particular sense of the Latin word 'vir' has thus been assimilated to the general sense of 'homo'. Woman appears as the negative, to the extent that every specifically female characteristic attributed to her is regarded as a limitation, though the same does not apply to the male. [...] In practical terms, just as the Ancients had an absolute vertical in relation to which the oblique could be defined, so there is an absolute human type, which is the masculine type. Woman has ovaries, a uterus; those are the peculiar conditions which enclose her in her own subjectivity; she is often said to think with her glands. Man proudly forgets that his own anatomy includes hormones and testicles.[18]

Beauvoir focusses primarily on the implications of the humanist sleight of hand for female identity, but in the process points to the loss of specificity which it entails for men. In particular they may not locate their identity in sexual or physiological difference. But in order for the *tourniquet* to operate successfully, it must secure an affirmation of masculinity within the envelope of humanity. The signs of the masculine-human, which may not be represented as physical properties, are therefore represented as social functions, as Rousset's text has indicated. Following Sartre's synopsis, the distinguishing social activities of the male may be characterized as work, ownership, and the exercise of power, especially military power. These male markers are to be found in every part of the culture of the Liberation period, across the entire political spectrum. Edith Piaf celebrates male power and ownership in her popular song 'La vie en rose'. Translated, the lyrics begin:

> Eyes that make me lower mine,
> A flicker of a smile on his lips,
> That's the honest picture
> Of the man to whom I belong
>
> When he takes me in his arms,
> He speaks softly to me,
> I see life through rose-coloured spectacles.[19]

The man's gaze is designated as carrying his power, to which the singer submits, lowering her own eyes, and proclaiming his right of ownership over her. His arms and his voice complete the conquest of her body and soul.

A slightly different construction from the opposite end of the political spectrum is offered by André Fougeron, in an image which in many respects maps the topology of gender politics in 1945 (see figure 6, p.125). Published in colour on the front of the 14 July 1945 issue of the Communist daily *Ce soir*, it depicts a woman, part madonna, part Marianne, suckling her child, supported on the shoulders of a soldier and a (male) worker. The trio are surrounded by red-white-and-blue flags and emblems of France and the Allies. Compressed into the picture are symbols of politics, religion, the nation, the state, class, and the family, orchestrated in terms of femininity and masculinity. The feminine is primarily marked by her body and motherhood, but also by the nation and spirituality. The masculine is primarily marked by the functions of labour and state (military) power, but also, in the worker, by hairy arms and large hands. The composition of the image emphasises the unity of this holy family, though its setting, in a PCF paper, might also remind readers that Marxism is based on the recognition of what Henri Lefebvre called 'contradictions in man and in human society'.[20]

Contradictions and conflicts were not lacking. Quite apart from the

Figure 6. Image by André Fougeron, *Ce Soir*, 14 July 1945. Reproduced on the back cover of Charles-Louis Foulon, *La France libérée 1944–1945*, Paris, 1984.

suppressed conflicts arising from the Occupation, there were new ones, or new versions of old ones, arising from the post-War situation. Class conflicts reemerged openly as the hardships of the reconstruction process weighed increasingly on the working population. Political conflicts intensified with the sharpening of party differences and the onset of Cold War polarizations. Military conflicts continued as the French army of Liberation set out to reconquer its lost colonial possessions in Indo-China. And gender conflicts simmered as the newly enfranchized female electorate were shepherded into their dual role as 'les mamans de France' and as a growing proportion of the lower-paid echelons of the workforce.

Far from undermining the humanist-masculine synthesis, these conflicts confirmed and supported it. As Lefebvre pointed out: 'When you say contradiction you also say problem to be solved, difficulties, obstacles – therefore struggle and action – but also the chance of victory, of a step forward, of progress.'[21] If solving problems, struggling against obstacles and striving for victory were the ethos of the Liberation, then it clearly offered every opportunity to reconstruct a masculine identity embodying Badinter's conception of it as 'a task which must be carried out'. As Fougeron's picture also suggests, this was the world into which the post-War baby boom was born. The child suckling at the mother's breast may be a boy or a girl, though the echoes of the Virgin and Christ Child would argue for a boy. Either way, the child of the Liberation was one of the generation of 1968, for whom the transformation of gender identities was also a struggle against what they had imbibed with their mother's milk. In this sense, the masculinity reconstructed at the Liberation is an absent presence whose influence will pervade French life and culture for many years yet.

Notes

Unless stated otherwise, the place of publication is Paris.

1. Elisabeth Badinter, *X Y de l'identité masculine*, Odile Jacob, 1992, p.15. This and all subsequent translations are my own.
2. Paul Colin, 'La Libération', reproduced in Pontus Hulten (ed.), *Paris–Paris 1937–1957*, Centre Georges Pompidou, 1981, p.455.
3. Hulten, *Paris–Paris 1937–1957*, p.454.
4. Gabriel Audiovisio, 'L'Air de la délivrance', *Poésie 44*, no.20, 1944, pp.83–4.

5. See Maurice Larkin, *France since the Popular Front*, Oxford, Clarendon Press, 1988, pp.101–2.
6. These are the concluding words of *Le Mythe de Sisyphe* (1942). See Albert Camus, *Essais*, Gallinard, 1965, p.198.
7. Reproduced in Hulten, *Paris–Paris 1937–1957*, p.129.
8. David Rousset, *L'univers concentrationnaire*, Editions du Parois, 1946, p.71.
9. Ibid., p.76.
10. Raymond Gid, *Retour à la France, retour à la vie*, in Stéphane Marchetti, *Affiches 1939–1945, Images d'une certaine France*, Lausanne, Edita, 1982, p.171.
11. Georges Bernanos, *Français, si vous saviez*, Gallinard, 1961, p.205.
12. Maurice Merleau-Ponty, *Sens et non-sens*, Nagel, 1948, p.331.
13. Simone de Beauvoir, *L'existentialisme et la sagesse des nations*, Nagel, 1986, pp.9–10.
14. The list includes Paul Alpert, *Economie humaniste*, Desclée de Brouwer, 1945; Louis Aragon, *L'Homme communiste*, Gallimard, 1946; Simone de Beauvoir, *Tous les hommes sont mortels*, Gallimard, 1946; Léon Blum, *A l'échelle humaine*, Gallimard, 1945; Pierre Bourgelin, *L'Homme et le temps*, Aubier, 1945; Adrien Ferrière, *Libération de l'homme*, Geneva, Editions du Mont-Blanc, 1944; Georges Friedmann, *Machine et humanisme*, Gallimard, 1946; André George, *et al. Les grands appels de l'homme contemporaine*, Editions du Temps présent, 1946; André Hauriou, *Vers une doctrine de la Résistance: le Socialisme humaniste*, Algiers, Editions Fontaine, 1944; Georges Izard, *L'Homme est révolutionnaire*, Grasset, 1946; André Lang, *L'Homme libre, ce prisonnier*, Les Editions de Paris, 1946; Louis de Lavareille, S.J., *Humanisme et prière*, Desclée de Brouwer, 1946; Henri de Lubac, *Le Drame de l'humanisme athée*, Spes, 1944; Jacques Maritain, *Principes d'une politique humaniste*, New York, Editions de la Maison française, 1944; Jacques Maritain, *Les Droits de l'homme et la loi naturelle*, Paul Hartmann, 1945; Charles Moeller, *Humanisme et sainteté. Témoignages de la littérature occidentale*, Casterman, 1946; Edward Montier, *Les jeunes devant l'humanisme intégral*, Spes, 1946; Jean Mouroux, *Le Sens chrétien de l'Homme*, Aubier, 1945; Jacques Rennes, *Du marxisme à l'humanisme*, L'Amitié par le livre, 1946; Fernand Robert, *L'Humanisme: Essai de définition*, Les Belles Lettres, 1946; Jean-Paul Sartre, *L'existentialisme est un humanisme*, Nagel, 1946; Luc Somerhausen, *L'humanisme agissant de Karl Marx*, Richard Masse, 1946; André Ulmann, *L'humanisme du XXe siècle*, Editions à l'Enfant Poète, 1946; Xavier de Virieu, *Métier de*

chef: Perspectives d'humanisme militaire, Grenoble, Prudhomme, 1946.

15. See Michael Kelly, 'Humanism and National Unity: the Ideological Reconstruction of France', in Nicholas Hewitt (ed.), *The Culture of Reconstruction: European Literature, Thought and Film, 1945–50*, London, Macmillan, 1989, pp.103–19.

16. Simone de Beauvoir, 'Idéalisme morale et réalisme politique', *Les Temps modernes*, November 1945, pp.248–68, 266.

17. Jean-Paul Sartre, *Situations II*, Gallinard, 1948, pp.22–3.

18. Simone de Beauvoir, *Le Deuxième Sexe*, Folio, 1991, pp.14–15 (first published 1949).

19. Edith Piaf, 'La vie en rose', in Pierre Saka, *La chanson française à travers ses succès*, Larousse, 1988, p.174.

20. Henri Lefebvre, *Le Marxisme*, P.U.F., 1948, p.10.

21. Ibid., p.10.

– 9 –

The First Women *Députés*:
'les 33 Glorieuses'?

Hilary Footitt

In the 'ordonnance' of 21 April 1944, women in France were to be given for the first time, at the Liberation, the right to vote and the right to stand for public office. In the first national elections after this, to the first Constituent Assembly on 21 October 1945, thirty-three women were elected as *députés*, 5.63 per cent of the total membership of the Assembly. In the two subsequent national elections – to the second Constituent Assembly on 2 June 1946 and the first National Assembly of the Fourth Republic on 10 November 1946 – thirty and thirty-five women respectively were elected, 5.11 per cent and 6.48 per cent of the total. This period is not only the first point of women's national representation, but also numerically by far its highest point until the Mitterrand era some forty years later.[1]

Given this, the relative lack of academic interest in the first women *députés* – 'les 33 Glorieuses' of the title[2] – is surprising. It is almost as if the narratives of transition and betrayal which hang heavily over interpretations of the 1944–46 period[3] have been accepted by and subsumed in feminist interpretations of the 'event' of women's suffrage and representation. For liberal-feminists, for example, the accomplishment of the vote in France was a short-lived triumph because it did not, as it were, 'deliver the whole package of goods' until very much later.[4] For socialist-feminists the implications of women's suffrage and representation are subsumed in the arguments and disappointments over the reestablishment of bourgeois democracy in France.[5] For radical feminists, the whole issue is anyway an irrelevancy to an essentialist agenda.

I want to argue however that we should reexamine the entry of women into the National Assembly in 1945 as a particularly propitious point at which to consider the contribution of gender to political discourse. Propitious because the immediate post-War period was one of profound institutional questioning, with a Provisional Government and a Constituent Assembly. The identity of the 'authorities', of who was in charge as it were, was far from clear for a very considerable time. From the assertion of the brand new Minister of the Interior in September 1944 that, 'the government's authority was limited to Paris, the suburbs and possibly the outer suburbs; no one knew what was happening in the departments',[6] through to the local disputes all over France about the competing powers of *Commissaires de la République*, *Milices patriotiques* and Departmental and Local Liberation Committees, there was genuine uncertainty about who or what constituted the government. With this went a hopeful belief that the very nature of politics and the identity of politicians had been irrevocably changed by the war experience: 'The political fight is neither a career, a leisure activity or an accident of life... it is a new order which has been formed... [politics] is the direct way of speaking... It's an accent.'[7]

Within this discussion of a new language and change, women as potential representatives were still largely perceived as outsiders who would need to be fitted in to ensure they understood the workings of the system, albeit a new one, and proved of benefit to existing interests. Women were the outsiders, the objects of the discourse. Léon Blum, writing in *Le Populaire* on 5 September 1945 about the importance of having women candidates on the election lists, did so in the guise of a personal observation to the Socialist party, slightly at right angles to the more pressing matters of political business. In Blum's discourse, women in politics were the objects of the verbs, a colony which the Socialist party had created and which it now intended to liberate to its advantage: 'The introduction of women into public life in our country is practically our own work... We put women in government... I hope we'll know how to exploit such a considerable and legitimate advantage...'[8]

The strangeness and essentially outsider status of new women *députés* was emphasized by the uncertainty with which press reports of their election handled the naming of the phenomenon: 'Femmes Constituantes', 'représentantes', all in inverted commas.[9] There is however contemporary evidence of a contrary expectation on the part of some women who appeared to believe that their women representatives should contribute to the debate on redefining politics, on changing the language of politics, rather than assuming a marginal status in an already agreed system. Simone Esprels in *Front National* for example ran a long interview with women voters in La Motte– Picquet market just before the October 1945 election, quoting such views as: 'It's high time that women were elected to change the legal situation of women and get social laws passed. Women know a lot more about everything to do with protecting the mother and child... and as for food? Women have a much clearer grasp of the needs of a family, of the nightmare of the high cost of living; perhaps they'll have more common sense, clearer solutions and be more persevering in improving the food situation.'[10]

An interview with the first MRP women *députés* underlined their belief that certain issues would be of particular relevance to women *députés*. Francine Lefebvre for example explained: 'Our role in the Assembly? But it's very clearly set. By their very essence women are called upon to defend the interests of the family,' while Simone Rollin believed that 'Social and political matters are sufficiently interconnected for them not to be isolated in artificial compartments... you see, the family is the cornerstone of society. That's why women, and especially Mothers, must participate in all the work of the Constitutional Assembly.'[11]

The suggestion, partial and party-limited though it may be here, that women should represent the preoccupations of all women in the whole country, that women are a specific group, with specific political concerns, is particularly interesting in relation to recent discussions of why the vote for women was delayed so long in France. Pierre Rosanvallon, sidestepping the clichés on the cultural influence of Roman Catholicism, the political fears of Republicans, and the institutional block provided by the Senate, compares the utilitarian view of democracy held by Anglo-Saxons with the French universalist view derived from the Revolution. In the former, women were given the vote precisely by virtue of their representative function, because they can represent the preoccupations and expertise of women. In the French model, he argues, voting rights are connected to the principle of political equality of individuals, so that women are deprived of the right to vote for the very reasons that had entitled them to it in the Anglo-Saxon model, because they are too marked by their female role in society to be seen as 'neutral' political individuals.[12]

The hypothesis that I want to examine here is that in the two Constituent Assemblies where the language of politics was still under discussion, the first women *députés* challenged the inherited construction of the political system by valorizing gender, the very issue which had previously served to exclude them from politics, and that this was, to use Geneviève Fraisse's words, one of these 'historic moments where women define themselves as women, as the subjects of history',[13] rather than marginalized objects to be fitted in to a pre-existing system. In 1946, with the establishment of the Fourth Republic, however, and the increasing polarisation of politics, this strategy can be seen to be abandoned or subordinated to other interests.

Gender

The Constituent Assemblies

Of 'les 33 Glorieuses', thirty-one were elected for metropolitan France, one for Algiers and one for Guadeloupe. From the original thirty-three elected in October 1945, twenty-four survived into the second Constituent Assembly of June 1946, and twenty-three into the first National Assembly of November 1946–June 1951. In background, at least nineteen had well attested activity in the Resistance and indeed twelve were decorated. Seven had been arrested and imprisoned in the war, three in Ravensbrück. In several cases, the women had clearly held key positions in Resistance organizations: Emilienne Galicier, PCF *député* for the Nord, for example, had assumed Front National responsibility for Union des Femmes Françaises (UFF) activity in the Nord region; Denise Bastide, PCF *député* for the Loire, had worked in the leadership of the Francs-Tireurs et Partisans Français (FTP) of the Allier from March 1943 onwards; Germaine Degrond, (SFIO) *député* for Seine-et-Oise, was secretary of Ceux de la Résistance. Six of the thirty-three were connected to politics, quite apart from their own actions, by famous partners: on the PCF side, Mathilde Gabriel Péri, Marie-Claude Vaillant-Couturier, Jeannette Vermeersch; in the SFIO, Eugénie Eboué-Tell, Madeleine Léo-Lagrange; and in the Parti Républicain de la Liberté, Hélène de Suzannet, *député* for the Vendée, whose deceased husband had sat for the same constituency between 1936 and 1940.

In party terms: of the thirty-three, seventeen were in the Communist party (PCF), six were Socialists (SFIO), nine were Christian-Democrats (MRP), and one was in the Parti Républicain de la Liberté (PRL). The evidence of their speeches in the two Constituent Assemblies suggests that gender was a more salient feature in the construction of discourse than party difference. Indeed, of the sixty-six speeches made by the women *députés* in the Constituent Assemblies, forty-one (62 per cent) adopt what might be described as a tactic of specificity, arguing explicitly as women and for women, and this tactic clearly crosses party divisions. Women *députés*, far from accepting their outsider status and seeking to integrate themselves into an existing political system, consciously adopted the language of specificity and in so doing challenged definitions of politics, in terms of political legitimacy, the delineation of political clienteles and the identification and redefinition of political issues.

Firstly, their contribution to debate established a specific political identity. Women presented themselves as a self-conscious political force which drew its legitimacy from their own activity in the years of War and Occupation. Jeannette Vermeersch (PCF) could provide a roll-call of heroines: 'The French women of Montluçon who lay down on the railway lines to stop their sons going on STO; Simone Jaffray killed in the fight to liberate Paris... Henriette Dumin, killed on a mission...'[14] The legitimacy claimed, however, was grounded on a wider definition of resistance than public action by acknowledged heroines. Thus Denise Ginollin (PCF) pointed out the range of activity in which women had been engaged in the War, finding food for the family as well as fighting and demonstrating.[15] For Francine Lefebvre (MRP), the heroism women had shown in the War in looking after their families and helping them to survive was of at least equal value to the more normally acknowledged acts of the Resistance: 'I don't know, Minister, if you realize what life was like for these women after 1940. They managed to keep their families going through a patience [...] a courage – one might almost say a heroism – to which not enough tribute is paid. Because it's a lot easier to accomplish one outstanding act than to carry on fighting day after day with the same difficulties.'[16]

Here political legitimacy is being firmly centred in the specificity of women, the separate spheres debate overtaken by a construction which puts public and private together: 'It's in the love of their home and country that they found the strength to persevere and fight.'[17]

Secondly, the speeches of these *députés* represent women as a specific political clientele. An intrinsic part of this tactic is a choice of language which, in the context of political discussion, seeks to valorize the traditional concerns of women. Germaine Degrond (SFIO) compared the role of women *députés* to that of good housekeepers: 'Here, where you need a magnifying glass to find a woman, I think it's helpful to recall that women are not people who systematically demolish things. Guided by an age-old habit, they see their role as tidying up the house. When something's not right, they try to put it right, without a fuss and with patience and simplicity.'[18]

Speeches by women members on the subject of food shortages could sound like a collage of examples drawn from the experiences of female constituents. One *député* took the minister round a verbal guided tour of the empty shops: 'If you please, we'll go out of the grocer's and stop in on the restaurant... Before we leave the restaurant, I want to point out the wine situation to you. The moral of my story, minister, is that children in Haute-Savoie don't have any potatoes... and whilst I'm on the subject of potatoes... we should have a little look at the bread problem...'[19]

In some of the speeches, particularly from the Communists, it is clear that women as a whole are being presented by their first women *députés* as a powerful clientele who will need to be heard politically. Emilienne Galicier called for the death penalty for black-marketeers with the words: 'Minister... women had high expectations of you when you took over... All the mothers demand that capital punishment should be applied as speedily as possible to black-marketeers.'[20]

Far from being the objects of the discourse, women became tactically the active agents. In Denise Ginollins's contribution, for example, there is an insistent incantatory repetition of women demanding and calling for change: 'Women are a little disappointed...' 'They know that...' 'They know that...' 'They're amazed that...' 'Foresight is a very feminine characteristic that they would wish successive Ministers to acquire...' 'They want...' 'They want...' 'What really upsets women...' 'Women demand...' 'Women are angry...' 'They expect this Assembly...'[21]

The third discernible theme is a conscious espousal by these women *députés* of issues which interest the specific group of women, and an assertion of the primacy of these issues against others. The first of these is undoubtedly 'ravitaillement' – food. In women's speeches, 'ravitaillement' is not just a vital issue, it is the central issue, and one that the women *députés* insisted was particularly theirs. Thus Renée Prévert (MRP): 'The women, who are sitting here for the first time, know what hope the country has placed in them, particularly in the area of food where women have such an important role to play...'[22]

Germaine Degrond (SFIO), who was indeed President of the Commission on 'ravitaillement' on which seven women *députés* sat, made explicit the radical stance of embracing specificity on this issue: 'Gentlemen, you have limited women's concerns and preoccupations for so long to matters of the home and the kitchen, that you won't be surprised if a woman attaches so much importance to the question of food in this Assembly.'[23] Given the chronic food shortages at the time and the well-attested public unrest on the issue,[24] food and feeding the family, previously considered an essentially female issue, could be seen as located centrally in the political debate, with women using their specialized knowledge to exploit the question: 'Allow me to give you some practical pointers on the question of food, a question which, I can assure you, concerns women, even *députés*, a good deal more than the rows upon rows of budget figures.'[25] There is no suggestion here that male *députés* did not contribute vigorously to the 'ravitaillement' debates – they did. Women *députés* however constructed with 'ravitaillement' a woman's issue which was central to politics. Formerly held definitions of high and low politics could be usefully challenged: 'We've discussed here, and we'll discuss a lot more in the future, problems that may seem nobler or more elevated to you. Ah, believe me, the solution to those problems is intimately linked to that of the food problem. A people can only accomplish great tasks when it is physically strong.'[26]

The second woman's issue eagerly espoused was that of the family. Here however the interpretation given to the family was a radical one, fitting in less to Third Republic/Vichy discourse and more into a reassessment forced by the context of war, deportation and changing circumstance. Certainly the immediate post-War period, before the surviving prisoners returned, was one of a radically altered gender balance. This had clearly been of some concern before the Liberation: indeed the March 1944 debate in the wartime Consultative Assembly had discussed the possibility of not allowing women the vote in the first post-War elections to obviate the danger of universal male suffrage being replaced by universal female suffrage.[27]

The family, as depicted by women *députés*, is a family which has no man, the family where the norm is a woman left alone with children. Here the notion of what traditionally constituted a war widow has to be widened to include Resistance war widows/deportee war widows, a point made by women across the political spectrum.[28] Alice Sportisse (PCF *député* for Algiers) took the argument on redefinition into new constitutional areas, arguing that in francophone Africa the status of widow as redefined should confer the privilege of citizenship on Muslim women, less, interestingly enough, on the grounds that a debt was owed by France, but rather because such women had to behave like their metropolitan sisters in the war in assuming total responsibility for their families.[29] More radically, the family could change its configuration because additional orphaned relatives were added, or because women chose to bring up children alone: 'We want... the mothers who have had children outside marriage, by choice often rather than of necessity, to have the right to bring them up with respect and dignity... there are women who will never be able to get married, given that women vastly outnumber men in our country... are you going to deprive these women of the joy of being mothers?'[30] In any case, the insistent domestic need to feed the family, and the national need to increase production were making the mother working outside the home a largely accepted norm. Such new definitions of the family required developed social support structures: crèches, after-school facilities, canteens, women police, all of which questions women *députés* raised and discussed.[31]

For the first women *députés*, the family was a major issue which they embraced overtly as a political tactic. In Germaine Peyroles' words: 'In the hands of all women, the ballot paper is a weapon, offensive or defensive, in the service of what they hold dearest in the world.'[32] For some women at least, the family could now join the canon of official French history: 'Children... could imagine, reading the history books of France, that the French nation was formed with the bayonet, at the foot of the Bastilles, at the Louvre, at the street barricades in Paris. But... below all these stirring episodes there is an invisible web, silently woven in the hidden homes of France.'[33]

The Fourth Republic

By the time of the first National Assembly of the Fourth Republic, however, (November 1946 to June 1951) the speeches of the twenty-three women *députés* reelected from the original thirty-three were displaying rather different characteristics. Whereas in the two Constituent Assemblies, 62 per cent of their interventions had adopted the tactic of specificity, in the National Assembly the percentage over the five years was 31.4. If however their speeches are reviewed on a year by year basis, it is evident than the percentage is sharply diminishing by the end of the Assembly's term of office, to 25–26 per cent.[34] The tendency for the same group of women to argue explicitly as women and for women is markedly less present in the National Assembly than in the Constituent Assemblies.

The themes identified in the Constituent Assemblies – political legitimacy, the delineation of political clienteles, and the identification and redefinition of political issues – occur in the *députés'* speeches in the National Assembly, but do so in significantly different terms. Thus for example, the political legitimacy which had been proclaimed as arising from the day-to-day activity of ordinary women in the Resistance – a construction which was clearly made by women equally across different parties – has become a matter of inter-party dispute, with Communist women like Denise Ginollin defending their Resistance records publicly in the face of accusations in the Assembly.[35]

With the imprisonment of Communists, the Resistance heritage of women became linked for PCF *députés* to the fate of their supporters. Thus Denise Bastide claimed in July 1950 that there were twelve women imprisoned by the government after demonstrations: 'These women are subjected to the same regime as common criminals. Raymonde Dien was in a cell with a German prisoner, a Gestapo agent. When she came in, the German was delighted: "Well, if the Communists are being put in prison, we'll soon be out."'[36] Two of the original thirty-three, Madeleine Braun, PCF *député* for the Seine, and Germaine Peyroles, MRP *député* for Seine-et-Oise, briefly clashed in the Assembly over the heritage of the Resistance and the preparation of a Resistance exhibition.[37]

Whereas in the Constituent Assembly speeches of the women *députés* there was evidence of the emergence of women as a potentially powerful but as yet undefined political clientele, the Fourth Republic speeches situated women in the current fraught party debates. For Communist *députés*, women were essentially pro-peace, a suggestion which only one speech in the Constituent Assemblies had made. Madeleine Braun set out with clarity the link woman/international peace/defence of home: 'If there is a strong link particularly binding women [...] it is the desire to build for peace... through their experiences, women believe that the security of the home and the happiness of their children are closely linked to the security of their country. Defending one amounts to defending the other,'[38] and the theme was repeated another five times, with PCF women portraying the specificity of women in terms which they thought would prove embarrassing for the government.[39] In May 1950, Gilberte Roca, Communist *député* for the Gard, roundly accused the government of forfeiting any rights to legislate for Mothers' Day.[40] In this sense, the clientele of women had been overtly annexed by one political party, and whilst Socialist and MRP women spoke about the needs of particular groups of women – Germaine Poinso-Chapuis about home helps, Rachel Lempereur about women civil servants[41] – the confident cross-party assertion of the political potential of women had disappeared.

Gone too was the powerful argument that there were specifically women's issues – 'ravitaillement', the family – on which the women *députés* had particular and unique knowledge. In the developing social and economic situation, discussions on the former were relatively rare, and the Commission on 'ravitaillement' was wound up at the end of 1949. Of the relatively small number of speeches on the issue made before this date by women *députés*, only one, Rose Guérin's in April 1948, gets anywhere near the menacing incantatory rhythms noted in Constituent Assembly offerings.[42]

On the family, however, the twenty-three survivors of the thirty-three women *députés* continued to make speeches – 15 per cent of all their contributions were connected to this subject. Whereas the Consultative Assembly speeches had amounted to a reappraisal of what constituted the family in post-War France, and a claiming of the area as one in which women *députés* had specialized knowledge, the speeches of the Fourth Republic addressed specific questions of family policy – family allowance, child support, nursery schools, support for mothers working outside the home, support for widows.[43] At times, women *députés* would call for all women in the Assembly to support them: 'I'd like to crave a few minutes' attention from this Assembly, and I'm particularly addressing my female colleagues who can hardly be insensitive to what the wives and mothers of France think and say.'[44] Or they would suggest that there was a female understanding of these issues which transcended party, as when Germaine Poinso-Chapuis, the MRP Minister of Health, assured her PCF colleague, Germaine François, *député* of the Nièvre, that her amendment would be considered by the ministry with the words: 'Madame François, the Minister of Health is a woman... I mean by that you can have confidence in a woman... I'm certain that Madame François at least will know what I mean by that...'[45] On the whole however, discourse on family policy was increasingly marked by the need to attack or defend government policy. Thus Emilienne Galicier, PCF *député* for the Nord, accused the government of pursuing an antifamily policy in its relations with the miners. Here women were added on to the end of the speech as an adjunct to the argument: 'That's why all the miner's wives are on the side of their husbands in the struggle. They're defending the lives of their children, and the well-being of their home.'[46]

Conclusion

The difference between the discourse of the same group of women *députés* in the Constituent and National Assemblies is striking. In the first assemblies to which they were elected, 'les 33 Glorieuses' staked out a particular place in a political system which was still developing and defining its language. In doing this they gave value to gender in a positive and assertive way, describing their political antecedents, their constituents, and the major issues they chose to discuss in gender-related terms. In the very different post-1946 situation, the same women either abandoned the gender-related terms or subordinated them to a more traditional set of political interests.

In their recent set of interviews with women who are currently local and national representatives in France, Régine Saint-Criq and Nathalie Prévost returned again and again to the problematic of who sets the rules and who sets the agenda in politics. One distinguished and experienced woman *député* expressed her fatigue and disappointments with the present political debate with the words: 'There is a coded language, and this coded language has been written by men.'[47] The issue of creating an identity within commonly agreed political structures is intimately bound up with the creation of an appropriate political discourse. Joni Lovenduski and Vicky Randall, reviewing the extent to which feminism has affected British political institutions, note that, 'where feminists have attempted entry on their own terms, they have sometimes been able to affect the rules of the game, normally where those rules are being contested...'[48]

The 1945 and 1946 Constituent Assemblies in France were precisely a period when the rules and the language of politics were being contested. The first woman *députés,* I have argued, entered politics very largely 'on their terms', staking out a political space which was new in French politics. With the rules of the political game re-established in the 1946-51 Assembly, the discourse of specificity was modified. The first thirty-three women *députés* did not permanently change the language of French politics, but they give us an unusual example of the creation, from scratch as it were, of a political identity through language. For this alone, in my view, they merit the title, 'les 33 Glorieuses'.

Notes

Unless stated otherwise, the place of publication is Paris.

1. For figures on women's parliamentary representation, see J. Pascal, *Les Femmes Députés de 1945 à 1988,* Jean Pascal, 1990.
2. 'Les 33 Glorieuses' is a reference to J. Fourastié's book, *Les trente Glorieuses, ou, la Révolution invisible de 1949 à 1975* (Fayard, 1979), which examines the post-War economic boom in France.
3. For example, P. Hervé, *La Libération Trahie,* B. Grasset, 1945; G. Madjarian, *Conflits, Pouvoirs et Société à la Libération,* Union Générale d'Editions, 1980; S. Kramer, 'The Provisional Republic: the Collapse of the French Resistance Front and the Origins of Postwar Politics', doctoral dissertation, Princeton, 1971.
4. J. Jenson, 'The Liberation and new rights for French women', in M.T. Higonnet *et al.* (eds), *Behind the Lines, Gender and the Two World Wars,* New Haven, Yale University Press, 1987, p.284.
5. For discussions of this, see G. Willard, V. Joannes, F. Hincker and J. Elleinstein, *De la Guerre à la Libération, la France de 1939 à 1945,* Notre Temps/Histoire, 1972; A. Lecœur, *L'autocritique attendue,* Saint-Cloud, 1955; A. Rieber, *Stalin and the French Communist Party 1941–47,* New York, Columbia University Press, 1962; A. Kriegel, *Les Communistes Français,* Seuil, 1970.
6. Hilary Footitt and John Simmonds, *France, 1943–45,* Leicester,

Leicester University Press, 1988, p.156.

7. *Le Combat*, 1 September 1944.
8. *Le Populaire*, 5 September 1945.
9. *Libération*, 14/15 October 1945; *Le Figaro*, 7 November 1945.
10. *Le Front National*, 14/15 October 1945.
11. *L'Aube*, 28/29 October 1945.
12. Pierre Rosanvallon, 'L'Histoire du vote des femmes: réflexions sur la spécificité française', in G. Duby and M. Perrot (eds), *Femmes et Histoire*, Plon, 1993.
13. Geneviève Fraisse, *La Raison des Femmes*, Plon, 1992, p.115.
14. *Journal Officiel* (JO), Assemblée Nationale Constituante (ANC), 17 January 1946, p.96.
15. JO, ANC, 18 January 1946, p.127.
16. JO, ANC, 2 August 1946, p.2920.
17. JO, ANC, 18 January 1946, p.127.
18. JO, ANC, 30 July 1946, p.2853.
19. Germaine Degrond, JO, ANC, 28 December 1945, p.480; F. Lefebvre, 2 August 1946, p.2920.
20. JO, ANC, 1 October 1946, p.4330.
21. JO, ANC, 18 January 1946, p.127–9.
22. JO, ANC, 22 February 1946, p.433.
23. JO, ANC, 21 February 1946, p.410.
24. Footitt and Simmonds, *France 1943–45*, p.213.
25. Germaine Degrond, JO, ANC, 28 December 1945, p.479.
26. Germaine Degrond, JO, ANC, 21 February 1946, p.413.
27. Footitt and Simmonds, *France 1943–45*, pp.42, 43.
28. See for example, M. Oyon, JO, ANC, 31 December 1945, p.624; R. Nédelec, JO, ANC, 27 December 1945, p.430.
29. JO, ANC, 4 October 1946, p.4552.
30. Germaine Degrond, JO, ANC, 19 March 1946, p.874.
31. See for example, Rose Guérin, JO, ANC, 30 December 1945, p.609; M. Méty, JO, ANC, 21 December 1945, p.324; G. Roca, JO, ANC, 27 August 1946, p.3332, 3; G. Poinso-Chapuis, JO, ANC, 30 December 1945, pp.604–6.
32. JO, ANC, 27 August 1946, p.3330.
33. G. Peyroles, JO, ANC, 27 August 1946, p.3330.
34. Figures on speeches adopting the tactic of specificity as a percentage of interventions by these women *députés* are as follows: 1947 – 26/74 (35 per cent); 1948 – 31/81 (38 per cent); 1949 – 23/63 (36.5 per cent); 1950 – 32/127 (25 per cent); 1951 – 18/69 (26 per cent).
35. JO, Assemblée Nationale (AN), 6 December 1947, p.5536; see also, Denise Bastide, JO, AN, 29 November 1947, p.5411.

36. JO, AN, 27 July 1950, p.6101.
37. JO, AN, 3 June 1949, p.3151.
38. JO, AN, 2 December 1948, p.7369.
39. M.-C. Vaillant-Couturier, JO, AN, 26 July 1947, p.3596 and 24 February 1949, p.887; Rose Guérin, JO, AN, 27 December 1948, p.8012 and 15 March 1949, p.1634; and E. Galicier, JO, AN, 9 April 1951, p.2975.
40. JO, AN, 16 May 1950, p.3693.
41. Germaine Poinso-Chapuis, JO, AN, 12 June 1950, p.4638; Rachel Lempereur, JO, AN, 17 June 1947, p.2143.
42. JO, AN, 27 April 1948, p.2313.
43. See for example: M. Péri, JO, AN, 29 November 1947, p.5301; Denise Bastide, JO, AN, 3 June 1948, p.3185; Rachel Lempereur, JO, AN, 6 August 1948, pp.5487, 5488 and 17 July 1950, p.5465; Germaine Poinso-Chapuis, 30 April 1951, p.4332.
44. Rose Guérin, 18 September 1948, p.6629.
45. JO, AN, 27 December 1947, p.6374.
46. JO, AN, 23 November 1948, p.7164.
47. Régine Saint-Criq and Nathalie Prévost, *Vol au-dessus d'un nid de machos*, Albin Michel, 1993, p.18.
48. Joni Lovenduski and Vicky Randall, *Contemporary Feminist Politics: women and power in Britain*, Oxford, Oxford University Press, 1993, p.174.

– 10 –

Reviewing Gender and the Resistance: the Case of Lucie Aubrac

Claire Gorrara

Autobiographical texts by women Resisters have been generally analysed, if at all, from a historical perspective. They have been studied in order to question prevailing notions of resistance, as well as to illustrate the diversity of activities women undertook in clandestine organizations. Yet little has been said about these women's awareness of gender as a key factor in their experiences. My discussion will focus, therefore, on the submerged contradictions between the presentation of the Resistance as a unified group experience and the often unacknowledged specifics of women's roles which mark many texts written by women Resisters from the early 1970s. I will look particularly at *Ils partiront dans l'ivresse* by Lucie Aubrac, translated into English as *Outwitting the Gestapo*.[1] This text illustrates how one writer combines an interpretation of her experiences as testimony – the author as witness to the events of the war years – with a gender-conscious presentation of her identity as a woman Resister.

Many autobiographical texts by women Resisters written during the 1970s and 1980s reveal their writers' anxiety at French revisionist attacks on the Resistance. Primarily calling into question the extent and even existence of the Nazi 'Final Solution', French revisionists were beginning to challenge post-War images of the Resistance.[2] This anxiety was exacerbated by the trial in 1987 of Klaus Barbie, a former Gestapo leader, for crimes against humanity.[3] Several women Resisters who testified at the trial, including Lucie Aubrac, claimed that it was a catalyst for their writing projects. Acting as a witness to events, such women writers felt they needed to reaffirm the moral and humanitarian beliefs for which they had fought and to counter charges of corruption levelled at the Resistance.

Writing such a politicized narrative about the war years meant that these women Resisters had to create models and structures for their life stories which deviated from the norms of women of their generation. During the 1970s and 1980s, historians had begun to debate the position of women as subjects in history. This new focus on female subjectivity would affect women Resisters' telling of their own experiences, but the extent to which gender became an issue, or was even accepted as a viable subject for comment, varied very much from writer to writer. Stressing their experiences as women Resisters would necessarily involve questioning images of the Resistance as a unified group experience.

Many women Resisters refused interpretations of their actions which emphasized their identity as women, believing this to be restrictive.[4] Women were active as explosives experts, evasions specialists or even leaders of whole Resistance organizations. Such women activists ranged in age and experience from single young women to married women with children and from politically unaware teenagers to experienced Communist activists. Their group affiliations, therefore, were rarely tied to issues of gender and there is a reluctance on the part of many women Resisters to conceptualize their experiences in such a way. Yet, in their texts, three areas stand out where it is clear that being a woman marked their ability to carry out clandestine tasks.

Firstly, many women Resisters were chosen as *agents de liaison*. An *agent de liaison* was the man, or more commonly woman, who transmitted messages, information and also arms and equipment to different groups and individuals. Young women were often chosen for this role because they stood less risk of being checked when travelling; as the War continued, young men travelling alone raised more suspicions because the Service du Travail Obligatoire[5] was meant to have sent many of them to work in German factories for the Nazi war effort. Women's relative 'invisibility' as members of the general populace was, therefore, the first marker of a gender specificity in their assigned Resistance roles.

Secondly, women's manipulation of gender stereotypes allowed them greater scope to dupe their adversaries. In *Ils partiront dans l'ivresse*, Lucie Aubrac exploits her femininity as a weapon of war by playing out a range of staged identities in dealings with the Vichy and Nazi authorities. Her most accomplished disguise was as the aristocratic pregnant fiancée of her husband Raymond. This identity is devised to get an interview with Barbie when the Gestapo capture and sentence Raymond to death under the name of François Vallet. Like an actress, she plans her persona and costume down to the last detail. When interviewed, Lucie Aubrac said 'I paid great attention to my appearance because perhaps they would have arrested a woman who had a scarf on her head, who was badly dressed. I paid great attention to my appearance because it was all part of the game.'[6] As with the 'invisibility' argument, women's exploitation of gender stereotypes meant that their contribution to the Resistance did not necessarily stand out as significant. In post-War France, the gender specifics which had been women's trade mark during the war years caused them to fade from mainstream historical accounts when the Resistance was examined in the light of more heroic and military models of action.[7]

The third area in which the gender contradictions of women Resisters' actions becomes evident is the image of the *combattante* or woman activist heading operations and using arms. Paula Schwartz argues that the 'gender tag' for such activities was generally male. This meant that those women who carried out such tasks often were redefined as honorary men rather than the tasks being redefined as non-masculine.[8] Many of the younger women Resisters foreground such contradictions, like Jeanne Bohec who was an explosives expert parachuted into France from England. In *La Plastiqueuse à bicyclette*, Bohec claims that she was accepted by the men on the ground for her expertise and that her gender was never an issue with the internal Resistance. However, this situation changes at the Liberation when the hierarchy of the official armed forces reasserts itself. As a woman, she is not allowed to be on the front line or carry a gun even though she has been well trained:

> I would have wanted to take part in the front line action in spite of my fears. I didn't know who to go and see about it. I was told politely to forget about it. A woman isn't supposed to fight when so many men are available. Yet I surely knew how to use a submachine gun better than lots of the FFI volunteers who had just got hold of these arms.[9]

Despite wishing to portray her Resistance experience as free of gender prejudices, Bohec reveals the inherent masculine/feminine divide for tasks which resurfaced in the last days of the Occupation.

It is clear, therefore, that women Resisters are working within complex and contradictory interpretations of their experiences. Their autobiographical texts engage with debates about the role of women in clandestine organizations which the Resisters themselves cannot resolve satisfactorily when writing from the standpoint of the 1970s and 1980s. Their self-perception is crossed through with contemporary concerns to promote a positive and unified image of the Resistance yet this hides a specific space for women in the history of the Resistance without which many of their actions cannot be recognized and theorized. I will now turn to look more closely at *Ils partiront dans l'ivresse* by Lucie Aubrac which successfully combines a presentation of her Resistance experiences as gender-neutral testimony with the importance of her identity as a woman.

Ils partiront dans l'ivresse was heralded as a great date in the historiography of *les années noires* by respected French historians.[10] However, the reception of the text was overshadowed by its connection to the trial of Klaus Barbie who had tortured and deported Jews and Resisters in the Lyon area. Barbie had been extradited to France in 1983 to face charges of crimes against humanity, and his lawyer, Jacques Vergès, was known to have prepared a defence of his client which pivoted on a counter-accusation of corruption within the Resistance. Speaking to Lucie Aubrac, it became clear that her text was first conceived as a response to Vergès's comments and as a testimony to the collaboration of the Vichy regime.

The notion of testimony as the written and spoken moment of an intersection between history and literature has only recently received significant critical attention, notably in a study by Shoshana Felman and Dori Laub.[11] They examine the testimonies of survivors of the Holocaust and the importance of their work comes from their emphasis on testimony as a text which does not simply reflect historical events and experiences but rather reshapes and reforms them. For Felman and Laub, the literature of testimony is interpreted as subjective and highly personal accounts of events whose consequences are still evolving. The writer as witness occupies a unique position, for s/he is placed as an individual whose experiences cannot be relayed or reported by another. The witness reaches out to a readership external to events which s/he wishes to persuade and instruct. The text produced is, therefore, more than a historical record, for it acts as a participant in the events it describes, striving to demolish the deceptive image of history as abstraction in favour of its impact on individuals.

Felman and Laub use the model of the courtroom situation to represent how the writer sees her/his text as on trial before a potentially hostile readership. Such a relationship has evolved, according to Felman and Laub, because of a crisis of truth in our present age. When widely accepted interpretations of history are under attack, such as knowledge about the Holocaust, then the urgency of testimony is most felt. In such circumstances, the model of the courtroom situation and the image of the juridical pledge symbolize the witness's feeling that s/he must take responsibility and tell her/his version of the truth before it is distorted and manipulated by others. This situation was played out for real in the use made of *Ils partiront dans l'ivresse* during the trial of Barbie.

In theory, as a member of the Nazi regime in France, Barbie was to be tried for his part in the systematic extermination of the Jewish population and not war crimes which related to his persecution of Resisters.[12] However, Jacques Vergès, notorious for his defence of Algerians accused of terrorism during the 1960s, had announced to journalists that he planned to conduct a counter trial of the West, and in particular the French Resistance, whom he wished to expose as morally unfit to pass judgement on Barbie.[13] Vergès referred specifically to the capture of Jean Moulin, General de Gaulle's representative to the internal Resistance, at Caluire on 21 June 1943. Although one former Resister, René Hardy, had been tried twice after the war for betraying the Resistance meeting to Barbie, he had never been convicted. Amongst those captured in the raid was Raymond Samuel, Lucie Aubrac's husband, and her successful bid to free him from prison after his arrest was to form the central drama of *Ils partiront dans l'ivresse*.

At the trial, Vergès chose not to name the Resister who had allegedly betrayed the group at Caluire, but he had already called into question the reputation of Moulin in the build-up to the trial. For contemporary commentators, this meant that the 'affaire Caluire' became an integral part of the debate surrounding the trial, although not formally part of the proceedings. Indeed, the trial was soon perceived to be not so much a judgement on Barbie as an explicit condemnation of the political system which had endorsed anti-Semitism. Some journalists even commented on the educational value of the trial and believed it would help educate French youth about the war years. By its end, the trial had allowed the nation to address some of the complex issues around the Resistance and collaboration but the controversy it raised did not stop with Barbie's conviction. 'L'affaire Caluire' resurfaced in October 1991 when Jacques Vergès appeared on television, shortly after Barbie's death, with the 'Testament de Barbie', a seventy-two page booklet which claimed that Raymond and Lucie Aubrac had been the double agents who had betrayed Jean Moulin and his colleagues.

This accusation was based on a reading of *Ils partiront dans l'ivresse* in which Barbie claimed that three days, from 11 to 13 May 1943, were omitted from the fictional diary and represented the period during which Lucie and Raymond had been in contact with him. It seemed that Vergès was using the text as a belated *pièce à conviction* and this highlighted the explicitly pedagogical nature of the trial, fought around conflicting accounts of the Resistance. The Aubracs denied such accusations but the situation revealed how *Ils partiront dans l'ivresse* had been read by some as a valued testimony against Barbie and collaboration which they needed to discredit.

Lucie Aubrac's training as an *agrégée d'histoire* has meant that she has always been aware of her role as a witness to historical events. In her text, this awareness comes, firstly, in her presentation of the ideological agenda of the Vichy regime and its collaboration with the German authorities and, secondly, in her defence of the Resistance.

At the beginning of the text, Lucie Aubrac reports Raymond's encounters with the French police: 'I shiver. Knowing about the collusion between the Vichy government and Hitler is one thing; to be confronted with the reality is another matter. I swear to remember this after the war: these were French policemen, real government employees, not just fascist rabble like the *Milice*, obeying German orders as a matter of routine.'[14] Lucie Aubrac's decision to remember such collaboration after the War immediately sets her up as a witness bearing testimony against the Vichy regime. By emphasizing that it is not only militant Fascist organizations, like the *Milice*, which follow German orders, she is portraying Vichy as a state which actively promoted collaboration with the Nazis.

The pedagogical role of the witness is played out literally in the text through the author's role as a teacher. Lucie Aubrac is aware that the classroom is a battleground for the control of her students' minds. She uses all possible occasions to show up the facile ideological basis of the Vichy regime. When a circular comes from the Ministry of Education asking teachers to praise Jeanne d'Arc on her saint's day and to show how the Maréchal Pétain is a worthy successor, the class makes a detailed comparison between the two emphasizing the differences in age, gender and actions. Such an exercise ridicules Pétain's pretensions to appear as the patriotic and spiritual leader of the nation. By showing the propagandist aims of Vichy reaching into the classroom, Lucie Aubrac places herself in opposition to those historians and commentators who would still regard Vichy as a group of pragmatists rather than ideologically committed politicians with a set right-wing agenda.[15]

Lucie Aubrac also acts as a defence witness for the Resistance. Published three years before the trial, her text ends with an afterword which confronts the strategies Barbie and Vergès had declared they would use at the trial and she defends 'the glorious and tragic history of the Resistance'.[16] Yet the text proves to be more than a catalogue of heroic actions. As a witness to the Resistance, Lucie Aubrac takes the reader into an everyday world of opposition to Vichy and the Nazis where women had an important role to play.

The merging of life in the Resistance with everyday life in occupied

France has been seized upon by some historians, like Dominique Veillon, as marking a break with previous representations of the Occupation.[17] By integrating a woman-centred vision of the war years with more traditional political and military narratives, Lucie Aubrac is seen to construct a different perspective on events where gender predominated. This perspective is seen firstly in the author's emphasis on the family unit and *le quotidien*.

Like many other married women Resisters with children, Lucie Aubrac highlights the daily routine of her life in occupied France. The food queues in Lyons and the forays into the countryside to persuade friends and relatives to sell precious foodstuffs are important aspects of her life. The family unit necessarily dominates this world, as family ties and connections are a way of recruiting new members for the Resistance. Both Lucie and Raymond view their involvement in the Resistance as a joint venture and Lucie Aubrac projects a vision of their family home as a safe haven for those who have gone underground. She encourages a presentation of the Resistance as a clandestine family unit which extends over the whole of France: 'We are no longer alone in this vast repression. Our family tragedy is subsumed into the tragedy of all of France.'[18] However, Lucie Aubrac's woman-centred interpretation of her wartime experiences also challenges narratives of women and the Resistance in more significant ways than many other texts by women of her generation.

In the preface to her text, Lucie Aubrac emphasizes the multiple roles and identities she assumed during the war years. As a woman she is forced to lead a double life as Mme Samuel, the history teacher and mother, and Catherine, the woman Resister who specializes in orchestrating prison escapes. Daily life and clandestine life are juxtaposed as Lucie Aubrac leads two parallel but separate lives, a situation which she sees as specific to women: 'Outside the underground life of the Resistance, with its more or less dangerous activity, daily life must be confronted – for a woman more than a man: a household to take care of, a husband and child to feed, clothes to be washed.'[19] Yet these two identities – Mme Samuel and Catherine – are not totally distinct entities, for Lucie Aubrac's perception of her Resistance activities is suffused with her identity as a pregnant woman.

The text begins with Lucie Aubrac in the maternity ward of a London hospital in February 1944. The rest of the text acts as a flashback of the last nine months so that the author's pregnancy frames her Resistance narrative. Lucie Aubrac fixes the child's conception as 14 May 1943, the day Raymond is released from prison a second time, suspected of being a black-marketeer and also a Resister. The conception of her first child, Jean-Pierre, is similarly related to important personal events as it comes after Raymond's escape from a prisoner of war camp. Such careful attention to the date and circumstances of conception suggests that Lucie Aubrac is encouraging a reading of motherhood as a personal response to public events – firstly, the Armistice and the prisoner of war experience and secondly, the persecution of Resisters which is symbolized by Raymond's capture.

The unborn child acts as a gesture of defiance. For Lucie Aubrac, the wife of a Jew, having a child in such conditions represents a victorious act of resistance. The Nazi 'Final Solution' and Vichy's active contribution to the deportation of thousands of Jews meant that if she had been captured, especially under her real name, her unborn child's chances of survival would have been slim. Lucie Aubrac's pregnancy could, therefore, be read as a direct challenge to the mass extermination of the Jews.

Another more symbolic reading of pregnancy in the text is one which was suggested by the author herself in interview. The unborn child is an image of hope which links with her activities as an evasions expert. The author stressed how her pregnancy could be used to represent her attempts to free men from prison: '[A] form of hope, one day I will bring a child into the world and while I wait for this child, there are men in prison like my child is in me and I get them out. I find that very symbolic – that you can free men at the same time as having a child.'[20] Lucie Aubrac, therefore, integrates her pregnancy into her clandestine life as both a motivating force and a symbolic reflection of her resistance.

Lucie Aubrac's position as a pregnant woman also enables her to recognize and challenge some of the gender prejudices within the Resistance which she has not acknowledged so far. She is given the status of an honorary man for her clandestine action by some members of the internal Resistance. Unlike other woman Resisters of her generation, Lucie Aubrac does not accept this as a sign of respect. In her text, she highlights how ridiculous socially constructed images of masculine prowess are when applied to a pregnant woman: 'I look down at my stomach, thinking back to all my ploys with the Gestapo, that same old story of my illegal pregnancy. Is there anything masculine about that?'[21] Disrupting associations of the masculine as the active and the feminine as the passive, Lucie Aubrac interprets her biological specificity as a woman not as a sign of weakness, but as evidence of her capacity to operate as a Resister in difficult conditions.

Lucie Aubrac's wartime record has been overshadowed by her status as an exceptional woman who freed her husband from prison three times. Her decision to write an account of the war years, over forty years later, is clearly an attempt to go beyond such clichés and to construct a gender-integrated image of her multiple identities as Resister, wife and mother. Rejecting a heroic and mythologized narrative of her past, Lucie Aubrac has used the writing experience to emphasize a woman's perspective on events. Although we, as readers, may regard privileging pregnancy, both formally and thematically, as a feminist gesture, Lucie Aubrac does not accept such an interpretation herself.

When interviewed, Lucie Aubrac rejected a sustained reading of her text as a feminist interpretation of the war years, saying 'I am not a feminist in the way suffragettes were before the War ... I am more a humanist.'[22] Her understanding of feminism as mainly a struggle for women's political rights reveals a generational divide in conceptualizing feminism. For women who were active in the women's movement in France and elsewhere during the 1970s, this interpretation would form only one part of their understanding of the term. The feminist movement was also seen as a more general campaign to reevaluate patriarchal narratives of women's experiences in history. Indeed, Lucie Aubrac's use of pregnancy in *Ils partiront dans l'ivresse* identifies her with this movement as a woman writer who challenges some of the more glorious and military 'master' narratives about the Resistance. It appears, therefore, that a different term is needed to encompass Lucie Aubrac's perspective of her past and that of gender-conscious historians and critics.

A recent article by Dorothy Kaufmann discusses her discovery of unpublished manuscripts by the historian, writer and Resister, Edith Thomas. Thomas is perhaps best-known for her part in the setting up of *Les Lettres françaises*, an influential clandestine journal.[23] In her article, Kaufmann mentions an unpublished anthology of works by fifteen French women writers, from Christine de Pisan to Simone de Beauvoir, entitled *L'Humanisme féminin* which Thomas wrote between 1947 and 1949. With its focus on questions of gender and writing, this would seem to be a text before its time. Unfortunately, Kaufmann does not outline what Thomas meant exactly by 'l'humanisme féminin' but when this term was put to Lucie Aubrac as a possible description of her wartime experiences, she replied: 'That is exactly the word. I think that it fits well because it goes beyond intellectual reflections and addresses real issues.'[24] As a merging of humanitarian concerns and women's issues, *l'humanisme feminin* could be used to describe many autobiographical accounts by women Resisters who grew up at a time when Nazis carried out one of the first systematic exterminations of a people during the twentieth century. By highlighting a woman-centred perspective on events, such a term draws the reader back to the different rhythms and patterns of women's lives. My study has aimed to show how *Ils partiront dans l'ivresse* can be read as this combination of testimony and gender-conscious narrative which allows Lucie Aubrac to place the Occupation within the context of women's experiences.

Notes

Unless stated otherwise, the place of publication is Paris.

1. Lucie Aubrac, *Ils partiront dans l'ivresse*, Seuil, 1984; idem, *Outwitting the Gestapo*, Lincoln, Nebraska University Press, 1993. All subsequent English translations of the text will be taken from *Outwitting the Gestapo*.
2. Henry Rousso, *Le Syndrome de Vichy de 1944 à nos jours*, Seuil, 1990, is an excellent account of the evolution in the collective memory of the Occupation in post-War France.
3. Two texts dealing with the debates surrounding the Barbie trial are Alain Finkielkraut, *La Mémoire vaine du crime contre l'humanité*, Gallimard, 1989, and Pierre Vidal-Naquet, *Les Assassins de la mémoire. 'Un Eichmann de papier' et autres essais sur le révisionnisme*, La Découverte, 1987.
4. Despite the refusal of many women Resisters to see their experiences in terms of gender, historians of women and the Resistance have started to redefine concepts of resistance in order to show the specifics of women's experiences: Dominique Veillon, 'Résister au féminin', *Pénélope*, no.12, Spring 1985, pp.87–91, and, idem, 'Elles étaient dans la Résistance', *Repères*, no.59, May/June 1983, pp.9–12; Paula Schwartz, 'Redefining Resistance – Women's Activism in Wartime France', in *Behind the Lines – Gender and the Two World Wars*, Margaret T. Higonnet *et al.* (eds), New Haven, Yale University Press, 1987, pp.141–153; and Margaret Collins Weitz, 'As I Was Then: Women in the French Resistance', *Contemporary French Civilization*, vol.10, no.1, Fall/Winter 1986, pp.1–19.
5. The STO came into effect in February 1943.
6. Interview with the author, Paris, 26 February 1994. All subsequent references are translated extracts from this meeting.
7. This lack of recognition for women is perhaps symbolized by the fact that only six of the 1,059 awards of *compagnon de la libération*, the most prestigious award for Resistance action, were given to

women. As Lucie Aubrac pointed out, four of these six awards were posthumous too – Berty Albrecht, Marie Hackin, Simone Michel-Lèvy, Marcelle Henry.

8. Paula Schwartz, '*Partisanes* and Gender Politics in Vichy France,' *French Historical Studies*, vol.16, no.1, Spring 1989, pp.126–51.
9. Jeanne Bohec, *La Plastiqueuse à bicyclette*, Mercure de France, 1975, p.186 (my own translation).
10. Jean-Pierre Rioux, 'Les Souvenirs de Lucie Aubrac – l'héroïsme ordinaire d'une résistante', *Le Monde*, 5 October 1989.
11. Shoshana Felman and Dori Laub, *Testimony – Crises of Witnessing in Literature, Psychoanalysis and History*, New York, Routledge, 1992.
12. For a detailed discussion of the debates surrounding the definition and application of crimes against humanity in post-War France, particularly in the cases of Klaus Barbie and Paul Touvier, see Nancy Wood, 'Crimes or Misdemeanours? Memory on Trial in Contemporary France', *French Cultural Studies*, no.5, 1994, pp.1–21.
13. For the connection between Vichy and Algeria, see Finkielkraut, *La Mémoire vaine*, and Vidal-Naquet, *Les Assassins de la mémoire*.
14. Aubrac, *Outwitting the Gestapo*, p.18.
15. One of the best known defences of this position being the *chambre d'accusation*'s report on the Touvier dossier in April 1992. The court declared a 'non-lieu' (no grounds) by, what many considered, rewriting the history of Vichy. The judges' report concluded that Touvier could not be tried for crimes against humanity as a Vichy civil servant because the régime he served could not be defined as ideologically totalitarian or fascist.
16. Aubrac, *Outwitting the Gestapo*, p.232.
17. Veillon, 'Résister au féminin', p.90.
18. Aubrac, *Outwitting the Gestapo*, p.213.
19. Ibid., p.23.
20. Interview with the author.
21. Aubrac, *Outwitting the Gestapo*, p.195.
22. Interview with the author.
23. Dorothy Kaufmann, 'Uncovering a Woman's Life: Edith Thomas (novelist, historian, *résistante*)', *The French Review*, vol.67, no.1, October 1993, pp.61–72.
24. Interview with the author.

11

'La Femme au Turban':
les Femmes tondues

Corran Laurens

During August and September 1944 an exceptional wave of shearings of women took place. Any attempt to discover why these shearings happened has to confront the silence of most historians of contemporary France on the subject, and the silence also of both shearers and the sheared, very few of whom have come forward to talk of their experience.[1] The whole phenomenon of the shearings, as well as the victims and perpetrators, disappeared after the war. The image of 'la tondue' has been noted by Henri Amouroux as one that is common to all France but claimed by no one today as a 'titre de gloire'.[2] Why, if people were so demonstrably proud of this act at the time, did it rapidly become unspeakable? Explanations offered primarily in terms of 'carnival' and national revenge have tended to subordinate the key feature of 'les tontes' – namely, their enactment of a gender-based violence inflicted by men on the bodies of women. But if seen as a form of male violence against women, a number of other explanations open up involving sexual jealousy, erotic violence and an assault on the degree of autonomy that women had obtained during the War.

The shearing of women's hair seems to have been one of the earliest acts of purging, although other punishments followed for many women accused of collaboration, including torture and summary execution.[3] There is evidence to show that shearing ceremonies commenced in some towns *before* they were liberated and that they were sometimes hastily interrupted so that the real war could go on. The shearings appear to span a period of between one and a half to two months and then come to an abrupt end as the technique was rapidly delegitimated and a conspiracy of silence among participants settled into place. There was apparently no national directive to shear heads but the practice was widespread. Estimates of the number of women shorn vary – and are hotly contested – but in view of the large number of photographs in official Allied war collections, and newspaper reports of the time, the least to be said is that the practice, although short-lived, was massive in its repetition.[4]

Calls for this traditional punishment for adultery appeared well before the Liberation and suggest that the shearings were not entirely spontaneous. As early as December 1943, a warning appeared in *l'Aurore* that women associating with Germans would be branded.[5] A story by James Wellard which appeared in the *Sunday Express* on 20 August 1944 concerning the ritual nature of the shearings in Chartres is said to have played a part in the wildfire spread of the practice when it was beamed back to France by radio. In this report, after being shaved, the women were ducked 'rear first' in buckets of water and then paraded before the citizens 'so that everybody would know them for ever after'. The next day, a call to violence, bordered in black, appeared in an FFI weekly newspaper in Dordogne-Sud where shearings were to be particularly violent and numerous. It was reported that the FFI in Bergerac, aided by the police, had inflicted a well deserved punishment on these 'créatures abominables'. The sight of these 'prostitutes' marched around the town under armed guard once they had been shorn of those 'seductive charms that had helped them to betray' was described as a memorable 'cortège carnavalesque', the shaven women having 'un succès fou' somewhat different from that which they had sought previously.[6] There is evidence in official Allied photographs of the shearings and in their captions that the FFI and the Resistance were heavily involved in these ceremonies (their headgear often giving them away). It seems that these local public appeals for men to embark upon what one victim called 'une chasse aux femmes'[7] had no trouble finding willing recruits.

Shearing has been a traditional punishment for adulterous women in France and appears to be one of those ancient types of reaction to a resentment that refuses to die. Marguérite de Bourgogne, queen of France from 1290 to 1315, was shorn as an adulteress, repudiated and strangled on the orders of Louis X. It was also applied to 'ces femmes de mauvaise vie' – prisoners at the Salpêtrière under the Ancien Regime.[8] Older Parisians who had experienced the siege of 1871 recalled that 'les filles publiques' who had been seen in the company of a Prussian general on the Champs-Elysées were publicly spanked. During the First World War, screaming women were seen being shorn on the Place du Marché at Renaix in Flanders on 11 November 1918.[9] Many of the women shorn at the Liberation were labelled as prostitutes and one of the principal arguments advanced in favour of the 'Loi Marthe Richard', which closed brothels in 1946, was the extent to which they had been centres of collaboration.

While stories concerning shearings have to be treated with caution since they are, like other episodes of collaboration, often recounted from conflicting viewpoints by those who have good reason to confirm or deny them, they nonetheless offer a glimpse of perceptions and judgements at the time.

A correspondent in the Gironde recalled the practice of tying women suspected of collaboration naked to the balconies of town halls.[10] A summary court was set up at the town hall in Libourne (Gironde) where a 'prostitute' denied contact with Germans. Her hair was shorn off all the same and she was stripped naked and forced on to the pedestal which had supported the statue of the first Duc Decazes which the Germans had removed to melt down the bronze.[11] Sartre encountered a 'sad procession' around a shorn woman on the Boulevard Saint-Michel but failed to intervene. While noting the medieval nature of the scene, he was of the opinion that the men guarding the victim were unhappy at carrying out this duty (though this view is not borne out in the numerous photographs of shearings).[12] Elsa Triolet saw shorn women at the Palais de Justice in Montélimar and noted that the men who guarded them 'did so with disgust but also with a certain sense of duty'. The next day she saw some of the same women, their heads hidden under multicoloured turbans.[13] Gertrude Stein expressed her shock at the *public* nature of the punishment: 'Nous voilà au Moyen Age. C'est très intéressant et c'est logique au fond.'[14] Two sisters in Paris were shorn simply because their 'judges' had mistakenly gone to the wrong floor. Nobody in the building intervened to help them.[15] Flora Groult recorded in her diary on 25 August 1944 that a neighbour who was a barber was requisitioned to shear women and returned in the evening 'fier comme un héros'.[16] The Fourth Republic historian Georgette Elgey wrote of the shock of coming across a shearing in August 1944:

> On the Place de l'Eglise, a crowd. A woman from a nearby village is on her knees, shaven. She is said to have 'collaborated', shared a bed with a German. Stones are thrown at her. I am horrified. The priest intervenes. I draw back. At the end of an hour the woman is taken away. I hated this scene. It spoilt my happiness for a long time.[17]

The shearing of a fifty-five-year-old teacher in Saint-Brieuc on 25 August 1944 was vividly described in his diary by the novelist Louis Guilloux. The woman was led to a chair within a semicircle to lewd cries of encouragement. 'La patiente', as she was disturbingly referred to, was ashen-faced and crying and her hideous convict-like appearance shocked the writer. Two days later he came across another ceremony, the victim's house now guarded by a young man with a gun. A photograph of the very young girl at an abundantly laden table and kissing a German was passed around the excited crowd waiting for her to be brought out. Guilloux overheard an old woman voicing a warning to a younger one, citing this punishment as an example of what would happen to her if she ever slept with a German. Guilloux found himself unable to sit at his desk and work after these episodes.[18]

Just being seen in a bar with German soldiers aroused a devastating degree of hatred and anger from male onlookers although the later legal concept of *indignité nationale*, elaborated in November 1944, stipulated that social contacts or intimate relations with German military personnel were not punishable unless accompanied by reprehensible acts.[19] The ubiquitous Father Raymond-Léopold Bruckberger – the FFI chaplain whose name is rarely absent from books on the Occupation and the Liberation – wrote in his diary of entering a café

> ...full of German soldiers accompanied by French girls. As we came in, we saw one directly in front of us with a German non-commissioned officer. I stared hard at her. She blushed to the roots of her hair. We were sad. Those girls could be dipped in tar and burned in the public square, and it would affect me no more than a fire in the fireplace of a neighbour's house.

One reason for this vengeful reaction may lie in the fact that, as his war diaries disclose,[20] Father Bruckberger had recently been shot by a German patrol and left for dead at the roadside. Even so, it is significant that his anger was not directed towards the real enemy – the German soldiers and officers. Father Bruckberger later said funeral masses for the FFI, who alone had the right to church services in the 'charnel-house odour' of Paris at the end of August 1944.[21] Paradoxically, he was to become one of the chief apostles of forgiveness and reconciliation throughout the official purge and, as chaplain to Darnand, argued for his life to be spared.[22]

While such testimonies contain their own indispensable insights, photographs of the shearings taken by Allied military personnel contain more information about the circumstances of the ceremonies (see figures 7 to 21, pp.159–173). Moreover, the captions that accompany these photographs suggest little sympathy on the part of Allied personnel for the sheared women. In several photographs, the first sentence of the captions gives its title as a collaborationist woman having her head shorn, and then the caption continues with a seamless

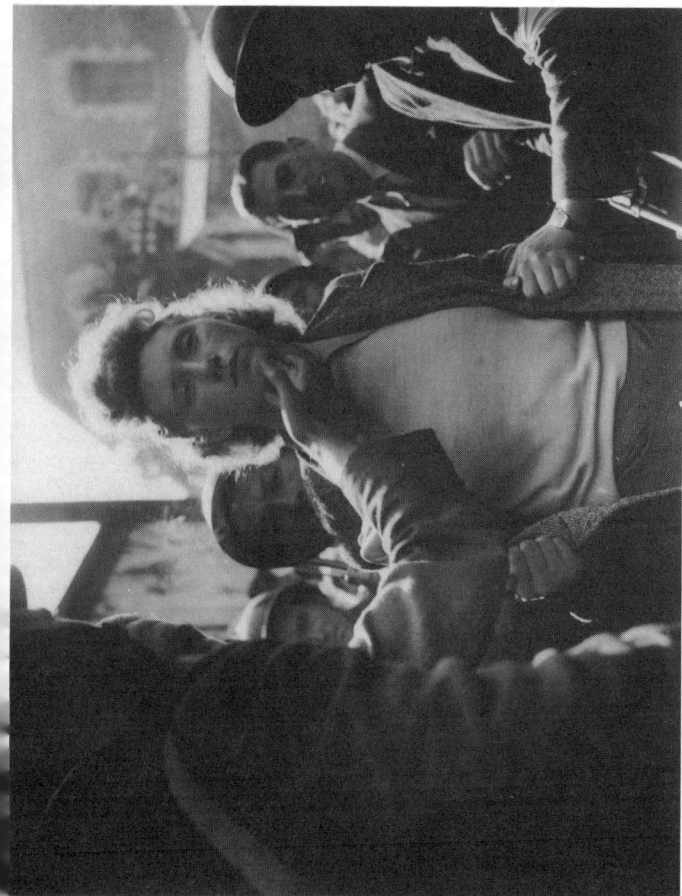

Figure 7. 'WOMAN COLLABORATIONIST SEIZED IN RENNES: Members of the French Forces of the Interior, armed and wearing their distinguishing Croix de Lorraine armbands and steel helmets, force a French woman suspected of aiding the Nazis to confess during a mass collaborationist round-up at Rennes soon after the city was captured by US troops, 4 August 1944' (original caption). © Imperial War Museum.

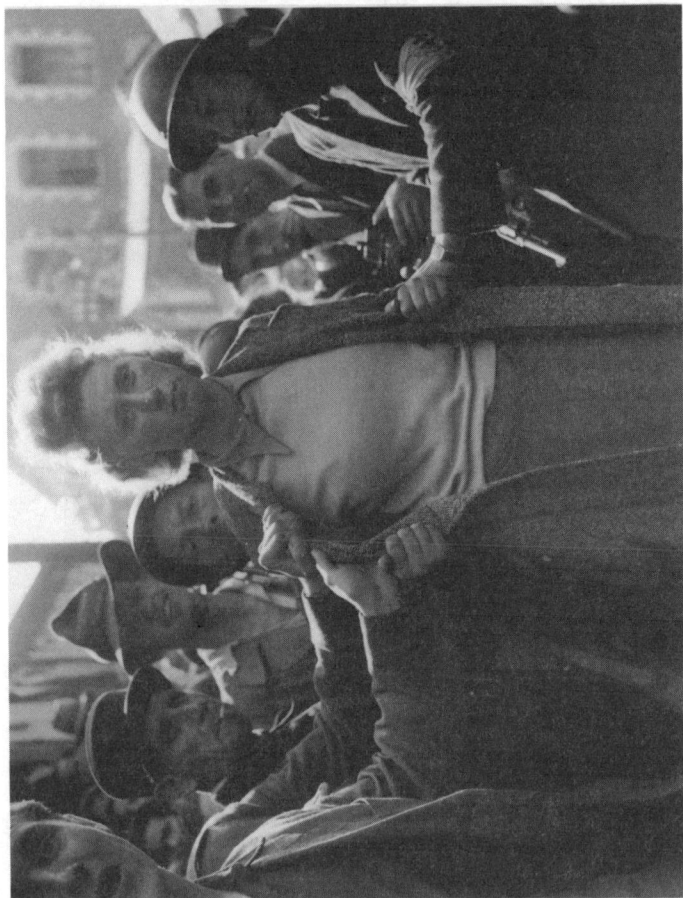

Figure 8. (Caption as for Figure 7.) © Imperial War Museum

Figure 9. 'In the local Town Hall, that is now the HQ of the Maquis, two women collaborators, who have had their hair shorn, are interviewed. 21.8.44' (original caption). © Imperial War Museum.

Figure 10. 'This woman collaborator put up some resistance, but the cropping was carried out with the aid of two Maquis holding her down. GISORS. 31.8.44' (original caption). © Imperial War Museum.

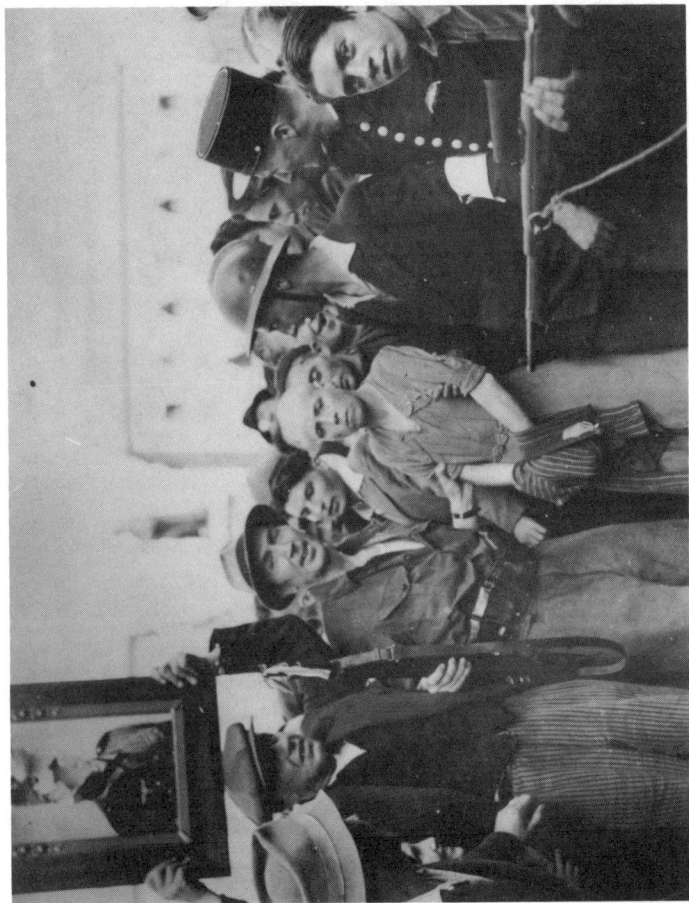

Figure 11. 'A Frenchman who collaborated with the Nazis is forced to hold the torn picture of a Nazi officer over his head as he is led through a crowd in Nancy, following the entry of General Patton's US forces. The French woman at the right has had her head shaven to brand her as a collaborationist' (original caption). © Imperial War Museum.

Figure 12. 'COLLABORATIONISTS IN FRANCE: Their heads shaved and their clothes partially ripped off, these two French women, accused of collaborating with the Nazis, are being turned over to the authorities by Paris crowds. The woman on the right is carrying her shoes and both have Swastikas painted on their cheeks' (original caption). © Imperial War Museum

Figure 13. 'COLLABORATIONIST JAILED IN MANTES: Her head shaved, a French woman collaborationist is escorted to the police station in Mantes, France, by patriotic resisters. A fighter of the French Forces of the Interior (left) is still armed with hand grenades and rifle after helping to rout the Nazis from the Seine River port' (original caption). © Imperial War Museum.

Figure 14. 'AXIS COLLABORATIONISTS DENOUNCED IN CHERBOURG: Girls accused of being Axis collaborationists as a result of violations of the rules of the French resistance party for conduct with the Germans, are paraded through the streets of Cherbourg. They were rounded up Bastille Day morning, 14 July 1944, and their heads shorn before they were driven through the streets. The placard reads: "Le Char des Collaboratrices"' (original caption). © Imperial War Museum.

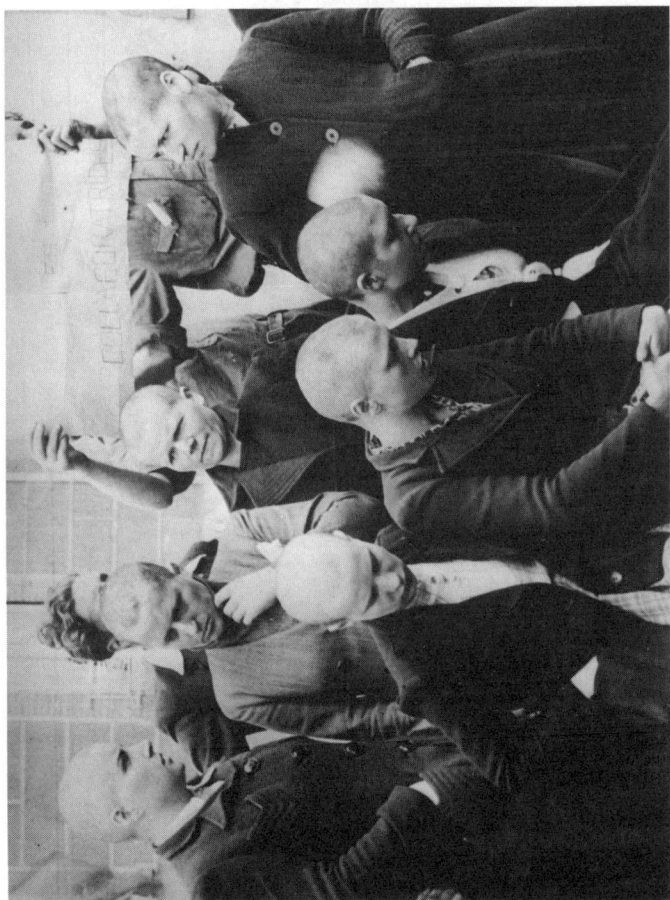

Figure 15. (Caption as for Figure 14.) © Imperial War Museum

Figure 16. 'This woman was quite ashamed when the barber had finished cropping her hair as a mark of disgrace. GISORS. 31.8.44' (original caption). © Imperial War Museum

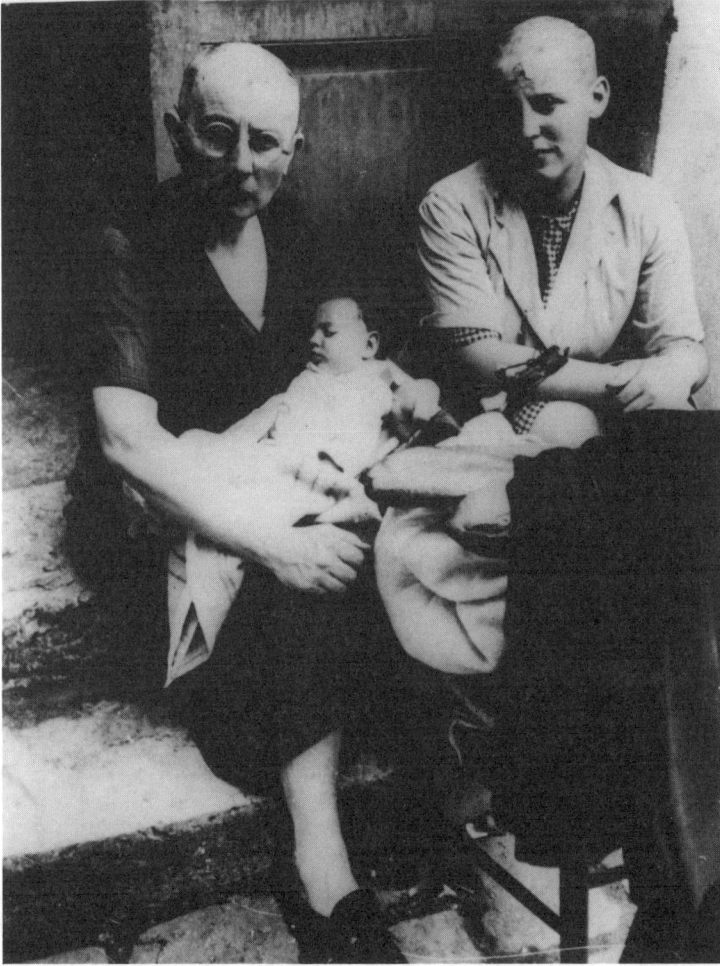

Figure 17. 'FIRST PICTURES OF THE CAPTURE OF CHARTRES. 23.8.44. A girl collaborator sits with her mother and her German fathered child' (original caption). © Imperial War Museum.

Figure 18. 'Liesville: The mother of Madaleine Bazise trying to protect her daughter against two French patriots' (original caption).
© Imperial War Museum.

Figure 19. 'THIS IS WHAT THE FRENCH PATRIOTS THINK OF COLLABORATORS: Grande Guillotte, 23 year old French girl collaborated with the Germans in Normandy. When her town was liberated by Allied troops, French patriots dragged her from her house and cut off all her hair . . .' (original caption). © Imperial War Museum.

Figure 20. '. . . Mme GUILLOTTE certainly looks awful with all her hair cut off' (original caption). © Imperial War Museum.

Figure 21. 'Mme Juliette Audieuve, age 35' (original caption). © Imperial War Museum.

story of local German atrocities against the Maquis in a sort of transference or displacement of blame onto the women for the barbarity. There is little evidence from the photographs that Allied troops tried to halt the shearings although it was reported that American officers spent a large part of their time rescuing suspected (male) collaborators from summary execution. Some young women are shown preferring to be arrested with German soldiers rather than by their compatriots or imploring American soldiers to protect them.

Photographs also reveal the extent to which the shearings were formalized *ceremonies* conducted with all the pomp of an administrative festival. Mona Ozouf's view that revolution is all about order and not disorder is confirmed with wide evidence of flag-waving, drum-rolls, busts of Marianne, statues, framed photographs, raised platforms or trundling vehicles and prolonged and noisy processions with stops at strategic public places.[23]

Arguments have been advanced to suggest that women were 'equal' partners in scenes of shearing but photographs do not provide evidence of this claim. They show women being manhandled by bands of laughing, smoking men, heavily armed with rifles, machine-guns and belts laden with hand grenades and ammunition. In the numerous photographs where women are visible among the 'chahuteurs', they are in a minority and always in secondary roles. A well known photograph of a shorn woman carrying a baby in the rue du Cheval Blanc at Chartres, taken by the celebrated American photographer Robert Capa on 19 June 1944, does indeed show women walking alongside the procession, though this female presence may well explain its worldwide diffusion and acceptability as an image of the Liberation. A second photograph taken the same day by Capa shows a woman being led to a shearing across the hair-strewn courtyard of Jean Moulin's Préfecture. A recent article on the shearings in the weekly magazine *L'Evénement du Jeudi*, mentions a short fictional film on shaven women made by a psychotherapist in Saint-Nazaire who apparently interviewed thirty-eight victims anonymously. One pregnant woman described 'la fête' with people shouting and dancing and her extreme fear for her unborn child because of not knowing how far the torture would go: 'I live alone with this memory, and the silence. This is the worst thing, this silence, all my life.'[24]

The stigma of 'les femmes au turban' extended by visual association alone to another category of victimized women. One survivor of the concentration camps said that for months after the Liberation, a woman who walked out with a scarf or a turban on her head was called a 'collabo'.[25] Fred Kupferman has also confirmed this guilt by association, noting that 'la marque d'infamie, c'est le crâne rasé. Celui des femmes déportées, celui des tondues de la Libération. Il s'agit d'humilier. Le résultat passe les espérances.'[26]

An attempt to categorize the different types of women who entered into relationships with Germans has been made by Célia Bertin, herself a messenger for the Resistance in Occupied Paris.[27] There were those who genuinely loved men they should not have loved but whose feelings were not inspired by Nazi ideology. Other women were motivated by self-interest and duplicity, rather than political opinions or racial prejudice and would have easily slept with American soldiers a few days later simply because this was their 'profession or way of life'. Others needed paid work desperately and worked for the Germans as house-cleaners and servants. And finally, there were mistresses of Germans or of French men who worked with the Gestapo. Célia Bertin's judgement of these women fifty years on is harsh and they still fill her with disgust. Yet, like Lucie Aubrac, who recalled that the number of women sleeping with Germans was very small and that in Lyon she often saw men smiling at Germans and giving up seats in buses to them,[28] Bertin also remembers that these women were in a minority and that most women in Paris sought to avoid contact with Germans. 'Les tondues', she felt, were women who had by their actions indeed excluded themselves from French society, but the price they paid was disproportionately high in comparison to the misdeeds of men. Her own explanation for this double standard is that it reflected contempt for women's bodies and sexual autonomy. Regarded as the property of 'males of the tribe', once the female body was used by others, the woman had to pay.[29]

Yet even as it was despised, this body was mobilized by male fantasy. 'La tondue' became a familiar figure in many fictional narratives which have the Occupation and Liberation as their background. An 'archétype de la femme au crâne rasé' – an image or 'scène de genre' appears to have captured the imagination of many male novelists and poets from Georges Brassens's song 'La belle qui couchait avec le roi de Prusse – A qui l'on a tondu le crâne rasibus' to Eluard's poem 'Comprenne qui voudra'. How, then, to explain this combination of disgust and desire, danger and pleasure which was projected onto the female figure?

An attempt at justifying the behaviour of some men towards suspected women collaborators can be seen in most historical accounts of the period. Stanley Hoffmann has noted that the official version of events had a 'therapeutic mission'[30] and indeed conventional explanations are couched in this apologetic and cathartic mode: hatred and passions were *bound* to explode during the Liberation and although the occasional mistake and summary executions were to be regretted, given the circumstances, they probably could not have been avoided. Only *occasionally* were women who were suspected of sleeping with Germans shaved bald and paraded through the streets of a village;[31] the outlaw habit of the underground days of personally settling accounts was *inevitably* going to continue for some time. 'Les tondues' had a sacrificial function in some accounts – 'It is more than likely that many girls who were shorn were, unbeknown to themselves or their barbers, the instrument of salvation for miliciens and collaborators who might otherwise have died to appease the rage of their fellow citizens'[32] – and a safety-valve effect in others: 'Without the release of accumulated tensions' by the blood-letting of the Liberation, the regular trials would not have been as lenient as they often were.[33] Father R. More, a Resistance chaplain in the Savoie who, when informed that some young women were surrounded by 'gardes de corps' and about to be shorn, told his partisans to let them do it. By allowing the shearing, the women would provide a 'firebreak', diverting energies from killing. 'For a long time after', the chaplain reported, 'women wearing turbans would no longer say hello to me. But blood did not flow.'[34]

Even in the face of warnings, women had not expected such treatment and were apparently taken by surprise, some fleeing to the surrounding forests as the Maquis descended from their hideouts. Some historians note that it must not be forgotten that acts of vengeance were a reaction to four years of suffering and the terrible misfortunes of the times are invoked. Others have hinted that this violence may have been excusable in the build-up of anger that occurred as discoveries were made about the true nature of German atrocities – as if there was some connection between the two.[35] A dismissal of the shearings as unfortunate but unimportant is widespread, as is the suggestion that it was preferable to undergo a public humiliation than to be shot in a discreet doorway in a 'private and privileged' execution[36] which was reserved for some members of the *Milice*.

The theory that the shearings represent a rite of passage from one era to another is more convincing. In the first book on the shearings, Alain Brossat notes: 'Ces tontes-là, par lesquelles l'individu se trouve réduit à un matricule, énoncent en clair les nouvelles tables de la Loi.'[37] But what is crucial to understand is why this new era seems to have *required* women's more general devalorization. Women's new-found independence and importance during the War – in economic life and in Resistance activity especially – contrasted sharply with the humiliation of French men (see Michael Kelly's chapter in this volume, pp.117–128). Given this crisis of male identity, the shearings could be said to represent both an attempted symbolic reversal of women's emergent power, and an exorcism of the image of threatened masculinity from public memory. It seems that this symbolic reversal *had* to take place at the Liberation to restore a familiar hierarchy and to act as a warning to women to revert to their expected socio-cultural peacetime role.

Notes

Unless stated otherwise, the place of publication is Paris.

1. Since the research for this chapter was undertaken, an important study of 'les tondues' has appeared. See Alain Brossat, *Les Tondues: un carnaval moche*, Editions Manya, 1992.
2. See Henri Amouroux, *Joies et Douleurs du Peuple Libéré, La Grande Histoire des Français sous l'Occupation*, Robert Laffont, 1988, pp. 530–5.
3. Ibid.
4. Cf. Marie-France Brive, 'L'Image des femmes à la Libération', in Rolande Trempé (ed.), *La Libération dans le Midi de la France*, Toulouse, 1986.
5. Cited by Marie-France Brive in 'L'Image des femmes à la Libération'. *L'Aurore* – organe du groupe 'Espoir et Courage' de la région R4, subventionné par les M.I.
6. 'France-Libre', organe officiel d'informations édité par l'Etat Major des Corps Francs de la Libération Nationale (F.F.I.) Dordogne-Sud, hebdomadaire, 21 aôut 1944.
7. *L'Evénement du Jeudi*, no.459, 19–25 August 1993. Articles by Véronique Chauvin and N.d.L.C.
8. Pierre Bourget, *Paris année 44: Occupation, Libération, Epuration*, Plon, 1984.
9. Conversation with Brigadier H.E. Hopthrow whose First World War trench diary has been photocopied by the Imperial War Museum.
10. Interview with J.-J. Lafon, June 1994.
11. Incident recounted by both Bourget in *Paris Année 44* and Brossat in *Les Tondues*.
12. Sartre writing in *Combat*, 2 September 1944, cited by Herbert R. Lottman, *The People's Anger: Justice and Revenge in post-Liberation France*, London, Hutchinson, 1986, pp.61–8, and by Brossat, *Les Tondues*, pp. 306–7.

13. Cited by Lottman, *The People's Anger*, p.67.
14. Cited by Brossat, *Les Tondues*, pp.35–6.
15. Marc Doelnitz, *La Fête à Saint-Germain-des-Prés*, Robert Laffont, 1979, pp.143–4.
16. Flora Groult cited by Florence Montreynaud in *Le XXᵉ siècle des Femmes,* Nathan, 1992, p.330.
17. Georgette Elgey writing in *La Fenêtre ouverte,* cited by Montreynaud.
18. Louis Guilloux, *Carnets: 1944–1974,* Gallimard, 1982, pp.410–14.
19. Lottman, *The People's Anger,* p.165.
20. Raymond-Léopold Bruckberger, *One Sky to Share,* New York, P.J. Kenedy and Sons, 1952, pp.23–4.
21. Catherine Gavin, *Liberated France,* London, Jonathan Cape, 1955.
22. See Dominique Veillon, *La Collaboration,* Livre de Poche, 1984, p.319, and Bertram Gordon, *Collaborationism in France during the Second World War,* Ithaca, Cornell University Press, 1980, p.169.
23. Mona Ozouf, *La Fête Révolutionnaire,* Gallimard, 1976. In a review of several recent volumes concerning the Occupation/Liberation period the link between the Revolutionary decapitations during the Terror and the shearing ceremonies has been noted by the reviewer as apt since the violent political struggle that started in 1789 with heads being paraded on pikes ended in 1944 with the shaven heads of collaborators, 'fortunately still attached', being displayed with equal ceremony and similarly gleeful triumph. See Robert Tombs, 'The Dark Years', *Times Literary Supplement,* no.4739, 28 January 1994.
24. *L'Evénement du Jeudi,* no.459, 19–25 August 1993.
25. Colette de Dampierre, interviewed by Ania Francos, in *Il était des femmes dans la Résistance,* Stock, 1978.
26. Fred Kupferman, *Les premiers beaux jours, 1944–46,* Calmann-Lévy, 1985, p.157.
27. Célia Bertin, *Femmes sous l'Occupation,* Stock, 1993, particularly chapter 4, 'Pour une raison ou pour une autre'.
28. Lucie Aubrac cited by Francos, *Il était des femmes dans la Résistance.*
29. In this context see also Siân Reynolds's fine analysis of a celebrated film: 'The Sorrow and the Pity Revisited: Or, Be Careful, One Train Can Hide Another', *French Cultural Studies,* vol.I, no.2, June 1990.
30. Stanley Hoffmann, *Decline and Renewal: France since the Thirties,* New York, Viking Press, 1974, p.50.
31. John F. Sweets, *The Politics of Resistance in France 1940–1944,* De Kalb, Northern Illinois University Press, 1976, pp.216–17.

32. Peter Novick, *The Resistance versus Vichy*, New York, Columbia University Press, 1968, pp.68–78.
33. Ibid. See also Sweets, *The Politics of Resistance in France* and his appraisal of Novick's comments on this matter.
34. Cited by Lottman, *The People's Anger*, p.68.
35. See for example Pierre Bourget, *Paris 1940–1944*, Plon, 1979, p.245.
36. Cf. Michel Foucault, *Surveiller et punir: Naissance de la prison*, trans. by Alan Sheridan as *Discipline and Punish: the Birth of the Prison*, London, Allen Lane, 1977.
37. Brossat, *Les Tondues*, p.226.

Part III

Epuration

12

From Resister to Knight of the Round Table: Jean Paulhan and the Liberation

Martyn Cornick

Our first reactions of violence and ill-humour, immediately after the Liberation, were only human. But it would be evil to persevere
— Jean Paulhan, letter to François Mauriac[1]

During the early summer of 1944, then in his sixtieth year, Jean Paulhan, editor of the *Nouvelle Revue française* (hereafter *NRF*), was forced to go into hiding until the Liberation of Paris in August. Over the months since early 1942 he had been the target of a number of denunciations, including that of Elise Jouhandeau (wife of Marcel Jouhandeau), who denounced Paulhan and his colleague Bernard Groethuysen to the Nazis.[2] Gerhard Heller, an officer in the Gruppe Schrifttum of the Propaganda Abteilung in Paris, himself a friend of Paulhan, stressed the role of French Nazis such as Lucien Rebatet in contributing to the denunciations,[3] whilst Paulhan himself refers to an article denouncing him in a collaborationist newspaper.[4] Heller learned that the German security police were investigating this information, and, just in time, he tipped off Paulhan, who managed to escape over the roof of his house on the corner of the rue des Arènes, near Jussieu metro station, but not before leaving a warning signal in a window. This signal, a red-covered issue of the review *Mesures*, was intended to alert possible callers, such as fellow resisters Jean Blanzat or François Mauriac, to the danger that the house was under surveillance. This dramatic escape began a period of clandestine existence which lasted until the Liberation.

This chapter offers an examination of Paulhan's rôle in the Resistance, and of the way his attitudes were perceived to change

I am grateful to Jacqueline F. Paulhan for her kind permission to consult and quote from material in the Archives Paulhan, referred to as AP.

suddenly at the Liberation. But why Paulhan? He is a central but neglected figure frequently characterized as an *éminence grise*, a personality who is sometimes difficult to fathom.[5] He is remembered principally for two works from this period, *De la paille et du grain*, published in 1948, and, most famous of all, the *Lettre aux directeurs de la Résistance*, published in 1952. His case is important because it is illustrative of the dilemmas facing those intellectuals who had participated in the Resistance, and who feared for French destinies in the post-War period.

During the summer of 1940 a violent press campaign was waged against the *NRF*. Some literary and cultural critics believed that far from constituting France's greatest cultural asset, the review distilled all that was bad and corrupting in the Third Republic. Paulhan learned that the weekly *Candide*, as early as 10 July 1940, had printed an attack on the review, 'French in name only'. 'For twenty years,' complained *Candide*, the *NRF* had been too 'preoccupied with Tibet and Kamchatka, and had never been truly interested in things French'.[6] For Vichy sympathizers the *NRF* was symptomatic of an overall political problem: like the Third Republic, it needed to be replaced.

The Germans, however, thought differently. Already in August 1940, after meetings with Otto Abetz, shortly to be appointed Hitler's ambassador in Paris, Pierre Drieu La Rochelle was encouraged to put his talents to good use by founding a quality review to promote Franco-German cultural collaboration in the new Europe.[7] Reports of this meeting gave rise to the apocryphal saying which averred that there were three centres of power in France: the banks, the French Communist party and the *NRF*. 'Let's start with the *NRF*,' Abetz is supposed to have said. Precisely because it had shone as one of the most brilliant stars in the Third Republic's cultural firmament before and after the First World War, the *NRF* undoubtedly warranted such attention. It is quite likely, however, given his liking for apocrypha, that it was invented by Paulhan after hearing reports from Drieu about the Germans' ambitions.[8] As a result of negotiations between German cultural counsellors, staff at the Propaganda Abteilung, and Gaston Gallimard, it was agreed that the review should be relaunched under the direction of Drieu La Rochelle as an operation separate from the publishing house. The Germans had no doubts at all as to why they wanted to appropriate the review: they wished to promote their own ideas about culture through the medium of French language and culture. As early as October 1940, the Gruppe Schrifttum in Paris was informed of Goebbels's directives: writers and publishers were to be told that French cultural influence was to be replaced by German cultural influence.[9]

Thus the *NRF* under Drieu, 'cleansed' of Jewish and other elements of 'anti-France', was relaunched to spearhead the Germans' cultural offensive. Drieu's *NRF* served to fulfil Goebbels's own wishes as they were relayed to Paris: Heller noted for instance that French writers and publishing houses were to be the major agents of cultural propaganda: '[T]he problem is to stop the cultural and civilizing influence that France has had in most European countries and to replace it by German action. In doing so we must create the conditions for our projects *to be explained by the French with the help of French literature* [my italic].'[10] Through his association with Drieu, Paulhan observed this process, and quickly learned that Drieu's *NRF* would be very different because Jewish contributors (such as Julien Benda, Benjamin Crémieux, Jean Wahl, André Suarès) were to be dropped in favour of 'new Nazis' (including Alfred Fabre-Luce, Jacques Boulenger, Abel Bonnard and Alphonse de Châteaubriant).[11]

As though to compensate for the 'sacrifice' of the *NRF*, Paulhan used his position as Drieu's right-hand man to provide cover for a number of Resistance activities. From the summer of 1940, Paulhan was in touch with a number of figures who would lead the intellectual Resistance, including Jacques Debû-Bridel, Claude Aveline, Jean Cassou, Jean Blanzat and François Mauriac. The first such group were the 'Amis d'Alain-Fournier', founded on 13 July 1940 by Cassou, Aveline and Pierre Abraham.[12] By December 1940, Paulhan had become associated with the group of resisters based at the Musée de l'Homme. As he would later testify, '[Anatole] Levitsky and [Boris] Vildé founded, in the summer of 1940, the first clandestine newspaper: *Résistance*.'[13] Paulhan was responsible for looking after the group's duplicating machine, and this involvement led directly to his arrest on 15 May 1941 and an interrogation at the Santé prison. Through Drieu's intervention, for which he sent a letter of thanks, Paulhan was released. Other members of the Musée de l'Homme group were not so fortunate, however. After the group had been penetrated and arrested, the leading members were imprisoned and tried, and seven defendants were executed on 23 February 1942.

By May 1941, the Front National, one of the most important Resistance organizations with cells in both zones, had been created.[14] Paulhan and Jacques Decour founded its literary offshoot, the Comité du Front National des Écrivains (CNE) and its clandestine publication *Les Lettres françaises*.[15] Paulhan was in contact with other groups, such as Combat: he corresponded at length with Pascal Pia, who, with Malraux and Martin du Gard, attempted to launch *Prométhée*, a sort of *NRF* in the southern zone, but unsurprisingly this project was refused by the Vichy authorities.[16] Claude Bourdet recollects that

Paulhan actively helped his movement by distributing copies of the clandestine newspaper *Combat*; moreover, although Bourdet pays a warm tribute to him, he underlines Paulhan's unsuitability with respect to the editorship of a future 'cultural' Resistance review because it was generally agreed that any such review should be located firmly on the Left.[17]

The fourth issue of *Résistance*, printed at his home, contained a text on the *NRF* written by Paulhan himself, in which he accused Drieu's *NRF* of betraying the interests of French culture.[18] The choices were clear: to collaborate with Drieu's *NRF* to construct a 'new France' under German domination, or to go underground and fight in the intellectual Resistance for another vision embodying the 'true France'. It was perceived that political differences in the Resistance were being set aside for the benefit of patriotic 'reconciliation', around the idea of 'true France' – 'a certain idea of France, or of the *patrie*', as Bernard Leuilliot puts it.[19] On this point there was no dispute between Paulhan and Aragon: resistance writers and poets were the 'custodians of French culture',[20] and it was this that united them in their clandestine activity.

From Drieu's perspective, Paulhan appeared to do his utmost to find authors and texts, all the while wishing to see the review disappear for good. As the months went by, Drieu began to tire of the difficulties besetting the compilation of each issue. In March 1942, Paulhan was made responsible for renegotiating terms in view of Drieu's wish to step down: 'Basically Paulhan is as much a Communist as he is a Gaullist,'[21] complained Drieu. In April he remained frustrated: 'Paulhan has promised me a committee [of advisers], but of course has ensured that nothing happens. The Germans are afraid that the firm will close. [...] The comical thing is that [Paulhan] is a Communist sympathizer and yet I want him to work with me.' Drieu finally announced on 20 March 1943 that he was to abandon the *NRF*, and although there was a plan to appoint Jacques Lemarchand to edit an 'apolitical' review, the last issue appeared in June 1943.[22] Drieu seized his chance: 'Leapt at the first opportunity Paulhan gave me (a poor article by him) to break the new arrangement whereby he edits the review under my name.'[23] For Paulhan the end of this ignominious episode in the history of the *NRF* came as a great relief. As for the CNE, a text in *Les Lettres françaises* rejoiced at the 'agony of the *NRF*', and again stressed that French culture would not submit to servitude.[24] For the rest of the Occupation, until he went into hiding, Paulhan returned to his writing, while continuing his clandestine activities for Combat, the CNE and Les Editions de Minuit.

Jean Paulhan and the Liberation: a Dissenting Voice

Paulhan's attitude at the Liberation would help to determine his and others' stance for much of the next decade. This stance originated in his dissidence from the CNE, and is explained by his disenchantment with the Liberation, brought about primarily by the literary purges.

The part he had played in the Resistance, in particular co-founding the CNE and *Les Lettres françaises,* brought Paulhan instant celebrity at the Liberation. He received offers of editorships and reviews, but almost immediately, Paulhan dissented from what had become the new prevailing orthodoxy. If one looks more closely, far from his actions representing a sudden volte-face which 'betrayed' his Resistance colleagues, Paulhan carefully premeditated his stance at the Liberation. Jacques Debû-Bridel, a key figure in the CNR, recalls that before August 1944 Paulhan already had grave reservations about the post-Occupation period, with its reprisals and purges.[25] His opponents' feigned surprise, their reproaches that he suddenly displayed inconsistency, treachery or ambiguity, are inimical, argues Debû-Bridel: Paulhan never concealed the way he thought, and could not tolerate the hypocrisy of sanctions against writers, when in reality these sanctions only served narrow partisan causes, not broader patriotic ones. This view is prefigured in a letter to Marcel Jouhandeau, who had accompanied a number of other collaborationist artists and writers on a Nazi propaganda visit to Weimar in October 1941; he had published his impressions in Drieu's *NRF.* For this Jouhandeau became one of the first victims of the CNE's blacklists. But Paulhan had written to reassure his friend that he would strive his utmost for what he called 'reconciliation':

> I think there are hatreds brewing amongst the French which are going to be more serious and terrifying than those we have already witnessed: it is going to be more difficult than ever to reconcile them. (But *we* are going to favour the reconciliation of the French, aren't we; and whether this is in opposition to the English or the Germans, it matters little...)[26]

The very day Leclerc's troops entered Paris (25 August 1944), Paulhan expressed his concern that Paul Eluard and other Communist writers would succeed in attracting numerous prestigious names to the CNE in order to dominate it by default: the Communists would benefit from a respectable cover, all the while undermining any effectual opposition.[27] Indeed, on 4 September, five days *before* the appearance of the first Liberation issue of *Les Lettres françaises,* a meeting of the CNE passed a motion to blacklist any members of the writers' group

Collaboration, any writers who had accepted invitations to travel to Germany (this included Jouhandeau, of course), and writers who had received payment from the enemy. Paulhan registered his disapproval by asking Maurice Noël, literary director of *Le Figaro*, to publish his protest which 'attempted to defend the writer's right to err [*le droit à l'erreur*]'.[28] This marks the beginning of Paulhan's campaign for the intellectual's 'right to err'. As he saw it, members of the CNE had taken it upon themselves to act both as 'judges' and 'informers' ('ni juges, ni mouchards' are Paulhan's terms in several letters at his time),[29] when they had no legal right to act in such a quasi-judicial manner. Furthermore their motion flew in the face of the fifth article of the CNE charter, which declared that its members should 'defend freedom of thought and expression by all possible means'. In order to distance himself Paulhan let it be known that he would take no further part in meetings of the CNE, stressing that the future well-being of France lay in the willingness (if not the duty) of the Resistance to continue to reconcile the nation by bringing back into the fold those who had strayed:

> You should *also* consider that you have to recreate unity, national unity, in which it will be necessary to admit everyone who shows goodwill (even if they happened to stray from the path). Don't allow yourself to be guided too much by the pride of having been right. You must consider what France will be tomorrow. If, like you, I am in favour of the purge [*l'épuration*], this is because it must quickly and unswervingly free us from any further worries about purges.[30]

Already in October 1944 Paulhan told several correspondents how disappointed he was with the press.[31] He claimed that it spoke with one voice; there was no genuine pluralism despite the explosion of titles. Claude Morgan, one of Paulhan's main adversaries, admitted in his memoirs that during the Occupation the Resistance press, much of which had been set up with Communist help, had facilitated the expression of diverse opinions, but after the Liberation they all became Communist papers.[32] For Paulhan the pendulum had swung too far towards uniformity, and he said as much in a text published in January 1945. The underlying problem was the 'mystery of the Liberation', as he put it, 'the rather vague sense of disillusion it has left behind. In the end, it has left a bitter taste in the mouth, a sense of disorientation.'[33] In another text (this time in *Les Lettres françaises*) he referred explicitly to his belief that 'the Liberation has resulted in the most serious outbreak of mental depression to be seen in France over the last century.' His disenchantment was tempered by a mock nostalgia for the Occupation:

> The Occupation had its pleasures too. Your duty was clear. You knew at every moment what you had to do, to think, to say. [...] You even had peace and quiet, and the added bonus of being free to behave badly. False identity cards, false declarations, lies, even assassination – so long as you did them for the right side – were all worthy of merit. That's what we have lost.[34]

His frustrations were compounded when in November 1944 the Purge Commission for Publishing (the Commission d'Epuration de l'Edition) called for the liquidation of the *NRF*: Paulhan was appointed 'special adviser' to oversee this.[35] Privately, Paulhan felt embittered by what amounted to a second sacrifice of the review to save the publishing house:

> [T]he company [i.e., the Gallimard publishing house] has been saved for the second time by throwing the review overboard. None of this is very pleasant, and the official notification is couched in venomous terms. (Incidentally, I was offered the chance to restart the *NRF* under another name, with the successor to Denoël!)[36]

Neither was this the end of the matter: when the Purge Commission finally investigated Gallimard in November 1945, the whole process began again to provide reasons why the publishing house had remained open during the Occupation. In a prepared deposition to the hearing, emphasis was laid on the fact that 'whatever could be done, openly or otherwise, to bolster the resistance of French culture to German propaganda, was done.' Gallimard's actions were defended on the grounds that had Drieu's appointment been objected to, the Germans would have appropriated the whole operation anyway – review and publishing house – to spearhead their cultural propaganda in Europe.[37]

When the Cour de Justice finally heard the case on 26 October 1946 the magistrates indeed decided that the suppression of the *NRF* was an adequate sanction against Gallimard.[38] But the loss of the *NRF* was keenly felt by Paulhan and Gallimard, for whom the ex-editor of the *NRF* was 'the very soul of the firm'.[39] The review's disappearance from the cultural scene certainly left a vacuum which was only partially filled by other ventures such as *L'Arche*, Sartre's *Les Temps modernes* (launched in October 1945), Paulhan's *Cahiers de la Pléiade* (April 1946), or *La Table ronde* (January 1948): but arguably this was as much to do with the disappearance of the Third Republic in July 1940 – the so-called 'République des Professeurs' – as it was the fault of the purges.

Paulhan's attitudes hardened in March 1946 when the Purge Commission decided to apply another series of sanctions. 'Certain writers are now subject to a "suspension" measure which is intended to ban the publication of their work for one or two years, depending on the case.'[40] Having been asked the question 'Do you approve or disapprove of this form of sanction, i.e., the ban on publication?', Paulhan sent a letter in reply which unleashed a long-running polemical exchange. He argued that the purge was lasting too long, and that one group of writers, with no legal status, were continuing to act as judges over other writers.

In November 1946, Paulhan's dissent came to a head. Having campaigned to have Pierre Benoit's name removed from the blacklist, he promised Jouhandeau that he would resign if, on his behalf, he was not successful. Although Benoit was struck off the list, the text announcing as much in *Les Lettres françaises* carried a reiteration of the CNE's intention to impose itself as a quasi-judicial authority with powers to impose sanctions even if an author had paid a judicial price for collaboration: in short, the CNE felt itself empowered to legislate on behalf of 'human conscience':

> Let us use this opportunity to recall that the entirely moral sanctions taken by the CNE after the Liberation are totally independent of any judicial decisions which may affect collaborationist writers. [...] The execution of Brasillach or of Paul Chack, or the suicide of Drieu La Rochelle do not mean that their names will be removed from the blacklist, and the CNE charter does not allow members of this association to publish a newspaper, book or review alongside those who may have paid a price in the eyes of the law, but certainly not in the view of human conscience.[41]

This text was the trigger for Paulhan's resignation. He explained himself to Aragon, one of the key players in the CNE: 'I said at the CNE from the very beginning that I have never wanted to be a judge or an auxiliary policeman. I feel this all the more if you are going to pronounce eternal sanctions in the name of "human conscience". So it is better that I resign from the CNE.'[42] After he had been joined by Georges Duhamel, Jean Schlumberger, Gabriel Marcel and others, the CNE went on the defensive. Vercors tried to alert Paulhan to the dangers his resignation would bring, and published an open letter to all the writers who had resigned.[43] It was left to Jean Cassou, president of the CNE, to reply directly to Paulhan's charges:

This is my response to Jean Paulhan: first, anyone can still write whatever they feel the irrepressible need to write. [...] The CNE has nothing to say on this, neither does it want to. It holds no sway over the literary world. It is content to act as a memory. [...] The CNE is a group of writers who, faithful to the principles of their clandestine activity, refuse contact with collaborationist writers, and in the more free and easy-going post-War climate it keeps up the memory of a time when every honest French writer was led to consider that his very function as a writer obliged him to respect his duty towards France. [...] Everyone must be persuaded that essentially this is what the CNE is, that it has no political meaning or intent, that it is not disposed to exercise any official authority, and finally that it must continue, today as yesterday, to reunite French people, whatever their origin or leanings.[44]

By resigning Paulhan dissociated himself from his former colleagues so that he could pursue what had become a crusade: the way was clear for a series of open letters to the CNE and other texts which would form *De la paille et du grain*.[45]

Paulhan's trajectory from authentic resister to scourge of the *épuration* was not, as he himself insisted, a betrayal of the Resistance:[46] it is more readily understood as a protest against those who, in Paulhan's view, had wasted the opportunities presented by the Liberation. In one sense this controversy may be considered with those identified by Henry Rousso in the context of the 'Franco-French cold war'.[47] Moreover, the corollary of Rousso's 'Vichy syndrome' is a 'Resistance syndrome', whereby the Resistance was mythologized after the Liberation into a *bloc*. As a consequence the diversity of the Resistance, as it had been experienced between July 1940 and August 1944, was lost. On the broader level of culture Paulhan's crusade may be viewed in the context of what Herman Lebovics has called 'wars over French cultural identity,'[48] especially considering the loss of the *NRF*. To whom would fall the custodianship of French literary and intellectual culture after 1944, in view of the end of the Third Republic in July 1940, and after the purges of French authors, reviews and publishing houses from 1944? During the Occupation, Paulhan – only half in jest – had anticipated how fortunes would change after 1944:

Paulhan [...] would prefer to see the *NRF* muddle along as best it can, and would only take over again after the German defeat, 'unless', he added, smiling, 'it is then the turn of the Communists, and we have to give way to Aragon... but our time will come again'.[49]

In the longer term Paulhan's stance may be viewed in the context of the Cold War: from 1947 onwards, real fears were frequently expressed about the proximity of a new conflict, whether European or global. In the case of another invasion of Western Europe, would not the occupying forces be Soviet, would not the 'collaborators' be drawn from the ranks of French Communists, already plotting fifth column activities? And who would form the Resistance? One major consideration must be whether Paulhan's changed attitude should be seen as a political shift towards the Right. There are parallels here with the conception of the 1930s *NRF*: whilst representing a pillar of the liberal, specifically radical-republican, cultural establishment, Paulhan was always prepared to take decisions which distinguished it from encroaching orthodoxies. Thus he appears to have favoured the Left when the Right held power, and the Right when the Left held sway.[50] If, as he told Aragon, he felt he could vote Communist in April 1945, as time went on Paulhan was increasingly swayed by Gaullism: he was delighted that the General approved of his later polemic, *Lettre aux directeurs de la Résistance*.[51] His crusade caused him to be seen by the Left as a leading 'knight of the Round Table' [chevalier de *La Table Ronde*], particularly when his name appeared among those featured in the first issue of the review of that name.[52] More importantly, however, his opposition to the CNE undoubtedly gave succour to the reemergent intellectual Right. Indeed Paulhan's position calls into question the rather too general view that 'for a decade at least, the left-wing intellectual occupied *alone* the ideological terrain [my italic]'.[53] Pierre Boutang, for instance, one of a new generation of Maurrassians and keepers of the Pétainist flame, militated in a clutch of right-wing periodicals and reviews at this time, and found encouragement in Paulhan's stance. *Paroles françaises*, one of these new periodicals, commented on Cassou's reply to Paulhan in terms which provide a chilling reminder of the streams of vilification characteristic of the right-wing press during the 1930s:

This Cassou, [...] guardian of the arbitrary 'blacklist', which, in the name of freedom deliberately prevents non-conformist writers, selected for the most suspect motives, from expressing their thoughts, two and a half years after the so-called triumph of the Liberation, this Cassou, who does not have a drop of genuine French blood in his veins, has tried, in a storm of protest and against all reason, to justify himself to his former associates, who, in a moment of conscience, have just inflicted their premeditated resignation on him. [...]
M Jean Paulhan, one of the latest defectors from the CNE, has finally noticed that their methods are fascist... [...] This Cassou has made the CNE

the instrument of a policy, of a strategy in which France is bound to lose, and to sacrifice on the altars of fear and treachery the best of itself and its people. Despite his treacherous denials, he admires the genial little father of all mankind [i.e., Stalin], and his government of the slaughterhouse and cultural intolerance.[54]

Thus were the battle-lines drawn: despite the *mystique* of the Liberation, and because of the factions which emerged as a result of the purges, the decade 1944-1954 would continue to be disturbed by the noisy battles of the Franco-French cultural wars.

Notes

Unless stated otherwise, the place of publication is Paris.

1. Jean Paulhan (JP) to Mauriac (letter dated 4 October 1944), in *Choix de lettres*, vol.2, *Traité des jours sombres*, Gallimard, 1992, p.379 (hereafter referred to as *Choix*).
2. Maria Van Rhysselberghe's unpublished journal relates: '[Paulhan] confided to me that he had left Paris in rather a hurry. He has been warned secretly, by a German friend of the *NRF* [Heller], that Jouhandeau's wife had gone to the Gestapo to denounce him and Groet[huysen] as convinced Communists, asserting moreover that the *NRF* was nothing but a nest of Communists! And she did so out of revenge because Paulhan had had the courage to say to Jouhandeau what he thought of his journey to Germany and the notes he had published in the review'; C. Martin, *La NRF de 1940 à 1943*, Lyon, Centre d'Études gidiennes, 1975, p. XLIII. For Jouhandeau's impressions, see *NRF*, December 1941, pp.649–51.
3. Gerhard Heller, *Un Allemand à Paris, 1940–1944*, Seuil, 1981, p.105.
4. 'I was told that it was Pierre Pascal who had publicly denounced me in his article'; unpublished interview with Dominique Aury (AP). See 'Certaine façon d'écrire au «goût américain»...', *L'Appel*, 5 November 1942.
5. Among many examples that could be given to illustrate this point, see Alexandre Astruc, writing in 1946: 'His liking for mystery and mystification has made him into a sort of *éminence grise*, working in the shadows through intermediaries...', *Combat*, 20–21 January 1946; cf. Maurice Toesca, 'Jean Paulhan, l'homme qui fait les écrivains', *Gavroche*, 21 February 1946.
6. Crémieux to JP (17 July 1940), referring to an article in *Candide*,

10 July 1940 (AP).

7. Pierre Drieu La Rochelle, *Fragment de mémoires*, Gallimard, 1982, pp.39–40, 42.

8. Its inspiration was Paul Bourget, who, on the eve of war in 1914, had declared: 'There are three sources of power in Europe: the French Academy, the Vatican and the German High Command'; see P. Hebey, *La Nouvelle Revue Française des années sombres, 1940–1941*, Gallimard, 1992, pp.14, 123.

9. Cf. G. Loiseaux, *La littérature de la défaite et de la collaboration*, Publications de la Sorbonne, 1984, p. 89.

10. Notes by Heller quoted in P. Fouché, *L'Edition française sous l'Occupation*, 2 vols, BLFC, 1987, vol.1, p.158.

11. JP to Pourrat [November 1940] (AP), and to Ponge (20 November 1940), *Choix*, p.201.

12. Hebey, *La Nouvelle Revue Française des années sombres*, p.214.

13. See the draft of 'Une semaine au secret', published at the Liberation in *Le Figaro* (9 September 1944), in C. Paulhan (ed.), *La vie est pleine de choses redoutables*, Seghers, 1989, p. 264. Paulhan adds: 'It was printed at my house. But Levitsky was arrested. With Jean Cassou we printed one more issue which someone took care to send to the Gestapo. This was an attempt to demonstrate Levitsky's innocence – because the newspaper continued to appear. [...] On the advice of Jean Cassou I destroyed the printing machine. It was an electric Roneo. The pieces were still so heavy that Jean Blanzat had to help me. We threw them into the Seine.'

14. The Front National was important because it welcomed Resisters of all political colours, despite being Communist in inspiration; see Henri Michel, *Les courants de pensée de la Résistance*, PUF, 1962, pp.6–13.

15. The first issue of *Les Lettres françaises* appeared in September 1942, after the arrest and execution of Jacques Decour on 30 May 1942.

16. 'I have just spent a week in prison (suspected of anglophile propaganda) at the Santé. It was nothing much, except for the worry and fatigue it caused Germaine [Paulhan]. Several insistent interrogations. Vichy has refused Pia's review [*Prométhée*]. They are going to try something different'; JP to Hellens (14 June 1941) (AP).

17. Claude Bourdet, *L'aventure incertaine*, Stock, 1975, p.311.

18. *Résistance*, no.4, March 1941.

19. L. Aragon, J. Paulhan, E. Triolet, *«Le Temps traversé»*, *Correspondance 1920–1964*, Gallimard, 1994, p.9.

20. Aragon to Fouchet (31 May 1941), quoted by Bernard Leuilliot in *«Le Temps traversé»*, p. 16.

21. Pierre Drieu La Rochelle, *Journal 1939–1945*, Gallimard, 1992, p. 290 (entries for 2 and 5 March 1942).
22. Ibid., p. 292 (5 April 1942), and p. 339 (20 March 1943). See also JP to Pourrat (27 May 1943): 'Lemarchand is to be editor of the *NRF*. The Germans are still insisting on using Drieu's name but I believe that L. will have a free hand: I've advised him to substitute (bad) politics with (good) German literature, ancient or modern. [...] Drieu will no longer submit his political essays'; *Choix*, p.306.
23. Drieu, *Journal*, p.347 (12 July 1943). For Drieu's public account of his attempts to run the *NRF*, see 'Bilan', *NRF*, January 1943, pp.103–11.
24. See *Les Lettres françaises*, July 1943, pp.3–4.
25. 'Before the Liberation, at the height of the underground struggle, he had already conceived most of the reservations he would develop later'; Jacques Debû-Bridel, 'Jean Paulhan, citoyen', in Jean Paulhan, *Œuvres complètes*, vol.5, Cercle du livre précieux, 1970, p.490 (hereafter referred to as *OC*).
26. JP to Jouhandeau (letter dated as 1941), in *Choix*, p.222.
27. JP to Lescure (25 August 1944), in *Choix*, p.371. Also to Debû-Bridel, ibid., p.373.
28. *Le Figaro*, 9 September 1944. See letter to Jouhandeau, *Choix*, p.374.
29. For example, see JP to Debû-Bridel (9 September 1944): 'That the first public act of the CNE should be to go to the law and demand the arrest of other writers seems to me to be absolutely appalling. I think I am more faithful than you to our principle agreed when we were still underground: neither judges nor informers'; *Choix*, p.374. See also letters to Eluard and Mauriac, pp.378–9.
30. JP to Debû-Bridel (3 October 1944), in *Choix*, p.378.
31. JP to Guérin, Mauriac and Bousquet (21, 22 October 1944; 4 November 1944), in *Choix*, pp.380, 381 and 387.
32. Claude Morgan, *Les Don Quixote et les autres*, Guy Roblot, 1979, pp.181–2.
33. 'Les morts', *Bulletin de la Fédération du théâtre*, no.1, January 1945, in *OC*, vol.5, p.300.
34. 'Quelques raisons de nous réjouir', in *Les Lettres françaises*, 12 May 1945 (*OC*, vol.5, pp.303–4).
35. *Les Lettres françaises*, 25 November 1944.
36. JP to Schlumberger [November 1944] (AP).
37. From *Note sur l'activité de la NRF pendant l'occupation* (AP).
38. For details see Fouché, *L'Edition française*, vol.2, pp.228–9.

39. Gallimard displayed the depth of his feelings in a letter containing a paean to Paulhan, and indicating that his sole ambition was to see the *NRF* reappear (AP).

40. *Le Figaro littéraire*, 30 March 1946.

41. *Les Lettres françaises*, 22 November 1946.

42. «*Le Temps traversé*», pp.200–1.

43. Vercors to JP (15 December 1946) (AP), and 'Lettre ouverte à MM. Georges Duhamel [...] et autres démissionnaires du CNE', *Les Lettres françaises*, 27 December 1946.

44. J. Cassou, 'Ce qu'est le CNE', *Les Lettres françaises*, 10 January 1947.

45. This work is based on eight different segments published variously as facsimile tracts or articles. For details see *De la paille et du grain*, Gallimard, 1948, and *OC*, vol.5, pp.313–406.

46. See his interview with Robert Mallet (1952), *OC*, vol.4, p.490.

47. Henry Rousso, *Le syndrome de Vichy*, Seuil, 1987, especially pp.38–71.

48. Herman Lebovics, *True France. The Wars over Cultural Identity*, Ithaca, Cornell University Press, 1992.

49. Quoted in Martin, *La NRF de 1940 à 1943*, p. XLIII (entry dated 15 May 1942).

50. 'Our position in the extreme-centre (as Gide used to say) makes us automatically seem too right-wing, when the Left dominates, like now, but too left-wing, when the Right is in power'; JP to Arland [1956], in *NRF* May 1969, p.1032.

51. 'I've written a little pamphlet on the injustice of the judicial system (since the Liberation). I must admit that only one man has talked to me about it with loyalty and kindness (but also critically): and that's General de Gaulle'; JP to Pourrat (4 January 1952) (AP).

52. P. Hervé, 'Les chevaliers de *La Table Ronde*', *Action*, 4 February 1948.

53. P. Ory and J.-F. Sirinelli, *Les Intellectuels en France de l'Affaire Dreyfus à nos jours*, A. Colin, 1986, p.146.

54. 'Ce qu'est le CNE', *Paroles françaises*, 17 January 1947.

– 13 –

France's Little Nuremberg: the Trial of Otto Abetz

Nicholas Atkin

On 12 July 1949 Otto Abetz, Hitler's wartime 'ambassador' to France and symbol of Nazi oppression during the Occupation, appeared at the Palais de Justice in Paris charged with war crimes. *L'Aurore* spoke for much of the French press when it predicted on 11 July that this would be the most dramatic trial of the Liberation era. The promise of excitement ensured that the tiny courtroom was packed for the ten-day hearing, and the intensity of the media's gaze attracted celebrities to the tribunal. Towards the close of events Edward G. Robinson, the American actor noted for his gangster roles, was spotted in the audience. Unable to understand French, he left after half-an-hour complaining of the intense heat.[1]

It is doubtful whether Hollywood could ever have made a good film of the Abetz trial. Certainly the setting was cinematic enough. Presiding over the court was the judge resplendent in his red robes; to his side were twelve jurors, all former members of the Resistance, bearing their wartime medals; and, in the centre of the *salle*, Abetz himself, watched from the gallery by his wife Suzanne, the former secretary of Jean Luchaire, her face overshadowed by a wide-brimmed straw hat.[2] Yet, as with so many trials of the *épuration*, the events themselves lacked passion. The proceedings were muddled; no great revelations were unearthed; and there were no unforeseen incidents. The lugubrious nature of the hearing was compounded by the intense summer sun and the court's magnesium lights. No one dared ventilate the room as the window-frames were riddled with bullets, a legacy

The author is indebted to the Centre de Documentation Juive Contemporaine (CDJC), Paris, for permission to consult and cite material held in its archives. He is particularly grateful to the archivist, M Vidar Jacobsen, for advice on the Centre's holdings on Abetz.

of the liberation of Paris. The stuffy atmosphere leant the proceedings a surreal flavour. Fending off the sun, foreign court reporters took to wearing paper hats as though they were following the Tour de France.[3]

Not surprisingly, then, the Abetz trial has largely been forgotten. Its proceedings have never been published in their entirety.[4] These hardly make for gripping reading and add little to our understanding of Franco-German collaboration. Nevertheless, the events of July 1949 are worth rediscovering for the light they shed on Abetz himself. He remains one of the more enigmatic figures of the war years. Although a faithful and obedient Nazi, he always maintained that he had acted in the best interests of France by playing a double game with his masters.[5] At his trial, the failure of the prosecution to destroy this defence helped consolidate his reputation as a Francophile and began the process of his rehabilitation.[6]

On 25 October 1945 two officers of the Sûreté Militaire made their way to an address in Baden where the former German ambassador to France had been in hiding under a false name for the past three months. On his arrest, Abetz was transported to Strasbourg and on 16 November arrived at the Gare de l'Est in Paris. From there he was escorted to the Cherche-Midi prison, his home until July 1949.[7]

His lengthy incarceration begs the question why the trial was delayed for so long. It might be speculated that this was due to the wish of the French authorities to avoid embarrassment. Certainly by 1949 tempers had cooled, and the hearing was conducted in a calmer atmosphere than some of those tribunals held immediately after the war. Yet such considerations do not appear to have concerned the Deuxième Tribunal Militaire de Paris which compiled the prosecution case against Abetz. Rather this body had to surmount a series of obstacles which held up proceedings.

Firstly, it should be noted that Abetz was frequently called away to give evidence at other trials of the *après-guerre*.[8] Secondly, and more importantly, his captors had to agree on where he should be tried. One option was to offer him up to the International Military Tribunal (IMT) at Nuremberg. Later on 21 July 1949 both *Le Monde* and *Le Figaro* criticized the way in which the prosecution was proceeding and argued that the issues of law raised would have been better handled by an international body. It was not up to a French court, they declared, to decide where the rights of an occupying power began and ended. Unfortunately, the present author has been unable to ascertain whether the name of Abetz ever figured on the lists submitted by the Allies when preparing for the Nuremberg trials. It seems doubtful. The

British, Americans and Russians had bigger fish to fry. It also appears improbable that Abetz was nominated by France. Given his role during the Occupation, it was always more likely that the French would wish to try him for themselves; and because he was such an important catch, it was intended that he should be judged in Paris rather than in Germany at one of the French zonal trials which followed Nuremberg.[9] Maybe there was an element of revenge in this determination. It was not forgotten that Abetz's appointment as ambassador in 1940 had, in part, been a snub to the French for his expulsion from Paris in August 1939 on spying charges. Now he would again return to the capital not in triumph but in chains.

Thus empowered to try Abetz, the Deuxième Tribunal had to resolve a third conundrum: under which law should he be charged? At one stage it seemed likely that he would appear in the High Court of Justice. This had been established by an ordinance of 18 November 1944 with the intention of trying all members of 'the governments or pseudo-governments which had their seat on metropolitan territory' between June 1940 and August 1944.[10] The possibility of punishing Abetz in such a way was floated in November 1946 as a result of the Luchaire trial. Henri Noguères, President of the High Court, was so dismayed at the means by which Abetz had betrayed the interests of France that he requested his dossier from the Deuxième Tribunal, possibly with a view to compiling a prosecution case.[11] Yet how could a German citizen and diplomat, who had never been a part of the Pétain régime, be judged in a court specifically designed for French nationals accused of betraying the interests of their country? To have brought Abetz to justice in this manner would have played into the hands of his defence.

Ultimately common sense prevailed and the case remained in the jurisdiction of the Deuxième Tribunal. The result was that charges were framed under the terms of the military code as revised by the ordinance of 28 August 1944. According to the *Acte d'accusation*, this ordinance was ideally suited as it had prefigured the definition of 'war crimes' later established at Nuremberg.[12] Even so, in their many interviews with Abetz, the military authorities were not certain that they had put together a water-tight prosecution. At hand they had numerous documents from the German Foreign Ministry, yet these could be interpreted in various ways and did little to undermine Abetz's claims that he had been playing a double game with Berlin.[13] Indeed, they underscored his lack of real authority. Always suspicious of the ambassador's avowed Francophilia, Hitler had been reluctant to entrust him with extensive powers. Thus it was always going to be difficult to link Abetz with his alleged crimes. Not until spring 1949 did the prosecution feel ready to proceed, only then to discover that the most suitable courtrooms were already reserved. The press had expected the trial to be heard in the *grande salle* of the *cour d'assises*. In the event, it was conducted in a tiny little room in the Palais de Justice adding weight to the claims of those who alleged that the authorities were attempting to sideline the affair. Whatever the truth, the location was seen as a poor reflection on French justice and augured badly for the trial itself.

The defendant led into the dock on 12 July 1949 presented a different figure to the one which he had cut during the Occupation. Although the French press commonly referred to him as the 'arrogant Otto', prison had aged him. His hair was now white, his face was lined and it was rumoured that he had a heart condition and might not survive the intense heat.[14] His mind, however, remained sharp and he stayed calm throughout the proceedings. He rarely required an interpreter and preferred to speak French when questioned. Whereas English and American newspapers were impressed by his linguistic abilities, the Paris press was less charitable. According to *Le Figaro* of 14 July, Abetz spoke the language of Voltaire as though he was having to translate everything. It was ironic that French journalists expected him to speak their mother tongue like a native, and a measure of how successful he had already been in convincing people that he was a true Francophile.

Once ensconced in the courtroom, Abetz sat patiently as two clerks read out in monotonous tones the 178 pages of the *Acte d'accusation*. This began by stating his importance in the German chain of command in France. It then went on to outline the brief highlights of his pre-War career – his job as an art teacher in Baden, his involvement in French and German youth movements, his position in the Dienststelle Ribbentrop and his links with the Comité France-Allemagne – before chronicling in more detail his actions during the Occupation. In the course of this recital, the *Acte d'accusation* betrayed its confused origins by admitting that Abetz could not be tried with pursuing a policy of collaboration as this charge could only be levelled at a French citizen.[15] Instead he stood trial as a war criminal on some sixty-four counts.

These charges fell into six broad categories pertaining to the role of Abetz in the following: the sequestration of French press and radio interests; the transfer of French stock in the Yugoslav Bor copper mines to German hands; the expulsion of Jews to Eastern Europe and the seizure of Jewish property; the deportation of French workers to Germany; the execution of hostages in France; and the murder of

Georges Mandel, the former minster of the Third Republic. This final charge carried with it the death penalty and was regarded as the most serious of all the accusations. Although it was not overlooked that Mandel was himself Jewish and a symbol of Jewish suffering during the war, it is striking that the prosecution regarded the callous murder of a former government minister as being of more significance than the extermination of thousands of Jewish lives. Yet this was not surprising. In the wake of the Occupation, few were prepared to admit or come to terms with Vichy's complicity in the Holocaust.

The prosecution's case attracted lively criticism in the press. More enlightened opinion argued that Abetz should have been tried at Nuremberg. How could a French court, it was asked, charge a German national with helping the German cause? Other newspapers noted that the *Acte d'accusation* had little to say about his role in France during the 1930s. Given that in 1946 Abetz had taken his captors to the Black Forest where he had unearthed the *livre d'or* of the German embassy,[16] this omission was viewed with suspicion. Was the government trying to shield the identities of leading French politicians who had been entertained by Abetz before the war? Was it attempting to cover up the circumstances surrounding his expulsion in 1939? Such possibilities offered ample scope to the satire of *Le Canard Enchaîné*. In its edition of 14 July, it doubted whether any Frenchman would have stepped inside the embassy on the rue de Lille and wondered whether the ambassador had ever existed. The whole affair was due to the phenomenon of 'Ottosuggestion', it concluded. Far less humorous was the tone of *l'Humanité* which held a particular grudge against the former diplomat. On 12 July it recalled how, in the aftermath of his expulsion in 1939, the journalists Lucien Sampaix and Gabriel Péri had been charged with libel for their part in highlighting the activities of Abetz. At the same time, it hoped that the trial would expose the activities of such fifth columnists as the trusts and Reynaud's mistress, the Comtesse de Portes. Thus *l'Humanité* was alarmed that the interrogation of Abetz on the 1930s only lasted five minutes. On 13 July the newspaper concluded that this was not the real trial of collaboration; it was instead the rehabilitation of Vichy.

Why was so little attention paid to the 1930s? There may be some truth in the claims of *l'Humanité*. The expulsion of Abetz had taken place in a feverish atmosphere of unproven allegations and it can be reasonably assumed that many leading politicians of that time had no desire for the trial to be investigating old ground. Yet it is also necessary to bear in mind other possibilities. Certainly the Deuxième Tribunal had looked into the pre-War activities of Abetz. On 21 November 1945 he had been interrogated on these matters.[17] This interview underscored the extent to which he had established himself in Parisian society. Yet at his trial the prosecution never questioned Abetz closely on the way in which he had exploited his vast network of contacts. Had it done so, it would have been in a stronger position to have revealed his true beliefs. Although Abetz undoubtedly possessed an affection for France, he was convinced of the superiority of German culture and was drawn to National Socialism precisely because this ideology offered an opportunity to assert Teutonic dominance over Western Europe. Through his pre-War cultural connections, he had been attempting to make the French recognize the merits of the Nazi system.[18] He had performed this task with considerable finesse, yet once France had been defeated militarily he had not hesitated to stoop to more ruthless means. These had been outlined in the so-called 'Salzburg memorandum' of July 1940. Here Abetz detailed his plans for the takeover of French publishing houses, the creation of a *parti unique*, the establishment of regionalist organizations and the founding of a German institute at Paris.[19] Although this document was quoted at length in the *Acte d'accusation*, the prosecution never appeared certain of its real significance. Accordingly, from the opening day of the hearing, Abetz had little reason to fear that the trial would uncover his real motives.

Given his long captivity, the former ambassador had enjoyed ample time to prepare a defence.[20] Not surprisingly, this emphasized his love of France and his lukewarm support for fascism. Under cross-examination on the opening day of the trial, he pointed out that he had put off joining the Nazi party until 1937; he only enroled then as he recognized that this was the most practical means of achieving his dream of Franco-German reconciliation.[21] Bearing in mind his Francophilia, he had been surprised at his appointment as ambassador to Paris. He had been deeply unsettled by this posting as he always knew that he would be unable to fulfil the wishes of his masters. Thus anything he had said or done during the Occupation could not be taken at face value. 'My true policy,' he claimed, 'was diametrically opposed to what I wrote in my reports.'[22] Nimbly, he skipped over the way in which he had held court on the rue de Lille by pursuing a ruthless policy of 'divide-and-rule' among the collaborators who gathered there. Instead, he focussed on how he had attempted to help France by calling for the liberation of French prisoners of war, a reduction in occupation costs and a plebiscite on the fate of Alsace-Lorraine. Eventually, he concluded, his actions brought about his disgrace and temporary recall to Germany. There he was chastised for not having arrested Giraud and for not having assisted Sauckel in his plans for the deportation of workers.

The force of this testimony was bolstered by the sharp mind of Abetz's lawyer, René Floriot. Having previously represented Luchaire, Floriot was well acquainted with the background to the case and was not afraid to broach sensitive issues. He soon developed a two-pronged defence. Firstly, he echoed the Francophile claims of his client. Never a committed Nazi and certainly no anti-Semite, Abetz, he argued, had been playing a double game with Berlin in order to save France from becoming an SS state. This line of argument was employed to counter such charges as the sequestering of Jewish property and the deportations of workers and Jews. These measures, it was claimed, would have been far worse had it not been for the interventions of Abetz. Secondly, the advocate played on the ambivalent diplomatic status of the defendant. This line of reasoning was used to fend off those charges relating to the pillage of French assets and the appropriation of information agencies. According to Floriot, such actions were within the rights of an occupying power; in his position as ambassador, Abetz could not be held directly responsible for them.

The elaborate nature of these arguments proved effective against the lugubrious cross-examining of the prosecution advocate, Maître Flicoteaux. Young and inexperienced, he drew on the diplomatic evidence at his disposal and often became entangled in minutiae. So too did the presiding judge Pihier.[23] Journalists thus looked to the witnesses to break the monotony of the proceedings, yet they did little to enliven events. Among the more notorious defence witnesses were the prominent SS men, Oberg and Knochen. Although their presence created a frisson of excitement in the courtroom, these hard-boiled Nazis merely attested to Abetz's obstructiveness and love of France. Far more disappointing were the witnesses appearing for the prosecution. They included leading republican politicians such as Daladier and Reynaud and former Vichyites such as Flandin and Tracou. *L'Humanité* of 18 July regarded the summoning of these Pétainists as further proof of the rehabilitation of Vichy. Their testimonies lacked passion with Flandin (like Daladier) electing to submit written evidence. As *Le Monde* of 21 July commented, the prosecution's men had hardly been accusers.

Only two witnesses generated any real excitement: Choltitz and Reynaud. Choltitz, the former military governor of Paris, appeared for the defence and spoke of how in August 1944 he, with the blessing of Abetz, had conspired to disobey Hitler's orders for the destruction of the French capital. It was not lost on observers that the trial was being conducted in the Palais de Justice on the Ile de la Cité close to the beauty of Ste-Chapelle and the magnificence of Notre-Dame. Choltitz, with his short-cropped hair and overbearing mien, was seen by the press as the archetypal Prussian general; nonetheless, he proved an effective and convincing speaker.[24] Reynaud, appearing for the prosecution, also left a lasting impression on the court. He spoke on the assassination of Mandel which, it will be recalled, was considered the gravest charge facing Abetz. Remaining calm and quietly spoken, Reynaud recalled how on three separate occasions – in 1941, 1942 and 1944 – the ambassador had demanded the execution of himself and Mandel.[25]

As always, Abetz had his double-game defence at hand. He freely admitted that he had indeed suggested the arrest and execution of Mandel and Reynaud. This course of action had been devised as a retaliatory measure for the killing of German parachutists and as an alternative form of reprisal to the shooting of French hostages, the option favoured by Berlin. Yet he knew that his government would not dare kill two such prominent politicians; thus the effect of his proposal was to have saved the lives of Reynaud and Mandel, and to have averted all other reprisals. The trick had worked and Mandel was deported to Germany where he was safe. It was unfortunate and outside of his knowledge, asserted Abetz, that Darnand's *Milice* had transported him back to France where he was shot. This transfer had been authorized by Laval, Abetz claimed, and it was the Vichy minister who was the real culprit in the affair.

The ingenuity of this defence appears to have sapped the confidence of the prosecution. At the summing up, and to the relief of the press box, Flicoteaux only spoke for four hours and did not call for the death penalty as was his right. Instead, he demanded twenty years of forced labour. By contrast, Floriot spoke for seven hours and made an impassioned plea for an acquittal. Like a refrain, the advocate returned to his client's commitment to Franco-German reconciliation. Here was an idealist, he proclaimed, who had struggled against overwhelming odds to realize his dream. To condemn such a man was to condemn the cause of international reconciliation.

In the traditions of military law, the verdict was communicated to the court on 23 July 1949 without the defendant present. He did not learn of his fate until later that evening when the decision was read out to him in private under military guard. Although it was acknowledged that his position as ambassador constituted mitigating circumstances, he had been found guilty on those counts relating to the deportation of Jews, the appropriation of works of art and the arrest of certain categories of French officials. He had been found not guilty on the charges pertaining to the press agencies, the Bor copper mines, the taking of hostages and the assassination of Mandel. Apparently it took the jury no more than ninety minutes to reach its verdict. The sentence also took little time to resolve: twenty years hard labour.[26]

The press was troubled by this outcome. Predictably *l'Humanité*, which had called for the death penalty, was outraged by what had happened. Scenting the influence of French and German trusts behind the decision, on 24 July the newspaper predicted that within years, maybe months, Abetz would again be free to spread his particular brand of treachery among French workers. Yet as *Le Monde* of 24/25 July reported, many communists were relieved that the affair was now over as it had reached farcical proportions. Indeed, it had offered wonderful opportunities for the ridicule of *Le Canard Enchaîné*. On 20 July, it had recommended as a sentence: '(1) 12 balles dans la peau comme mauvais allemand de la part des bons allemands. (2) A la croix de fer de la 1ʳᵉ classe comme bon allemand, de la part des mauvais allemands. (3) A douze balles dans la peau comme allemand ennemi de la France pour ses trahisons. (4) A la croix d'officier de la légion d'honneur comme allemand ami de la France, pour les services rendus.'

More sober sections of the press also commented on the inconsistency of the verdict. Yet, apart from agreeing that the case should have been heard before an international tribunal, journalists could not decide on the sentence that the French court should have awarded. Given that Abetz had been found not guilty on a number of counts, *Le Figaro* of 23/24 July admitted that the twenty years hard labour could be interpreted as too severe a punishment. Writing on the same day in *L'Aurore*, Jean Bernard-Derosne argued that the whole trial had been a mistake. Had Abetz, in his position as ambassador, been judged as a symbol of the Nazi party and all of its crimes, there could have been only one verdict: the death penalty. Instead he had been charged as a war criminal even though none of the evidence linked him with the atrocities he had supposedly committed. *Combat* of the same date adopted a different perspective. While it acknowledged that, as a representative of the enemy, Abetz had been no hard or cruel foe, it could not forgive the ambassador for the way in which he had poisoned the spirit of the French people. For this crime, he should have paid with his life.

The diversity of press opinion reflected the complex origins of the trial. Given that Abetz had come to personify Nazi rule in France, it was only to be expected that the French would wish to judge him themselves. Yet how best to proceed? Confusing the matter throughout was the much vaunted Francophilia of the one-time ambassador. This proved extremely pervasive and bore testimony to the extent to which Abetz had been successful in convincing Parisian society that he was a Greek among Romans.[27] Thus at one stage it appeared likely that he would be tried in the High Court charged as a collaborator. Even when that option was ruled out and he was brought before a military tribunal, it seemed as though he was being accused not with war crimes but with the betrayal of France. This muddled thinking only served the cause of the former diplomat. By stressing his betrayal of French interests, the prosecution appeared to be testifying to his Francophilia thus lending credence to his double-game argument. It failed to display convincingly how his love for France was dwarfed by his devotion to Germany. Ironically, the prosecution was hampered by the evidence at its disposal; this only bolstered the case for the defence. However much Flicoteaux raked through the official correspondence of the Reich's Foreign Ministry, Abetz could always claim that his dispatches should not be accepted at face value. Consequently it was difficult to pin down his precise role in many of the alleged crimes. As ambassador, he often appeared as a mere intermediary in the execution of Hitler's wishes. In many ways, this was an accurate depiction of his real powers. It will be recalled that his Francophilia had not only impressed the French; it had also troubled Berlin which was suspicious of his true intentions. When these concerns were read out to the court, Abetz again emerged as the lover of France who had indeed thwarted the designs of his German masters.

Thus the trial failed to uncover the real Abetz. Never the Greek among Romans, he was instead the committed Nazi determined to use his limited powers to demonstrate to the French the errors of their ways and the superiority of German culture. And for pursuing this task he probably paid with his life. In 1958, released from prison and working as a journalist in his native country, he and his wife were killed in an automobile accident.[28] The car was brand new and the incident has remained shrouded in mystery. Yet the suspicion must be that ultimately he was tried and sentenced not in Paris by a military tribunal but in Germany by partisans of the French Resistance.

Notes

Unless stated otherwise, the place of publication is Paris.

1. *Le Populaire*, 23/24 July 1949.
2. *Le Figaro*, 13 July 1949.

3. Ibid.
4. These proceedings are published as *D'une prison. Précédé du procès, vu par Jean Bernard-Derosne. Les quatre témoignages principaux, le réquisitoire et la plaidorie de Me Floriot*, Amiot-Dumont, 1949. A fuller transcript of the trial may be found in *Le Figaro*, 13 July–23/4 July 1949.
5. Abetz makes this defence in his memoirs, *Das öffene Problem. Ein Rückblick auf zwei Jahrzehnte deutscher Frankreichpolitik*, Cologne, Greven Verlag, 1951.
6. On the rehabilitation of Abetz, see J.E. Wallace, 'Otto Abetz and the Question of a Franco-German Reconciliation, 1919–1939', *The Southern Quarterly*, vol.13, no.3, 1975, pp.189–206. For a more critical assessment see J.P. Fox, 'German Bureaucrat or Nazified Ideologue? Ambassador Otto Abetz and Hitler's Anti-Jewish Policies, 1940–44', in M.G. Fry (ed.), *Power, Personalities and Policies. Essays in Honour of Donald Cameron Watt*, London, Frank Cass, 1992, pp.175–232.
7. Information from *Le Monde*, 27 October 1945 and 17 November 1945.
8. Among other court appearances in 1946, Abetz attended the Luchaire trial, a government enquiry into the Cagoule, and the International Military Tribunal at Nuremberg. See *Le Monde*, 26 January 1946 and 29 May 1946.
9. By Control Council Law Number 10 of December 1945, any one of the four forces that were occupying Germany was permitted to arrange its own zonal trials. For a guide to the French tribunals see N.E. Tutorow (ed.), *War Crimes, War Criminals and War Crimes Trials. An Annotated Bibliography and Source Book*, Westport, Greenwood Press, 1986, pp.381–6.
10. Ordinance of 18 November 1944 cited in G. Warner, *Pierre Laval and the Eclipse of France*, London, Eyre and Spottiswoode, 1968, p.408.
11. *Le Monde*, 11 and 15 November 1946.
12. CDJC CII-2, Tribunal Militaire Permanent de Paris, 'Acte d'accusation dressé par Nous, Capitaine Flicoteaux, Substitut du Commissaire du Gouvernement près du Tribunal Militaire de Paris dans l'affaire du nommé, Abetz Otto Friedrich', Paris, 1949, p.167. The definition of 'war crimes' as established by the ordinance of 28 August 1944 did indeed correspond with that outlined in Article 6 (b) of the Charter of the IMT at Nuremberg of 8 August 1945. Nonetheless, it also overlapped with the definition of 'crimes against humanity' as laid out in Article 6 (c) of the Nuremberg Charter. On this point see Nancy Wood,

'Crimes or Misdemeanours? Memory on Trial in Contemporary France', *French Cultural Studies*, no.5, 1994, pp.1–21.

13. Half-way through the trial it was discovered that the Quai d'Orsay was sitting on a large cache of German documents which had not been seen by the defence. It remains unclear whether they had been viewed by the prosecution. See *Le Monde*, 19 July 1949.

14. On the appearance of Abetz see *Le Monde*, 12 July 1949, *New York Times*, 13 July 1949, and *Newsweek*, 25 July 1949.

15. CDJC CII-2, Tribunal Militaire, 'Acte d'accusation', *passim*.

16. *Le Monde*, 30 April 1946.

17. CDJC LXXI-113, *procès verbal* of the Commissaire de Police à la Direction des Renseignements Généraux à résidence à Paris, 'Relations d'Otto Abetz avec certaines personnalités Françaises', 21 November 1945.

18. M. Larkin, *France Since the Popular Front. Government and People, 1936–1986*, Oxford, Clarendon Press, 1988, p. 86, and M. Ferro, *Pétain*, Fayard, 1987, pp.170–2.

19. CDJC LXXXI-28, 'Politische Arbeit in Frankreich', Salzburg, 30 July 1940.

20. In 1948, Editions Gaucher of Paris published *Pétain et les allemands. Mémorandum d'Abetz* containing documents testifying to this Francophilia.

21. Abetz's testimony reported in *Le Figaro*, 13 July 1949.

22. Abetz quoted in *New York Times*, 13 July 1949.

23. *Combat*, 16/17 July 1949.

24. See L. Doblhoff, 'Traitor or Patriot', *The Commonweal*, vol.50, no.19, 19 August 1949, pp.461–2.

25. Reynaud's testimony reported in *The Times*, 18 July 1949.

26. The press appears extremely confused over which counts had been proven. Maybe this is not surprising given the number of charges facing Abetz. The verdict as cited here is taken largely from *L'Aurore*, 23/24 July 1949.

27. Larkin, *France Since the Popular Front*, p.86.

28. *Le Monde*, 7 May 1958.

– 14 –

Pacifism and the Liberation

Norman Ingram

The Second World War did a great deal of damage to the fortunes of the French peace movement, which has always been a rather tender plant anyway. The title of an article published in 1991 by Karl Holl in the German weekly *Die Zeit* describes French pacifism of the inter-War period as 'permanently discredited'.[1] This is certainly the prevailing view in France where in common parlance pacifism has become associated with defeatism, collaborationism, and the Vichy experience. As one French commentator has written, 'In denying the virtue of war, rendered sacrosanct by tradition, pacifism shakes established ideas. It is lumped together with defeatism, with cowardice, with treason. Pacifism has, therefore, often taken on a pejorative connotation. It is perversion. It is to peace what formalism is to form, simplism to simplicity, sentimentality to sentiment.' And he goes on to say that 'pacifism played its role in the birth of the Vichy regime'.[2] Recent French attempts to 'rediscover' their pacifist past have been marked in many cases by an apparent unwillingness to define precisely what was meant by pacifism in the inter-War period and subsequently. Pacifism has, moreover, been overwhelmingly treated in France as a subset of other political or social movements, and not, as in British, American or German historiography, as an historical subject worthy of consideration in itself.

French pacifism has become history's pariah, in particular the inter-War pacifism known as absolute or integral pacifism.[3] If, as Dieter Riesenberger has written, German pacifism belongs to the 'losers' of history, this must be doubly so in the case of France.[4] The men and

The author wishes to thank the Concordia University Faculty Research and Development Fund, the Social Sciences and Humanities Research Council of Canada, and the Fonds pour la Formation de Chercheurs et l'Aide à la Recherche (du Québec) for the ongoing funding which made possible the preparation of this chapter and attendance at the Sussex conference.

women who struggled for peace in inter-War France have by and large been discredited by a posterity transfixed by what Henry Rousso has called 'le syndrome de Vichy'. By 1939, because of its dissent regarding the question of the origins of the First World War and its rejection of French political society, integral pacifism in France found itself on a shrinking island of political despair. The politics of inter-War dissent begat in turn the politics of wartime and post-War pacifist despair. The political introspection of French inter-War integral pacifists caused them to define the enemy as French rather than German. Whereas Martin Ceadel has convincingly shown that British pacifism of this period represents an 'ethic of ultimate ends',[5] to use Weber's phrase, in France integral pacifism represented a stance of political and historical dissent *vis-à-vis* the rest of French society which ultimately took precedence over the fact of Nazi aggression and atrocities.

The result was that over the course of the four years of the Vichy régime, one finds a constellation of inter-War integral pacifists writing in what was clearly the collaborationist press, and arriving at conclusions in this same press which reflected ideas that only a few years earlier might well have seemed anathema to them. One of the best examples of this sort of pacifist/collaborationist newspaper is *Germinal* whose publication dates (28 April to 11 August 1944) conveniently encapsulate the period of the Liberation of France. In the first number of the paper one finds the names of Marcelle Capy, Félicien Challaye, Pierre Hamp, Claude Jamet, Maurice Rostand, Gérard de Lacaze-Duthiers, and Armand Charpentier among the contributors – all of them people who had been contributors to the pre-War *Patrie humaine* or *Le Barrage*, and in some cases had held office in the Ligue Internationale des Combattants de la Paix (LICP) which had been the prime example of new-style, integral pacifism in France in the 1930s. Other names are conspicuous by their absence. One such is that of René Gerin who, although he wrote a literary column for *L'Œuvre* of which Marcel Déat was editor, seems to have taken it as a point of honour in the post-Liberation period that he had never soiled his hands at *Germinal*.[6] One of the noteworthy characteristics of this erstwhile left-wing, integral pacifism was its veneration of the memory of Jaurès and its attempt to incorporate him into its new-found emphasis on a 'national' socialism.[7] Nationalism alone was not enough. On this count Félicien Challaye rejected out of hand any notion of a link between his wartime political views and the ideas of Charles Maurras, Maurice Barrès, or Charles Péguy. All three of these intellectual leaders were suspect, and ultimately rejected, because they were all afflicted by the same fault – a hatred of Germany.[8] Challaye attempted to make the 'idealistic socialism' of Jaurès fit the needs of the Vichy régime and of occupied France. He insisted on the spiritual side to Jaurès' socialism, on its 'national' character, as well as on its inherent pacifism which, according to Challaye, saw Franco-German reconciliation – even during the Second World War – as a necessary precondition for general European peace and stability.[9]

The link with pre-War integral pacifist analyses is seen in Challaye's complete antipathy towards the French war effort which flowed largely out of his belief that the war was not Germany's fault, but in fact had been imposed on Germany by a bellicose France: 'In a war which, without consulting the people, or even Parliament, our leaders declared on a Germany which did not in the least declare it on us, our country has suffered the most terrible disaster.'[10] According to this view, 1939 was indeed 'la guerre de l'imposture'.[11]

For Léon Emery, the link with Jaurès was less obvious. He seemed to include Jaurès in the group of 'naïve prophets' who held that 'The union of the workers will bring peace to the world.' Having said that, socialism, according to Emery, was to the twentieth century what liberalism had been to the nineteenth. The humanization of this 'statist socialism' would only be possible in peace and therefore, 'One can only hope to loosen the iron corset in which the peoples live to the extent that the conflict can be attenuated. Thus, modern socialism, intimately connected to the wars of class and of nation, child of a tragic epoch, now needs to find peace once again.'[12] This socialism had nothing whatsoever to do either with classical Marxism or with the variety practised in the Soviet Union: 'Marx and his line have nothing but disdain for pacifist Utopias, and it is superfluous to insist on the disastrous case of bolshevism.' It is worth noting, too, that Emery's view of the war was as profoundly anti-American as it was anti-Soviet. For him, Germany was a bulwark against Sovietization; the German defeat would bring a Russian hegemony over the continent, and this would mean 'not only the dictatorship of a summary and materialist communism, harmful to the elites and to real culture, but [also] the beginning of a new and gigantic conflict between American imperialism and a Russian imperialism probably allied to Japan, a conflict in which Western Europe would once again be squeezed'.[13] The only way to avoid this 'apocalyptic dance' lay in cooperation between the four great West European nations – France, Germany, Italy, and Spain – to which he hoped Britain might add itself when faced with the final reality of the disintegration of its empire. These West European nations were the cradle of civilization, and whether one liked it or not, they were made of a different stuff, formed by a different historical tradition, from either of the 'vast barbaric empires constituted by the United States and Russia'.[14] The Euro-centricity of Emery's argument, even in the face of Nazism which was the antithesis of the great European values and historical tradition he professed to cherish, continued to find an echo in the independent French peace movement of the early 1950s.[15] The moral ambivalence of Emery's position is evident in his hope that France and Germany, 'realizing their common destiny in a world in which their quarrels of yesterday have definitively taken on the look of absurd anachronisms', would opt for genuine reconciliation.[16] The Franco-German conflict in the Second World War was thus reduced to a simple, albeit pernicious, dispute of long standing between two neighbouring peoples; not a word was said about the ideological nature of the conflict, nor indeed of the atrocities being committed by the Nazi régime.

These sentiments were also echoed by a feminist pacifist of some note, Marcelle Capy, who continued to argue that because women were 'closer to the very source of life, less encumbered by formulas, less deformed by minuscule political routines and vanities' they would be better able to bring about a peaceful and reconciled world. Nazism and the struggle for Europe were thus reduced to a 'minuscule political vanity'. Where did the fault lie? Precisely in France's inter-War failure to 'save the peace'. But she also blamed women, and in particular mothers, for the new war: 'If [the] mothers [of France] had thrown their hearts in the balance, we would not be where we are. They were lacking in Love.'[17]

By the beginning of June 1944, *Germinal* seemed certain that the Allies were about to make their move. Sowing fear, Claude Jamet sought to remind readers of the horrors of the Allied landings in Italy: cities utterly destroyed, churches ruined, the earth scorched, fire and blood under the bombs and cannons. Recognizing the divided nature of French society, Jamet seemed also to plead for some sort of French reconciliation so that the nation could face the onslaught united.[18] One week later, in the wake of D-Day, *Germinal* issued a call for a united front of Frenchmen against the second front opened up by the Allies. 'They' had landed. The 'liberation' – 'like a plague' – had been declared, and this meant that war was once more upon France:

War! Total, inexpiable. War is on our soil. It already reddens our coasts as would a cancer of fire and of blood. War! With consequences, more or less distant, which no one can foresee. But with its immediate cortège of sorrows, of destructions, of increased miseries, of multiplied ruins. And for the sake of interests, of which the least one can say is that they are not ours.[19]

Paul Rives, the political director of *Germinal*, wrote two weeks later that the Anglo-Americans had not invaded light-heartedly but rather because of the pressure brought to bear on them by Stalin. They were thus in a no-win situation because if they lost their gamble, Stalin would draw the obvious conclusion from their weakness, but if they were successful, they would then find themselves face to face with their sometime ally. Either way, Rives saw nothing but future wars between the Anglo-Americans on the one hand and the Soviets on the other, wars fed by ideological and economic differences. The lesson he drew from this scenario was that out and out collaboration with the Nazis was called for; he hoped for a German victory. France's destiny was inseparable from that of Europe which in turn depended on a German victory. He called all French people to facilitate the German victory in whatever way possible.[20]

On 7 July this call for collaboration took an interesting semantic turn when the paper issued an appeal to the French people: 'Let us all be Combattants de la Paix.' The name of the largest and most influential new-style pacifist group of the inter-War period had now become a slogan in a defeatist, collaborationist newspaper. *Germinal* came out in favour of full-scale collaboration with the Nazis and resistance to the Allied invasion:

> Thanks to our liberators, our soil has again been transformed into a battlefield, thanks to them thousands of Frenchmen have perished. Thanks to them yet again, thousands of others are without shelter.[...] The situation worsens day by day; it is time to face up to it. The means are offered, let us avail ourselves of them.
>
> No one can deny any longer that to work at forging armaments here or in Germany is to work for our own personal defence, it is to work for the European victory which will bring true liberation – total liberation, that of all the foreign armies by a return to peace. Therefore, take heart, let us work with diligence.[21]

The call for collaboration certainly did not come merely in the closing months of the war as the Liberation unfolded across France; it was not simply a cry of desperate, last minute bravado. Félicien Challaye, for example, had been preaching collaboration with the Germans in the service of European reconciliation since 1941 at least; he had also been the apostle of Vichy's National Revolution. For Challaye, the Second World War was 'the most absurd of wars', 'an abominable blow against the security of France'.[22] He vehemently defended pacifists 'who were the only ones for twenty years to denounce the idiotic Treaty of Versailles', and in contradistinction to his views on politicians he heaped praise on Maréchal Pétain 'who had "saved the country by imposing the armistice" and who had had the courage to go to Montoire'.[23] He denounced the political class and the journalists responsible for pushing France into war, and suggested that the guilty amongst them should be sentenced to prison terms and be stripped of their civic rights. He proclaimed the 'duty' to collaborate with Germany and preached his own pseudo-socialist version of the National Revolution with amongst other things a call for 'a society freed from capitalist liberalism'.[24]

Once the Liberation had been accomplished how did it treat French pacifists, and what was their reaction to its political claims and to those of the *épuration*? Can one speak of an 'image' of the Liberation which is separate from the actual 'event'?

Perhaps not surprisingly, the *épuration* was not kind to some pacifists. Given what some of them had written during the war, this was probably inevitable. Some post-War pacifists, though, saw in the *épuration* a politically motivated patriotic-communist catharsis. Gérard Vidal, for example, was sentenced to five and a half years in prison for refusing to bear arms in May 1940. He was offered a reduced sentence if he agreed to go and work in Germany. This he refused. As the internal memorandum of the War Resisters' International (WRI) put it:

> When France was liberated in 1944 he also refused to be enroled in any way in the FFI parties, which would have meant his release. So that when the prisons were emptied, he remained behind. He told me he had refused because he did not wish to take part in armed acts of violence, but that he would have agreed to unarmed action which would have endangered him but been of a beneficial kind. He has always come up against the same lack of understanding and the same intolerance, so that he is still in the Bergerac prison.[25]

Three integral pacifists of note – Félicien Challaye, Léon Emery, and René Gerin – were tried by the courts of the Liberation or the Fourth Republic for collaboration. Challaye benefitted from a *non-lieu*.[26] Gerin was sentenced to eight years of hard labour, ten years of banishment (*interdiction de séjour*), and national *dégradation* for life. This was eventually reduced to one year's imprisonment and national indignity for life.[27] As for Emery, he was sentenced to five years in prison, a 1,200 franc fine, and national indignity for life. He obtained an early release from prison in March 1946 after the fine was paid apparently by friends, and eventually he was able to regain his civic rights and with them his pension as well.[28]

In the case of Challaye and Emery, it is interesting to note that they formed the core of the minority group within the Ligue des droits de l'homme (LDH) over the course of the entire inter-War period. This minority within the LDH consistently demanded revision of the Versailles Treaty, criticized French foreign policy, and became increasingly anti-Communist in the thirties. The debate within the LDH on the question of war and peace was a key forum of transmission of pacifist ideas from the peace movement into more mainstream French society. The great divorce between the minority and the rest of the LDH occurred at the Ligue's 1937 Congress which had as its theme 'How to defend both democracy and peace.' There were two somewhat related issues at stake in 1937: one was the Moscow Purge Trials, and the other was the position France should take *vis-à-vis* the challenges of the dictatorships. In the wake of the Congress, Challaye and Emery both resigned from the Central Committee of the Ligue.[29] Michel Alexandre, a *professeur agrégé* at the Lycée Henri-IV in Paris, was also part of the minority group within the LDH. He, together with his wife, Jeanne Halbwachs Alexandre, were active in both the Ligue and in integral pacifist circles from the First World War onwards.

Despite Challaye and Emery's clearly ambiguous position during the Second World War, Michel Alexandre came fulsomely to their defence during the *épuration*. The experience of Vichy and of the measures against the Jews, to say nothing of his incarceration by the Gestapo at the Compiègne camp, seem not to have lessened one whit Alexandre's commitment both to integral pacifism and to his friends Challaye and Emery.[30] In July 1945 he wrote:

> Hunted and more or less on the run, I saw very little of Challaye in the years 1940–44. I only read in a piecemeal fashion the articles that he published in this period, but in which I always found his ideas of yesteryear. In any case, at each of our meetings, I noted the admirable firmness of [unclear] his indignation against any sort of tyranny (including, of course, the Nazi tyranny). All persecution – and especially racial – horrified him. At the most critical moments he did not cease to offer me sanctuary in his home, and that with the most fraternal *élan*...[31]

As for Emery, Alexandre wrote that the man was an ascetic, someone who drove himself in his work to the limits of human endurance, an effort which eventually caused him to go almost blind. His total commitment to pacifism caused something to snap in Emery's mind when the Second World War broke out:

But the war of 1939, the length and the horror of which he had only too well foreseen, was for him the final blow which he could not overcome. Lost in his despair, seeing before us only chaos and irremediable decadence, this man who was normally so lucid, thought a quick end to the conflict possible as early as 1940; and he resigned himself to it as to a lesser evil; and since then he has not ceased to dream desperately of some compromise between bloodied peoples.

Thus, the purest pacifism found itself the source and the *unique* source of the errors of attitude which he has committed during the past three years.[32]

Alexandre admitted that Emery was a collaborator because he had been convinced after the defeat that the democratic ideal was unrealizable for years to come. Emery had therefore supported the Vichy régime, albeit without much conviction. He continued to believe that European civilization was completely lost without a Franco-German *entente* which would form the basis for an occidental one. Collaborationist opinion could only be considered a crime, according to Alexandre, if it could be demonstrated that some sort of treasonous thinking had insinuated itself into the mind, or if *in fact* these opinions led to odious or reprehensible acts. As to the first, he declared that Emery at all times acted 'with the most complete good faith', and as for the second, 'the "collaborationism" of Emery really stopped at the threshold.' Emery had indeed joined Déat's Rassemblement national populaire – 'not without reservations and distaste' – but despite allegations to the contrary, Alexandre continued, he had never taken an active role in any collaborationist group, nor had he had anything to do with the occupying authorities.[33]

On the other side of the balance sheet, Alexandre testified to the help Emery gave throughout the war to persecuted people, 'for, if on the political and military level Emery had resigned himself to what he believed to be inevitable, never on the human plane did he cease to condemn and to fight against the injustices and the horrors of the Nazi oppression, and notably against the racial persecutions.'[34] Alexandre's letter ends, as does the accompanying draft petition to be signed by people who knew Emery, with a plea for the 'Gaullist absolution' in his case:

It seems to me the humane and understanding words of General de Gaulle in his speech of 14 October apply most precisely to M[onsieur] E[mery]. 'Many people have fallen into error at one moment or another since 1914... Who is it who has never given in to illusion or discouragement? Come on! France is made up of all French people, it needs them all.' We ardently hope that the Justice of our country will not disappoint our desire, and that it will return a Frenchman of good faith to freedom and our common work.[35]

René Gerin was an *ancien normalien*, an *agrégé des lettres*, and a journalist. He had been cited for bravery during the First World War, had risen to the rank of captain, and was a Chevalier of the Legion of Honour, from which he was expelled in 1934 largely because of his pacifist beliefs and his spirited defence of Georges Demartial.[36] He had also engaged Raymond Poincaré in a debate over the origins of the First World War.[37] During the Second World War he wrote a literary column for *L'Œuvre* which was the origin of the legal proceedings against him following the Liberation. Alphonse Barbé, the editor of the inter-War libertarian newspaper *Le Semeur* which had been published in the Calvados and which had consistently advocated conscientious objection and an integral pacifism, believed that Gerin's troubles with the *épuration* had more to do with the fact that he was a pacifist than with his journalistic activity, as such, under the Occupation:

> For René Gerin it has been made a crime to have worked at *L'Œuvre* under the Occupation. [L]ike many anti-fascist French people, I read this newspaper, not having had much to choose from, and never did I read anything by Gerin which incited to collaboration in the slightest.
>
> In reality, it is less the columnist for *L'Œuvre* who is being attacked here than the pacifist who always affirmed his faith in the rapprochement of the peoples...[38]

Barbé had other criticisms to make of the entire process of the *épuration* which he seemed to believe was based on moral quicksand, to say the least. The Pétain trial, for example, would not serve to 'cleanse the Augean stables' because the rot went back much further than the old Marshal. He emphasized that he was not trying to defend Pétain, but merely to point out that in the spring of 1940, with one sixth of the population of France on the road as 'miserable refugees', and with the French army quite literally disintegrating, it was hardly any surprise that ninety-nine per cent of French people saw in Pétain a saviour.[39]

Fernand Gouttenoire de Toury took this analysis even further the following year in an article in which he examined the options open to pacifists in the elections to the second Constituent Assembly in the spring of 1946. According to de Toury there was not a single candidate in whom a sincere pacifist could put his trust. No one was willing to condemn the policies followed since the war, while at the same time all of the former *Pétainistes* were falling over themselves in an attempt to distance themselves from the Vichy period. In de Toury's mind there was nothing to distinguish the Gaullist policies from those which had preceded them. His principal complaints about de Gaulle's policies were threefold: first, that the Gaullist régime was built on the lie that those Frenchmen who supported the Armistice in June 1940 were evil or traitors. Such a view bore no relation to the reality of the defeat and to the fact that there were virtually no 'resisters' in 1940. De Toury concluded: 'The "Gaullist" régime is therefore built on a fundamental lie.'[40] Secondly, he charged that de Gaulle had 'regilded the escutcheon' of the Communists whom he castigated, not for being Communists as such, but for being in the service of a foreign government. This behaviour was not something new in the Communists; they had shown the way before in their official support of the Molotov–Ribbentrop pact in August 1939. Above all, though, de Toury condemned the Gaullist régime for the *épuration*, for having

> made a mockery of justice and of its fundamental principle which demands that in a trial no one, ever, can be both judge and prosecution: in constituting these Courts of Justice composed of the political adversaries of those whom one is to judge, this régime has permitted parodies... such as that which constituted the trial and execution of that Pierre Laval, of whom today even the worst adversaries hesitate to say what they think after the ignoble fashion in which his trial and execution were carried out.[41]

Having said that, de Toury clearly condemned the Vichy régime – 'not for having signed the Armistice – but for having spoken of "collaboration" and for having thrown its lot in with Germany, at a moment when the strictest neutrality was called for between victor and the Allies, in the same way that the Gaullist régime merits our condemnation for having sowed the seeds of hatreds throughout the country which are far from being extinguished'.[42] De Toury concluded by saying that if he were running for office, it would be on the platform 'Ni Pétiniste [sic], ni Gaulliste'.

Unlike the wartime pacifists examined above, those of the post-Liberation period did condemn the atrocities of the Nazi régime, but they tended to do so in muted terms, and to continue to insist on the primary need for Franco-German reconciliation – with almost no questions asked. For example, in a letter to the War Resisters' International written in May 1945, Alphonse Barbé condemned not the death camps, but rather merely the 'deportation camps'; he seemed to think that there was not much difference between the latter and the famine which ravaged Russia following the end of the First World War. As far as the German nation was concerned, he argued, 'one ought to condemn unceasingly the executioners, but to accuse an entire people of the crimes of a few is more than shameful, it is a mistake of which we could repent.'[43] This criticism of Allied policy towards the vanquished Germans, with its concomitant apparent denigration of the magnitude of Nazi atrocities, was echoed by de Toury, who claimed that the victors were exacting a Carthaginian peace from Germany:

> Since you ask me what I should insist upon... here it is: the necessity for pacifists to denounce without fail the harmfulness of the policies presently being used by the Allies with regard to defeated Germany. We have killed millions of human beings under the noble pretext of defending liberty and justice against the Nazis, and now that Hitler has been beaten we are using his methods and his procedures: as victor he could not have crushed us, torn us apart, tortured us any more than we are doing to Germany since its disaster... Thus, alas, not only is Peace made a mockery of, but its immediate future is irremediably compromised...[44]

Pacifism was vitally affected by the Liberation of France and the events which flowed out of it. The political theses of pacifism – especially those of the new-style, integral pacifism of the 1930s – seemed hard to accept in the cold light of post-War France. The moral equivalence which some pacifists seemed to make between the Nazi new European order, and their pre-War desires for Franco-German reconciliation, led to political choices which were unfortunate to say the very least. Politics makes strange bedfellows, and no stranger coupling can in principle be imagined than that of men like Félicien Challaye, with impeccable liberal-socialist credentials, writing in a newspaper such as *Germinal* which preached outright collaboration with the Occupier. And yet the moral quicksand on which French political pacifists stood from 1940–44 is reflected in other areas of French society in these years; one has only to think of the 'Knight-Monks' of Uriage to see the truth of that.[45] The fact that French political society in 1940 generally seemed so ready to reject liberal democracy together with Soviet communism goes some way to explaining the case of the wartime pacifists. The reaction to them at the Liberation was perhaps predictable. Not without reason did Alphonse Barbé warn in the spring of 1945: 'For years to come, pacifist propaganda in France will be dangerous given the present state of mind...'[46]

Notes

Unless stated otherwise, the place of publication is Paris.

1. Karl Holl, 'Pazifismus in Frankreich, 1919–1939: Dauerhaft diskreditiert. Die Irrtümer der französischen Friedensbewegung – damals', *Die Zeit*, 8 February 1991, p.38.
2. Jean Defrasne, *Le Pacifisme*, Collection 'Que sais-je?' PUF, 1983, pp.3, 111.
3. Because of the vagueness of the term 'pacifisme' the expression 'pacifisme intégral' came into common use in the late 1920s, and by 1930 had come to denote a political movement of quite a different sort from the mainstream of French pacifism which had a long history. For the inter-War period, for questions of definition and for the historiography of pacifism in France see my *Politics of Dissent: Pacifism in France, 1919–1939*, Oxford, Clarendon Press, 1991. See also Norman Ingram, 'L'Envers de l'entre-deux-guerres en France: Ou à la Recherche d'un passé pacifiste', in Maurice Vaïsse (ed.), *Le Pacifisme en Europe des années 1920 aux années 1950*, Brussels, Editions Bruylant, 1993, pp.17–42. For the nineteenth-century origins of French, and indeed European, pacifism, see Sandi E. Cooper, *Patriotic Pacifism: Waging War on War in Europe, 1815–1914*, Oxford, Oxford University Press, 1991. Most of the recent French work on pacifism is being done by a new generation of historians. In particular, see Nicolas Offenstadt and Philippe Olivera: 'Pour une histoire de l'engagement pacifiste en France 1919–1939: sources et bibliographie', *Bulletin de l'Institut d'Histoire du Temps Présent*, no.51, March 1993; Offenstadt and Olivera (eds), *Matériaux pour l'histoire de notre temps*, no.30, sur le pacifisme, January–March 1993.
4. Dieter Riesenberger, *Geschichte der Friedensbewegung in Deutschland: von den Anfängen bis 1933*, Göttingen, Vandenhoeck und Ruprecht, 1985, pp.7–8.
5. Martin Ceadel, *Pacifism in Britain, 1914–1945: The Defining of a Faith*, Oxford, Clarendon Press, 1980, p.5.
6. See *Germinal*, no.1, 28 April 1944 for a list of contributors to the first number of the paper. Challaye and Capy had both been presidents of the LICP. For Gerin's comments see René Gerin, *Un Procès de la Libération*, Editions des Cahiers de Contre-Courant, 1954, p.46. Gerin writes: 'J'ai refusé, de même, de collaborer à *Radio-Paris*, à *Germinal*, à d'autres feuilles dirigées et payées par la propagande allemande. J'ai refusé aussi, malgré les propositions très avantageuses qui me furent faites en octobre 1940, de faire

reparaître *Le Barrage*, l'hebdomadaire dont j'étais le rédacteur en chef avant la guerre.'

7. See for example, Armand Charpentier, 'Jaurès, étudiant et professeur', *Germinal*, no.1, 28 April 1944, p.4.
8. See Félicien Challaye, 'L'Actualité de Jaurès', *Germinal*, no.2, 5 May 1944, p.2.
9. Ibid.
10. Ibid.
11. The expression comes from the title of Georges Demartial's book *1939: La Guerre de l'imposture* (Editions Jean Flory, 1941), which is another denunciation by an integral pacifist of the origins of the Second World War.
12. Léon Emery, 'Le Socialisme et la paix', *Germinal*, no.2, 5 May 1944, pp.1–2.
13. Ibid., p.2.
14. Ibid.
15. See Ingram, 'Ambivalence in the Post-World War Two French Peace Movement', in Harvey L. Dyck (ed.), *The Pacifist Impulse in Historical Perspective*, Toronto, University of Toronto Press, in press.
16. Emery, 'Le Socialisme et la paix', p.2.
17. Marcelle Capy, 'Sur Terre ou sous terre?' *Germinal*, no.5, 26 May 1944, p.1.
18. Claude Jamet, 'L'Heure H, moins 5', *Germinal*, no.6, 2 June 1944, p.1.
19. Germinal, 'Face au deuxième Front! Front Unique', *Germinal*, no.7, 9 June 1944, p.1.
20. Paul Rives, 'Pour la France et pour l'Europe', *Germinal*, no.9, 23 June 1944, p.1.
21. 'Soyons les Combattants de la Paix', *Germinal*, no.11, 7 July 1944, p.2.
22. Félicien Challaye, preface in Raoul-Albert Bodinier, *Vérités d'avant-paix,* Les Editions de 'Mon Pays', n.d. [1942], p. 17. Challaye's preface is dated December 1941.
23. Ibid., p.18.
24. Ibid., pp.18–21.
25. Note on Gérard Vidal, April 1945, WRI archives, International Institute for Social History, Amsterdam.
26. Mentioned in 'Discours de Gérard Vidal (France) à la Conférence Préparatoire WRI, Cambridge, 30 décembre 1946', in WRI archives.
27. See Gerin, *Procès de la Libération*, pp.41–2. See also Vidal, 'Discours de Gérard Vidal'.

28. See Maurice Moissonnier, entry on Emery in Jean Maitron, *Dictionnaire biographique du mouvement ouvrier français*, part 4, vol.17, pp.31–3.

29. I have dealt with this, in embryonic form at least, in a paper delivered at the Second International Conference of Peace Historians at Stadtschlaining, Austria, in September 1991 ('Defending the Rights of Man: The Ligue des droits de l'homme and the Problem of Peace').

30. It is possible Alexandre was not aware of a scurrilously anti-Semitic novel which Challaye wrote during the war, entitled *L'Etrange Chemin de la paix*. It exists only in manuscript form at the Bibliothèque Nationale in Paris. I am indebted to Professor William D. Irvine for drawing this to my attention.

31. Michel Alexandre à Monsieur le Président, Limoges, 12 July 1945. Typescript in Bibliothèque de Documentation Internationale Contemporaine (BDIC), Nanterre, Dossiers Jeanne et Michel Alexandre. It is unclear from the typescript precisely who 'Monsieur le Président' is.

32. 'Témoignage de M.A. pour Emery: Notes Justificatives', in BDIC Dossiers Jeanne et Michel Alexandre.

33. Ibid.

34. Ibid. There is also a list of the people helped or saved by Emery in the same file.

35. Draft petition in favour of Léon Emery in BDIC Dossiers Jeanne et Michel Alexandre.

36. See René Gerin, *Honneur et Patrie: ou comment j'ai été exclu de la Légion d'Honneur*, Ligue Internationale des Combattants de la Paix, 1934.

37. Raymond Poincaré and René Gerin, *Les Responsabilités de la Guerre: Quatorze Questions par René Gerin, Agrégé des lettres: Quatorze Réponses par Raymond Poincaré de l'Académie Française*, Payot, 1930.

38. Alphonse Barbé to André Philip, Minister of Finance (copy), Falaise, 10 February 1946, in WRI archives.

39. Alphonse Barbé, 'The Outlook in France', translation of 'Points de vue', August 1945, and published in an unnamed journal in France. English translation in WRI archives.

40. Fernand Gouttenoire de Toury, 'Un Pacifiste devant les urnes', *Les Cahiers du Pacifisme*, no.2, May 1946, p.1.

41. Ibid.

42. Ibid.

43. Alphonse Barbé to the War Resisters' International, Falaise, 20 May 1945, WRI archives.

44. Message from Fernand Gouttenoire de Toury, cited in 'Discours de Gérard Vidal'.
45. See John Hellman, *The Knight-Monks of Vichy France. Uriage, 1940–1945*, Montreal, McGill-Queen's University Press, 1993.
46. Alphonse Barbé to WRI, Falaise, 20 May 1945, WRI archives.

Part IV

Outre-Mer

– 15 –

'Nos journées de juin': the Historical Significance of the Liberation of Martinique (June 1943)

Richard D.E. Burton

When news of the Armistice reached Martinique on 24 June 1940, the first reaction of the local mayors and Conseillers Généraux had been to pass a motion pledging the island-colony and its inhabitants to 'the continuation of the struggle alongside the Allies with the French overseas Empire'.[1] Any hopes that Martinique and France's other Caribbean possessions, Guadeloupe and Guyane, would become an early focus of anti-Vichy resistance were, however, dashed when, the same day, Admiral Georges Robert, commander in chief of the west Atlantic fleet and Haut Commissaire de la République aux Antilles et en Guyane française, accepted the armistice and placed himself and the 2,500 sailors and 400 soldiers he commanded under the orders of the new government in France. The island was promptly blockaded by an American fleet and would remain so for the following three years during which, in conditions of near complete isolation from the outside world, an improbable Caribbean version of the Révolution Nationale took place with Robert as its figurehead and architect and with the officers and men of the *Emile-Bertin*, the *Béarn* and the *Jeanne d'Arc*, backed by the bulk of the colonial bureaucracy under Governor Yves Nicol, providing the physical and administrative muscle without which Vichy would have been unable to impose its authority, at a distance of 7,000 miles, on a local population of 200,000. The local Catholic Church, headed by Mgr Varin de la Brunellière and manned principally by French or French Canadian priests, also provided invaluable ideological support.[2] But, crucially, Robert could also count on significant support amongst the islanders themselves, at least until the beginning of 1943. His principal backing came from the white creole population, descendants for the most part of the slaveowners of old and known locally as *békés*, who returned to an active and visible political role for the first time since the installation of the Third Republic had transferred formal political power to the coloured (i.e. mulatto or mixed race) middle classes and the preponderantly black lower classes who, by and large, supported them. Creole whites were installed as mayors of many of the island's *communes* and certainly constituted a majority on the twenty-five-strong Conseil Local which was established in late 1942, but no serious study of Vichyism in the Caribbean can gloss over the significant backing the regime received from sections of the local coloured and, to a lesser extent, black populations: it was, in particular, coloured and black *anciens combattants* who made up the bulk of the membership of the local Légion des Combattants et des Volontaires de la Révolution Nationale.

By the end of 1942, however, such coloured and black support was visibly dwindling. The local version of the Vichy régime, which claimed to transcend racial as it did class divisions, was reduced, in effect, to the white officers and men of the immobilized west Atlantic fleet, to white colonial officials and to the much feared white *gendarmes à cheval*, backed still by a majority of the local white creole population though, here too, support for Robert and his associates was likewise in decline. This 'racialization' of the regime had a profound impact on the local perception of white people which, since at least the abolition of slavery in 1848, had clearly distinguished between 'bad' local whites (*békés-pays*) and 'good' metropolitan whites (*békés-France*) – priests, teachers, colonial officials – who, with at least some reason, were believed to constitute the principal resource of the local coloured and black populations against the perceived threat of the creole whites. Ever since 1848, coloured and black Martinicans had sought legal and political assimilation into metropolitan France as a means of furthering their interests over and against the local white elite, to counter the brute economic and social power of the *béké-pays* with the institutions and values of the *béké-France*. Now, however, *békés-France* and *békés-pays* were in open and explicit alliance with each other and the historical distinction between 'good' and 'bad' white men began to blur as the sailors of the beleaguered French fleet started to act, in Frantz Fanon's words, in the manner of 'authentic racists' towards the non-white population. Fights became commonplace on the streets and in the rum shops of Fort-de-France and, as the food crisis brought about by the American blockade worsened, sailors and peasant farmers came to blows over the commandeering of food crops for the use of the occupying forces. For the first time since the abolition of slavery, whites *as such* became hate-figures for non-white Martinicans, leading in some instances, and for a very brief period only, to a calling into question of the idea of France itself. In Fanon's words once more, 'an extraordinary sight' was witnessed in late 1942 and early 1943: 'West Indians refusing to take off their hats while the 'Marseillaise' was being played.'[3]

The significance of this gesture should not be exaggerated and, if there was any questioning of the relationship to France *as such*, it was rapidly countered by knowledge of the existence of 'another France' – the France not of Robert, Nicol and Pétain but of General de Gaulle – which became widespread in 1941 and 1942, as did knowledge of the first Allied victories against the Axis powers. In an interesting aside in his otherwise turgid apologia *La France aux Antilles de 1939 à 1943*, Robert states that many Martinicans believed de Gaulle to be 'a black general wanting, exactly like Toussaint L'Ouverture, to liberate the coloured population from the yoke of the white landowners'.[4] This image of de Gaulle as Black Messiah is confirmed by an amusing story told – in creole – in *Le Clairon* shortly after the Liberation: it is 14 July 1943 and, as cries of 'Vive de Gaulle! Vive la dissidence!' ring out in downtown Fort-de-France, one elderly black woman asks another, 'Ça qui de Gaulle?' ('Who is de Gaulle?') 'Pas occupé ou ma fie,' replies her friend, 'de Gaulle cé nègue can-marade nous.' ('Don't worry dear. De Gaulle is a black friend of ours.') The first woman is still not happy: 'Et cé qui moune qui Ladissidence?' ('And who is Ladissidence?'), only to get the more or less proverbial reply: 'Comment non, ma chè, ou pas save ku Ladissidence cé Madame de Gaulle?' ('What dear, you don't know that Ladissidence is Madame de Gaulle?')[5]

By the middle of 1942 acts of opposition, if not of active resistance, to the Robertist régime were widespread. Vichyist posters were being systematically defaced, people were listening to Gaullist broadcasts more or less openly, agents and supporters of the regime were lampooned semi-publicly,[6] and, above all, hundreds of Martinicans began, like their forebears during the last years of slavery, to flee their native island by boat, raft or other means to gain freedom in the nearby British islands of Dominica and St Lucia whence, after transiting via Trinidad and the United States, most enlisted in the forces of la France Combattante. By April 1943 there were as many as 5,000 such new-style maroons from Martinique and Guadeloupe in transit camps in the British West Indies . In November 1942 a public petition urged Robert to rally to la France Combattante. Another was organized in April 1943 by the much esteemed ex-mayor of Fort-de-France, Victor Sévère, who was by now the focal figure in the growing opposition to Vichyism in the island. By early 1943, a Comité de Libération

Martiniquaise was in existence and in contact with Gaullist networks in the Caribbean. Despite the *ralliement* of Guyane and Guadeloupe to la France Combattante in March and May 1943 respectively, these networks urged caution on the Martinican dissidents, anticipating that Vichy would make a stand in the colony in order to secure control of the west Atlantic fleet and, not least, of the 300 tons of gold bullion that had been placed in Fort Desaix in Fort-de-France at the beginning of the war. The Comité included pre-War Radicals like Sévère, Socialists such as Paul Symphor and Emmanuel Véry, Communists like Joseph Del and Georges Gratiant, and had its more or less public headquarters at the Fort-de-France home of Emmanuel Rimbaud, a member of a well known *béké* family. According to Eugène Honorien, writing in the immediate aftermath of the Liberation, the Comité was supported by 'political groups from the reddest to the colourless', not least the powerful Masonic Lodges of Fort-de-France that had withstood Robertist attempts to suppress them. With the exception of Rimbaud, all of its leading figures appear to have been coloured or black and most had a background in local politics under the Third Republic.

It was the decision of the Comité de Libération Martiniquaise to commemorate the third anniversary of the signing of the armistice that triggered off the sequence of events that led to the collapse of the Robertist regime in the last week of June 1943. A demonstration planned for 24 June at the Monument aux Morts on the Savane in central Fort-de-France was banned by Governor Nicol but took place notwithstanding, with the more or less willing consent of the Gendarmerie.[7] In the course of the demonstration, a prominent Vichyist supporter, the French-born director of the post and telegraph services (PTT), one Poimiro or Poimiroo, was held to have insulted the *tricolore*. Vigorous protests ensued and, that evening, Robert and Nicol arranged for the internment, the following morning, of the leading dissidents: Rimbaud, in the military camp at Balata just north of Fort-de-France; Réjon and Cognet, at Fort Desaix in the capital; Sévère under house arrest safely away from Fort-de-France. These measures not unnaturally excited rather than quelled public discontent which other members of the Comité, notably Symphor, Calvert and Castaing, did their utmost to foment 'at crossroads in the suburbs and even on certain public squares in the centre of town, protected by serried ranks of demonstrators'.[8] In desperation, Robert and Nicol appealed to Emmanuel Véry, president of the pre-armistice Conseil Général and himself a member of the Comité, to do what he could to contain the mounting disorder. This he agreed to do, on condition that the internees were released forthwith. Two days of uneasy calm ensued.

Thus far opposition to the Robertist régime had been essentially a Martinican affair, led by members of the old coloured political class of the Third Republic, with little active participation, as yet, from the black lower classes of Fort-de-France. It took a split within the occupying forces themselves to move events into a higher gear and to bring the whole population of the island, and particularly of the capital, into open resistance to the régime. Throughout the régime's existence, there had been a marked tension between the officers and men of the west Atlantic fleet on the one hand and, on the other, the much smaller military force – some 400 strong – which was based at Balata, north of Fort-de-France, under the command of the French-born career officer Commandant Henri Tourtet who was widely suspected of harbouring pro-Gaullist, or at least anti-Robertist, sentiments. There is much uncertainty concerning the ethnic composition of the force Tourtet had at his disposal, a subject on which Tourtet himself says nothing in his official report on the events of June 1943. The officers were undoubtedly French and white, as were a significant proportion of the ordinary ranking soldiers, but the majority – or so I am told by a Martinican informant, M René Clerempuy – were coloured or black Martinicans. There was also an important contingent of *tirailleurs sénégalais* though these, according to the same informant, were considered 'too black' and 'too primitive' by their Martinican counterparts, and had for the most part been regrouped in a separate military camp near Saint-Pierre. Whatever their race or origin, the soldiers were strongly opposed to the increasingly pro-German stance of the Vichy government and ashamed, according to their commander's post-Liberation account, of their passivity, as officers and men in other colonies, most notably Guadeloupe and Guyane, were openly rallying to la France Combattante. Closer to home, they were disgruntled by the demeaning agricultural work they were required to perform and enraged that their counterparts in the navy were allegedly receiving 50 to 100 per cent more pay than they were. On 27 June the seventy men of the 3ᵉ Compagnie (including twenty-two Senegalese) effectively mutinied and, through their commanding officer Lieutenant Renvoisé, put pressure on Tourtet to declare for De Gaulle and lead an uprising against Robert. Tourtet demurred but entered into secret negotiations with the Comité de Libération while sending the 3ᵉ Compagnie on a round trip to Saint-Pierre and back. Everywhere along the road the troops were hailed by the local population with cries of 'Vive de Gaulle!' On 28 June, Robert reiterated his support for Vichy and did everything he could to prevent the dissidents from moving from Balata to Fort-de-France, promising them a free passage to Saint Lucia or Dominica if they wished. His offer, needless to say, was turned down with contempt.

The following day, 29 June, Tourtet at last decided to take personal control of the insurrection in order, in his own words, 'to conduct it in an orderly and dignified fashion,without bloodshed'.[9] As more and more soldiers from other bases in Martinique declared for la France Combattante, Tourtet formally proclaimed the insurrection at 4.45 p.m. of the 29th and, in conjunction with the Comité de Libération, urged the population of Fort-de-France to take to the streets. By 6.00 p.m. over two thousand Foyalais had gathered at the Place Galliéni where they demonstrated against Robert and all that he stood for until 2.00 a.m., by which time the Admiral himself, knowing that the end was near, had taken refuge on board the *Emile-Bertin* which, with ironic appropriateness, was in dry dock at the time. 'Public opinion,' Tourtet wrote in his report, 'did not fail to comment on the humour of such a situation.'[10] During the night many sailors decided to throw in their lot with the insurgents and, with demonstrations continuing in the morning, the end came at 3.00 p.m. on the 30th when Robert signalled his capitulation to the commander of the American fleet. At no time would he accept to negotiate with Tourtet or the Comité de Libération. A few naval officers continued to hold out as best they could until 2 July, but Vichy in the Caribbean was effectively destroyed by the demonstrations of 29–30 June when the black population of Fort-de-France responded *en masse* to the joint call of a white French military commander and a mainly mulatto Comité de Libération to overthrow the by now almost exclusively white Vichyist clique that had ruled them for the past three years.[11] After an uneasy lull of almost a fortnight, the representative of la France Libre, Henri Hoppenot, arrived in Martinique on the destroyer *Le Terrible* on 14 July and, with the resounding words 'Je vous ramène la France et la République,' formally enlisted the island-colony into the Gaullist camp. The same day Governor Nicol was replaced by the Gaullist nominee Ponton and on the 15th Robert and his aides and acolytes were shipped off the island. Vichy's improbable three-year 'reign' in the Caribbean had come to its suitably bathetic and incongruous conclusion.

Thus summarized, the events that led to the liberation of Martinique in June 1943 seem clear enough: an unsurprising instance of civilian and military discontents combining to overthrow a by now wholly discredited authoritarian regime. But, replaced in the general trajectory of Martinican history since 1848, the events of June 1943 – 'nos journées de juin', as one member of the Comité de Libération significantly called them[12] – reveal a number of ambiguities and problems. In the first place, who liberated whom? Was it the Comité de Libération's initiatives that prompted the military into action, or was it the military insurrection that prompted the civilian uprising, or were the two elements so closely interrelated that it becomes impossible, and indeed meaningless, to attempt to separate them? In short, did Martinicans liberate themselves in 1943, or were they liberated by others? The question would be otiose but for the fact that it revives one of the most burning issues in French West Indian historiography: were Martinican slaves liberated by the French republican government's decree of 27 April 1848 or did they liberate themselves by virtue of their revolt of 22 May 1848, which took place before news of the abolition decree had reached the island?[13] Were Martinicans, in 1848 and 1943,[14] truly the protagonists of their own history or were they in both instances merely objects unleashed and directed by others? Was the liberation of Martinique just a further illustration of the alienated, overdetermined character of the island's history as a whole, or did it represent a true assertion of subjectivity on the part of a historically objectified people? Were the *événements* of June 1943 in reality just so many *non-événements*, in the sense understood by the Martinican novelist Edouard Glissant: 'What is an event for us? Something which happened elsewhere, without us, and which nonetheless has repercussions here and in us?'[15] In short, does Martinique have a history, or is that 'history' in reality, as Glissant claims, a 'non-history', merely a by-product or refraction of the history of metropolitan France? My own feeling is that, in 1943 as in 1848, Martinicans were co-producers, alongside progressive metropolitan forces, of their own history, but that without the participation of those forces, neither the Liberation of 1848 nor that of 1943 would have occurred exactly how and when they did, though clearly neither could or would have been much delayed. On the other hand, the historical significance and consequences of the Liberation of 1943 (as of 1848) would be rather different had only Martinicans been involved in each instance.

As we have seen, the essential feature of the Robertist régime by early 1943 was that both its agents and its supporters were overwhelmingly, if not exclusively, *white*. The limited coloured and black support of 1940 and 1941 had almost totally evaporated, and the open alliance between Robert, his officers and men, on the one hand, and the creole whites, on the other, meant that the traditional opposition of 'bad' *békés-pays* and 'good' *békés-France* had collapsed as far as the non-white population of the island was concerned.[16] It is clear that both Robert and Tourtet, from their different viewpoints, feared that opposition to the régime could easily degenerate into a straight confrontation between whites (local and metropolitan alike) and non-whites, and that it was partly to prevent this occurring that Tourtet intervened on 29 June and Robert capitulated during the afternoon of the 30th.[17] Tourtet's intervention permitted the traditional opposition of 'good' and 'bad' whites to be reconstructed in a somewhat different form. It was no longer a question of simply opposing 'good' metropolitans to 'bad' creoles, as it largely had been in the past, but, as the newspaper *Libération* put it on 6 August 1943, of distinguishing 'once and for all the "good Frenchmen" that we have always known here from the "bad Frenchmen" that Vichy had imposed on us'. Thanks to the involvement of Tourtet and his mixed force of white and black troops,[18] the Liberation could be projected not as the overthrow of whites by non-whites but as the crushing of a clique of 'Mauvais Français' by a united force of 'Bons Français' of all colours and origins acting in concert, namely Metropolitans, coloured, black, and even a few white Martinicans (notably the leader of the Comité de Libération, Emmanuel Rimbaud), plus, of course, the Senegalese contingent. Or, as the new governor put it in his address to the Conseil Général in November 1943, in June and July: 'France has triumphed over anti-France.'[19]

By this time, Robert and his associates were being projected not simply as 'Mauvais Français', but as barely French at all. Honorien, for example, speaks derisively of the oddly named Vichyist head of the PTT as 'le mussolinicule Poimiroo',[20] while Tourtet makes much of the fact that the still more unfortunately named Lieutenant Colonel Jung (or Yung) was a holder – or so he claims – of the German Iron Cross.[21] But it was above all the demonization of 'Robert le Diable' – Honorien's phrase – that permitted the reconstruction of the myth of the 'Bon Français' which the experience of 1940–43 had so radically called in question. As depicted by Honorien, Robert is a demonic mixture of slaveowner and Nazi fiend – 'a maniac, a man stupefied by racism whom the merest shadow of a person of colour plunged into the darkest thoughts', a sadist as intent on 'the annihilation of the black population of the Caribbean Sea' as his master Hitler was on the destruction of the Jews: 'Hitler instigated the mass annihilation of Jews by gunfire, poison gas, famine and disease. The Haut-Commissaire of Vichy, less *kolossal* but just as diabolic, resolved to put an end to the niggers [*la négraille*] of the islands by the least costly of these scourges: famine.'[22] In this perspective, the expulsion from Martinique of the principal Vichyists on 15 July 1943 conforms to a classic scapegoating scenario whereby a double catharsis was achieved. On the one hand, many coloured and black Martinicans must have felt guilt either at having supported Robert in 1940–41 (or, in a few cases, even later) or at having failed actively to oppose him and his regime until the very last. One such person was honest enough to write, without concealing his identity, to *Libération* in August 1943 and confess his shame at having lent Robert, that 'false democrat, deeply imbued with the principles of a slave-owner', his 'collaboration as the grandson of liberated slaves'.[23] There must have been many such who, less candid than he, were able to project 'the horrible fault' they subliminally felt onto the departing diabolized figures of Robert, Bayle, Poimiroo, Jung, Roques, Constantin and the rest. On the other hand, the pre-War image of a pure and benevolent *mère-patrie* was successfully reconstructed through the ritual banishment of a band of 'Mauvais' or even 'Non-Français'. Any ambivalences that may have arisen since June 1940 in the local perception of France and the French were forthwith resolved: the *mère-patrie* may have been momentarily sullied, but in herself she was virtue and generosity incarnate.

The Liberation, then, plays a significant part in what I call the 'family romance' of Martinican history.[24] According to Frantz Fanon, the defeat of 1940 was nothing less than a 'murder of the father' for Martinicans whose whole history and upbringing had conditioned them to identify with *la mère-patrie* and to look to it for succour and protection against the perceived threat of the local whites.[25] For a brief period, Robert and, beyond him, Pétain had functioned as a surrogate white father (or, in the case of Pétain, grandfather) for some non-white Martinicans,[26] but by 1943, Robert, his associates and the creole whites who supported them had coagulated into a single, overwhelmingly negative image: they were *mauvais blancs*, pure and simple. In June 1943, coloured and black Martinicans joined forces with a group of 'bons Français' to overthrow a negative white father-figure, Robert, but only to replace him with a new, and still more potent, paternal image, a white superego of quite prodigious charismatic force – Charles de Gaulle.[27] On 14 July 1943, de Gaulle sent a personal telegram to the people of Martinique and Guadeloupe assuring them of 'l'amour de la Mère-Patrie pour les Antilles Françaises,'[28] and, during the weeks that followed, he (and, to a lesser extent, Tourtet, Hoppenot and even General Giraud) was projected, by Metropolitan and Martinican speakers alike, as little less than the saviour of the Martinican people, and even of the black race as a whole, a Messiah-figure fit to be placed alongside the supreme incarnation of the 'Bon Blanc' in the French West Indian psyche – Victor Schoelcher, the benevolent, paternal 'liberator' of the slaves in 1848 and, since that time, the object of a veritable cult in the French West Indies to which the name 'Schoelchérisme' has been given.[29]

The continuity between 1848 and 1943 is a leitmotiv of post-Liberation discourse in Martinique, whether the speaker be Martinican or Metropolitan, white, coloured or black. Thus Emmanuel Véry, coloured member of the Comité de Libération and Vice-President of the new Conseil Général, on the occasion of that body's inaugural session stated:

> On 14 July Henri Hoppenot came to deliver us from the yoke of the men of Vichy in Hitler's train. He represents for us the France that made the Revolution of 1789, the France which drew up in the face of humanity the immortal principles of the Rights of Man, the generous France of 1848, the France which, after the reverses of 1940, faithful to its past and its traditions, resumed the conflict alongside the Allies, the France, in short, that we shall never be able to separate from the Republic, for we cannot forget that it is the Republic which made of us men and citizens.[30]

For his part, Governor Ponton, speaking on the occasion of the annual commemoration of Victor Schoelcher just a week after the formal *ralliement* of Martinique to la France Combattante, insisted on the direct line that ran from Schoelcher, via Clemenceau, to de Gaulle and Giraud: 'It is the only way by which you, French men and women of the West Indies, united with the other provinces and territories of the Empire, will have the great honour of returning to our Motherland, by delivering her from the Boche, what she gave to you almost a century ago – Freedom.'[31]

'Français et Françaises des Antilles ....' It is, finally, this insistence on the *Frenchness* of Martinique and its inhabitants that provides the unifying theme of the discourse of Liberation in Martinique. Before the war, and before Robert, it had been primarily Martinicans themselves who had insisted on their integral Frenchness, whereas Metropolitan France, for diverse and complex reasons, had always placed obstacles in the way of the islanders' desire for complete assimilation into *la mère-patrie*. Now, in 1943, with Robert gone, and with fears of American designs in the Caribbean at large, *petite patrie* and *mère-patrie* spoke the same language of identity. Martinique and Guadeloupe, asserted Henri Hoppenot in September, are 'not possessions or colonies of France, but fragments of its territory that are as inseparable from it as if they were located at the centre of the garden of France.'[32] It followed that the insurrection of June 1943 had been made not by an alliance of *Martiniquais* and *bons Français*, but of *bons Français tout court*. Birthplace and colour were seen as irrelevant: all were French in essence and spirit. The non- or trans-racial ideology of French assimilation had triumphed yet again. The way to complete assimilation of the *vieilles colonies* as overseas departments of France in 1946 now lay open.

Notes

Unless stated otherwise, the place of publication is Paris.

1. Quoted in Camille Chauvet, 'La Martinique au temps de l'Amiral Robert (1939-1944)', *Historial antillais*, Société Dajani: Pointe-à-Pitre, vol.5, n.d., p.424. This study (hereafter referred to as HA) is the best overall survey of Vichy in the Caribbean.
2. On Vichyist ideology in Martinique, see Richard D.E. Burton, 'Vichyisme et Vichyistes à la Martinique', *Les Cahiers du Centre d'Etudes Régionales Antilles-Guyane*, no.34, February 1978, pp.1–101.
3. Frantz Fanon, *Pour la révolution africaine*, Maspéro, 1964, p.32.
4. Admiral Georges Robert, *La France aux Antilles de 1939 à 1943*, Plon, 1950, p.28. According to Claude Lévi-Strauss, who passed through Martinique in 1941, many Martinicans believed that 'Hitler n'était autre que Jésus-Christ redescendu sur terre pour punir la race blanche d'avoir, pendant les deux milles ans qui précèdent, mal suivi ses enseignements' (*Tristes Tropiques*, Plon, 1955, p.15).
5. *Le Clairon*, 31 August 1943.
6. Eugène Honorien speaks of the semi-public lampooning of 'le Commandant pro-boche et négrophobe Delpech', 'le *Von Muller* des gamins de Fort-de-France' and of Governor 'Coco' Nicol, 'l'homme le plus niais que les lambris du Palais de Gouvernement à Fort'de-France aient jamais abrité' ; 'Coco' means 'cock' in creole. See Eugène Honorien, *Le Ralliement des Antilles à la "France Combattante" (Juin–Juillet 1943)*, T.I.: *la Martinique*, Imprimerie Officielle, Fort-de-France, 1945, pp.71 and 61.
7. The following account is based primarily on Commandant Henri Tourtet's own official report (reproduced in Honorien, *Le Ralliement des Antilles*, pp.8–18), supplemented by Chauvet's account in HA, pp.462–4, and by the relevant pages of Alice Delpech's well-informed documentary novel *La Dissidence* (L'Harmattan, 1991, pp.194–215).
8. Honorien, *Le Ralliement des Antilles*, p.62.
9. Ibid., p.12.
10. Ibid. A distinct carnivalesque element was present in the demonstrations of 29–30 June, and is well brought out in Alice

Delpech's account in *La Dissidence* (pp.206–7).

11. The increasingly racial character of the 'divorce' between the régime and the local population is stressed in a telling editorial in *Le Sportif* on 10 July 1943: 'Le peuple a vu se creuser chaque jour davantage le fossé entre les métropolitains et l'élément de couleur.'

12. 'La Révolution a grondé et nous avons eu nos journées de juin' (Emmanuel Véry, Vice-President of the post-Liberation Conseil Général speaking on the occasion of the Conseil's opening session, cited in *Libération*, no.61, 6 August 1943).

13. The literature on this issue is considerable, and is magisterially reviewed by Edouard de Lépine in his *Questions sur l'histoire antillaise*, Fort-de-France, Editions Emile Désormeaux, 1978.

14. Parallels between the two liberations were commonly drawn in 1943. One writer even says of the members of the Comité de Libération: 'Ils étaient onze comme ceux du Governement provisoire [of 1848]', Ludger Xavier, 'Les Journées', *Libération*, no.7, 3 August 1943.

15. Edouard Glissant, *Le Discours antillais*, Editions du Seuil, 1981, p.100. For a discussion of this view of Martinican history, see Richard D.E. Burton, 'Comment peut-on être Martiniquais ? The Recent Work of Edouard Glissant', *Modern Language Review*, vol.79, no.2, 1984, pp.301–12.

16. Not all *békés* backed the Vichy régime: the de Reynal de Saint-Michel family was noted for its opposition to Robert and one of its members had been interned for six months for having painted a red, white and blue 'V' on his car (HA, p.460).

17. On learning of Tourtet's intervention, Robert telegraphed his superiors in France as follows: 'Je crois de mon devoir d'éviter l'effusion imminente du sang entre Français et surtout entre Armée et Marine. Au point de surexcitation où sont les esprits, les déchaînements raciaux menacent déjà d'accompagner de pareils événements' (Robert, *La France aux Antilles*, p.181). For his part, Tourtet claims, probably correctly, that the sailors had been told by their officers that 'il s'agissait d'un mouvement de Noirs contre Blancs' (Honorien, *Le Ralliement des Antilles*, p.16).

18. There remains some uncertainty, to repeat, about the racial composition of Tourtet's forces. Robert (*La France aux Antilles*, p.170) claims that they consisted 'pour les trois quarts d'indigènes se trouvant quotidiennement au contact de la population et aussi sensibles qu'elle aux excitations du moment'. It is unclear whether by 'indigènes' he means Martinicans or Senegalese, or both. What is clear, however, is that the critical 3ᵉ Compagnie was composed

preponderantly of white professional soldiers (Honorien, *Le Ralliement des Antilles*, p.9). Needless to say, the principal officers involved in the insurrection (Renvoisé, Savary, Franco, Laine) were all whites.

19. *Journal Officiel de la Martinique*, no.47, 11 November 1943, p.451.
20. Honorien, *Le Ralliement des Antilles*, p.71.
21. Ibid., p.13.
22. Ibid., pp.36–50 *passim*.
23. Félix Jouanelle in *Libération*, no.16, 13 August 1943.
24. Richard D.E. Burton, *La Famille coloniale. La Martinique et la Mère-Patrie 1789–1992*, L'Harmattan, 1994.
25. Fanon, *Pour la révolution africaine*, pp.31–2.
26. On the 'cult' of Robert and Pétain in Martinique, see Burton, 'Vichyisme et Vichyistes', pp.43–7.
27. For the image of De Gaulle in Martinique, see Burton, *La Famille coloniale,* pp.171–6.
28. *Journal Officiel de la Martinique*, no.29, 17 July 1943, p.270.
29. On the cult of Victor Schoelcher in Martinique, see Richard D.E. Burton, 'Trois statues: le Conquistador, l'Impératrice et le Libérateur. Pour une sémiotique de l'histoire coloniale de la Martinique', *Carbet*, no.11, 1991, pp.147–64.
30. *Libération*, no.6, 2 August 1943.
31. *Journal Officiel de la Martinique*, no.30, 22 July 1943, p.274.
32. *Journal Officiel de la Martinique*, no.38, 11 September 1943, p.353. 'Abordez à Fort-de-France ou à Pointe-à-Pitre,' he continued, 'et vous verrez dans chaque ville et dans chaque village autour des clochers comme autour des humbles mairies où flotte un pauvre drapeau délavé aussi bien que vous le verriez sur les bords de la Seine et du Rhône ce qu'est pour nous cette profonde réalité spirituelle de la France et cette fraternité essentielle de tous les Français.' See also his speech on 14 July, *Journal Officiel*, no.29, 17 July 1943, pp.269–70.

– 16 –

African Perspectives: the Liberation of France and its Impact in French West Africa

Tony Chafer

Given the key role played by France's empire in black Africa in lending credibility and legitimacy to de Gaulle's claim, in the crucial early years of the war, to be the authentic representative of a France still free, it is surprising how little attention has been paid to the way the Liberation was experienced in French black Africa. In focussing on the Liberation in Afrique Occidentale Française (AOF),[1] this chapter aims both to reorientate perspectives on the Liberation and offer a different angle on the concept of 'liberation'.

Clearly, the context in which 'liberation' took place in AOF was very different from metropolitan France: there were no Germans and no fighting in AOF and for much of the period from 1940–44 the colony was largely cut off from events in Europe. Although events in France were followed as closely as possible, particularly by the French population of AOF, for most people the Liberation was a 'secondhand' experience (the only exception to this was the small minority of the population who took part in the Liberation campaigns in Europe or North Africa). Since they did not experience it directly, the question therefore arises: how was the period of the Liberation actually experienced in AOF? What did it mean from the perspective of AOF? First of all, chronology is important here. With French black Africa largely cut off from the *métropole* for much of the war, the key events that marked and structured life in the *métropole* and life in the empire were different. So what were the key events in terms of the 'liberation' of France's African empire, and how were they experienced there? Is an alternative chronology needed when studying the Liberation period in AOF? Secondly, the concept of liberation itself needs to be examined. Who was to be liberated? And where was 'liberation' expected to come from? This depended partly, of course, on whether you were French or African, although it is notable that Africans did not at this time apparently see the Liberation of France as an opportunity to press for their own liberation from foreign occupation and control, whereas such a demand was articulated in both Indo-China and Algeria. Colonial reform was certainly demanded, but the severing of links with France and political independence were not yet .on the agenda of African political leaders and groups.

An alternative chronology

Both AOF and France's other colony in sub-Saharan Africa, the federation of Afrique Equatoriale Française (AEF) were cut off from the *métropole* for most of the war. Whereas AEF under Governor-General Félix Eboué declared for de Gaulle by the end of July 1940, AOF under Governor-General Boisson declared for Vichy. It was only on 23 November 1942, after the Allied landings in North Africa, that Boisson decided to rally to Darlan in Algiers, mainly because the French army in AOF had no stomach to fight the Americans.[2] However, the decision to rally AOF to the North African *bloc* was not seen as a decision to rally to de Gaulle, but was presented by Boisson as reflecting continuing loyalty to the real spirit of Vichy and thus in keeping with his original decision in 1940,[3] which he had justified by the need to keep the empire together, to keep foreign troops out of AOF and to maintain continuity of administration. Overall, the change from Vichy to Algiers was presented as a change in AOF external policy which, it was implied, had no significance for internal policy.[4] But no words, however carefully chosen, could hide the significance of what had taken place: AOF had changed allegiance and the whole of France's African empire was now on the side of the Allies and, in effect, economically and militarily dependent on them.[5] It was also cut off from France: even postal links with the *métropole* were cut, only to be restored towards the end of 1943.

Boisson was replaced as Governor-General by the Gaullist Pierre Cournarie in July 1943 and wide-ranging colonial reforms were recommended by the Brazzaville Conference in January–February 1944. This meeting of colonial officials and representatives of the Provisional Government was held against the background of growing concern about American plans for the French colonial empire after the war. The Atlantic Charter of 1941 had declared the right of all peoples to choose their own government and the idea had been circulating in American government circles that the colonies should be removed from imperial control and placed under international trusteeship once the war had ended. In response to this, and to show that France intended both to retain its colonies and reform its colonial system after the War, the Brazzaville Conference was organized.[6] Proposals were put forward for the election of representatives of France's African empire to the National Assembly in Paris, an increase in African participation in the colonial administration and in internal policy-making, putting an end to forced labour, abolishing the native administrative code, the *indigénat*, improving education and health provision, and drawing up a plan for the economic development of France's African empire.[7]

Within AOF however, the emphasis was on continuity even after the Governor-General had been changed and the Brazzaville Conference had taken place. There were sound and, from the French point of view, understandable reasons for this. A joint Anglo-French force, which included de Gaulle, had attempted to land at Dakar on 23–25 September 1940 and had been repulsed by French forces based there. For the following two years, Vichy propaganda in AOF had presented the British as enemies and de Gaulle as a traitor, yet three years after the abortive attack on Dakar, on a flying visit to Dakar in January 1944 on his way to the Brazzaville Conference, de Gaulle was welcomed in Dakar as a hero. Against this background, it is hardly surprising that some Africans were said to be confused as to who was the enemy.[8] More seriously from the French point of view, the colonial administration knew that, as a result of France's defeat and the Occupation in 1940, the image of French superiority had been undermined and French authority seriously weakened. It was therefore important to create an aura of continuity and stability, which meant playing down the significance of the Brazzaville Conference within AOF. Thus, according to Cournarie in his address to the December 1944 meeting of the Conseil de Gouvernement, the aim of the conference had not been to: 'invent a new philosophy, but to extract from the experience and generous traditions of the French Republic general principles applicable to the African *bloc* and capable of overseeing the evolution of very diverse countries towards a harmonious and solid federation'.[9] Furthermore, changes of personnel were limited to the top of the colonial hierarchy, and even here changes were not necessarily immediate: the governors of Côte d'Ivoire and Dahomey were changed in August 1943 and those of Dakar and Senegal later that year; the Governor of Guinea, who gained a certain notoriety as a result of his decision to take security measures against Gaullists in his colony in November 1942, nevertheless remained in post until March 1944; and the governors of the other territories of AOF were not changed until after the War.[10] Further down the colonial hierarchy there were very few changes of personnel, mainly because of the shortage of staff to replace them.

This emphasis on continuity was maintained throughout 1943–44 and into the early part of 1945. Even the restoration of republican institutions in March 1943 did not necessarily mean substantive change. After all, the colonies had, under the Third Republic, been subject to an authoritarian regime under which, apart from the Four Communes of Senegal where the *originaires*[11] had since 1848 elected a deputy to the National Assembly in Paris, African subjects did not enjoy political rights. It cannot therefore really be said that there were any republican liberties to 'restore'. Admittedly, the *indigénat* was applied less rigorously after 1942 than under Vichy and the right to form trade unions had been introduced in AOF in 1944, but as far as possible the impression was created of 'business as usual'. There was also no real pressure for internal reform from the Provisional Government in Algiers and the approach of the colonial authorities within AOF to reform remained timid.

A number of factors combined to change this state of affairs in 1945. First of all, there was the massacre of thirty-five African ex-POWs at the Tiaroye barracks near Dakar in December 1944. On their return from Germany, they had been rounded up in camps in France and sent to Dakar, where they awaited repatriation to their territory of origin. They were entitled to various payments and arrears of salary, which still had not been paid by the time they reached Tiaroye. Concerned that the money would not be paid at all and that, once split up and back home, they would be in a weaker position to press home their rights, they organized protests, one of which, on 1 December 1944, seems to have sown panic among the soldiers guarding them, with the result that they opened fire, killing thirty-five and seriously wounding a further thirty-five. The colonial authorities in Dakar presented this as a mutiny,[12] which seems to have been successful in defusing any immediate African political reaction to the massacre, although it sent shock waves through the office of the Governor-General who cabled Paris that the use of force 'could not be permitted to be repeated, under any pretext whatsoever'.[13] The consequence of Tiaroye was 'to delegitimize naked force as a political instrument'[14] in AOF.

When news of the massacre reached the Provisional Government, now reinstalled in Paris, it was already beginning to worry more generally about the future of France's colonial empire unless the pace of reform was accelerated. Pressure for the government to clarify its colonial policy came from delegates to the Constituent Assembly in March[15] and news of events in both Indo-China and Algeria in the first half of 1945 further increased government fears about losing control of the situations now developing in the colonies. Lamine Gueye's reported comment at a meeting of 3,000 people in Dakar in May 1945, that the Senegalese were 'ready to do anything to have their freedom',[16] doubtless further fuelled these worries. At the same time, pressure was growing within the Colonial Ministry for the government to take a more proactive role with respect to colonial reform. In June 1945, Henri Laurentie, its Director of Political Affairs, drafted a memorandum for the Minister which he started with the words 'We are in the middle of a colonial crisis' and continued:

> Feelings of disappointment, disaffection, distrust and hate are manifest on so many points as to create a dangerous whole. There is little to counteract this: the apathy of the masses cannot counteract the nationalism that is being born or taking shape everywhere...
>
> The new system... will provide renewed hope, [and] at the same time will give the government the authority without which the mismatch between the promises that were loyally received and the necessities of everyday life would culminate in anarchy and eviction.[17]

Minister Giacobbi clearly took the warnings seriously, since he issued a circular on the eve of the Constituent Assembly elections informing colonial officials that the conditions in which they exercised their authority had 'entirely changed' since 1939: 'The truth is that colonialism is condemned and that certain forms of colonization at least are outdated.' He went on to explain that indigenous populations demanded, and expected, new freedoms and equal treatment with Europeans and that, if France did not respond, then they would look elsewhere and the very future of France's empire was at stake 'since these people are subject to the attractions of American wealth, or Soviet ideology, or the illusions of Pan-Africanism, or more probably all of these at once, which promise them a better and freer life, in any case *something else* [my italic].'[18]

A number of new appointments were made in 1946 which kept up the momentum for reform: Marius Moutet took over as Minister for Overseas France, as the Colonial Ministry was now called, in January; the left-wing Gaullist, André Latrille, was reappointed Governor of Côte d'Ivoire in March; Cournarie was replaced as Governor-General by the more progressive Barthes in July; and Jean Capelle, who came from outside the colonial establishment and was rector of an *académie*[19] in metropolitan France, was seconded to head the education service in AOF from 1 January 1947. Also, all forms of forced or obligatory labour were outlawed on 11 April and the distinction between subjects and citizens was abolished on 7 May, although this did not mean that Africans immediately acquired the same rights as citizens of metropolitan France.[20]

We can therefore see that the rhythm of political developments in France and AOF from 1943–45 diverged. This is not surprising, since the pattern of events to which they were responding was different. In metropolitan France in 1943–44, the primary concern was liberation from German control. Within the Conseil National de la Résistance (CNR) and the Comité Français de la Libération Nationale (CFLN), the political emphasis was on breaking with the past and the need for far-reaching economic, political and social reform. In 1945–46, however, France's political leaders, now reinstalled in Paris, increasingly stressed the need for reconciliation and consolidation, and by the time the new Constitution was adopted in October 1946 widespread political disillusionment had set in. In AOF on the other hand, the period from 1943–44 was characterized by an attempt to maintain an aura of continuity and stability. It was only when the government in Paris began to fear losing control of the situation in the Empire that this changed. From 1945–46, the pace of reform thus accelerated dramatically and some of the most unpopular colonial practices, such as forced labour and the *indigénat*, were abolished. The Brazzaville Conference, the significance of which had been played down by the colonial authorities in 1944, now became an important point of reference, a benchmark for both Africans and French colonial reformers by which the government's commitment to reform was henceforth to be measured.

Concepts of Liberation

Returning African soldiers remained for the most part loyal to France,[21] despite the fact that many of them had every reason to feel resentment about the way they had been treated. Having fought in the battles for the Liberation of France, they had then been rounded up in camps in France in preparation for their repatriation to Africa and, as a result of the process of 'whitening' of the French army in 1944–45,[22] had been denied the opportunity to take part in the victory marches and celebrations. Many had had to fight hard to obtain their pay at the end of the war or had not been granted their full pensions, culminating for some, as we have seen, in the tragedy of Tiaroye. Nevertheless, having had the idea of white superiority inculcated into them since childhood, many African soldiers were impressed by the fact that, during the War, they fought as equals alongside the white man. Many also came into contact for the first time with 'another France', that is to say with French people who were not colonialists or racists, who were committed to the cause of freedom and believed in the possibility of a 'new deal' for Africans once the War was over. Combine this with the effect of military discipline and it is not so difficult to see why most African soldiers, while demanding colonial reform, nevertheless remained loyal to France after their return to Africa.

It was not only African *soldiers* who remained loyal to France. No popular movement for liberation from French control emerged in AOF after the war, and the 'modern' elite of African *évolués*,[23] who now emerged as the political representatives of the population of AOF, also continued to declare their allegiance to France. Africans, it seems, joined in the events organised in AOF to celebrate the Liberation of France from German occupation, but remarkably few used the weakening of the French position during the War as an opportunity to press for their own liberation from foreign, that is French, domination.

In this context it must be remembered that, after sixty years of French colonial rule, most Africans had never known anything else. The French were not perceived as an occupying force in AOF in quite the same way as the Germans were in France. Furthermore, if the 'new' France of the Liberation was a force for civilization and progress, and if de Gaulle really was the great liberator,[24] as his actions since 1940 and his visit to AOF in January 1944 seemed to suggest, then it was reasonable for Africans to expect that progress and freedom would come not through secession from France but through maintaining close links with it.

The studied ambiguity of de Gaulle's public pronouncements on colonial matters is worthy of note here. Whereas he openly celebrated the Liberation of France, in the colonial context he eschewed the word 'liberation', which had more actively political connotations and could have been taken to suggest that freedom might be won through winning liberation *from* France, and referred instead to the 'union' and 'cohesion' achieved during the war between the *métropole* and the colonies in their common struggle for liberty.[25] This can be seen as a calculated appeal to the new political leaders of Africa to envisage their future as being with France rather than separate from it, and it is not difficult to appreciate why such an appeal was attractive to many of them. Like the rest of the 'modern' elite of African *évolués*, they had received a French education, they had cultural and emotional ties to France and they were also well aware of the state of dependency of AOF on France, both because of its economic underdevelopment and the acute dearth of French-educated Africans. Against this background, it is not so surprising that they chose to seek a new deal for Africans within the context of maintaining continued links with France, rather than secession. The petition presented to de Gaulle in Algiers in early 1944 by Lamine Gueye on behalf of the people of AOF exemplifies the belief among African *évolués* in a 'new France', committed to the cause of freedom:

> It is unfortunately a fact that some French people have... since 1940 introduced a racist policy into this country...
>
> We believe that we are carrying out a pressing duty and acting as good Frenchmen by protesting against criminal plans, by asking the CFLN to put an end without delay to the acts that are the product of these plans... and to remedy the situation to which we have drawn their attention...
>
> May we... return to Senegal with outcomes and assurances that confirm to... all the peoples of AOF that they were right to remain loyal to France and to keep faith with her.[26]

In this text, republican France, the France of the Liberation, represents a tribune, a kind of court of appeal, to which French-educated Africans could appeal over the heads of French colonialists in AOF, who were seen as having betrayed the 'true' France of liberty, equality, justice and fraternity. This theme, of a 'new' French colonialism as a force for progress, was taken up by the new African political leaders of Senegal, Lamine Gueye and Léopold Senghor, in their manifesto for the 1945 Constituent Assembly elections: 'Children of Senegal, totally devoted to the destiny of these ancient French lands, our only ambition is to serve, as effectively as possible, within the framework of a Republic which gives a little reality to the fine slogan "Liberté, Egalité, Fraternité". Long live France! Long live Socialist Africa! Long live the Republic.'[27]

The political discourse of the French left, both Communist and Socialist, played a key role here. Neither supported African nationalism after the War, and the SFIO in particular promoted closer integration between France and its empire. In its pronouncements, French colonialism was seen, in the true republican tradition, as progressive and civilizing, a force for economic, social and political progress, and the 'civilizing mission' reemerged as a key aim of, and justification for, empire.[28] This idea was also taken up in 1945 by the Director of Political Affairs at the Colonial Ministry, Henri Laurentie, when he suggested that the choice for colonial peoples at that time was between on the one hand, an illusory independence that would lead to tyranny and on the other, real freedom that, by implication, would be achieved through continued association with France: 'We are resolved that the *liberation* of colonial peoples should not become a *tyranny*, the only merit of which would be that it is modern.'[29] The aim of French colonialism, according to the newly-appointed Minister for Colonies, Paul Giacobbi, was thus to: 'lead our overseas peoples, without conflict... from dependency to liberty *within the Union Française* [my italic]'.[30]

It was not only government spokesmen who preferred to use the word 'liberty' rather than 'liberation' to describe their aspirations for colonial peoples, but also African political leaders and the main political parties in AOF who, after 1945, largely avoided the term 'liberation' and preferred instead to use the word 'emancipation'. Whereas the former implied the act of people freeing themselves from external domination or occupation, the latter was associated with the struggle for equal rights[31] and suggested a process of people being freed from those political, economic and social constraints that prevent them from realising their potential.

This emerged clearly in the manifesto of the main political party in AOF, the Rassemblement Démocratique Africain (RDA), which was founded at Bamako in October 1946. The party's aims were expressed as follows: 'equal political and social rights; individual and cultural liberties; local democratic assemblies; a union of the peoples of Africa and France based on consent'; and the manifesto went on to explain that: 'Our membership of the Union Française... is justified... by the certainty that... we shall obtain the liberal, democratic and human conditions which will allow the free development of the original potentialities of the African genius.'[32]

It was against this background that the decolonization of education became a major campaigning issue, not only for the RDA but for all the new political leaders of AOF after the War: 'It is through education that we shall be able to emancipate ourselves.'[33] Until the War, the only education offered to all but the tiny minority of Africans who had alternative sources of financial support was narrowly vocational in nature. Even this was restricted to less than 5 per cent of the African population and the curriculum in most schools was a diluted version of that taught in the *métropole*. Furthermore, the two secondary schools in AOF were effectively closed to Africans and there was no higher education. The expansion and development of educational opportunities in AOF thus came to be seen by the new political leaders of AOF as the key to African emancipation since, without it, the process of development would be held back and Africans would not achieve their full potential as individuals.

In sum, apart from the brief period following the rejection of the first draft of the constitution in the referendum of May 1946, when some of them appear briefly to have flirted with the idea of independence,[34] African political leaders after the War did not want to secede from France. On the contrary, they saw their future development as taking place within the context of the Union Française, into which they wished to be more fully integrated as equal partners.[35] Lamine Gueye's article, published in October 1945 on the front page of *L'AOF* under the title 'Libération', was doubtless written in a flush of enthusiasm after the Liberation of France. It was not, however, a word that was subsequently to be very much used by the political leaders of AOF.

Conclusion

As in the *métropole*, the Liberation marked a turning-point in the political evolution of AOF. However, with the colony cut off from the *métropole* for much of this time, the key events that determined the rhythm of political developments – the Allied landings in North Africa, the Brazzaville Conference, the Tiaroye massacre – were not the same, and did not have the same significance, as in the *métropole*. The emphasis on continuity from 1942–44 gave way to a realization that change was unavoidable if France was to maintain the loyalty of its colonial population. The reforms that were introduced from 1945–46 were successful in defusing nationalist aspirations, at least for the time being, but the pace of change remained hesitant and they were ultimately to prove insufficient to satisfy African demands.

Within AOF, the transition from Vichy to the Free French had been made reasonably smoothly, but once the Liberation of France was complete and the initial euphoria at the liberation of the *métropole* from foreign domination had passed, the French population in AOF viewed the future with increasing apprehension. They were well aware of the weakening of France's position in AOF as a result of the War, and the colonial reforms introduced in the immediate aftermath of the Liberation left them feeling, politically, on the defensive and unsure about the future.

For Africans, however, the period 1943–45 marked the definitive end of the old system of French colonial rule through chiefs and traditional authorities. The function of representing the views and political aspirations of the population transferred to the 'modern' elite of African *évolués*, from among whom the new political leaders of AOF now emerged. Western-educated Africans, who grew rapidly in both number and political effectiveness after the war, were determined to take advantage of the display of French weakness during the War to press home their demands for change. They were not, however, secessionists and initially sought to attain their goal of African emancipation through the achievement of equal rights with Europeans within the context of the Union Française, as the French empire was now to be called. Thus, African liberation was to be achieved through closer integration *into* France, and not through liberation *from* it. But as the pace of political, economic and social progress in AOF increasingly fell short of African expectations, French-educated Africans began to turn in increasing numbers to new political horizons. This would initially take the form of a demand for autonomy within the context of the Union Française, but would lead within a few years to the demand for independence.

Notes

Unless stated otherwise, the place of publication is Paris.

1. AOF covered the modern African states of Mauritania, Senegal, Guinea, Côte d'Ivoire, Mali, Niger, Burkina Faso and Benin.
2. Document dated 18 November 1942, Archives Nationales, Section Outre-Mer, Aix-en-Provence (hereafter ANSOM) Aff.Pol. 895/4.
3. ANSOM Aff. Pol. 872/13.
4. D. Bouche, 'Le retour de l'AOF dans la lutte contre l'ennemi aux côtés des Alliés', *Revue d'Histoire de la 2ᵉ Guerre Mondiale*, no.114, 1979, p.41.
5. M. Michel, *Décolonisations et émergence du tiers-monde*, Hachette, 1993, p.73.
6. Cf. C. Levy, 'Les origines de la Conférence de Brazzaville, le contexte et la décision', in Institut Charles de Gaulle/Institut d'Histoire du Temps Présent, *Brazzaville. Janvier–Février 1944*, Plon, 1988, p.28.
7. See H. Michel and B. Guetzevitch (eds), *Les Idées politiques et sociales de la Résistance*, Presses Universitaires de France, 1954, pp.339–57.
8. Document dated 24 November 1942, Archives de l'Afrique Occidentale Française, Dakar (hereafter AAOF) 13G/15.
9. AOF, *Conseil de Gouvernement*, December 1944, p.9, ANSOM 50480.
10. D. Bouche, 'Le retour de l'AOF', p.49.
11. The term '*originaires*' refers to non-Europeans born in the first

French settlements in Senegal: Saint-Louis, Dakar, Gorée and Rufisque.

12. Report from Governor-General of AOF to Minister of Colonies, marked 'Secret' and dated 17 January 1945, AAOF 17G132/17.
13. Quoted in M. Echenburg, 'Tragedy at Tiaroye: the Senegalese soldiers' uprising of 1944', in P.W. Gutkind *et al.* (eds), *African Labour History*, vol.2, London, Sage, 1978, p.120.
14. Ibid.
15. *Journal Officiel* (hereafter *JO*), débats de l'Assemblée Consultative, 19 and 20 March 1945, pp.556–74, 579–96.
16. Report from Governor-General of AOF to Minister of Colonies, marked 'Secret' and dated 22 May 1945, AAOF 17G127/17.
17. Document dated 20–21 June 1945, Archives Nationales, Paris (hereafter AN) 72AJ/535.
18. Document dated 20 October 1945, ANSOM Aff. Pol. 2167/1.
19. In France, a rector is both head of a university and director of education in the region.
20. For example, suffrage remained restricted to selected categories of Africans, mainly those with a French education, until 1956.
21. The first independence movement in AOF, the Mouvement Nationaliste Africain, was created by African soldiers after the War. It published a monthly newspaper, *La Communauté*, 'Organ for the defence of the interests of former colonial career soldiers, war widows and orphans, and for the defence of the political, economic and social interests of AOF.' However, it had no mass following and seems to have disappeared at the end of 1947.
22. Cf. A. Clayton, *France, Soldiers and Africa*, London, Brasseys, 1988, pp.141–9.
23. Under French colonial rule two separate elites, one traditional and the other 'modern' (i.e. French-educated), coexisted in AOF. Before the War, the French had used chiefs and traditional authorities as their intermediaries, but the political changes introduced at the end of the War meant that the 'modern' elite of African *évolués*, as they were called, now emerged as the spokesmen for the African population of AOF.
24. The extent to which de Gaulle was regarded by many Africans as a 'messiah' and a 'liberator' cannot be overemphasized. Cf. report dated 9 April 1945 by Papa Gueye Fall, a captain in the Colonial Infantry, to the Governor-General of AOF, in which de Gaulle is seen as a 'liberating messiah', AAOF 17G127/17; and the scene in F. Oyono's novel *Le Vieux nègre et la médaille*, Julliard, 1956, p.68, in which we are told that, after the war, portraits of de Gaulle were displayed in every household and

many African children, both boys and girls, were named after him!

25. Cf. *JO*, débats de l'Assemblée Consultative, 20 March 1945, p.596; C. De Gaulle, *Discours et messages*, vol.1, Plon, 1946, pp.364, 375.
26. The full text of the petition is in ANSOM Aff. Pol. 2098/7.
27. Published in *L'AOF*, 5 October 1945, p.1. Also in AAOF 17G419/126.
28. See, for example, the contributions of Socialists and Communists to the debate on the colonial budget, *JO*, débats de l'Assemblée Consultative, 20 and 21 March 1945, pp.556–74, 579–96. See also articles published in the review *Renaissances*, 1943–45, *passim*, and Moutet's preface to L. Mérat, *Fictions et réalités coloniales*, Librairie du Recueil, 1947.
29. H. Laurentie, 'Les colonies françaises devant le monde nouveau', *Renaissances*, October 1945, p.12.
30. ANSOM Aff. Pol. 2167/1.
31. Cf. interview with Doudou Gueye, broadcast on Radio France Internationale on 11 April 1979, published as 'L'Itinéraire intellectuel et politique d'un militant du RDA: Doudou Gueye', Radio France Internationale, 1986, p.14.
32. In J. Dalloz, *Textes sur la décolonisation*, Presses Universitaires de France, 1989, p.35. At the meeting of its coordinating committee in Dakar in October 1948, the RDA unanimously reaffirmed its objective as the 'struggle for political, economic and social emancipation *within the framework of the Union Française, based on equal rights and duties* [emphasis in the original]'. Cf. also P. Kipré, *Le Congrès de Bamako*, Editions Chaka, 1989, pp.136–9.
33. *Le Démocrate*, no.202, 6 November 1950, p.1. As an RDA paper, it took a leading role in the campaign for better education in Côte d'Ivoire.
34. Even the indefatigable advocate of close links with France, Senghor, used the word 'independence' in public at this time: Léopold S. Senghor, 'We no longer wish to be subjects, nor to undergo a régime of occupation', *Gavroche*, 8 August 1946, p.7.
35. This situation contrasts with that in Algeria, see chapter 17 in this volume by Martin Evans, pp.255–67.

– 17 –

Algeria and the Liberation: Hope and Betrayal

Martin Evans

In September 1958 Ferhat Abbas became the first president of the Algerian Provisional Government which was located in Tunis. Writing in 1962, at the end of the Algerian war, he wished to underline that the expectations he had invested in the French Resistance of 1940–44 were very real. At the time, the impending Liberation was a beacon of hope. He was convinced that the Occupation had transformed France in a fundamental manner and would provide a unique opportunity to rebuild Franco-Algerian relations. From the perspective of 1962 he frankly admitted:

> Personally I was confident. The France which emerged from the Resistance was not going to desert us. In the eyes of a lot of friends, it was unthinkable that the French people, which had been subjected to four long years of Hitlerian domination, would not recognize our legitimate aspirations. The Occupation had prepared France for the reception of new ideas.[1]

For Abbas it was inconceivable that the revolution which the Liberation entailed would not extend to Algeria, above all because of the way in which hardline colonialism was now hopelessly tarnished by its enthusiastic endorsement of the Vichy régime. Again in 1962 he wrote:

> The extremists in Algeria had compromised themselves with Hitlerism under the Vichy regime. They lowered their heads. French Resisters were in power. Everywhere, liberty and peaceful cooperation were being established [...] between former colonies and former *métropoles*. Why was this lawful 'revolution' also not valid for Algeria, Tunisia and Morocco?[2]

When this revolution was not realized and when, far from introducing fundamental reforms, the end of the Second World War witnessed a violent reassertion of colonial rule, this generated a powerful sense of betrayal amongst Algerians. A new generation of Algerian activists emerged who drew bitter lessons from this experience. A rejection of reform and a belief in the armed struggle now became the basis of their activity.

In examining the impact of the Liberation on Algerian nationalism this chapter will explore three closely related themes. Firstly it will reorientate perspectives by moving the focus away from metropolitan France to a consideration of how the Liberation was viewed from Algeria. This aspect has been largely overlooked despite the fact that since 1848 Algeria had been administered as an integral part of France under the control of the Ministry of the Interior. It is useful to bear in mind that the Liberation of France did not begin in June 1944, but in November 1942 when the Allied landings in North Africa brought Algeria into the Free French camp. Secondly, this chapter will outline an alternative chronology to the one experienced by metropolitan France with differing dates, memories and events, all of which played a crucial role in forging a radical consciousness directly opposed to colonialism. And, thirdly, it will explore conflicting concepts of 'liberation'. At the end of the Second World War French administrators viewed reform for the empire in terms of assimilation or some sort of federation.[3] Within this debate the left-wing nationalism articulated by much of the Resistance saw liberation in the colonies in terms of assimilation. According to this schema, liberation meant the extension of citizenship rights to colonial subjects who would be transformed into fully-fledged French citizens. Liberation, therefore, was something handed down to the empire by the Republic. Raising colonial peoples to the level of French culture and values was the logical outcome of France's civilizing mission.[4] However, between 1942 and 1954 Algerian nationalism began to posit an alternative definition of liberation. Drawing on the tradition of anti-Nazi Resistance, this strain of thinking saw liberation as coming not from France through a grand paternalist gesture, but from Algerians themselves who would win liberation through armed struggle.

The Significance of the Popular Front

It is impossible to separate the radicalization of Algerian nationalism during the Second World War from the events of the Popular Front. To understand the change in nationalist rhetoric from 1936 to 1945 the two experiences must be kept in a state of permanent interconnection. Certain conclusions flowed from the disappointment with the Blum government which inevitably structured subsequent attitudes. Above all its failure to carry through even a limited programme of reform in Algeria ensured that in November 1942, following the Allied Liberation of Algeria, nationalist discourse was noticeably more combative. In the wake of the Popular Front, assimilation, and anything which resembled it, was a dead letter.

In 1936 there were four political movements which saw themselves as either an expression of nationalist aspirations, or as pressurizing for the extension of citizenship rights to Algerians. These were the Ouléma movement, the Étoile Nord-Africaine, the Fédération des Élus Indigènes and the Algerian Communist party. Differing aims and outlooks meant that each movement viewed the other with hostility and suspicion. Consequently, Algerian politics was riven with deep-seated clashes of style, leadership and strategy.

The Ouléma movement (i.e. *'ulamā* in Arabic – men learned in theology and the law), formed in 1931 under the leadership of Sheikh Ben Badis, was primarily a religious and cultural movement. Strongly critical of the marabouts – leaders of mystic orders – whom they accused of corrupting Islam and thereby acting as the tools of colonialism, it called for a return to basic Muslim values. Through a network of schools, religious circles and youth movements, the Ouléma sought to promote the values of Arabic as a language and Algeria as a separate national entity. The Étoile Nord-Africaine was established by North African immigrants in Paris in 1926. Led by Messali Hadj, the Étoile Nord-Africaine demanded independence not only for Algeria but also for Tunisia and Morocco. In terms of practical measures, it called for the freedom of the press and association, abolition of the *code de l'indigénat*, and the establishment of an Algerian parliament.[6] Open anti-capitalism allied with a concern for the rural masses marked the Étoile Nord-Africaine out as the most revolutionary of the opposition movements. Actively supported by the French Communist party (PCF) it was dissolved by the French government in November 1929. Re-formed again in June 1933, at which point there was a severing of links with the PCF, the Étoile Nord-Africaine was broken up by the Popular Front government in January 1937, only to be reconstituted by Messali two months later as the Parti Populaire Algérien (PPA).[7]

The assimilationist strain of thinking within Algerian politics was represented by the Jeune Algérien movement. The initial impetus behind the movement was the introduction of military conscription for Algerians in 1912. The reward for such military service, Jeune

Algérien argued, should be greater equality, and in June 1912 the movement presented the French government with a list of precise political and social demands. As a grouping the movement was the expression of a Gallicized élite whose objective was not independence, but equality of rights within a framework of French sovereignty. In 1927 the supporters of assimilation sought to increase their effectiveness by forming the Fédération des Élus Indigènes. At its inaugural conference in Algiers the Fédération adopted a clear programme which called for native representation in parliament, the abolition of the *indigénat*, and the extension of metropolitan social legislation to Algeria. The most prominent protagonist within the Fédération was Ferhat Abbas. Born in 1899 in the Constantine area, a pharmacist by training, Abbas was very clear that he did not identify France with the colonial system. Against the oppressive structures of colonialism Abbas poised an alternative France, inspired by the democratic ideals of 1789. Strategically speaking he saw this alternative France as a tribune to which Algerian democrats could appeal. His hope was that once in power the metropolitan Left would overcome colonial intransigence and extend citizenship rights to Algerians. Significantly, in order to reinforce the argument for assimilation, Abbas denied the existence of the Algerian nation. In 1936, in a speech which provoked the hostility of the Ouléma and the Étoile Nord-Africaine, Abbas declared:

> I will not die for the Algerian nation, because it does not exist. I have not found it. I have examined History, I questioned the living and the dead, I visited cemeteries; nobody spoke to me about it. I then turned to my Koran and I sought one solitary verse forbidding a Muslim from integrating himself with a non-Muslim nation. I did not find that either. One cannot build on the wind.[8]

The final strand within Algerian politics was the Communist movement. Up until October 1936 the Communist federations were extensions of the French Communist party, at which point it was decided to change tactics and create a separate Algerian Communist party (PCA). Predominantly European, the Communist movement was hampered by its failure to maintain a consistent policy over Algeria. In the 1920s the PCF had unambiguously supported independence, but by 1936 the major focus of Communist rhetoric was the international fight against fascism, and with this strategy in mind militant anti-colonialism was put on the back-burner. In March 1939 at a speech given in Algiers, Maurice Thorez, the PCF general secretary, redefined official policy and introduced the concept of

Algeria as a 'nation in formation'.[9] According to this formula Algeria was not yet a nation, but a melting pot of some twenty races which were in the process of creating a nation. For Thorez it was the Algerian Communist party which was the most progressive force within Algeria, because it was the only party which was uniting all the various races into one political organization. Importantly too, Thorez stressed two further themes: firstly the positive role played by the Republic in terms of the ongoing creation of the Algerian nation; and secondly the fact that, given the international fight against fascism, it was in the best interests of Algeria to strengthen ties with France. As regards practical demands, the PCA supported reform and was hostile to radical nationalism.

For all four movements 1936 was a key year. It was widely hoped that the Popular Front government would enact far-reaching reforms to do away with the colonial system. In June 1936 a Muslim Congress, grouping together the supporters of Ferhat Abbas, the Ouléma and the Communist movement, was established to act as a pressure group upon the Popular Front and to this end a charter of demands was drawn up. Central to this charter was the call for equal voting rights. Significantly the charter demanded: 'Unity pure and simple with France, with the abolition of special structures: *délégations financières, communes mixtes*, and the Government General.'[10] In contrast the Étoile Nord-Africaine was much more guarded; Messali Hadj unambiguously reiterated the demand for Algerian independence, to be achieved by the immediate establishment of an Algerian parliament.

Practically speaking the reforms proposed by the Popular Front were prudent and modest. In December 1936 the Blum-Viollette Bill was brought before the French Assembly.[11] Under its provisions 25,000 out of six million Algerians would have been offered citizenship, but even this meagre legislation provoked the wrath of the colonial lobby within the French Assembly, who did all they could to sabotage the bill. Confronted with this pressure Blum vacillated, with the result that when the Popular Front collapsed in October 1938 the Blum-Viollette Bill collapsed with it.[12]

The Popular Front must be seen as a fracturing moment which polarized Algerian politics. In concrete terms the failure of reform led to a hardening of strategies into two tendencies. On the one hand, the supporters of Abbas continued to press for equal political rights; on the other, Messali Hadj and the PPA mobilized around the theme of militant nationalism, and it was this second viewpoint which rapidly began to gain ground, especially among the working class and the lower middle class in large towns and cities. Uncompromising and radical, the PPA asserted a new set of priorities with the slogan 'neither assimilation nor separation, but emancipation'.[13] Most of all it underlined the need for changed perspectives. Faith in the metropolitan Left as a democratic tribune was dangerously misguided. For Messali the fact that the Popular Front had not only reneged on reform but, more crucially, dissolved the Étoile Nord-Africaine on the grounds that it represented a threat to the territorial integrity of the Republic, demonstrated the validity of his conclusions.

The outbreak of the Second World War inaugurated a period of intense dislocation for the nationalist leadership. In autumn 1939 it was subjected to a blanket repression, which then intensified under Vichy. The PCA and PPA were dissolved, while Ben Badis, the Ouléma leader, was consigned to house arrest. When in March 1941 Messali rejected overtures for collaboration from Vichy, he was sentenced to sixteen years of hard labour.

The period must also be understood as one of complex ambiguities, where choices of action were far from clear. The most obvious example of this was the career of Ferhat Abbas. In September 1939 he volunteered for military service as a gesture of solidarity with the Republican war effort. The fall of France left him deeply disillusioned, but within the Vichy régime, initially at least, he saw an opportunity to press the Algerian cause. On 10 April 1941 he sent a detailed report to Pétain detailing the economic and social hardships suffered by Algerians. Forty years later he justified his action with the argument that, at the time, he naïvely believed that the National Revolution had created a new climate which could transform the old structures.[14] Retrospectively Abbas admits that he was misguided, but he was unaware of the extent to which Pétain was in the pocket of the colonial lobby. Similarly, following the logic that your enemy's enemy is your friend, a small minority of the PPA members were tempted to see Nazism as a possible ally against the French. Overall, therefore, September 1939 until November 1942 was a time of confusion and fragmentation. The catalyst which radically transformed the situation was to come from outside. It was the Allied landings in North Africa and the Liberation of Algeria from Vichy which provided the dramatic spur for the reemergence of a dynamic national movement.

The Impact of the Allied Liberation of Algeria

On 8 November 1942 the Americans landed in Algiers and quickly overcame the puny resistance offered by the Vichy army. For Algerian nationalists the arrival of the Americans was to be of enormous significance. Firstly it revealed the weakness of the French. Henceforth French military force no longer had the aura of invincibility. Secondly it brought Algerians into contact with the new ideas of the Atlantic Charter.[15] Signed by Churchill and Roosevelt in August 1941, and trumpeted as a clear statement of democratic ideals directly opposed to Nazism, the Charter unambiguously asserted the right of peoples to choose their own forms of government. Almost immediately Algerian leaders drew upon the language of the Atlantic Charter to challenge the legitimacy of colonialism. Abbas met the American envoy, Robert Murphy, in Algiers, and Murphy's sympathetic response led him to present a short list of demands not only to the French authorities, but also to the Allies. Therein he emphasized that Algerian support for the war was not unconditional. Instead it was dependent upon the nature of the war aims: 'If this war was, as has declared the President of the United States, a war of liberation for peoples and individuals, without distinction of race or religion, Algerian Muslims would join, with all their strength [...] in this liberating struggle.'[16]

Rapidly this initiative was followed up by the Manifesto of the Algerian People. Drawn up in February 1943 by Abbas and the *élu* leadership and presented to Governor-General Peyrouton at the end of March, the nine-page document catalogued Algerian demands in greater detail. It stressed that, in the face of the internal divisions within the French community, the lot of the 8.5 million Algerians had been ignored.[17] The explicit purpose of the manifesto was to voice Algerian aspirations and put the issue of Algerian nationhood onto the political agenda. Colonialism was comprehensively condemned as an outmoded system based upon subjugation. The manner in which attempts to extend rights to Algerians had been consistently sabotaged demonstrated that the system could not be reformed and for this reason the manifesto rejected assimilation as a viable policy. Now the keyword was 'liberation', as the manifesto called for the recognition of the Algerian right to self-determination.[18]

Reflecting the temporary weakness of the French, the response of the Governor-General was to ask the signatories of the manifesto to produce a comprehensive programme of reform. Presented to Governor-General Catroux on 11 June 1943, the resultant document reiterated the need to break with the past in a fundamental manner. The imminent defeat of fascism was seen to represent the opportunity for a new beginning. The task of the French authorities was to grasp this opportunity and establish an Algerian nation, where all, settler and native alike, would be treated equally. At this point the Algerian leadership drew attention to the enormous sacrifices being made by

Muslim soldiers who made up 90 per cent of the forces commanded by General Giraud. These soldiers, it was emphasized, needed to have the firm guarantee that in fighting for the liberation of France they were also fighting for the liberation of Algeria. Such a radical tone was repeated by Abbas in January 1944. He warned the authorities that the world, as in 1789, was experiencing a revolutionary epoch which, in extending democratic principles to the whole of the globe, signalled the end of colonialism.[19]

During the spring of 1944 the hopes of Abbas and his supporter rapidly dissipated. Demands for independence were ignored and reforms introduced on 7 March, granting citizenship to 65,000 Algerians, were widely perceived as too little too late. The concrete expression of the new mood was the Association des Amis du Manifeste et de la Liberté (AML), established in Sétif on 14 March. Supported by Abbas, the Ouléma and the PPA – although significantly not the PCA who attacked it as a nationalist organisation controlled by foreign powers – the intention of the AML was to propagate the ideas contained within the manifesto. The central goal of the AML was the creation of 'an autonomous Republic federated with a renovated and anti-colonialist France'.[20]

In the ensuing months the AML mushroomed into a genuine mass movement, attracting a membership of 100,000. During the course of this expansion serious divisions began to appear, separating the leadership, which favoured legal methods, from a grass roots dominated by the PPA and committed to a more radical contesting of colonialism. Rapidly, the latter came to predominate over the former, creating a combative discourse which militants became increasingly impatient to actualize. At a special conference in Algiers on 2 April 1945 the vast majority of delegates voted for the immediate creation of an Algerian parliament and government rather than for an autonomous republic federated to France. In the remoter parts of Algeria, most notably in the Kabylie and the Constantinois, the PPA created networks of paramilitary cells, as the grass roots prepared for a military confrontation, which the leadership viewed as rash and ill advised.

The militant atmosphere caused a flurry of anxiety within the colonial administration. As a precautionary measure Messali Hadj was deported to Brazzaville on 23 April 1945, but this only served to heighten tensions, as it offered the nationalists a precise issue, Messali Hadj's freedom, around which to mobilize. On top of this, April was a time of acute economic hardship for Algerians. A long, cruel winter, following a very bad harvest, led to famine in the countryside. Thousands of starving Algerians flocked to the major towns which provided a fertile ground for the diffusion of AML ideas. Large numbers of Algerians now looked forward to the end of the war with anticipation, believing that it would lead to a general amelioration of their lot. In this way economic deprivation and hope fed each other and fuelled a climate of rebellion which was to climax with the cataclysmic events of Sétif in May 1945.

The imminence of Allied victory brought a major expansion of activity. Large numbers of Algerians were self-consciously aware of the immensity of the moment and wanted to use VE day to assert a separate national identity. Through an impressive show of force the AML aimed to move the Algerian nation out of the shadows and into the open, thereby making an explicit link between victory over fascism and the end of colonialism. Thus, 8 May witnessed huge popular demonstrations calling for national independence. Most passed off without incident but at Sétif in the Constantinois events escalated into bloodshed. There, police attempts to break up the demonstration provided the spark for a general and violent insurrection which quickly engulfed the whole region. The government response was ferocious and allowed the army a free hand to launch a savage campaign of repression. The AML was dissolved and its moderate leadership, including Ferhat Abbas, imprisoned. In terms of the scale of the retaliation, the French government spoke of 1,500 Algerian dead, while Algerian estimates have put the figure as high as 45,000.[21] Initially at least, such repression was supported right across the political spectrum. Both the PCF and the PCA denounced the uprising as the work of Nazi agents, and this at a time when Nazi Germany had just capitulated.

For the French government, Sétif was symbolic of a general desire to stamp its authority both within France and the empire. In this sense, if the Liberation was a reassertion of French national sovereignty, then defeat of the Algerian rebellion was part of the continuing logic of that Liberation. For a large number of Algerian nationalists, on the other hand, Sétif was the point of no return. Much more than the Liberation of metropolitan France, experienced as a second-hand event, and much more than November 1942, Sétif was to stand out during the following decade as a focus of remembering for nationalists. It was seen as a betrayal, proof that even a new France based upon Resistance principles could not transform colonialism. Sétif carried the national struggle onto a new stage in that it represented the fusion of modern nationalism, which was urban in origin, with the disaffected rural masses. Importantly too, Sétif politicized a new generation, and here it is necessary to emphasize the importance of Algerian ex-servicemen returning from the war in autumn 1945.[22] For many of these demobbed soldiers, such as Ahmed Ben Bella one of the founder members of the Front de Libération Nationale (FLN), news of French atrocities turned them instantly into militant anticolonialists. For nationalists such as Ben Bella the liberation of Europe from fascism was not an end, but rather it was the beginning of a new struggle for Algerian self-liberation.[23]

Post 1945, this emerging generation, shaped by the events of Sétif, began to develop a new political strategy. It was a strategy which rejected electoralism, rejected assimilation and federation as solutions, and rejected the image of metropolitan France as a tribune of appeal. Instead of addressing demands to France, this new generation looked directly to the Algerian people. For them it was the Algerians alone who could achieve liberation, through the logic of the armed struggle. This current of thought, represented by activists such as Mohammed Boudiaf, Hocine Aït Ahmed and Belkacem Krim, fed into the FLN, which launched the uprising of 1 November 1954, now recognized as the beginning of the Algerian war. From the outset the discourse of armed liberation was central to the FLN. Militant and uncompromising, it fashioned an identity based upon revolt, disavowal and resistance.

The most radical expression of this perspective was to be found in the writings of Frantz Fanon, the Martinican psychiatric doctor working in Algeria, who joined the FLN in 1956. In *Wretched of the Earth*, published in 1961, he claimed that the true liberation of the colonized could only be achieved through violence, that is the physical destruction of the colonial oppressor.[24] Writing two years earlier in *A Dying Colonialism* he set out to show how national and social liberation went hand in hand.[25] In Fanon's opinion the revolutionary struggle was transforming Algerian society. Through it, age-old taboos were being reassessed and attitudes towards new cultural forces, such as radio, were being clarified; family structures were shifting. The physical participation of women in the struggle, Fanon argued, was highly positive. Through their action, Fanon claimed, women were breaking free from the constraints of traditional religious values. The liberation of Algeria and the liberation of women were indissolubly intertwined. In this manner the armed struggle was laying the basis for a fundamental redefinition of their role within the post-independence era.

The power of Fanon's vision moved François Maspero, one of the small minority of French left intellectuals who actively supported the FLN, to accuse the Republic of a betrayal of the spirit of Resistance, a spirit which he had internalized as a twelve-year-old in 1944.[26] In his opinion the cruellest irony was that the personal and collective liberation embodied in the Resistance was no longer located in France, but within the very Algerian rebels against whom the French army was fighting. Writing in 1959, Maspero's conclusion was as simple and straightforward as it was provocative. For him the FLN in particular, and third-world liberation struggles in general, were the true inheritors of the Resistance tradition.

Notes

Unless stated otherwise, the place of publication is Paris.

1. Ferhat Abbas, *Guerre et révolution d'Algérie. La nuit coloniale*, Julliard, 1962, p.151.
2. Ibid., p.152.
3. For a detailed discussion of these debates see Andrew Shennan, *Rethinking France: Plans for Renewal 1940–1946*, Oxford, Oxford University Press, 1989, chapter 6.
4. Claude Bourdet, one of the leaders of the Resistance movement 'Combat', has emphasized the paternalism of Left Resistance discourse. As he has put it: 'The men of the Left of my generation did not understand the colonial problem. I spent all my years in the Resistance without thinking for one second about the emancipation of the colonized peoples. The idea that they could aspire to anything else other then being French appeared to me incongruous. To explain this mystification, I think that you have to go back to the French Revolution. The men of 1793 wanted to establish equality where all citizens would be free and benefit from the same rights. The abolition of slavery by the Convention seemed to confer a certain reality on this plan... During one hundred and fifty years young French people continued to learn about the generous and civilizing role played by France. And the activists and leaders of the Left have been steeped in this same paternalist and universalist ideology.' Quoted in Hervé Hamon and Patrick Rotman, *Les porteurs de valises: la résistance française à la guerre d'Algérie*, 2nd edn, Seuil, 1982, p.28.
5. For a history of Algerian nationalism see Mahfoud Kaddache, *Histoire du nationalisme algérien. Question nationale et politique algérienne. 1919–1951*, 2nd edn, Algiers, Société nationale de l'édition, 1981. See also Benjamin Stora, *Les sources du nationalisme algérien*. L'Harmattan, 1989.
6. The *code de l'indigénat* was imposed on Algerians during the 1870s. Under its terms Algerians could be punished for offences such as

being disrespectful to a colonial official or insulting the Republic.

7. By 1928, the Étoile Nord-Africaine had attracted 4,000 members in France. Despite harassment the movement continued to grow and by 1934 its paper, *El Ouma*, had a circulation of 43,500 in France. Figures from John Ruedy, *Modern Algeria*, Indianapolis, Indiana University Press, 1992, p.138.

8. Quoted in Claude Collot and Jean-Robert Henry, *Le Mouvement National Algérien: Textes 1912–1954*, 2nd edn, Algiers, Office des Publications Universitaires, 1981, pp.66–7.

9. Maurice Thorez quoted in Benyoucef Ben Khedda, *Les Origines du 1 novembre 1954*, Algiers, Éditions Dahlab, 1989, p.292. For an analysis of the Communist movement see Emmanuel Sivan, *Communisme et nationalisme en Algérie, 1920–1962*, Presses de la Fondation nationale des sciences politiques, 1976, and Danièle Joly, *The French Communist Party and the Algerian War*, London, Macmillan, 1991.

10. Collot and Henry, *Le Mouvement National Algérien*, pp.72–3.

11. Maurice Viollette had been Governor-General in Algeria from 1925 to 1927, where the experience had convinced him of the necessity of reform.

12. For a detailed analysis of the reaction of Algerian parties to the Popular Front, see Benjamin Stora, *Nationalistes Algériens et Révolutionnaires Français au Temps du Front Populaire*, L'Harmattan, 1987.

13. Collot and Henry, *Le Mouvement National Algérien*, p.144.

14. Ferhat Abbas, *De la colonie vers la province. Le jeune Algérien*, 2nd edn, Garnier, 1981.

15. Mohammed Dib's trilogy of novels covering this period climaxes with the arrival of the Americans who are presented as liberators. See Mohammed Dib: *La Grande Maison*, Seuil, 1952; *L'Incendie*, Seuil, 1954; and *Le Métier à tisser*, Seuil, 1957.

16. Collot and Henry, *Le Mouvement National Algérien*, p.154.

17. In the wake of the Allied landings the French army and the settler communitry were riven with divisions over whether to support de Gaulle or Giraud.

18. Collot and Henry, *Le Mouvement National Algérien*, pp.152–70.

19. Ibid., pp.175–6.

20. Ibid., pp.186–91.

21. For a detailed analysis of the events of 8 May 1945, see Radouane Ainad-Tabet, *Le mouvement du 8 mai 1945 en Algérie*, Algiers, Offices des Publications Universitaires, 1985.

22. For the writer Kateb Yacine, who experienced the May events at first hand, Sétif became a recurrent reference point in his

writing and poetry. In particular see *Nedjma*, Seuil, 1956, and *Le cadavre encerclé*, Seuil, 1959.

23. Militant nationalism of this kind was evident elsewhere in the Empire, most notably Indo-China. However, in West Africa the demands of the political élites were more moderate in tone. For them liberation was still seen in terms of closer links with France. On this last point see the chapter by Tony Chafer, pp.241–53.

24. Frantz Fanon, *Les Damnés de la Terre*, Maspero, 1961.

25. Frantz Fanon, *L'An Cinq de la Révolution Algérienne*, Maspero, 1959, with introduction by François Maspero.

26. Ibid., p.12.

– 18 –

The Inescapable Allusion: the Occupation and the Resistance in French Fiction and Film of the Algerian War

Philip Dine

The subject of this chapter is a double substitution within the French collective memory. For on the one hand, as I have argued elsewhere, a multiplicity of more or less partisan narratives has emerged in France in the absence of a broadly consensual history of that country's final war of decolonization in Algeria.[1] On the other hand, this same Franco-Algerian conflict has been read by the French in terms appropriated from the lexicon (and thus the symbolic order) of their own *années noires* – the 'dark years' of Nazi occupation, 1940–44.

This double substitution is particularly striking, and particularly revealing, in those very many works of fiction and rather fewer feature films which take the Algerian war as their subject. For it is here that the essential plurality and mutual hostility of the competing narratives generated by the French experience of defeat, occupation, resistance, and liberation are brought into a powerfully affective interaction with the similarly plural and equally hostile narratives competing for dominance in the French consciousness of Algeria. That interaction, or interference, may be either positive or negative, both with regard to the relevant narratives' value as repositories for the French collective memory of events in the period 1954–62 and to their status as art.

However, in many cases we shall encounter what we might, with apologies to Henry Rousso and with obvious reference to Camus's *La Peste* (1947), call 'the Oran syndrome', in which Algeria becomes for French writers and film-makers a mere backdrop for the reliving of the Second World War, and, in many cases, for settling its old scores. For in the Algerian context, one war may all too easily hide another. More than this, in the imagined Algeria of French fiction and film, one liberation from foreign occupation may actually serve to deny another.

For if the Algerian war has emphatically not been forgotten in the way that France's immediately preceding colonial conflict in Indo-China undoubtedly has, then neither has it been established as a suitable subject for public commemoration to compare with 1914–18 and 1940–44.[2] French historiography has had to fall back on alternative 'mnemonic sites' (what Pierre Nora terms *'lieux de mémoire'*[3]), and above all fictional narratives, in order to preserve the national memory of that conflict. Many of the producers of such narratives have looked to the apparent certainties of France's own recent loss and recovery of political sovereignty and territorial integrity in an attempt to make sense of the troublesome specificity of the Algerian conflict. The result is a systematic literary and cinematic recourse to historical analogy across the political spectrum – from the 'Sartrean' Left to the pro-colonial Right – in the face of an insurgent Algeria's radical challenge to still unconsolidated French values and identities.

The Algerian war occurred in a land which, for all its supposed 'Frenchness', remained profoundly alien to the mass of the metropolitan French population. Moreover, the hostilities were officially denied *qua* war, being referred to instead by a string of euphemisms, such as 'operations to maintain law and order' and 'pacification'. With no clear onset, no identifiable front, and no real high spots, events in Algeria did not fit easily into the established pattern of French wars and their national commemoration. More than this, the 1954–62 troubles were actually read by contemporary participants and observers, just as they were destined to be reread by subsequent commentators, as other, more memorable – and frequently Franco-French – conflicts. Of these often highly idiosyncratic attempts to make sense of the bewildering specificity of the Algerian conflict, by far the most important was what Henry Rousso has famously termed 'the Vichy syndrome', i.e. the indelible memory of the Occupation of France which had ended a mere decade before the Algerian war began.

However powerful the appeal of other historical parallels may have been, the memory of France's *années noires* is an almost obligatory point of reference for any French commentator on the Algerian question. Such references may be characterized as negative or positive to the extent that they confirm readers and viewers in their established world-views or encourage them to consider new mental pictures of France's experiences both in 1940–44 and 1954–62. Whether comforting or challenging, however, there can be little doubt that the recent experience of occupation served to structure French perceptions of Algeria, at all levels, and across the political spectrum. The appeal of clandestinity to opponents of the government both on the Left and on the Right is only the most obvious example of a broad tendency to mimetism in French responses to this new conflict.

The preeminence of the Second World War as a common symbolic store is as clear on the level of personnel recruitment as it is on that of political, especially extra-parliamentary, and military practice. This fact underlines the essential flexibility of key concepts such as 'Occupation', 'Collaboration', 'Resistance' and 'Liberation'. So, for instance, student opposition to conscription may well have led to a 'Jeune Résistance', as the principal organization to help deserters and draft-dodgers to flee France was significantly named. However, the memory of Resistance heroism also led idealistic young Frenchmen like Gilles Perrault to join the parachute regiments which had sprung from de Gaulle's Free French Forces during the Second World War and which were themselves shortly to be likened to the Gestapo as a result of their use of torture for the gathering of intelligence in Algeria.[4] By the same token, there are several examples among the defenders of French Algeria which demonstrate what Rousso calls 'the complex posterity of resistance participation' and which could hardly be further removed from nostalgia for the Maréchal as the basis for opposition to de Gaulle. Rousso notes that:

> Authentic former résistants, many of them well known, numbered among the most intransigent opponents of Algerian independence. Château-Jobert, a leader of the OAS [the Organisation armée secrète, a French Algerian terrorist group] and zealous defender of the 'Christian West,' was a veteran of the FFL [*Forces françaises libres*, or Free French Forces] and Compagnon de la Libération, as were Jacques Soustelle and Georges Bidault. Bidault's case is especially noteworthy, because in 1962 he did not hesitate to support the OAS by founding what he called the Conseil National de la Résistance, a name that evoked memories of the organization of which Bidault became the head in 1943 after the death of Jean Moulin.[5]

However, not everyone was alive to the fact that 'the resistance heritage was not the sole possession of those who opposed the war in Algeria'.[6] In particular, there were many on the Left who were only too ready to attach the epithet 'fascist' to anything and anyone that did not conform to their vision of Algeria and its future.

The most self-assured, and, indeed, the most self-righteous, appeal to the 'resistancialist' heritage is to be found on what we might conveniently refer to as the 'Sartrean' Left – the Left of *Les Temps Modernes*, 'Young Resistance', and the Jeanson network. For Sartre himself, there was never any doubt that the French struggle against the Nazi invader and the campaign waged by the Algerian Front de libération nationale (FLN) against French colonial rule were the same in kind. Indeed, he went further than this, famously equating de Gaulle's Fifth Republic with the colonial régime in Algeria: 'Colonialism over there, fascism back here: they are one and the same thing.'[7] What is more, even de Gaulle's enemies on the far Right were not averse to equating his return to power in June 1958 with the National Assembly's desperate appeal to another old war hero exactly eighteen years earlier. So, for instance, the embittered ex-Gaullist Jacques Soustelle brings to a close his polemical *L'Espérance trahie* by laying the blame for the Algerian tragedy squarely at the feet of his former leader, 'a man who had once been great (and whom we, the generation of the Resistance, had made the mistake of recalling, as the generation of Verdun had recalled Pétain)...'[8]

Others on the Sartrean Left have taken the historical analogy even further. Perhaps the most notable of these is former antiwar militant Georges Mattéi, whose *La Guerre des gusses* (1982) depicts a fictional France in which the social divisions revealed by the Algerian conflict map unproblematically onto those of the Occupation years. As his conscript hero explains, in the wake of his desertion to the FLN: 'When I was a child, I was brought up to admire those who fought against the Nazis in occupied France, those whom we called the "resisters". Here, I now know which side the resisters are on. I've chosen my side.'[9]

If those who oppose the war in Algeria represent the Resistance, then those who support the cause of French Algeria must be tarred with the brush of collaboration. So we are presented in turn with an old soldier who shouts 'Death to the Jews!' as he attacks a group of antiwar demonstrators, a military torturer who wears the Iron Cross on his uniform, and French soldiers who describe themselves as 'the Boche'.[10] For Mattéi, in short, there is no doubt that all those who support the French cause in Algeria can be lumped together and condemned as 'worthy heirs to the colonial conquerors, grandsons of the Marshal [Pétain], sons of the General [de Gaulle], and sons of bitches'.[11]

This mechanical equation of *la France gaullienne* with Vichy is symptomatic of a broader failure on the part of the French Left to comprehend de Gaulle's willingness to decolonize. Wholly unexpected, because essentially pragmatic, the General's unsentimental recognition of the impossibility of retaining French colonial control in the post-War world was to remain a mystery to Sartre and thus to those, like Mattéi, who were guided by him. This ideologically motivated blindness to de Gaulle's genuine achievements in Algeria undermines what is, perhaps, the most valuable aspect of Mattéi's novel, its commemoration of the still largely forgotten massacre of some two hundred Algerian men, women, and children in Paris on 17 October 1961.

Mattéi's representation of the murderous repression of an FLN-orchestrated, but wholly peaceful, demonstration, although nobly inspired, is spoiled by caricature and an overdependence on historical analogy: in this case, with the persecution by the Nazi occupier and the collaborationist French authorities of the country's Jewish population. In consequence, the real continuities of administrative personnel and repressive practices which may be identified between these two atrocities are signalled by Mattéi's narrative in a way which is altogether too heavy-handed to be effective. So, for instance, when the fictional Prefect of Police, 'Marcel Pantobe' – a figure transparently based on his real-life counterpart, Maurice Papon, previously a key figure in Vichy's deportation of Jews – is confronted with a group of Algerian prisoners, he initially orders their removal to the 'Vél d'hiv' (the 'Winter Velodrome', notoriously used in the 1942 roundup of Jews) rather than to the planned holding centre at the Porte de Versailles sports complex.[12]

This 'knee-jerk' use of the historical analogy is similarly visible in the post-1968 Algerian war cinema of the radical Left. Such films as René Vautier's *Avoir vingt ans dans les Aurès* (1972) and Yves Boisset's *RAS* [i.e. '*rien à signaler*' or 'nothing to report' in military jargon] (1973) were essentially a response to that radical questioning of the past which had been prompted by the quasi-revolutionary events of May–June 1968. This movement undoubtedly had its finest cinematic expression in *Le Chagrin et la Pitié* (1971), Marcel Ophuls's pioneering documentary study of Vichy, and *Lacombe Lucien* (1974), Louis Malle's disturbing portrait of youthful collaboration. Against this background of sophisticated reassessment of national guilt, the belated attempts of confirmed leftists like Vautier and militant ex-conscripts like Boisset to equate the French army in Algeria with the Nazi occupier in France stand revealed as clumsy diatribes.[13]

For the pro-colonial Right, and its literary defenders, the Left's charge of fascism predictably rankled. In particular, for the French army's élite troops in Algeria, the historical analogy with the Occupation period was extremely hard to accept. Critical journalistic pieces such as Claude Bourdet's famous 'Votre Gestapo d'Algérie' had their effect, but undoubtedly the single most influential contribution to the French intellectuals' campaign against the army's use of torture in Algeria was *La Question* (1958), the celebrated account by Henri Alleg, the Communist editor of *Alger Républicain*, of his own experiences at the hands of the paratroopers of General Jacques Massu's 10th Parachute Division.[14] Published, very significantly, by Minuit, an ex-Resistance imprint which had famously made its first appearance under the Occupation with Vercors's *Le Silence de la mer* (1942),[15] *La Question* was ineptly seized by the authorities only after it had become a best seller. In this harrowing work, Alleg explains his ability to resist the tortures to which he was submitted: 'Every blow left me more dazed, but at the same time strengthened me in my determination not to give in to those brutes, who flattered themselves that they were the equals of the Gestapo.'[16]

Very few defenders of French Algeria were ready to accept the charge of 'fascism' which was so routinely levelled at them from 1957 onwards.[17] For the majority of the supporters of the French colonial cause such a historically loaded analogy remained anathema. Moreover, for a veteran of the Vercors like Colonel Yves Godard, one of the most influential and the most intransigent of the paratrooper colonels, even the most extreme personal ideology could not ignore the fact of his own historical commitment to the anti-fascist cause in France itself.[18]

It is in the light cast by this rather more complex history of personal continuities and ideological changes that we need to examine the properly 'reactionary' depiction of the parachute corps in a contemporaneous novel such as Jean Lartéguy's best-selling *Les Centurions* (1960). For in the character of Captain Philippe Esclavier – who was, incidentally, to be played by Alain Delon in Mark Robson's 1966 Hollywood adaptation of Lartéguy's novel – we have not only the son of one of the leading lights of the Popular Front, but also a veteran of the Resistance, who has survived arrest, torture, and deportation to Mauthausen. His critique of the social and moral decline of post-War France may thus have strong echoes of the Pétainist case against the Third Republic, but his assault on its replacements is deemed to have been inspired by the experience of life in the concentration camp. As he puts it himself: 'I stayed in the army... out of disgust at what I saw when I came back from deportation.'[19] For Lartéguy, then, the paratroopers are by no means the betrayers of the Resistance heritage, but rather its stoutest defenders in the face of a national capitulation to the forces of decadence.

A rather more productive use of the occupation analogy occurs in the work of another best-selling novelist, Bernard Clavel. In his *Le Silence des armes* (1974), Clavel tells of a young French soldier who returns to his native Jura profoundly traumatized by his experiences in Algeria. One night, unable to sleep, the hero climbs by moonlight up to a plateau reminiscent of the Vercors and the Glières. There he comes across an ancient tree which raises troublesome memories of the recent past. Still bearing traces of wartime messages cut into its bark by members of the Resistance, the tree is preserved as a shrine to the local struggle against a brutal occupier. The struggle seems all too painfully familiar to the veteran of the French army's anti-insurgency operations in Algeria.

In this appeal to the Second World War analogy, Clavel's lovingly evoked Jura does undoubtedly provide just the sense of place required for the French commemoration of the Algerian war in the absence of the physical mnemonic sites associated with earlier conflicts. The undeniable specificity and historicity of the earth which the protagonist scoops up in his hand, in an attempt to wring out of it the blood of the Resistance martyrs, is extended, by a process of association, to that of an Algeria generally unknown to the metropolitan French reader.[20] This narrative strategy also serves to emphasize the motive force of the remembering of history and of the interference which may occur between powerfully affective memories. In this case, memories will very shortly and very visibly function as motivations, leading first to Jacques's refusal to return to Algeria and thus to a suicidal last stand against 'the forces of order' in his own land.

Published a good decade after the Algerian war ended, Bernard Clavel's novel is obviously the product of an extended period of political reflection and artistic maturation, in marked contrast to the two works which represent the best known and most critically celebrated artistic applications of the Second World War analogy to the Franco-Algerian hostilities: Jean-Paul Sartre's *Les Séquestrés d'Altona* (1959/60) and Alain Resnais's *Muriel* (1963).

Such was the intensity of Jean-Paul Sartre's commitment to the cause of Algerian nationalism, or, more accurately, of his hostility to the colonial policies pursued by his native land, that the Algerian war has seriously been described as 'Sartre's war', a substitute for the Resistance campaign which he never, in fact, waged.[21] The intense debate among French intellectuals which was prompted by the Algerian war – 'a battle of the written word', as Michel Crouzet has famously described it[22] – is thus equated with one man's vicarious settling of a psychic debt to the Resistance. Such a conception of the war, although obviously schematic and reductive, may usefully be borne in mind as we consider Sartre's sole contribution to the fiction of the Algerian war. For Sartre's creed of artistic commitment would lead him to use every available opportunity to denounce French Algeria and its defenders: polemical journalism, petitions and manifestos, and, most intriguingly, a play dealing with the characterizing taboo of the Algerian war: torture.

First produced at the Théâtre de la Renaissance in Paris on 23 September 1959, *Les Séquestrés d'Altona* was extremely successful both on stage and, from 1960, as a book.[23] Given the climate of censorship which reigned at this time – the botched seizure in 1958 of Alleg's *La Question*, the banning of Jean-Luc Godard's film *Le Petit Soldat* (1960) – it is small wonder that Sartre should have recourse to a parable to tell his tale of Algeria which presented the France of 1954–62 in terms of the Germany of 1939–45.

As Rhiannon Goldthorpe has pointed out 'this highly complex play can be interpreted on a number of different levels [which] can be separated [...] only with some contrivance.'[24] However, in the present context, the most obvious interest of Sartre's tale of a former SS man who, for the past fifteen years, has hidden from the world in the family home at Altona, near Hamburg, is to be found in its allegorical references to the Algerian conflict. Locked away from a rapidly modernizing and increasingly prosperous West Germany, the protagonist – whose very name, 'Frantz', is itself an accurate indicator of the character's symbolic value – seeks, in vain, to escape from his memories of war on the Eastern Front, where, we eventually discover, he was nicknamed 'the butcher of Smolensk'. As Catherine Brosman has observed, following Michel Contat, 'Sartre wants to show the French that they *are* Germans, that is, in exactly the same relationship to the native Algerians as the Nazi occupants were to them,' a point which Sartre himself makes most forcefully in an important article on Alleg.[25]

So, the Frantz who tortured during the war and now locks himself away from the West Germany of the *Wirtschaftswunder* is, in fact, the France of the *trente glorieuses*, the thirty years of economic expansion and social restructuring 1945–75, that remains silent about the suffering done to the Algerians in its name, and for which it, like the German nation, is held collectively responsible by Sartre.[26] Indeed, it is this analogy which underpins the play's status as allegory, for throughout its length, from his introduction, through his painful facing of the truth about his actions, to his eventual suicide, Frantz can be equated with France. As 'the rosy glow of half-truths' gives way to 'the cold light of whole truths and perfect lies' (Act I, Scene IV), we are presented with an impassioned indictment of the capacity for self-deception of a frenetically modernizing France ever more concerned with individual consumption. A similar mood of cynicism in the face of French hypocrisy pervades Alain Resnais's classic juxtaposition of the troubled and troubling memories of the Second World War and the Algerian conflict in his masterly *Muriel* (1963).

Like Sartre, Resnais was a signatory of the famous 'Manifesto of the 121' of September 1960, in which leading intellectuals had taken a very public stand against the conscription of French youth for service in the Algerian war. Moreover, he shared Sartre's awareness of the need to tread warily in dealing with the Algerian question. The director himself has gone so far as to suggest that his celebrated documentary treatment of the Holocaust, *Nuit et Brouillard* (1955), is to be read on one level as an allegory of the French army's activities in North Africa.[27] Rather more plausibly, *Muriel* is of particular interest to us for its sophisticated use of the Second World War analogy.

For Celia Britton, *Muriel* is 'a film whose most salient structural characteristics are generally seen to be fragmentation and decentredness; and, of course, a film whose principal theme is that of torture'.[28] Moreover, she explains, these facts are closely linked, and themselves relate directly to the film's treatment of its setting, Boulogne-sur-Mer, the 'ville martyre' of the Second World War: 'The Algerian war as it were explodes within Boulogne, shattering the social structure of the town just as decisively as the bombs had shattered its material structure in 1940.'[29] While post-War reconstruction may be able to repair the physical fabric of Resnais's Boulogne, the psychological trauma suffered by those, like Bernard, the central figure, who return to the town from France's 'dirty war' in North Africa proves to be untreatable because it remains unavowed on all but the individual level, and even there may be denied or concealed.

Indeed, the best efforts of those in authority to harmonize and sanitize the French experience of occupation and liberation only serve by their omissions to highlight failures of the French collective memory, and this as regards the darker sides both of the Second World War and of the Algerian conflict. As Resnais's insistent situating snapshots of Boulogne's reconstruction make plain, by putting up a few street signs commemorating the Resistance, the guardians of public memory only serve to draw unwanted attention to those areas of the nation's recent history which remain in darkness, most notably collaboration at home and torture abroad.

In contrast to the celebrated, and much analysed, contemporaneous works just described, there are interesting uses made of the Second World War analogy in three lesser-known novels dating from the mid-1980s: Guy Lagorce's *Le Train du soir* (1983), Alain Le Carvennec's *La Mémoire chacale* (1983), and Didier Daeninckx's *Meurtres pour mémoire* (1984). These three narratives share a common preoccupation with the childhood experience of the Second World War as a key factor in adult perceptions and motivations.

Guy Lagorce's story of childhood love and courage in the later stages of the war takes place against the background of German reprisals in the once 'Free' but now occupied Southern Zone in the summer of 1944. At the heart of this tale is the love of two French schoolboys, Antoine and Julien, for their Jewish classmate, Monique. This love will lead the boys to hide and protect Monique as the vengeful occupiers regroup and retreat before the Allies' advance. As adults, the three will eventually grow apart before Antoine's suicide forces Monique and Julien to reassess their complex set of relationships. Of central importance, we discover, is Antoine's military service in Algeria, during which he actively participated in the torture of suspect insurgents. It is the contrast between this adult behaviour and the friends' childhood hopes that Antoine underlines in his suicide note: 'I feel that we three cannot behave with one another as ordinary people do. It is not that we are extraordinary, but that our summer of 1944 story was. It should have made us splendid people. We got a bit lost on the way. Me especially.'[30]

How can this transformation from victim into torturer, the epitome of that symbolic and psychological shift from the cellars of the Gestapo to those of the Villa Sésini, El Biar, and the other Algerian interrogation centres, be comprehended? Julien explains to Monique that the two aspects of Antoine's personality can, in fact, be reconciled by recognizing that Antoine's only real moral imperative was that of 'action': 'With that, one moment you fall into one camp, the next you fall into another.'[31] This explanation is reminiscent of Louis Malle's *Lacombe Lucien* in which the protagonist becomes a collaborator only after having been turned down by the local Resistance, and might even serve to throw light on the militantly pro-colonial 'activism' of ex-*résistants* like Bidault and Yves Godard. It is also a key theme in Antoine Le Carvennec's novel, *La Mémoire chacale*.

As its title indicates, this novel's emphasis is placed throughout on the problematic of memory, or rather memories, as the essential plurality of the processes of individual and collective remembering is regularly stressed by means of a combination of chronological layering and narrative fracturing not unlike that noted in Resnais's *Muriel*. The partial (both incomplete and biased) nature of all recollection is thus foregrounded by Le Carvennec's narrative as we learn of the difficult wartime childhood and blighted Algerian manhood of Karl, the novel's central figure. Having been a loyal disciple of Marshal Pétain in the early years of the war, the mature Karl reflects that, one fine day, for no very obvious reason, he 'went over' (the verb used is *basculer*, meaning literally to topple or tip over) to the side of the Resistance. As a result of this shift, his personal experience of the collective euphoria of the Liberation will retain a powerfully affective force in later life, and particularly during his period of military service in Algeria: 'I have never got over the Liberation and what it taught me! Now, it's strange to say it, but I feel like the Boche of Algeria! And that is something which I cannot bear!'[32]

Yet the power of memories of the Second World War to structure the French experience of colonial conflict is only fully revealed in those instances where, as in Resnais's *Muriel*, wartime recollections and the Algerian events which they serve to render so painfully intelligible to the individual children of the Occupation are formally denied by the official and academic guardians of the French collective memory. In his 1984 detective story, Didier Daeninckx makes brilliant use of an apparently unassuming, but in the context perfectly adapted, narrative mode to cast light on the all too easily forgotten French crimes of 1940–44 and 1954–62. This is in direct contrast to Mattéi's bludgeoning 1982 work on the same theme. For by subtly linking the murder of a troublesome French historian to both the Paris police's massacre of Algerian demonstrators on 17 October 1961 and the French authorities' active participation in the deportation and extermination of Jews, Daeninckx's novel presents an indictment of the national will to forgetfulness with regard to these apparently very different, but fundamentally similar, rejections of the non-European 'Other' in the French midst. In a memorable dream sequence, Daeninckx's hero, a basically conventional but not altogether hard-boiled detective, comes as close as the novel gets to an overt statement of this ever present subtext, with a stream of bloodied Algerians staggering out from between piles of human bones transported along a ghostly railway in cattle-trucks.[33]

It is to be hoped that the foregoing analysis will have given some indication of the range of uses to which the Occupation and Resistance analogies have been and continue to be put in the context of the French experience of the Algerian war. However, perhaps the one historical analogy which really needs to be drawn is between the role played by the emerging American superpower in the liberation of Europe from Nazi domination and its support for the emancipation of those territories and peoples previously ruled by the European colonial powers. Indeed, this is precisely the significance of the child's-eye view of wartime American landings in North Africa presented by nationalist writer Mohammed Dib as he brings his celebrated 'Algeria' trilogy to a close.[34] In the face of indigenous revolt and international condemnation, France could not for long maintain the illusion of the 'Frenchness' of great swathes of Africa and Asia.

Against this background, the regular appeal by French artists to the Liberation theme must ultimately be reckoned a reduction, and thus part of a wider occultation of the radical ideological challenge of militant colonial nationalism. This is the result of the inherent limitations of the francocentric perspective, even in its most apparently sympathetic and committed forms. For the Algerian struggle for national liberation is ultimately conceived – and is, perhaps, only ever conceivable – as a pale reflection of the processes and personnel of the Liberation of France. Indeed, the FLN's armed challenge to the colonial order may even be recuperated as an expression of 'resistancialist' Frenchness – and thus as a manifestation of Algeria's essential colonizability – rather than be recognized as a profound rejection of everything French: that is to say, as Algerian nationhood in the making.

Unsurprisingly, the Liberation thematic casts far more light on the France of 1954–62, and since, than it ever can on the Liberation struggle in colonial Algeria. However, it might genuinely tell us something about the France of 1940–44. For as Henry Rousso has observed: 'The real anachronism is not to confuse the two sets of issues [raised by the Occupation and Algeria] but to ignore memories of the Second World War as a factor in the Algerian conflict.'[35]

Notes

Unless stated otherwise, the place of publication is Paris.

1. Philip Dine, 'Reading and remembering *la guerre des mythes*: French literary representations of the Algerian war', *Modern and Contemporary France*, NS2 (2), 1994, pp.141–50; idem, *Images of the Algerian War: French Fiction and Film, 1954–92*, Oxford, Clarendon Press, 1994.
2. Jean-Pierre Rioux (ed.), *La Guerre d'Algérie et les Français*, Fayard, 1990, pp.499–503.
3. Pierre Nora (ed.), *Les Lieux de mémoire: 1. La République*, Gallimard, 1984.
4. Gilles Perrault, 'La Gangrène morale', in François and Max Armanet, 'La guerre d'Algérie: 30 ans après', *Le Nouvel Observateur*, Collection Dossiers, 9, 1992, p.45; Claude Bourdet, 'Votre

Gestapo d'Algérie', *France-Observateur*, 13 January 1955.

5. Henry Rousso, *The Vichy Syndrome: History and Memory in France since 1944*, London, Harvard University Press, 1991, p.79; (originally published as *Le Syndrome de Vichy: de 1944 à nos jours*, Seuil, 1990).

6. Ibid., p.76.

7. Jean-Paul Sartre, *Situations V: Colonialisme et néo-colonialisme*, Gallimard, 1964, p.163. (All translations of French sources, with the exception of Rousso, are my own.)

8. Jacques Soustelle, *L'Espérance trahie*, Editions de l'Alma, 1962, p.263.

9. Georges Mattéi, *La Guerre des gusses*, Balland, 1982, p.111.

10. Ibid., pp.16, 162, 172.

11. Ibid., p.210. The Vichy régime and de Gaulle's Fifth Republic are also equated on p.214.

12. Ibid., pp.212–14.

13. See Jean-Pierre Jeancolas, *Le Cinéma des Français: La V* République (1958–1978)*, Stock, 1979, pp.200–1.

14. Henri Alleg, *La Question*, Minuit, 1958.

15. Under Jérôme Lindon's guidance, Minuit was to play a particularly active role in the campaign against both the conduct and the continuation of the Algerian war. See A. Simonin, 'Les Editions de Minuit et les Editions du Seuil: Deux stratégies éditoriales face à la guerre d'Algérie', in Jean-Pierre Rioux and Jean-François Sirinelli (eds), *La Guerre d'Algérie et les intellectuels français*, Brussels, Editions Complexe, 1991, pp.219–45.

16. Alleg, *La Question*, p.36.

17. An important exception was future OAS ideologue Jean-Jacques Susini at the 'Procès des Barricades' in 1960, as Eugen Weber has noted. See Eugen Weber, *My France: Politics, Culture, Myth*, Cambridge and London, Belknap/Harvard University Press, 1991, p.261.

18. See Soustelle, *L'Espérance trahie*, p.252.

19. Jean Lartéguy, *Les Centurions*, Presses de la Cité, Collection 'Presses Pocket', 1960, p.267.

20. Bernard Clavel, *Le Silence des armes*, Robert Laffont, Collection 'J'ai Lu', 1974, pp.179–81.

21. Annie Cohen-Solal, *Sartre*, Gallimard, 1985, p.563; cited and discussed by David Schalk, *War and the Ivory Tower*, New York and Oxford, Oxford University Press, 1991, pp.102–5.

22. Michel Crouzet, 'La Bataille des intellectuels français', *La Nef*, nos.12–13, October 1962–January 1963, pp.47–65; p.47 for the quotation.

23. See Philip Thody's introduction to his edition of the play (London, University of London Press, 1965). The title, which is difficult to translate convincingly, refers to the family's sequestered existence at Altona.

24. Rhiannon Goldthorpe, *Sartre: Literature and Theory*, Cambridge, Cambridge University Press, 1984, p.137.

25. Catherine Brosman, 'Sartre, the Algerian War, and *Les Séquestrés d'Altona*', *Papers in Romance*, vol.3, no.2, Spring 1981, pp.81–9; p.84 for the quotation. Brosman goes on to point out that 'Simone de Beauvoir [in *La Force des choses*] repeatedly noted that she felt like a German when she thought of how the Algerians judged the French, and often looked at her fellow citizens on the street the way she used to look at the occupiers'; see Sartre, 'Une victoire', *Situations V*, pp.72–3.

26. Sartre, *Situations V*, p.66.

27. See Alan Williams, *Republic of Images: A History of French Filmmaking*, Cambridge and London, Harvard University Press, 1992, p.369.

28. Celia Britton, 'Broken images in Resnais's *Muriel*', *French Cultural Studies*, vol.1, no.1, February 1990, pp.37–46; p.38 for the quotation.

29. Ibid., p.46.

30. Guy Lagorce, *Le Train du soir*, Grasset, 1983, p.216.

31. Ibid., p.226.

32. Alain Le Carvennec, *La Mémoire chacale*, Hachette, 1983, p.274.

33. Didier Daeninckx, *Meurtres pour mémoire*, Gallimard, Collections 'Série Noire' and 'Folio', 1984, pp.180–2.

34. Mohammed Dib, *La Grande maison*, Seuil, 1952; idem, *L'Incendie*, Seuil, 1954; idem, *Le Métier à tisser*, Seuil, 1957.

35. Rousso, *The Vichy Syndrome*, p.75.

Part V

The Contested and Ambiguous Image

The Literature of the Right and the Liberation: the Case of the 'Hussards'

Nicholas Hewitt

Correctives to the Resistance and Gaullist 'myths' of the Occupation and Liberation are generally assumed to have come relatively late to France. Until the death of de Gaulle, the French are perceived as having subscribed to an historical vision often expressed as a fable, as Colin Nettelbeck noted in his seminal article of 1985. The fable ran:

> France, after being badly demoralised in the 1930s by incompetent leadership and the divisive struggles of party politics, was crushed in 1940 by superior weaponry and rather let down by its British allies. Even while she was being bled dry by the brutally repressive army that occupied her for four years, she resisted bravely: from the outside, with de Gaulle's Free French, and from within, through various clandestine movements. Thus France regained her freedom and honour by driving the Germans out – with a little help, of course, from the Allies. The few villains who had helped the Germans were purged: the collaborationist Vichy government in the first place, with the ignoble old Marshal Pétain being sent off into exile, and the even more ignoble Laval being shot; scurillous intellectuals, too, like the novelist-journalist Brasillach, were sent before the firing squad or to jail. France could once again stand proudly as a united people, joined by their historic participation in the unrelenting struggle against the Hitlerian Occupant.[1]

Nettelbeck argues that this harmonious vision, crucial to Gaullist domestic and international politics, was finally challenged in the 1970s by novelists such as Patrick Modiano[2] and films such as Louis Malle's *Lacombe Lucien*, scripted by Modiano, in a process of rectification which coincided uncomfortably with the revisionist history of writers such as Robert Faurisson.

In point of fact, however, this unificatory vision of French history in the period 1940–44 was not the monopoly of Gaullism nor confined to the time-span of the Fifth Republic. Rather, it was crucial to the establishment, legitimacy and survival of the Fourth Republic, and, as such, was questioned from the very beginning of the post-War period, initially by a vociferous and unrepentant extreme Right, but very rapidly by a more eclectic grouping which included non-aligned figures, even ex-Resisters, whose disquiet at the progress of the new Republic led them to express reservations concerning its founding myths. In this context, it is important to explore the exact nature of this right-wing, essentially literary, rectification and the reasons for its increasing attractiveness to a broader political and cultural spectrum. A crucial feature of this right-wing 'counter-culture' is the role of a younger generation of writers, who had published little or nothing before the Liberation and who, for the most part, had remained untainted by collaborationist politics, but who, nevertheless, took sides vehemently against the prevailing political and cultural orthodoxy of the Fourth Republic. They were represented most clearly by the group known as the 'Hussards'.

The Liberation is commonly believed to have destroyed the French Right as a political force. As René Rémond writes: 'En 1945–1946, on peut dire que la droite n'existe plus comme force politique.'[3] This is undoubtedly true as far as the parliamentary Right is concerned, which, for obvious electoral reasons, remained eclipsed until the return of Paul Reynaud to the Cabinet in 1948 and, particularly, the appointment of Antoine Pinay as Président du Conseil in 1952. However, it disguises the fact that, right from the end of the Occupation, there was a vigorous semi-clandestine extreme Right, uncompromising in its hostility to the Provisional Government (and later the Fourth Republic), and totally unrepentant regarding its role from 1940 to 1944. As Rémond himself recognises, this Right emerged with surprising speed and surprising resilience:

> Que l'on étudie la droite strictu sensu ou que l'on étend la notion à une réalité plus vaste, nous saisissons un même phénomène qui est la reconstitution, la remontée des profondeurs d'une droite qu'en 1945 on pourrait croire appartenir exclusivement au passé.[4]

It was constituted by three major groups: Vichy 'ultras', still committed to the policy of collaboration and often ex-members of the *Milice*; members of extreme right-wing or fascist groupings under the Occupation, who had worked closely with the Germans or who had joined the Légion des Volontaires Français contre le Bolchevisme (LVF) or Division Charlemagne; and, most important, figures who belonged to royalist groupings during the inter-War years or the

Occupation and were even more sympathetic to the values of Action Française following the perceived victimization of Maurras at his trial in 1946. The importance of Action Française as a formative influence on a significant sector of the post-War generation of French writers and as a continuing mobilizing force for the French Right in the 1940s is a crucial factor in the intellectual and political history of the Fourth Republic. In particular, it exerted considerable influence through its publications, such as *Aspects de la France*, and its student organizations, especially in the *quartier latin*. In *Paris-Montpellier*, Emmanuel Le Roy Ladurie recalls leading the Communist students of the Ecole Normale Supérieure in weekly pitched battles during the 1940s against Jean-Marie Le Pen's Royalists from the Law Faculty in the Rue d'Assas.[5] The young writers who made up the group known as the 'Hussards' all came from Action Française backgrounds in the inter-War years and the Occupation.

On the political level, it is doubtful whether this extreme Right ever constituted more than a harmless irritation for the régime, though it fed into the parliamentary careers of figures such as Jacques Isorni and Tixier-Vignancourt, converged with the rise of Poujadism, and played a real, if ultimately doomed, role in the formation of the OAS at the end of the Algerian war. With its leaders René Malliavin and René Binet, its shadowy financier Christian Wolf, and its plethora of constantly changing, constantly reconstituting organizations, the extreme Right of the 1940s resembles nothing so much as the 'groupuscules' of the extreme Left in the 1960s.[6] Culturally, however, it has a broader significance for the post-Liberation period, particularly through its ability to attract and channel disaffection with the new régime from a base which came to extend way beyond its own narrow ideological confines. In particular, this self-styled 'Opposition Nationale' served as a rallying point for three convergent anxieties: broad and increasing disquiet at the extent, arbitrariness and severity of the *épuration*; the perceived inefficiency and corruption of the Fourth Republic (through phenomena such as the Félix Gouin wine scandal or the Joanavici case); the onset of the Cold War internationally, and the perceived threat of the PCF nationally, which fostered a broad and profound incipient anti-communism and appeared to justify in retrospect one of the main planks of collaborationist policy during the Occupation. In parallel with these political concerns, the non-parliamentary Right was able to construct and foster a genuine and sustainable counter-culture, through literature, theatre, publishing houses, and journalism, which is significant both for its richness and extent and for its relative eclipse by a particular orthodox culture of the period.

Paradoxically, in the post-Liberation period the semi-clandestine Right exhibits many of the characteristics of the early Resistance. Denied real political power and unable to achieve much in military terms, it resorted of necessity to the written word as its primary form of activity. In the same way that the Resistance is enshrined in the work of Vercors, in the publication of *Les Lettres françaises*, and in the poems of Aragon, so the impact of the non-parliamentary Right in the 1940s and 1950s is predominantly textual. Its history is the history of writers, journalists, reviews and publishing houses: hence the significance of the founding, by Roland Laudenbach in 1945, of Les Editions de la Table Ronde, which was to become the major publishing outlet for right-wing creative and polemical writing,[7] and the enormous importance of weekly and monthly periodicals: *La Revue de la Table Ronde*, founded in 1948 which, in its staunchly anti-communist line, grouped the Maurrassian Thierry Maulnier with ex-Resistance personalities such as Camus, Paulhan, Mauriac and Raymond Aron; *La Parisienne*, founded by Jacques Laurent in 1953 with the express intention of countering the influence of Sartre's *Les Temps Modernes*; *Opéra*, under Nimier's editorship, the finest general arts publication of its time until its closure in 1952; *Arts*, originally a specifically fine arts review, which, in the 1950s, particularly under Jacques Laurent's editorship, took up the general arts brief of the defunct *Opéra*; and *Rivarol*, founded by Christian Wolf in 1951 and staffed by the former *Je suis partout* team, which became a high-selling forum for anti-republicanism and anti-Semitism. What is interesting about these publications is that, whilst some of them, notably *Rivarol*, *La Parisienne* and *La Table Ronde*, have, to a greater or lesser extent, a specific and explicit political content, others, especially *Opéra* and *Arts*, whilst directed by figures associated with the Right (Nimier for *Opéra*, Louis-Pauwels and Jacques Laurent for *Arts*), achieve their impact precisely through a non-political stance, and are able to broaden their base significantly. In the mid-1950s *Arts* even attracted figures from the libertarian Left such as Boris Vian.

An examination of the writers who make up this right-wing counter-culture shows it to be extensive and strongly linked to preceding periods: not merely the Occupation, but also the inter-War years. Indeed, it is the continuity of culture, on the Right as on the Left, and in personnel as well as in form and content, which dominates over the supposed turning-points of 1940 or 1944. The courts of the *épuration* and the 'listes noires' of the Comité National des Ecrivains have little permanent impact upon the continuing production of the major literary figures of the French Right: Céline, Montherlant, Jouhandeau, Morand, Marcel Aymé. What is striking about the immediate post-Liberation period, however, is not just the continuity with the pre-War period, but the repetition, almost consciously contrived, and explicitly so in the case of Nimier, of that first 'après-guerre' of 1918 and the 'années folles' which followed. In 1945–46, France embarked upon its second Jazz Age, with the same combination of music, alcohol and Americanization which characterized the first, and whilst this was the common culture of right- and left-wing groupings in Saint-Germain-des-Prés, its thematic significance was largely exploited by the Right and repressed by the Left. An intriguing parallel between the two 'après-guerres' is to be found in the case of *Le Diable au corps*, Radiguet's novel of 1920, which relegated the First World War to 'de grandes vacances pendant quatre ans' and shocked the official morality of the France of the 'Chambre bleu horizon'. Autant-Lara's film of 1946, starring Gérard Philipe, similarly offended the sensibilities of the Resistance-dominated Assemblée Nationale. In both cases, the celebration of frivolity and hedonism constitutes a calculated insult to the puritanism and moral high ground of the régime. It is significant in this context that the major figures who influenced the younger generation of French writers – Jean Cocteau, Paul Morand, Jacques Chardonne and, crucially, the fascinating ghost of Drieu la Rochelle – all stem from that epicentre of the first Jazz Age, the nightclub Le Bœuf sur le Toit.

If this group hand on to their successors one key ingredient in post-War right-wing culture it is a sometimes empty mondanity, and Marcel Aymé is the pivotal influence, both as a demystifier and as the founder of a certain 'tone'. Aymé's novels constitute a systematic, if partisan, demystification of France's recent history of the Popular Front, the Occupation and the Liberation: *Travelingue* mercilessly lampoons the intellectual vapidity of the fashionable Left at the time of the Popular Front; *Le Chemin des écoliers* shows the confusion of Occupied Paris in which the black market appears more attractive than the plodding seriousness of the Resistance; and *Uranus* unveils a post-War France dominated by the PCF, in which wartime black-marketeers are readily tolerated, whilst minor collaborators are hunted down. That Aymé achieves this by employing a fictional form which combines comedy (heavily indebted to Molière and *Les Précieuses ridicules*, for *Travelingue*), fantasy and whimsicality, and that this can, in its own right, constitute a powerful weapon, is a lesson not lost on his younger disciples.

These disciples, who owe much to the 'mondain' personalities of Le Bœuf sur le Toit, and even more to the perspective and technique of Aymé, all published their first significant work in the immediate post-War period and presented such similarities of stance and tone that they became grouped together under the name of 'les Hussards', taken from Roger Nimier's novel *Le Hussard bleu* (1950). In fact, the label, first conferred on them by Bernard Franck in an article in *Les Temps Modernes* in 1952,[8] was as arbitrary as the term 'Existentialiste', given to Sartre and his friends in 1946. The central figures in the group, which never once actually met together, were Nimier, Jacques Laurent and Antoine Blondin, with a broader grouping including Michel Déon, Kléber Haedens and Stephen Hecquet. What is important for the political significance of this group is that they come to anti-parliamentary right-wing politics as much for aesthetic as for political reasons, and with no dramatic prior record. All came from royalist backgrounds: Nimier served in a light armoured regiment of 'Hussards' in the winter of 1944–45, though in the Pyrenees rather than the Germany depicted in *Le Hussard bleu*; Blondin was conscripted into the STO; the most implicated was Laurent, who served in Angelo Tasca's department in the Ministère de l'Information in Vichy.[9] In other words, for these writers, the adoption of a right-wing stance is less the product of a past commitment than a reaction to political and artistic circumstances in the post-War period itself.

In this context, the Right constituted a genuine counter-culture in that its main target was a cultural phenomenon, albeit with considerable political and historical significance – Existentialism. Quite apart from its literary or philosophical content, Existentialism was an historical phenomenon, born of the Resistance, growing to the height of its popularity in the aftermath of the Liberation, and declining with the moderation of the Cold War which followed the death of Stalin. If, as Michael Scriven suggests,[10] Existentialism was the 'glue' which held post-War French society, or at least ideology, together, it was glue which was not applied by chance. In a very real sense, this 'philosophie officielle'[11] of the new régime was marketed by the Fourth Republic as a means to self-legitimation. Heir apparent to the engagé political writer of the 1930s, in particular Malraux, Chamson, Nizan and Guilloux, the existentialists were, above all, with their insistence on recognition of situation, choice, action, responsibility and sacrifice, expressing the ideals of the Resistance. The continued popularity of Existentialism in the post-War era guaranteed the survival of Resistance values into a period when the moral credentials of the régime were under intense scrutiny. Ironically, therefore, in spite of its radicalism – indeed, because of its radicalism – Existentialism served the cause of the Establishment it so despised, just as its leading figures were obliged to reject the honours which a grateful government attempted to bestow upon them.

This ambiguous, but highly powerful, position of Existentialism allowed it to set a dominant literary tone which privileged the moral, and in which high seriousness and humourless didacticism became the orthodox aesthetic code, encapsulated, albeit confusedly, in Sartre's *Qu'est-ce que la littérature?* At the same time, this dominant aesthetic sought, with some considerable success, to exclude from the contemporary literary canon those works which did not meet its own high ideals of engagement: works by writers whose political pedigrees were suspect, whether of the Communist Left or, more usually, the Right, but also works of an experimental, sometimes comic, nature by non-conformist authors such as Vian or Queneau, neither of whom have received the attention their innovation merits.

The 'Hussards' reacted against this perceived literary and political hegemony by the adoption of a tone and tradition, quite separate from subject matter, which clearly demarcated them from their opponents. Where Existentialism found its origins in 1830s Romanticism, the 'Hussards' went back to the libertinism of the Eighteenth Century or to admiration for Stendhal (the Fourth Republic being, after the 1880s, the second period of resurrection of 'Beylisme'). If the roots of 'engagement' are to be found in the fiction of the 1930s, the 'Hussards' took their models from the 1920s. If Existentialism was bourgeois intellectually and democratic politically, the 'Hussards' adopted a tone of aristocratic 'hauteur' and the term 'insolence' is a favourite one in the description of their heroes' manner. If *Qu'est-ce que la littérature?* sought to impose an essentially didactic mode of fictional writing, the 'Hussards' vowed to restore to the fictional text its literary autonomy, and if that didacticism implied the adoption and maintenance of a tone of high seriousness, the 'Hussards', true to their masters Cocteau and Aymé, countered with wit, comedy and fantasy.

This antipathy to both the doctrine and the doctrinaire aesthetics of Existentialism was expressed at its clearest in Jacques Laurent's pamphlet of 1951, *Paul et Jean-Paul*, in which he compared Sartre to the late nineteenth-century novelist Paul Bourget, and detected in both the same subordination of the literary to the abstract.[12] In his 'Présentation' to the first number of *La Parisienne* in January 1953 he wrote:

> La littérature est devenue un moyen. Elle est mal vue dès qu'elle est autre chose qu'un moyen. Si des critiques aussi peu engagés que M. Robert Kemp ne peuvent parler d'un livre sans commenter l'attitude de l'auteur sous l'Occupation, c'est qu'il y a eu ces dernières années une victoire de la littérature-moyen sur la littérature...Voici une nouvelle revue littéraire qui ne souhaite servir rien d'autre que la littérature.[13]

What is curious is that, for a brief moment at least, there appears to have been an inversion of the traditionally associated aesthetics of Left and Right. Undoubtedly this was due in large part to the shifting fortunes of power and opposition by which, in the Fourth Republic, it was the Left that became the defender of the moral and political orthodoxy and laid itself open to charges of pomposity and hypocrisy, especially after the 1946 Marthe Richard Law closing the brothels, whereas the Right chose comedy and irreverence as its favoured means of expression and its most appropriate political weapon. It was this sardonic irreverence which brought it close to the left-wing libertarianism of a Vian or a Prévert, and which enabled the editor of *Le Crapouillot*, Jean Galtier-Boissière, with thirty years' experience of libertarian sniping at successive, almost exclusively conservative, governments, to fit easily into the post-War Right. At the same time as it adopted a privileged tone, which enabled it to champion the cause of non-doctrinaire literature, the new Right carefully exploited the mechanisms which that tone revealed to unpick the received view of the Occupation which Existentialism was forced to defend and which constituted the legitimate base of the morality of the Fourth Republic. The way in which it does this is illustrated by three novels: Jacques Laurent's *Le Petit canard* (1954), Roger Nimier's *Le Hussard bleu* (1950) and Antoine Blondin's *L'Europe buissonnière* (1949), in which the dominant tones are, respectively, pathos, insolence and humour.

Of all the 'Hussards', it was Jacques Laurent who was the most identified with right-wing politics. His uncle was Eugène Deloncle, founder of the 'Cagoule', and he had been involved in royalist student journalist circles since his days at the Lycée Charlemagne. A soldier in the Armée de l'Armistice, he moved to Vichy where he became a relatively important official in Angelo Tasca's section of the Ministère de l'Information, though not so important as to be seriously disturbed at the Liberation.[14] His post-War literary career took three distinct, but significant, directions: firstly as a serious novelist, beginning with the highly inventive and ambitious *Les Corps tranquilles*; secondly as a popular novelist, writing under a variety of pseudonyms, the best known of which is Cécil Saint-Laurent, author of the phenomenally successful *Caroline chérie* (1947) and its sequels; and finally as a successful polemicist and journalist, using the proceeds from his popular writings to finance such ventures as *La Parisienne*.[15] *Le Petit canard* is a carefully controlled exploitation of a banal case history, which illustrates, as does *Lacombe Lucien* twenty years later, the accidental and arbitrary nature of political involvement and the injustice of severe punishment for it. It recounts the story of an adolescent whose lycée moves from Paris to the Normandy coast during the 'Phoney War' and who then falls in love with a young girl who has been similarly located. During the rout of the 'Exode' following the German advance, the two become separated from their families and sleep together. It is then that the hero discovers that the girl has already had a lover, a Polish officer billeted in the same coastal town in Normandy, and the first part of the narrative ends with his abandoning her. In the second part, the reader discovers that the protagonist has subsequently joined the LVF, has been arrested at the Liberation, and is now under sentence of death. The initial theme of the arbitrariness of the connection between betrayal by mistress and subsequent betrayal of country, with the tenuous link of the Polish Allied officer as sole motivation, is given pathos by the device of narrating the second part of the novel in the second person singular. Here the boy's father, grief-stricken and remorseful, addresses his condemned son, the 'petit canard', who, as the result of an adolescent infatuation, has turned into a goose and not a swan. Informing the narrative throughout is a controlled and compelling anger at the uncomprehending severity of the *épuration*.

Among the 'Hussards', it was Roger Nimier who came closest to the mainstream of post-War French literature. This is illustrated by his constant association with the publishing house of Gallimard, with whom he invariably published and for whom he worked as a reader, whereas his colleagues were more often associated with La Table Ronde. His literary career was marked by its precocity, with his first novel, *Les Epées* (1948), making a considerable impact, and his subsequent development being carefully nurtured by two prominent members of the previous generation, Paul Morand and Jacques Chardonne. Indeed, so precocious was his career that his inventiveness as a novelist clearly began to suffer and, after the publication of *Les Enfants tristes* (1951), Jacques Chardonne advised him to suspend novel-writing for ten years in order to allow his talent to mature. In his fiction, Nimier showed a predilection for the cultivation of the superior, tortured, sardonic hero, which ultimately did not lend itself to development, whereas, on the evidence of a novel like *Perfide* (1950), it is possible that his talent lay equally strongly and more productively in the areas of the comic and the burlesque. His best-known novel, *Le Hussard bleu*, is an ambitious, multifaceted account of the advance of a light armoured regiment, the 'Hussards' of the title, into Germany in the winter of 1944–45 and its subsequent occupation of the Black Forest. The thrust of the novel is to show the French participation in the military campaign in the final months of the war as an absurd gesture, and unbearably costly in terms of casualties, designed solely to establish some French prestige before the final victory. Against this background of futile but dangerous military posturing, Nimier traces two parallel careers: that of the flamboyant, light, Stendhalian Saint-Anne, the 'Hussard bleu' of the title, so called because of his theatrical blue uniform, and the disabused, cynical François Sanders, the central character of *Les Epées*, disfigured by a German flame-thrower during the winter's advance, and marked by a curious experience – as a Resister he had been sent to infiltrate a group of *Miliciens*, and found them to exhibit the same qualities of camaraderie and courage as his previous comrades. Here, Nimier raises one of the familiar arguments used by revisionists of the orthodox view of the Occupation, and one employed repeatedly to castigate the post-Liberation governments: namely, that true Resisters and *Miliciens* were equally chivalrous and patriotic and had more in common than those who subsequently spoke in the name of the Resistance in the Fourth Republic. At the end of the novel, Sanders returns to Paris even more disabused as the result of the murder of Saint-Anne in his place and the suicide of his former *Milice* comrade, Besse. The novel concludes with the reflexion by Sanders as his train enters Paris: 'Tout ce qui est humain m'est étranger,'[16] a negation of the traditional humanist 'Homo sum, humani nihil a me alienum puto' of Terence, and a specific rejection of the unifying humanist philosophy of post-Liberation France.[17] Whereas *Le Petit canard* calls into question the justice of the *épuration*, therefore, *Le Hussard bleu*, through the aristocratic, insolent Sanders, extends its critique to the French military venture of 1944–45, to the 'artificial' distinction between Resisters and *Miliciens*, and, crucially, to the humanist 'glue', of which Existentialism was an essential ingredient, which held post-War French ideology together.

Of all the 'Hussards', it was arguably Blondin who was the most talented. An effective right-wing polemicist who began his career in Pierre Boutang's clandestine *La Dernière lanterne* in 1946 and went on to play a key role in *Rivarol*, he also became one of France's most distinguished sports journalists and wrote regularly for *L'Equipe* on cycling and rugby. As a novelist, his work exhibits a whimsical quality and a lightness of touch which his two counterparts rarely achieve and which makes him the direct heir of Marcel Aymé. In particular, the very title of *L'Europe buissonnière* (1949) is an acknowledgement of Aymé's *Le Chemin des écoliers*, with its theme of war and Occupation as truancy, and, beyond that, of Radiguet's 'grandes vacances' in *Le Diable au corps*. The comic and burlesque tone of the novel is reinforced by the adoption of a picaresque hero, the literally larger-than-life Muguet, who, with more than a nod in the direction of Voltaire's Candide and Céline's Bardamu in *Voyage au bout de la nuit*, sets off on a voyage through the Second World War which will take him from the Battle of France to Occupied Belgium, the French Resistance, exiled *maquisards* in Spain, the STO in Austria, and, finally, the Liberation. The very adoption of the picaresque mode serves, in addition to the comedy it generates, to heighten the importance of the accidental and the arbitrary and to question that clear vision of history and that belief in volition which were central to the self-legitimation process of post-War France and which, by no coincidence, are essential components of Existentialism. The vision of the war is one of an arbitrary chain of events in which heroism has no place. To the question 'Qu'as-tu fait?' Muguet's friend Superniel answers, 'Acte de présence'.[18] This answer, I would argue, is a more accurate reflection of the experience of the vast mass of French people during the war than the official 'myth' to which Nettlebeck draws attention.

A close examination of French culture in the post-Liberation period reveals a pattern which is considerably more complex than the fable criticized by Nettelbeck. The process of rectifying the legitimizing historical vision of the Fourth Republic began with the birth of the Republic itself and anticipated the later revisions of the 1970s. Initially, that rectification was carried out by a surprisingly vigorous anti-parliamentary Right, which was able to draw upon both a cultural tradition and a broader constituency in the wake of historical events such as the *épuration* and the Cold War. Viewed in this light, the culture of the Right exhibits a remarkable continuity from the 1920s to the 1950s, and, in the post-War period, clashes with the temporary Establishment culture of the Left, represented in particular by Existentialism, on issues which appear to be exclusively aesthetic, but which in reality are concerned with the interpretation and expression of the recent past. An examination of this alternative literature indicates the narrowness of what is normally assumed to be the cultural canon of the France of the Liberation, and also permits a certain circumspection towards French history from 1940 to 1945.

Notes

Unless stated otherwise, the place of publication is Paris.

1. Colin Nettelbeck, 'Getting the Story Right: Narratives of World War II in Post-1968 France', *Journal of European Studies*, vol.15, 1985, pp.77–116.
2. Colin Nettelbeck and P. Hueston, *Patrick Modiano: Pièces d'identité*,

Minard, collection 'Archives des Lettres Modernes', 220, 1986.

3. René Rémond, 'La Droite en France sous la IVe République', in *La Quatrième République*. *Bilan de trente ans après la promulgation de la Constitution du 27 octobre 1946*. *Actes du Colloque de Nice, les 20, 21 et 22 janvier 1977*, Librairie Générale de Droit et de Jusrisprudence R. Pichon et R. Durand-Anzas, 1978, p.277.

4. Ibid.

5. See Emmanuel Le Roy Ladurie, *Paris-Montpellier, PC-PSU, 1945–1963*, Gallimard, collection 'Témoins', 1982.

6. J. Plumyène and R. Lasierra, *Les Fascismes français*, Seuil, 1963, chapter 3; Nicholas Hewitt, '1944/1793: la droite intellectuelle et le mythe de la Terreur Rouge', *French Cultural Studies*, no.15, 1994.

7. See Patrick Louis, *La Table Ronde: Une Aventure singulière*, La Table Ronde, 1992.

8. Bernard Franck, 'Grognards et Hussards', *Les Temps Modernes*, no.86, 1952, pp.1005–18.

9. See Marc Dambre, *Roger Nimier. Hussard du demi-siècle*, Flammarion, 1989; Jacques Laurent, *Histoire égoiste*, Gallimard, collection 'Folio', 1978; Angelo Tasca, *Vichy 1940–1944: Quaderni e documenti di Angelo Tasca. Archives de guerre d'Angelo Tasca, a cura di Denis Peschanski*, Milan, Feltrinelli, 1986, pp.517, 648–82.

10. Michael Scriven, 'L'Etre et le néant 50 Years on', *French Cultural Studies*, no.13, 1994, p.105.

11. Jean-Louis Curtis, *Les Justes causes*, Julliard, 1954, p.213.

12. Jacques Laurent, *Paul et Jean-Paul*, Grasset, collection 'Les Cahiers irréguliers', 1951.

13. Jacques Laurent, 'Présentation', *La Parisienne*, January 1953, p.9.

14. Laurent, *Histoire égoiste*.

15. See Colin Nettelbeck, 'The Chameleon Rearguard of Cultural Tradition: the Case of Jacques Laurent', in Nicholas Hewitt (ed.), *The Culture of Reconstruction. European Literature, Thought and Film, 1945–1950*, Basingstoke, Macmillan, 1989, pp.153–71.

16. Roger Nimier, *Le Hussard bleu*, Gallimard, collection 'Folio', 1977, p.434.

17. See Michael Kelly, 'Humanism and National Identity: the Ideological Reconstruction of France', in Hewitt, *The Culture of Reconstruction*, pp.103–19.

18. Antoine Blondin, *L'Europe buissonnière*, Livre de Poche, 1961, p.435.

– 20 –

War and Victimization through Children's Eyes: Caen – Occupation and Liberation

Jill Sturdee

During the Bataille de Caen, which raged for two and a half months of summer 1944, sixteen-year-old Janine Espiasse kept a journal. This is her entry for Thursday, 29 June 1944:

> As I sit on a mattress in the cellar of the Convent of the Petites Sœurs des Pauvres, I begin here the account of the dreadful events of June 1944. In spite of the whistle of shells above our heads and the planes dive-bombing, I can remember every single hour of anguish which we have already suffered. I await those to come.[1]

The people of Caen paid a high price for their freedom. M Jean-Marie Girault, present Mayor-Senator of Caen who was himself a boy living in the city throughout the Occupation and the Battle, estimates that 600,000 Allied and German shells as well as thousands of high explosive and incendiary bombs fell in a devastating seventy-eight-day siege starting on 6 June and lasting as long as the Battle of Normandy itself. Casualty figures are estimated by him to have been 3,000–5,000 in a city of less than 60,000 inhabitants. Of the 18,000 homes, 10,000 were completely destroyed and a mere 400 were found by the end of 1944 to be unscathed.[2] Even after the liberation on 9 July of the left bank of the city, Caen continued to be the victim of numerous German counter-offensives until the last shell landed on 18 August, only eight days before de Gaulle's triumphal procession through the streets of newly-liberated Paris.

Within the context of childhood, the images and events associated with the liberation of Caen, both during and before 1944, offer a fresh insight into both the liberation of Caen and the four years of

Nazi Occupation which preceded it. Mia Kellmer Pringle's acknowledgement of the overriding importance of environment in the development of the child[3] brings into focus the fact that Caen children too, like Caen adults, lived, first through four years of Occupation, then through the brutal reality of liberation, which for many of them constituted bombardment, homelessness, bereavement and death. The detail of children's individual experience in grappling with the events of the period must not be neglected if we are to form a complete picture of this period in Caen's history.

It seems at first sight that memories of this period by adults who were then children do conform to the established categories of public memory of the Battle as outlined by Etienne Fouilloux and Dominique Veillon.[4] Memories of the night of 5/6 June appear for former children as for adults to have been universally and painstakingly preserved. M Jacques Perret recalls that on the night of 5/6 June, the pounding of shells was such that he and his brothers and sisters had the impression that a tremendous storm was raging all night on the coast.[5] M Jean-Paul Corbasson remembers that 'the night before the 6 June and the morning were very noisy. I didn't go to school. Lots of people were queuing early at the baker's.'[6]

A second constant in public memory pinpointed by Fouilloux and Veillon is the mass exodus from the city. This evacuation of an estimated 40,000 men, women and children[7] is recalled too by witnesses who were then children or who as parents were concerned for the safety of their families. Mme Annik Gires, living at her grandparents' farm in the country, remembers people beginning

> to stream out of Caen. I helped my grandmother to make soup in enormous cooking pots so that we could give something to eat to people who came to the farm. There were people sleeping in the barns and cowsheds. They took to the roads again the next day, but it was dangerous to travel, and my grandfather gave away his horses and carts as nobody had any transport.[8]

Mme Leullier recalls in a letter dated November 1944 to her cousins that 'we found shelter six or seven kilometers out of town, with a butcher and his family. We had to find someone who could take all twelve of us. The children slept four to a bed with their children.'[9]

Contributing to the impact of the scattered images collected by Fouilloux and Veillon of those rendered homeless by the bombing are the vivid images of devastation in the town in the wake of bombardments. Dr Guibé recounts his memories of the walk to the Bon Sauveur hospital from his ruined home. He recalls how we crossed the rue Saint-Jean, and I can still picture the houses burning, the rubble in the streets, and the rooms ripped open, still with pieces of furniture left inside... When we crossed the rue Bertrand there were German tanks camouflaged with greenery and manned by frenzied German troops. I remember being struck by the extraordinary impression of power.[10]

M Corbasson relates his journey across town to the Lycée Malherbe. He tells how 'houses were still standing on both sides of the street... Things jumped in flames from the window holes... These minutes remain today the most dramatic picture of war in the eyes of the nine-year-old I was.'[11]

Another constant in public memory are the centres of refuge which sheltered thousands of homeless families. As many as 20,000 of those who lost their homes stayed in Caen, finding shelter at one of the five official refugee centres set up in the town.[12] In the heart of the city, the area consisting of the Abbey Church of Saint-Etienne, the Lycée Malherbe and the Bon Sauveur hospital was relatively successfully designated a safe haven. Here a juxtaposition of childhood memories gives the impression of contrasting scenes of peace and war. M Jean-Paul Corbasson recalls: 'In the Lycée we settled in a vaulted passage called the Archbishop's Walk ... One of my friends was there with his parents. He was lying ill without toys and books and I gave him my teddy bear to keep him company.'[13] Mlle Marcelle Pommier, an orphan from the Saint-Vincent de Paul Orphanage in Caen, on the other hand, paints a scene more suggestive of a battlefield. She remembers that 'we all went to the Lycée Malherbe to take refuge but we couldn't stay because there were so many casualties there. I remember walking past all the wounded and dead bodies, and I can still picture the scene.'[14] In the same way, two portraits of life at the Bon Sauveur hospital paint contrasting images, suggestive of a semblance of normality on the one hand and images of appalling suffering on the other. Dr Guibé, whose father, a surgeon, spent all his waking hours in the operating theatre, remembers that 'we played in the grounds of the hospital. The whole place was full of refugees as well as all the wounded. There were a man and a woman who had a small trunk with them, and I remember somebody opening the lid, and it was full of poultry.'[15] Conversely, Dr Jean Olivier recalls transferring to the Bon Sauveur hospital a little girl of about six who was brought to him on a stretcher with extensive head injuries and having lost a leg. Relating how she fixed him with terrified eyes, he wonders: 'What became of this little martyr and her mortified parents?'[16]

Then there were the limestone quarries outside the town where up to ten thousand people took refuge during the Battle. The most celebrated of these are at Fleury, where by the morning of 7 June there were as many as 1,500 refugees sheltering.[17] Mme Gires remembers going there with her mother, her brother and sister. She relates:

> My uncle used to bring us food while we were at the quarries, and once the Germans told him if he came again they would shoot him. There were miles of underground galleries, and several entrances, so each time he came to see us he took a different route. We were frightened for him, though: at least I was because I understood what would happen to him. He used to bring us bread and milk. It was dark in the galleries except by the entrances, where there was always the danger of being fired on... I was frightened because the Germans told everybody to leave, and my mother said she was staying unless they forced us at gunpoint to go. I hated big lights afterwards, because they used to come looking for us with huge lamps.[18]

Many other specific instances of suffering to which children were subjected during the Battle have been recollected by witnesses. Mlle Baudre, headmistress of the Saint-Pierre Church School in Caen, recalls:

> I lost thirteen children from my school. Paulette Lamy was killed on 7 July: the sides of the dugout where she was sheltering collapsed and the whole family – the father, mother and seven children – were suffocated. The only boy was found in his father's arms, and the mother was lying on top of the girls as if to protect them.[19]

M Perret relates how he and his family sheltered in a doorway at daybreak watching the city of Caen in flames. He remembers that his youngest brother Dominique, then three and a half years old, had lost a shoe and was crying, and he kept repeating 'Little Jesus, save us, Little Jesus, save us.'[20] Then there is the history of fourteen-year-old Pierre Favier, a member of the Equipes d'Urgence de la Croix-Rouge, which played a significant role in assisting the emergency services during the Battle. Mme Brédiger, who worked with the Red Cross, remembers visiting the boy in hospital after he was mortally wounded by falling glass while working to clear rubble from the Galéries Lafayette store in town. She records: 'I shall always remember the scene. He was terribly badly wounded – he died 48 hours later – and I had tears in my eyes. He said to me, "You mustn't cry, Madame Brédiger, I'm dying like a soldier."'[21]

Within these images of the Liberation, as experienced by children in Caen, there are two major clusters. A first set of images demonstrates that the predominant sentiment among children during the Battle was one of sheer terror. An overt manifestation of a child's extreme fear is the girl's 'terrified eyes' when she was brought to Dr Olivier with massive head injuries and an amputated leg. Fear is also both named and evoked by Mme Gires when relating her experiences in the quarries. She remembers that 'we were frightened' for her uncle who brought them food, and even qualifies this with 'at least I was'. Other images suggest that the symbol of the dark served additionally to represent this child's primary terror of the Germans. She admits that she was 'frightened' when the Germans told them to leave, that 'it was dark in the galleries', and that she 'hated big lamps afterwards'.[22]

The child's use of symbolism is evident too in M Perret's evocation of the 'tremendous storm' which appeared to him to be raging on the coast on the night of the Normandy landings. An analogy may easily be drawn in the child's mind between the natural phenomena of thunder and lightning and the possibility of bombardment. Clearly to the child the latter is the more terrifying possibility. A storm, although a threat, is something previously experienced, while bombardment constitutes a human phenomenon of nightmarish quality capable of exciting an inconceivable degree of alarm. Thus the substitution of the storm image serves to suppress the terrifying image of bombardment.

The notion of terror may also be linked to M Corbasson's recollection that he gave his teddy bear to a friend 'who was lying ill'. Paul Fussell attests to the miraculous powers attributed by First World War soldiers in the trenches to talismans which were widely credited with the power to deflect bullets and shell fragments.[23] The same qualities may clearly be attributed by a small boy to a teddy bear which, credited by him with magical powers, will ward off danger and thus protect him, and his sick friend, from the object of their terror.

A second cluster of images demonstrates unequivocally that Caen children had no real understanding of the meaning of war. Caen had escaped bombardment in the 1940 German advance, so that war for the Caen child, unlike Occupation, was a concept which he or she was quite unable in June 1944 to understand. Anna Freud and Dorothy Burlingham provide corroboration that 'we may often be wrong in assuming that children "understand" the happenings around them.'[24] Thus, Dr Guibé's image of the 'extraordinary impression of power' offered by the German tanks and troops ties in with their theory that children may instinctively turn towards incidents of wholesale destruction with primitive excitement. Dr Guibé's fascination with this potent image is reminiscent of the similar boyish attraction, reported by Jerzy Kosinski in his autobiographical tale of childhood in occupied Poland, towards the SS officer whose 'entire person seemed to have something utterly superhuman about it'. The latter's 'resplendent being, armed in all the symbols of might and majesty,'[25] has the same fascinating magnetism for the Polish boy as do the German tanks and troops for the Caen child.

Inability to comprehend what is happening around him is manifested too in M Corbasson's evocative description of the devastation which he witnessed when he crossed the town after a major air raid. His image of 'things [which] jumped in flames from the window holes' is a scene reminiscent of a horrific fantasy in a fairy tale. A surreal world is conjured up too in Dr Guibé's images of life at the Bon Sauveur hospital. Here was a horrifying world of death and bereavement; yet Dr Guibé's lasting image is that 'we played in the grounds of the hospital.' Equally, the image of the trunk lid being opened to reveal that it was 'full of poultry' has the innocence of a magic show. Thus he has effectively obliterated the real world of corpses and mutilated bodies and substituted an imaginative world of magic and play. This ties in, through Mia Kellmer Pringle's notion that make-believe games allow the child to find temporary refuge from being small, inexperienced and without any real power,[26] with Paulette in *Jeux Interdits*, who contrives to eradicate the horrific image of German aircraft machine-gunning the defenceless cortège of 1940 evacuees by imagining zoo animals in the procession, and portraying the German pilot as a wolf wearing a tin helmet.[27]

Such interpretations of the child's view of the Battle of Caen indicate that those seventy-eight days constituted for some a world of sheer hell, perpetrated by constant terror, and that there was also an underlying lack of understanding of what it was all about. The significance of this finding is that these Caen children do not appear to corroborate the dominant public view that the Liberation of France constituted a joyous and hopeful event wherein all the images of assault, destruction, fire, tears, blood and death were contributors to the final goal, that of freedom from Nazi domination.

The fundamental difference between adults' and children's images of the Battle for Caen centres around the very concept of liberation. Dominique Veillon contends that, contrary to national public memory in France, the D-Day landings were seen by the people of Caen, Saint-Lô and Cherbourg as an ineluctable event for which a terrible price was paid, and which they judge with hindsight to have been too costly.[28] Nevertheless, there was no doubt among the Caen population at the time that liberation was of the highest priority. A May 1944 report from the Renseignements Généraux stated that 'there is a unanimous feeling that the war is becoming unbearable and that everybody is prepared to endure a short and terrible struggle in order to be liberated from the heavy burden which the Occupation represents'.[29] This sentiment is echoed by M André Heintz, then a young member of the Organisation Civile et Militaire (OCM) Resistance network, who declares simply that the Occupation by the Germans 'was so dreadful that we were prepared to put up with anything to get rid of them'.[30] Twenty thousand inhabitants elected to stay and endure a state of siege, the Prefect having refused to evacuate the city in spite of the Kommandantur's warning that the Battle had the makings of a second Stalingrad.[31]

By contrast, how were children to envisage liberation? That they also experienced feelings of expectation and deliverance is manifested in oral evidence. Mme Gires remembers that in May 'people started talking about the Allied landings. All the women and children were advised to leave the towns, so we went to live with my grandparents.'[32] But what exactly was liberation? The Occupation had been going on for so long that many children had only vague memories of what life was like before. To children, surely liberation from Nazi Occupation could not mean an increase in air raids, terror and death? The air raid warning which sounded in Caen shortly after midnight on the night of 5/6 June 1944 was the 1,020th in the town: and many had been victims of air attacks for over a year. *Bonhomme Normand* of 16–23 April 1943, reporting that the boys' primary school in Vaucelles had been hit, went so far as to declare that 'schools are always targeted by the Anglo-American raids. These pirates of the sky seem to derive pleasure from taking it out on children'[33]: while the Vichy departmental Delegate for Information was able to report a year later, in April 1944, that 'the sweet and joyous Liberation is no longer heralded. People are pleading with the skies that the attack should take place elsewhere.'[34]

I would argue that two oral statements are particularly significant here. M Perret recalls:

We older children had never imagined that this German Occupation would finish in blood. We were beginning to discover the meaning of the word 'War'... The Occupier had, without our realizing it, normalized our days. And we had visualized the Liberation with a certain naïveté, as if one beautiful day we would no longer have to argue amongst ourselves about our 350 grammes of bread and our squares of chocolate.[35]

And there was Mme Jeannine Flambard's recollection that 'we knew nothing: all we knew was that we were afraid, just as we were during the whole Occupation.'[36] Adults were able to rationalize, and to justify the fact that liberation might represent a battle high in casualties. Children did not imagine that liberation could be perpetrated by terror. This judgement opens up the possibility that many Caen children felt betrayed by the battle for liberation. The reality of four years of Occupation which preceded D-Day had been a relentless reign of terror for children who found themselves victims within the Nazi system. For them, the Battle constituted a prolongation or even intensification of the experiences of Occupation. Particularly from 1942 onwards, and coinciding with the appointment in Paris of Oberg as Chief of Police, terror had been a public and everyday occurrence. Children were exposed to brutal actions which took place before their eyes. Mlle Pommier claims to remember vividly 'the scene at Place des Petites Boucheries. We were coming out of Saint-Etienne church with the Nuns, and there was a girl saying "Qu'est-ce que c'est moche!" A German thought she had said "Boche" and he shot her dead in front of everybody.'[37] This aura of terror is echoed by Mme Gires, who recalls that

> one day when I was at my grandparents' farmhouse, the door was thrown open and a German SS rushed in, dressed in black and carrying a machine-gun. I thought he was going to kill the lot of us starting with me. He took my grandfather and uncle away because of some story about fuel which they had hidden for the tractor.[38]

There were many occasions on which children witnessed the arrest of their mother or father. M Jean-Paul Corbasson, whose father, Lieutenant-Colonel Gaston Corbasson, was a member of Ceux de la Résistance (CDLR),[39] recalls: 'I discovered the Gestapo in December 1943 when they arrested my father. We were in the dining room... The Gestapo rang the bell and banged at the door and rushed in. My brother Robert wept and my mother told him "Don't ever cry in front of these people."'[40]

Young boys were among those victimized in German reprisals. Two brothers aged fifteen and sixteen, Marcel and Lucien Colin, younger sons of the headmaster of the Ecole Primaire Supérieure in Caen,[41] were among the 120 taken hostage after the April and May 1942 derailments near Moult-Argences of two trains carrying German soldiers. While they were interned in Paris, and before being deported to Auschwitz, where both boys died, Lucien Colin compiled a journal. This is how he records his arrest: 'On Thursday 7 May 1942 at 10.15

p.m., two German policemen came to our house to arrest my brother Marcel and me... We spent a dreadful night at the Petit Lycée sleeping on the floor... Why were we there?... Why us?'[42]

Children were also used as pawns by the German police in measures to put a stop to Resistance attacks. In July 1942 an edict by Oberg was published in Caen stating that in the event of the perpetrators of a Resistance attack not being apprehended within ten days, members of their families aged eighteen and over would be shot or sentenced to hard labour, while all children of these family members would be sent to remand homes.[43]

Jewish children, as well as adults, in Caen were victims of terror. Among the total of 118 Jews from Caen listed in the Caen synagogue who died in deportation there are four large families. One is the Kirtzner family. Maurice Kirtzner aged six was deported from Drancy on 3 November 1942 for Auschwitz with his father, mother and four sisters.[44] Madame Moreau remembers him. She recalls that 'in my class at school there was a Jewish boy called Maurice. He was the eldest of five children, and the whole family were deported. I had no idea that they were Jewish until my mother told me years later.'[45]

Another child taken for deportation was Mme Guina Tresser, who remembers 'the morning when the SS in long leather coats came to the house. They put my mother in one car, and my sister and I went in a second car. I saw my mother waving goodbye to us from the car in front. The SS took us to an Orphanage and said they would come back for us the next day.'[46] In the event, the two sisters, then aged five and three, were rescued by the Resistance and spent the rest of the Occupation on a farm in Lisieux. Their cousin, Louis Juris, was not as fortunate as they were. He was taken from Pithiviers for Auschwitz on 31 July 1942 – the day before his sixteenth birthday – together with his father in a convoy of 1,049 Jews including 131 adolescents aged fifteen to twenty.[47]

Young boys and girls who themselves became involved in Resistance work clearly ran the risk of becoming victims of the Nazi system. Jacques Sabine, a pupil at the Lycée Malherbe and an active member of the Front Patriotique de la Jeunesse, was sixteen when he was arrested in February 1943. Condemned to seven years' hard labour, Jacques was deported to Breslau, where he died of tuberculosis in August 1944. A later tribute by a fellow prisoner affirmed Jacques to have shown 'more courage as a boy than many grown men'.[48]

Oral reminiscence cannot simply be taken at its face value, and always needs to be interrogated. Nevertheless from the very consistency of the oral evidence it is arguable that the perpetuation of terror from the Occupation into the Battle for Caen should be registered both as fact and image of the Liberation, if children's experiences are to be given historical value. The terror is summarized in the fatalities already mentioned: Paulette Lamy, who died of suffocation in a dugout on 7 July along with her brother and five sisters; Pierre Favier, who 'died like a soldier' after being mortally wounded by falling glass in the Galéries Lafayette; the Jewish children who died in deportation: Maurice Kirtzner with his four sisters, and Louis Juris who was deported to Auschwitz in a convoy of 131 young boys and girls; the *résistant* Jacques Sabine, who died of tuberculosis.

The Tresser girls' mother came home from Belsen to Caen, but the elder girl, Guina, was so traumatized by her experiences that she confesses: 'Those dark years deprived me of my childhood. For me there was no beauty in life any more. I became antisocial and I never got on properly with either my mother or father. Mine was an unhappy childhood. They never understood me.'[49] Mme Annik Gires's father, M Pierre Bouchard, was head of the Normandy section of the CDLR Resistance network.[50] Arrested in Caen in December 1943, he died in deportation. She records:

> For ages I refused to believe that my father was dead... Then in 1948 every deportee's family was given the chance to go and see the concentration camps. My mother wanted to go, and she took me with her. I was thirteen... At the concentration camp we saw buildings which had been designed way back ... expressly to perform a specific function: the gas chambers, the actual door they made them go through, and the one where they dragged the corpses out. My whole world caved in that day. Somehow it's not the same when one is grown up. Adults can distance themselves from things, but children are still developing. They need to have a firm foundation on which to build their world so that mankind can continue to benefit from such tradition. I felt I couldn't trust anything any more.[51]

If nothing else, these final records of trauma give telling personal emphasis to the statistics of loss and destruction which constitute the specificity of Caen in the Liberation of France. Within that particular history of the city dubbed 'Anvil of Victory'[52] there is the further specificity of children's experience. In the debate over the Liberation as end or beginning, their images, both at the time and since, point to a third historical dimension, that of continuity.

Notes

Unless stated otherwise, the place of publication is Paris.

1. Mme Colette Cormier (née Espiasse), private papers.
2. Jean-Marie Girault, 'Des ruines à la reconstruction', in François Bédarida (ed.), *Normandie 44. Du débarquement à la libération*, Albin Michel, 1987, p.240.
3. Mia Kellmer Pringle, *The Needs of Children*, London, Hutchinson, 1974, p.15.
4. Etienne Fouilloux and Dominique Veillon, 'Mémoires du débarquement en Normandie', in Bédarida, *Normandie 44*, p.215.
5. Jacques Perret, 'Une Famille pendant la Bataille de Caen', Musée Mémorial (hereafter MM), Caen, p.3.
6. M Jean-Paul Corbasson, written account to author, 21 May 1992.
7. Jean Quellien, *La Normandie au cœur de la guerre*, Rennes, Ouest-France, 1992, p.160.
8. Author's interview, 6 August 1990.
9. Mme Alix Leullier, private papers.
10. Dr Jean-Pierre Guibé, written account to author, 11 September 1990.
11. Corbasson, written account.
12. Quellien, *La Normandie au cœur de la guerre*, p.160.
13. Corbasson, written account.
14. Author's interview, 1 September 1992.
15. Guibé, written account.
16. Dr Jean Olivier, 'Souvenirs de la Bataille de Caen', Archives Municipales, Caen.
17. André Gosset and Paul Lecomte, *Caen pendant la Bataille*, Caen, Ozanne, 1946, p.223.
18. Author's interview, 6 August 1990.
19. Author's interview, 9 August 1989.
20. Perret, 'Une famille', p.13.
21. Author's interview, 31 August 1991.
22. Cf. Nick Tucker, *What is a Child?* London, Open Books, 1977, p.53, for children's fear of the dark.
23. Paul Fussell, *The Great War and Modern Memory*, Oxford, Oxford University Press, 1975, p.124.
24. Anna Freud and Dorothy Burlingham, *Infants without Families. Reports on the Hampstead Nurseries 1939–45*, New York, International Universities Press Inc., 1973, p.158.
25. Jerzy Kosinski, *The Painted Bird*, London, Arrow Books, 1982, pp.118–19.

26. Pringle, *The Needs of Children*, p.45
27. François Boyer, *Jeux Interdits*, Denoël, 1968, p.10.
28. Dominique Veillon, 'Le Débarquement de Normandie vu par la population civile', Colloque de Nice, 14–15 December 1990, pp.1–2.
29. Archives Départementales Calvados (hereafter AD) M11786, Rapport des renseignements généraux du Calvados, 20 May 1944.
30. Author's interview, 6 April 1990.
31. Quellien, *La Normandie au cœur de la guerre*, p.160.
32. Author's interview, 6 August 1990.
33. *Bonhomme Normand*, 16–23 April 1943.
34. AD M11480, Rapport du délégué général à l'Information, 29 April 1944.
35. Perret, 'Une famille', pp.14–15.
36. Author's interview, 2 September 1992.
37. Author's interview, 1 September 1992.
38. Author's interview, 6 August 1990.
39. Archives Nationales (hereafter AN) 72.AJ.105, Rapport du Lieut-Colonel d'Artillerie en retraite Gaston Corbasson sur l'activité du mouvement CDLR Calvados.
40. Corbasson, written account.
41. Author's interview, M Gaston Déterville, 4 June 1992.
42. Cahier des Frères Colin pendant leur détention à Drancy, MM, Caen.
43. *Bonhomme Normand*, 17–23 July 1942. Avis des Höhere SS und Polizeiführer im Bereich des Militärbefehlshabers in Frankreich.
44. Centre de Documentation Juive Contemporaine (hereafter CDJC), Paris, Convoy Lists.
45. Author's interview, 29 August 1991.
46. Mme Guina Tresser, written account to author, undated.
47. CDJC, Paris, Convoy Lists.
48. Dossier Jacques Sabine, MM, Caen.
49. Tresser, written account.
50. AN 72.AJ.105, Rapport du Lieut-Colonel d'Artillerie en retraite Gaston Corbasson sur l'activité du mouvement CDLR Calvados.
51. Author's interview, 6 August 1990.
52. Cf. Alexander McKee, *Caen: Anvil of Victory*, London, Souvenir Press, 1964.

– 21 –

Memory by Analogy: *Hiroshima, mon amour*

Nancy Wood

Shortly after the release of *Hiroshima, mon amour* in 1959, an interview with Alain Resnais entitled '*Hiroshima, mon amour*, film scandaleux?' appeared in *Les Lettres françaises*.[1] The 'scandal' referred to was the film's withdrawal from competition at the Cannes Film Festival of that year following pressure exerted by the French political and cultural authorities. Contemporary viewers might be tempted to jump to the conclusion that what French officialdom found most provocative was the film's representation of scenes that tarnished national memories of the Liberation, notably that most unsavoury image of 'les femmes tondues' – women whose heads were shorn because of their (usually sexual) liaisons with the German occupiers. However the scandalized sensibilities originated elsewhere: it was in fact French anticipation of *American* displeasure with the scenes of Hiroshima which was allegedly behind the film's exclusion from festival competition.[2]

In the intervening thirty-five years, *Hiroshima, mon amour* has attained the status of a classic of European art cinema – it has enjoyed ongoing theoretical attention, and the recent release of a new print (and video) in Britain to much critical acclaim confirmed its enduring renown in this corner of film culture. But if we look at the film from the perspective of its treatment of memory and catastrophe – of memories of catastrophe – I would suggest that a whiff of 'scandal' continues to linger over *Hiroshima, mon amour*, though it is not of the order which rankled French official sensibilities. Nor, for that matter, does it lie simply in the harrowing images of 'la femme tondue' – images which, according to Alain Brossat, continue to provoke a 'memorial agitation' that historians of the Liberation have yet to explain.[3] The unease which the film is still capable of generating arises from the *kind of analogy* it constructs between the personal memories of 'une femme tondue' and the collective commemoration of a nuclear conflagration.

Of course, a certain discomfort about the film's manner of linking these two events through the vehicle of memory was registered by critics at the time of the film's release and in a number of interviews that Resnais gave in 1959–60, he was quick to refute the charge that any simple equation or comparison had been proposed between the individual drama of 'Elle' (played by Emmanuele Riva), and the enormous tragedy of Hiroshima. Resnais argued that 'any pain is incommensurable' with another and that the film had merely attempted to draw these two dramas – two kinds of grief – closer ('nous avons rapproché ces deux drames') in order better to apprehend each of them.[4] But the distinctive feature of the film's 'mise en relation' of two incommensurable kinds of pain lies precisely in the compelling force of an analogy which the film elicits. The first task, then, is to identify the types of correspondences which are being proposed.

There are at least two meanings of 'analogy' that might prove helpful here. The first derives from the sphere of logic, wherein analogy involves a 'process of reasoning from similar cases'[5] (i.e. because Situation A is like Situation B, it follows that...); however in biological usage, analogy denotes a 'resemblance of function between organs essentially different'[6] (i.e. while Situation A and B are irreducible, they both have in common the function of...). If these distinctions are applied for heuristic purposes to *Hiroshima, mon amour*'s 'mise en relation' of personal memories of a traumatic love affair and collective commemoration of the atomic firestorm that destroyed Hiroshima, we might ask what interpretation of the film's analogical strategy is most appropriate: one that stresses a common relation to the past arising from the traumatic nature of the events themselves (the 'logical' meaning of analogy), or one that posits the incomparability of the events, but a memorial affinity which the process of 'working through' their respective legacies necessarily entails (the 'biological' definition)? The stakes of this enquiry are not so much definitional, but a matter of the implications – historical, moral, memorial and filmic – which arise from the film's negotiation of *both* these analogical possibilities.

The problem of interpreting the film's analogical strategy is immediately evident in two contrasting interpretations of *Hiroshima, mon amour* of recent years, both of which are critically attuned to the issues involved in representing memories of a traumatic past. The French film critic Marie-Claire Ropars-Wuilleumier offers a reading of the film in which the story of Elle's traumatic past serves as the narrative scaffolding bearing the weight of the otherwise 'unrepresentable' nature of Hiroshima's nuclear holocaust.[7] By contrast, philosopher Alain Brossat emphasizes that the disaster of Hiroshima provides the necessary corollary for an understanding of the calamity that History (with a capital 'H') inflicted on the women who become 'les femmes tondues'.[8] To draw the contrast more starkly, in one reading the stakes of the film's analogy are the 'limits of representation' of this – and perhaps any other – holocaust; in another, they are the indifference of History to the claims of a love exempt from political judgement.

In a discussion about the film in 1959 in the pages of the review *Cahiers du Cinéma*, the critics – among them directors Rohmer, Godard, and Rivette – assert that *Hiroshima, mon amour* is a quintessentially *modernist* film because, in true modernist fashion, it has reconstituted reality out of 'a kind of splintering'. They go on to speculate about the jarring effect this might have on spectators, but when the question is posed as to whether this sense of disequilibrium would be moral or aesthetic in nature, Jean-Luc Godard chimes in, with impeccable timing: '[I]t's the same thing. Tracking shots are a question of morality.'[9] This tongue-in-cheek comment perhaps protests too much the New Wave's need to have their own brand of cinematic modernism taken more seriously by French political culture. However it also provides Ropars-Wuilleumier with a basis for redefining the film's modernism as a 'rupture' of conventional cinematic codes and an attempt to activate new 'mechanisms of integration' of meaning and form appropriate to its subject matter. In particular, the film's *écriture* – in Barthes's sense of a textual rather than referential production of meaning[10] – is first put to work to articulate a historical sensibility which refuses a separation of the political and aesthetic, the public and private, 'the worldwide cataclysm and the individual trauma'. But in order for these relations to be grasped in their indissociability, Ropars-Wuilleumier argues that the film deliberately resists the documentary impulse to provide only the familiar repertoire of signs of the historical event they designate – the 'evidence' of Hiroshima's nuclear holocaust – and instead employs an *écriture* of simulated memory traces, sounds and images that designate by their very 'syntax' the impossibility of their referential task.

The fifteen-minute opening sequence is for Ropars-Wuilleumier the clearest expression of this textual engagement with the 'limits of representation' of the atomic firestorm that engulfed Hiroshima. Rather than beginning the film by documenting the effects of the bomb, the film's *écriture* figures its destructive residues via the glittering dust that falls gently and covers the fragmented bodies we see in a perpetual embrace. The 'horror of the destruction' is thus initially evoked via the abstractions of an erotic encounter. A referential testimony follows, accompanying Elle's account of what she has seen in the museums of Hiroshima, which brutally demetaphorizes the vision of fragmented corporeality which the preceding extreme close-ups have created. Here, the very *literality* of these images – of destroyed flesh, disfigured limbs – would seem to function as an indictment of the abstract figuration of the bomb's effects. But Ropars-Wuilleumier argues that critical attention that focussed only on the impropriety of drawing a figural analogy between the minutiae of extreme pleasure and the magnitude of extreme pain obscured the real motivation for introducing this 'disorder... into our scale of values' – namely, to acknowledge the 'impotence of sight and knowledge' faced with an event which, by its very nature, exposes the limits of familiar representational and moral categories.[11]

Hiroshima, mon amour's initial deployment of a cinematic *écriture* is by no means offered as a privileged solution to this representational quandary, for this would undermine the very problematic Ropars-Wuilleumier believes the film seeks to address. To avoid remaining trapped in the hermetic eroticism of the opening sequence, the film then harnesses *écriture* to the mechanisms of narration, thus making the 'event readable by inserting it into a logical continuity'. And this is where the function of the Nevers story assumes its full representational significance. Ropars-Wuilleumier maintains that the 'unrepresentable' of Hiroshima's catastrophe is transferred onto the 'narratable' of Elle's story of a doomed love affair in Nevers.[12]

This notion of 'transference' introduces another level of analogy into the film – between a narration that absorbs the force generated by cinematic *écriture* and the position of the analyst in the psychoanalytic encounter onto whom is transferred the affective charge of the analysand's discourse. Indeed, for psychoanalysis, the very condition of 'working through' in the therapeutic situation depends on the analysand's memories activating the 'affect' that was originally attached to them.[13] By reviving the affect and then adopting a role in the accompanying recollections of the analysand, the analyst helps to give form and expression to an emotive force which has until then exercised virtual blind rule over the analysand's psychic landscape. As Ropars-Wuilleumier points out, Lui, the Japanese lover, assumes exactly this identificatory position of the analyst in relation to Elle's discourse of Nevers at the moment when he accepts being addressed as her dead German lover, when he demands of Elle: 'Quand tu es dans la cave, je suis mort?' But, consistent with Ropars-Wuilleumier's reading of *Hiroshima, mon amour*'s analogical strategy, she insists that we should not see this 'psychoanalytic simulacrum' as operating primarily on behalf of the 'working through' of the traumatic memory of a 'femme tondue'. Rather, the elaboration of the Nevers story in this transferential mode implicitly poses the question of what it means to 'work through' the legacy of a nuclear catastrophe (or indeed any mass catastrophe), what comparable labour of mourning can release survivors – and societies – from the 'psychic numbing' which the devastation induced as the very condition of survival?[14] The 'simple story' of Nevers is thus designated to assume the enormous affective weight of 'the opaque memory of an event whose importance cannot be formulated'.[15]

In early sequences, when Elle relates the 'evidence' of destruction she has seen on her visits to hospitals and museums, and of the life which rose from the ashes and was captured by newsreels 'for all eternity', Lui tells her: 'Tu n'a rien vu à Hiroshima... Tu ne sais rien.' Elle in turn insists that she has seen 'everything', knows 'everything' and thus has come under the 'illusion' that she will never forget Hiroshima. But it is only after the transmission of her story of Nevers in the three flashback sequences[16] that Lui – and by extension the film's spectators – apprehend that it is not a certainty of knowledge of the catastrophe and its aftermath that Elle has been seeking from the sights of Hiroshima, but a confrontation with the forces of forgetting that overwhelm even the strongest compulsion to remember. Early in the film, Elle tells Lui that they both share the desire to resist any attenuation of the memories which bind them to their respective traumatic pasts: 'Comme toi, je connais l'oubli... comme toi, je suis douée de mémoire... come toi, moi aussi, j'ai essayé de lutter de toutes mes forces contre l'oubli. Comme toi, j'ai oublié. Comme toi, j'ai désiré avoir une inconsolable mémoire, une mémoire d'ombres et de pierres.' The first intrusion of another memory that also once seemed unforgettable makes her realize that her conviction that she will preserve an indelible memory of what she has seen in Hiroshima is just an illusion (recall that her first 'involuntary' memory flashback, a fleeting close-up of the hand of her dead German soldier, occurs as she stands staring transfixed at the hand of her sleeping Japanese lover, as if trying to register a mental imprint of this erotic moment).[17] It is the fate of traumatic memories which the film goes on to explore, and by setting this investigation of the vicissitudes of memory in motion, *Hiroshima, mon amour* manages to resist any simple identification of the city's traumatic past with Elle's own tragic love affair.

Once the story of Nevers is told, and Elle's labour of mourning approaches completion, this same traumatic but nonetheless precious memory of her German lover lying dead on the Quai de la Loire, which has made Elle captive to her past, begins to be consigned to oblivion. This, the film suggests, is the ambiguous fate awaiting individual and collective memories of Hiroshima. In the final scene, when Elle cries out in anguish 'Je t'oublierai! Je t'oublie déjà!' we know that she is not only experiencing the pain of forgetting the dead German soldier, but that she suffers by anticipation the pain of forgetting Lui and Hiroshima. From this perspective, then, the agency of subjective memory of a traumatic past is shown to be generative of a therapeutic process of forgetting, wherein forgetting is not simply the consequence of repression or social neglect, but of a cathartic 'letting go' of the traumatic memory itself. Or as Ropars-Wuilleumier puts the matter, in *Hiroshima, mon amour*, 'the horror of Hiroshima is not eclipsed, but it becomes the object of a secret reflection upon the terms of both enunciation and expulsion of the historical event.'[18]

However I have by now strayed very far from the specific representation of 'la femme tondue' and I want to return to this question because however convincing Ropars-Wuilleumier's emphasis on the film's engagement with the 'limits of representation' of catastrophe, the personal catastrophe of Elle cannot be so easily subsumed into this larger problematic. Let us recall the words with which Elle describes her youthful self towards the end of the film: 'Petite fille de Nevers. Petite coureuse de Nevers... Petite fille de rien... Morte d'amour à Nevers. Petite tondue de Nevers je te donne à l'oubli ce soir. Histoire de quatre sous.' According to the analysis of Alain Brossat, the voice which disparages Elle's own loss and subsequent humiliation is the voice of 'History', which condemns a love that remained indifferent to the demands of public morality. What Elle realizes by these words, observes Brossat, is that she was '"collabo" au même titre qu'elle fut amoureuse'.[19]

Brossat's discussion of *Hiroshima, mon amour* forms part of his larger study of 'les femmes tondues'. Brossat's own interest in these women derives in part from the failure of historians of the Liberation to account for the 'affect' attached to images of 'les femmes tondues' in French collective memory. He maintains that 'les tontes sont une question d'"intensité"... pas de quantité.'[20] The fact that this 'intensity' increases with time (Brossat speaks of 'l'inépuisable *resonance* de la scène des tontes dans le présent') affirms the traumatic nature of these collective memories in the sense that their affective impact was not – and by definition could not be – registered at the time of their occurrence but has only 'returned' belatedly and as confirmation of the peculiar emotive force which originally accompanied these 'baroque scenes' of 'la tonte'. He notes that far from being 'absent from history', these women are manifestly present. However their presence is not primarily registered in the historiographical work that now abounds on the *épuration* and Liberation, but in more nomadic and 'capillary' cultural channels – the novel, film, songs, 'le fait divers', rumours – i.e. outside the main fields of social visibility. Here they function as a 'painful spasm' ('une douloureuse contracture') reminding French collective memory of 'a past that will not pass'.[21]

There is not space here to discuss Brossat's provocative and fascinating study, but I do want to consider briefly several aspects of his analysis of *Hiroshima, mon amour*. As suggested above, for Brossat, what the film primarily exposes is the impossibility of an innocent love during this historical event. The 'amour fou' shown in the second lyrical flashback of the film, when we see a rapturous Elle in clandestine meetings with her young German lover, cannot be tolerated precisely because it tries to evade the fact of 'choice' which 'History' has imposed on intimate life ('tout mouvement, tout pas constituent un *choix* et une prise de responsabilité face à l'Histoire').[22] Elle's 'crime' is therefore not to bow to History's diktat, to regard her 'innocent love' as immune from History's demand that desire, too, take sides. And for this naïveté, she pays the price of madness in the cellar, remorse that she did not 'die of love' on the Quai de la Loire and subsequent psychic imprisonment by the repetitive, hallucinatory memory of her lover's death. Certainly this is one of the film's most flagrant moves: in defiance of the moral code of Resistance narratives, our empathetic identification is solicited with the loss suffered by 'une femme tondue' – the death of her *German* soldier-lover on the Quai de la Loire.

In the erotic encounter of Lui and Elle, argues Brossat, the 'infinite spiral' of time in which each of them is caught by their traumatic memories is merged with the time of *their amour fou*, a time which by virtue of being exclusively devoted to sensual ecstasy, is one of emphatic presentness. In surrendering to this temporality, they suspend the modalities of their 'normal' lives, wherein trauma can only exist for each of them as the legacy of a secret and 'unmasterable past', and become the 'midwife' of each other's pain.

Brossat also highlights the indispensability of Lui to Elle's reexternalization of her traumatic memory, but he stresses that this role is overdetermined by an analogy which the film mobilizes between the historical definitions ascribed to each of Elle's lovers. It is Lui's *alterity* – his designation 'in the time of History, as the absolute Other' – that permits him to occupy the phantasmic place of the dead German soldier in the transference. Like her German lover whom History defined solely as 'the enemy', Lui occupies a place in a system of binary oppositions which opposes the French woman to the Japanese man, the victor to the vanquished, the European to the Asiatic, the democrat to the ex-fascist.[23] (It is interesting to note that Resnais commented in an interview that he and Duras had imagined the German soldier as anti-Nazi, though they had deliberately not made this explicit in the film in order to allow the public 'the liberty of judgement' and 'pour ne pas dédouaner trop visiblement l'héroïne'.[24])

This leads us to an issue which it seems to me that Brossat overlooks. If we accept the view that History has ascribed to each of Elle's lovers an alterity which in turn determines the fate of these love affairs, is it not also the case that Elle is shown to desire these men precisely for this quality? Elle knew her lover was objectively 'un ennemi de la France' as she tells Lui and yet this knowledge, far from impeding her actions, gives her memories of her *amour fou* for the young German soldier their particular *élan*.[25] Resnais also observes that Elle is 'une adolescente qui s'est opposée à son milieu. La vie à la pharmacie, le piano, Nevers... l'amour allemand était aussi une façon de nier tout cela.'[26] In other words, the transgressive nature of Elle's love for a man objectively defined as 'the enemy' provides her desire with the force it needs to act out the rebellion of her youth, to express her emergent sexuality, and her sense of social confinement. When she suffers the punishment of 'la tondue', her spirit of transgression continues in her refusal to feel any remorse for her lethal desire. She tells Lui: 'Je suis d'une moralité douteuse, tu sais,' and when he asks her what this means, she replies that it is 'douter de la morale des autres'. The 'innocence' of which Brossat speaks is thus shown in the film to be not so much the consequence of *l'amour fou*, but of the belief that such transgression would *not* incur the vengeance of History's moral arbiters. Moreover, Elle does not even concede to sit in judgment of her torturers. She describes them as young patriots and 'des héros sans imagination' whom she has no will to condemn because she is too consumed by her own suffering. (Indeed, in the treatment of the script Duras attributes to Elle the 'scandalous' confession: 'Je n'avais plus de patrie que l'amour même'.[27])

By the same token, Elle's desire for Lui is conditioned by the very fact that it, too, cannot endure. Once its force is expended in the reenactment of an earlier *amour fou*, she *must* leave Hiroshima, despite his pleas that she stay. This Brossat does acknowledge and he goes on to note that the price of her cure, of mastery over the 'tyranny' of her traumatic memory, is a return to 'normal time' and hence her departure.

This leaves us with the question of the function that Hiroshima serves in this intimate scenario. Brossat argues that by refracting the tale of this 'petite tonte... sans nom' of the 'petite ville de Nevers' through the mirror of 'l'événement universel par excellence qu'est Hiroshima', the film establishes a 'symbolic equivalence' between the legacy of a disaster at the level of intimate life and one that must embrace the annihilation of an entire city.²⁸ We must be careful here – the function of the symbolic analogy which Brossat seeks to emphasize is not to equate the scale or significance of these respective disasters, but to highlight the common, debilitating relation to a memory of catastrophe that they both sustain: 'c'est dans ce rapport désastreux au passé qui se dévoile l'homonymie symbolique entre Nevers et Hiroshima.'²⁹ Though it could be argued that in this respect, the *time* occupied by the testimony of Nevers relegates Lui's memories to a textual marginality, the laconic – and bitterly ironic – nature of his recollections of world reaction to the bombing of Hiroshima is suggestive not only of the intensity of his psychic pain, but of its ultimate resistance to narrative representation: 'Le monde entière était joyeux... C'était un beau jour d'été à Paris... j'ai entendu dire...'

From their struggle to extricate themselves from the 'tyranny' of a cataclysmic memory, the combatants of the film finally emerge as 'survivors' of its violent legacy: '*Hiroshima* énonce une... modeste ambition: vivre, malgré tout, avec ce souvenir de la balle mortelle et des ciseaux pour l'une, de l'éclair meurtrier pour l'autre.'³⁰ Elle and Lui's common status as 'survivors' of modern History's catastrophic legacy thus emerges as the final level of analogy which Brossat identifies. In this regard, it is relevant to note that the psychoanalyst Robert Jay Lifton, who has investigated the psychic effects of the bombing of Hiroshima among the city's inhabitants, has described every death encounter as a 'reactivation of earlier survivals'.³¹ Elle and Lui come to experience and ultimately affirm their own 'survivorship' of catastrophe through an intimate encounter with the spectre of death which has compulsively haunted the other. In her commentary which is appended to the film's script, Duras affirms that it is this 'gift' of her story, and of her own death encounter, which Elle offers as a memorial homage to the pain of Lui and Hiroshima: 'Elle livre à ce Japonais – à *Hiroshima* – ce qu'elle a de plus cher au monde, son expression actuelle même, sa *survivance* à la mort de son amour, à *Nevers*.'³² The film ends with the reciprocal gesture by which Lui accepts the name of 'Hiroshima' as his survivor-appellation and confers on Elle an analogous title of 'Nevers-en-France'.

But if, as Brossat suggests, it is modern History which has inflicted the 'grand' and 'infinitesimal' legacies of catastrophe, is not one implication of his argument that the analogy of 'survivorship' which the film inscribes potentially embraces all of us who must live under History's tyrannous shadow? In this vein, literary critic Cathy Caruth has argued that '[i]n a catastrophic age [...] trauma itself may provide the very link between cultures...'[33] In other words, it is the *latency* inherent in the traumatic event – the belated, assimilation of its affective legacy – that confers on all of us the status of emotional survivors of this catastrophic era. From this perspective, *Hiroshima, mon amour* affirms not only the shared survivorship of Elle and Lui, but elicits an empathetic identification between them and the psycho-historical position of the film's spectators.

Yet however appealing this inclusive notion of 'survivorship' might first appear, if we stretch this analogy too far, we may find that we run up against the 'limits' of the analogical enterprise itself. If we are all nominated as History's 'survivors', we risk losing sight altogether of the specific sufferings of real survivors of this century's catastrophes, diminishing by such comparisons the 'incommensurable pain' that a film like *Hiroshima, mon amour* sets out to represent and commemorate.

Must the final judgement on *Hiroshima, mon amour* therefore be that it ultimately falls prey to the abstracting tendencies inherent in analogical strategies of memorialization? Real survivors – notably the residents of Hiroshima – reportedly thought so, since they resented the film's association of grotesque death imagery and amorous union.[34] Yet alternative modes of representing the catastrophes of Hiroshima and Nagasaki have encountered their own 'limits of representation', and have often fuelled the nationalist sentiments such commemorative practices are intended to condemn.[35] Moreover, if, as is the guiding premise of this volume, French collective memory has still not come to terms with the 'disorder' of the Liberation and *épuration*, perhaps recourse to analogy and the 'disorder in our scale of values' (Ropars-Wuilleumier) which it induces should be regarded as a highly appropriate means of working-through this profoundly ambivalent memorial legacy.

Notes

Unless stated otherwise, the place of publication is Paris.

1. 'Alain Resnais: *Hiroshima, mon amour*, film scandaleux?' *Les Lettres françaises*, 14–20 May 1959.
2. Georges Sadoul, 'Un grand film, Un grand homme', *Les Lettres françaises*, 14–20 May 1959.

3. Alain Brossat, *Les Tondues, Un carnaval moche*, Editions Manya, 1992, p.13.
4. 'Réponse à *Clarté*', in *Alain Resnais, Premier Plan*, no.18, October 1961, p.47.
5. *The Concise Oxford Dictionary*, Oxford, Clarendon Press, 1976, p.34.
6. Ibid.
7. Marie-Claire Ropars-Wuilleumier, 'How history begets meaning: Alain Resnais's *Hiroshima, mon amour*', in Susan Hayward and Ginette Vincendeau (eds), *French Film: Texts and Contexts*, London, Routledge, 1990.
8. Alain Brossat, *Les Tondues: Un carnaval moche*, Editions Manya, 1992.
9. 'Jean Domarchi, Jacques Doniol-Valcroze, Jean-Luc Godard, Pierre Kast, Jacques Rivette, Eric Rohmer: 'Hiroshima, notre amour', in Jim Hillier (ed.), *Cahiers du Cinéma 1: the 1950s, Neo-Realism, Hollywood, The New Wave*, London, Routledge and Kegan Paul, British Film Institute, 1985, p.62 (originally appeared in *Cahiers du Cinéma* 97, July 1959).
10. Cf. Roland Barthes, 'From Work to Text', in *Image–Music–Text*, London, Fontana/Collins, 1977.
11. Ropar-Wuilleumier, 'How history begets meaning', pp.179–80.
12. Ibid.
13. Cf. J. Laplanche and J.-B. Pontalis, 'Transference', in *The Language of Psycho-Analysis*, London, The Hogarth Press and the Institute of Psycho-Analysis, 1980, pp.455–62.
14. I borrow the notion of 'psychic numbing' from Robert Jay Lifton, whose study, *Death in Life: The Survivors of Hiroshima* (London, Weidenfeld, 1967) is a moving and indispensable exploration of the psychological effects of the bomb on Hiroshima's survivors, or '*Hibakusha*'. Cf. especially pp.500–10 for an elaboration of the concept. The following testimony of one *Hibakusha*, a physicist, renders the concept vividly: 'As I walked along, the horrible things I saw became more and more extreme and more and more intolerable. At a certain point I must have become more or less saturated, so that I became no longer sensitive, in fact insensitive, to what I saw around one. I think human emotions reach a point beyond which they cannot extend – something like a photographic process. If under certain conditions you expose a photographic plate to light, it becomes black; but if you continue to expose it, then it reaches a point where it turns white...Only later can one recognize having reached this maximum state', p.33.

15. Ropars-Wuilleumier, 'How history begets meaning', p.181.
16. An excellent analysis of these flashback sequences is offered by Maureen Turim, 'Disjunction in the Modernist Flashback', in *Flashbacks in Film: Memory and History*, London, Routledge, 1989.
17. On this 'involuntary memory', cf. Turim, 'Disjunction in the Modernist Flashback', pp.211–12.
18. Ropars-Wuilleumier, 'How history begets meaning', p.182. In her remarks on *Hiroshima, mon amour* in *Black Sun*, Julia Kristeva suggests that the tenacity of Elle's memory of the death of her lover is a function of a melancholia in which '[t]o love, from her point of view, is to love a dead person'. Hence her attachment to Hiroshima might be formulated as: '*I love Hiroshima for its suffering is my Eros...*' Cf. Julia Kristeva, 'The Malady of Grief: Duras', in *Black Sun: Depression and Melancholia*, New York, Columbia University Press, 1989, pp.231–6.
19. Brossat, *Les Tondues*, p.55.
20. Ibid., p.10.
21. Ibid., p.179.
22. Ibid., p.54.
23. Ibid., p.60.
24. 'Réponse à *Esprit*', in *Alain Resnais, Premier Plan*, no.18, October 1961, p.57.
25. Maureen Turim perceptively identifies the transgressive desire embedded in this lyrical flashback: 'Within the second set of flashback images, the full weight of the ideological taboo crossed by this love affair is unspoken, and the lyricism of the images, the racing across fields for clandestine encounters, counteracts the charged context of the War.' See 'Disjunction in the Modernist Flashback', p.213.
26. 'A propos d'Hiroshima dans *Image et Son*', in *Alain Resnais, Premier Plan*, no.18, October 1961, p.75.
27. Marguerite Duras, *Hiroshima, Mon Amour: scénario et dialogues*, nrf/Gallimard, 1960, p.133.
28. Brossat, *Les Tondues*, pp.62–3.
29. Ibid., p.63.
30. Ibid., p.62.
31. Cited by Eric L. Santner, 'History Beyond the Pleasure Principle: Some Thoughts on the Representation of Trauma', in Saul Friedländer (ed.), *Probing the Limits of Representation*, London, Harvard University Press, 1992, p.364.
32. Duras, *Hiroshima Mon Amour*, p.140.
33. Cathy Caruth, 'Introduction', *American Imago*, vol.48, no.1, 1991. In describing history as trauma, Caruth mobilizes the following

definition of trauma's particular pathology: 'The event is not assimilated or experienced fully at the time, but only belatedly, in its repeated *possession* of the one who experiences it. To be traumatized is precisely to be possessed by an image or event' (p.3). This notion of 'possession' is particularly useful for understanding the modality of Elle's traumatic memory of Nevers.

34. See Robert Jay Lifton's remarks on the reaction to the film among Hiroshima residents in *Death in Life*, p.468.
35. See Ian Buruma, *The Wages of Guilt: Memories of War in Germany and Japan*, London, Jonathan Cape, 1994.

22

Liberation in Novels of May '68: the Intertextual Image

William Kidd

The context of this enquiry is the familiar one of appropriation and recuperation. My thesis is that student exploitation of the Freudian 'mort du père gaullien',[1] and the historical specificity of May–June 1968 generated a return to a more problematic past, the years 1940–44, which in turn found expression in literature. This chapter focusses on images of liberation and their historical prototype, the Liberation of August 1944, as mediated in Jean-Louis Curtis's *L'Horizon dérobé* (1978), Dominique Fernandez's *L'Etoile rose* (1978), and Pascal Lainé's *L'Irrévolution* (1971). The order of study is from Curtis (the latest in terms of the manifest subject-matter) to Lainé (the most contemporaneous), a regressive démarche which mirrors the textual 'project' of each work, though manifestly not their individual authors' political stance.

May–June 1968 evoked many historical parallels, from the nineteenth-century revolutionary 'journées' (1830, 1848, the Paris Commune), to the Popular Front strikes and factory occupations in 1936, and more recent episodes such as the deaths at Métro Charonne during the Algerian crisis in 1962, recalled in student cartoons.[2] But the most significant echo was surely the wartime occupation of Paris. The increasingly few trains leaving the capital, the lengthening food queues (flour and sugar disappeared in panic-buying), the gas and electricity shortages, the unofficial rationing of cigarettes and petrol, recalled 1940–44: 'on n'a pas vu ça depuis la guerre', 'ça me rappelle 1940', were commonly heard observations in streets and cafés. There were other parallels. In a comment which recalled misplaced official optimism in 1940, Jacques Brel said of the students: 'ils vaincront, parce qu'ils sont les plus jeunes',[3] while the threat of intervention by French troops garrisoned in Germany added an ironic counterpoint to what was from the providential 'homme du 18 juin 1940' – the students issued an 'Appel du 18 juin 1968' – a parodic reenactment of the founding event of Gaullism: only the flight this time was not to London but to Baden-Baden, to Massu and the 'traitors' of 1958. 'CRS–SS', the subject of chanting, posters and cartoons is an obvious slogan, but in the atmosphere of the period little imagination was required to transform the booted and helmeted CRS into German soldiers, an identification exploited by novelists such as Curtis, one of whose protagonists sees in the CRS the 'chevaliers teutoniques' of Eisenstein's *Alexander Nevsky*, thus dehistoricizing the forces of repression into the mythical guardians of (Western) civilization.[4] Student 'nazification' of the police prompted criticism even from those otherwise well disposed towards them. In 'Mes Universités', Philippe Clay juxtaposed the German victory parade on the Champs Elysées in June 1940 and the students' symbolic resistance there on 11 November 1940, with the less awesome opponents faced by their successors:

Mes Universités,
C'était pas Jussieu, c'était pas Censier, c'était pas Nanterre,
C'était le pavé, le pavé d'Paris, le Paris d'la guerre.

On parlait peu d'marxisme.
Encore moins d'maoïsme,
Le seul système – c'était le système 'D'...

Nous, quand on contestait,
C'était contre les casqués
Qui défilaient sur nos Champs Elysées.
Quand on écoutait Londres – dans nos planques – sur les ondes,
C'était pas les Beatles qui nous parlaient.[5]

Historical allusion was not of course the prerogative of one side only; the very nature of Gaullism made that unthinkable. In his radio broadcast on 30 May, the General vowed to restore order by every means, including the resumption by the Prefects of their Liberation role as 'commissaires de la République'. A hostile tract issued on 27 May contrasted student defiance of the Occupier on 11 November 1940 (cf. Clay, above) and the presence now of 'foreign agitators' on French soil,[6] a sinister echo of the earlier period, and one in which the old Gaullist-Communist resistance coalition found common ground. By 22 May, Daniel Cohn-Bendit, described in *L'Humanité* on 3 May as 'l'anarchiste allemand', had become a 'juif allemand'. This grotesque political miscalculation gave the students one of their most effective propaganda weapons, alongside 'nous sommes un groupuscule', 'la chienlit, c'est lui', and the cartoon of the CGT and CRS linking arms to proclaim, 'la révolution ne passera pas': immediately they adopted as their own slogan, 'Nous sommes tous des juifs allemands'. When on 30 May, Gaullists singing 'La Marseillaise' marched up the Champs Elysées to the tomb of the unknown soldier (the opposite direction to the Liberation march of 25 August 1944), the chanting included, in another parodic recall of events twenty-four years earlier, 'la France aux Français'.[7]

Given the intensity of the 1968 'events', their historical and ideological specificity, and the abiding importance in France of intellectual and cultural mediation, it is unsurprising that writers of all political persuasions seized upon them, and that wartime echoes should loom large in their writing. Jacques Prévert's poem 'Mai 1968', which caricatures the régime as a museum janitor calling closing time ('On ferme!') and the students as revolutionary 'openers' is apposite and revealing. For what the régime seeks to close down are not just buildings but the essential freedoms – 'On ferme la cinémathèque et la Sorbonne avec/ On verrouille l'espoir/ On cloître les idées/ ORTF bouclée/ Vérités séquestrées/ Jeunesse baillonnée.'[8]

The closure of 'la cinémathèque et la Sorbonne avec' and the 'ORTF bouclée' are of course contemporary with May '68, as are subsequent references to police truncheons ('matraques') and riot control gas, and the cheeky allusion to the then pioneering technique of heart transplant 'cri du cœur à greffer' (in a cartoon entitled 'on va tenter une greffe', surgeons tend an anaesthetized 'vache' and an injured CRS in adjoining beds). But the poem's themes and metaphors of enforced silence ('espoir verrouillé', 'vérités séquestrées', 'jeunesse baillonnée'), contrast with the 'opening out' ('on ouvre') of the second stanza to enduring values of solidarity, liberty, and lucidity. They belong also to the register of wartime clandestinity, while the desire to free the media from government control which in May inspired slogans such as 'chassez le flic de votre tête', 'pas de rectangle blanc pour un peuple adulte' and the portrayal of de Gaulle behind a microphone, manipulating the truth, do not differ fundamentally in inspiration from the 1940s 'Radio-Paris ment! Radio-Paris ment! Radio-Paris est allemand'. In this context, the poet's depiction of youth forcing the doors of a 'passé mensonger' may be read as simultaneously recalling Resistance rejection of 'la fausse parole'[9] and undercutting the (largely Resistance-inspired) official history since the Liberation in the name of a new liberation (the student revolution).

Prévert's poem evokes wartime indirectly. The same thematic structure and contrasting moral/metaphorical values were articulated explicitly in a prose text written much closer to the Occupation, 'Une journée au milieu d'août 1944' from Curtis's *Les Forêts de la nuit*:

> Et maintenant c'est le jour!... Et toute la France s'éveille et exulte dans cette lumière. Partout, l'ombre est déchiquetée, les forêts de la nuit se dissolvent comme les fantasmagories d'un rêve d'épouvante, et la lumière ruisselle, le jour éclate, parmi les cris, les exclamations, le délire: et les combattants qui tombent aux barricades de Paris recueillent dans leurs prunelles mourantes une fulguration de soleil et de liberté, et savent avec certitude que leur sacrifice n'est pas vain.
>
> C'est le jour. Ceux qui se cachaient osent surgir à la lumière, et personne ne leur demande s'ils sont purs ou impurs. C'est un jour de fraternité universelle, de joie et d'embrassade; toutes les fois et toutes les croyances, toutes les classes et tous les visages sont mêlés et confondus derrière les barricades et la même délivrance pétille dans tous les yeux.[10]

Even in 1947, Curtis had cast doubt on the 'deliverance' which identified national victory with Resistance victory and achieved unity not by ending division but by selective exclusion (the political 'épuration', 'les tondues', other minority reprisal victims). Nonetheless, with its night/day, occupation/liberation antithesis,[11] and its carnivalesque atmosphere of exaltation and solidarity in freedom rediscovered (cf. Prévert), it functions both as idealized representation and as generally legitimized part of the French historical memory (with jeeps and GIs and de Gaulle),[12] an iconic image abundantly present in photographs and documentary footage of the period, available for replication by novelists and film-makers, or an unstated but powerful 'hors texte' informing and shaping their work and the reader's response to it.

L'Horizon dérobé is the first volume of a trilogy whose action begins in the mid-1950s, and but for one episodic reference elides the war years. But it recalls *Les Forêts de la nuit* by its initial location (Sault-en-Labourd in the south-west), by its narrative and interpersonal structures – the criss-crossing itineraries of three protagonists from childhood to adulthood – and by its characterization. The young 'gauchiste' Thierry Landes (*sic*) is a less naïve descendant of the ill-fated Francis de Balansun; Catherine Comarieu, torn between her inner life, a career and the security of marriage recalls his sister Hélène. Nicolas Marcilac (the surname previously designated the industrialist who offers sanctuary to the collaborationist Mme Costellot at the Liberation...) is a homosexual whose secret, long suspected by the others, finds expression in the liberated atmosphere of 1968. Parental figures are recalled by the improbable Mme Saint-Aygulf whose enthusiastic adoption of student slogans undercuts their revolutionary aims, and by her reactionary, wimpish husband Tancrède, who, like their predecessors in *Les Forêts de la nuit*, take us back to the 1880s and to a mock-Proustianism present in all of Curtis's work, including his May '68 pastiches, *La Chine m'inquiète*.[13] There are differences, of course: no one in *L'Horizon dérobé* has the leonine, amoral ferocity of Mme Arréguy or her son Philippe, successively collaborationist hit-man and Resistance fighter, and the work lacks the powerful concentration afforded by the circumscribed timespan. Nonetheless, these parameters and a number of specific textual dynamics inscribe the wartime past intertextually into the later novel.

In revolt against his deferential 'employé' parents, Thierry volubly rejects official attitudes and established institutions just as he silently resents the social superiority of Catherine and Nicholas. His political sympathies predispose him to militant, revolutionary action. If he is 'sans réserves du côté des exploités (les masses du tiers monde)', his views on a problem nearer home – the Algerian war – are presented as both anachronistic (hatred of Marshal Lyautey and le Père Foucauld, in 1956!) and jejeune: 'Thierry voit le colonialisme français sous les couleurs les plus sinistres (une bande de prédateurs sans scrupule, pratiquant le pillage systématique d'un pays sous prétexte de mission civilisatrice)' (p.20). Moreover, we have already been warned by the authorial voice that 'Chez Thierry, c'est presque toujours la rancœur qui l'emporte sur l'attendrissement' (ibid.). Thus, when we read that 'Si la Révolution éclate un jour, Thierry sera au premier rang des émeutiers. Drapeau rouge ou drapeau noir, peu importe, pourvu que les choses changent et qu'on en finisse avec le règne de l'inégalité et de l'injustice. Alors les nantis trembleront' (p.21), self-conscious adolescent exaggeration suggests that this scenario is fundamentally false, an emotional response to injured self-esteem, not a considered critique or passionate commitment. And when Curtis links Thierry's revolutionary fervour to parental memories of the Liberation, which, like the great 'Revolution' of 1789, he recreates in his imagination as '[une] de ces époques pendant lesquelles le monde explose, un ordre ancien est renversé, une classe jusqu'alors asservie se libère et domine à son tour' (ibid.), we scarcely need to be told that 'Thierry n'est pas dupe – il ne croit qu'à demi à toutes ces fictions où il se complaît' (p.22). And since the Utopian misapprehension in this early vision is manifest to the reader, the ultimate demise of May itself is already signalled here, to be confirmed by developments in the story. In Curtis's didactic and narratological project, the compressed image of 1944, the Liberation-as-social-revolution, functions as a representation to be used, not as a value system to be reaffirmed.

A more important and more indirect textual appropriation corroborates this interpretation. The novel opens with Nicholas, as yet unidentified (only the masculine adjectival endings provide a clue to gender), day-dreaming beside a sunlit pool. Two lines recalled from Mallarmé's unnamed but immediately recognizable 'L'Après-midi d'un Faune',[14] and then a neo-classical decor – 'Un paysage pastoral se déploie dans sa tête, oliviers, cyprès, buissons de lauriers roses, des taillis, un bocage' (p.8) – progressively unfold the literary trope which establishes the character's self-perception: 'embrasé de soleil, mais d'un autre soleil, celui peut-être d'une ère préhumaine', he is 'une créature sylvestre, une jeune bête heureuse, sans conscience et sans nom, à peine distinct de ce qui l'entoure' (ibid.). This reverie is interrupted by the intrusion of the outside world, by Catherine calling his name. As he experiences the nostalgia for his earlier state – 'il était si bien... il y a tout juste trente secondes, trente mille ans, mi-garçon mi-faune, sans loi, aux aguets dans le taillis, mâchonnant une herbe à goût de menthe' (p.9) – the unstated filmic as well as the stated literary derivation, and hence the ideological prototype, become explicit: the beginning of *L'Horizon dérobé* is the end of *Lacombe Lucien*.[15] It starts at the point at which Lucien has regressed to, or more completely become, what he always truly was, an apolitical pagan whose collaborationism was as meaningless as would have been his original intention to join the Resistance.

Androgeny, nostalgia for the unity which existed before the unwelcome insertion into temporality (history) and social division (politics), are subthemes of *L'Horizon dérobé*. They are central to *L'Etoile rose*, narrated from a 1970s vantage point by David, a man in his forties, who is scarred by the circumstances of his early life and by the prejudice which obliges him to conceal a homosexuality historically condemned as a sin (by the Church), as an unnatural perversion (Voltaire), or as neurotic symptom which might be cured (Freud) and one which was ultimately, in its concept of unproductive love, subversive of the capitalist ethos.[16] Its denunciation of contemporary intolerance in the French provinces where David first seeks freedom and anonymity, in Cambridge, England, where sexual repression finds symbolic expression in the choral tradition, and the United States where 'gay' liberation preceded its advent in Europe, makes this a hybrid as well as an 'apologetic' work whose narrative and ideological climax is May '68.

It is also semi-autobiographical. Dominique Fernandez, born in 1929, is the son of literary critic, novelist and 'committed intellectual' Ramon Fernandez (1894–1944) who, briefly aligned with the Left in 1934–35, joined Doriot and in 1940 became a prominent member of the Parisian collaborationist establishment. In the novel, David is the son of a former Socialist who abandons his wife and child to fight with the Légion des Volontaires Français contre le Bolchevisme (LVF) on the Eastern Front (the year is 1943), thereby betraying both family and country. This basic ambivalence – the child still loves his father despite the faults and derelictions – is reflected in David's situation at school; drawn to classmates like Daniel who are on the threshold of joining the Resistance, he is rejected as a 'fils de collabo'. Scholastic and social divisions are mutually reinforcing: Tubert, the Citroën worker's son from the Quai de Javel, is made to feel a failure by traditionalist teachers who describe a good essay as 'brilliant' and a poor one (Tubert's) as 'terne', epithets meaningful in a metal-polishing context but impenetrable to him in literature (pp.40–1). The wartime circumstances of another persecuted group, the Jews of 'l'étoile jaune' explain the novel's title (homosexual prisoners in the camps wore a pink triangle), and form part of David's psychological drama: he is seduced by an older man while travelling in the 'wagon de queue du métro' to which Jewish travellers were confined (pp.83–4), an event which reveals his homosexuality and becomes linked to the need to retain the ambivalent father-identification by betraying himself.[17]

The social and sexual strands are drawn together symbolically at the liberation of Paris on 25 August 1944: Tubert, of whom the narrator has lost sight since his humiliation at school, has been fighting with the Communist Francs-Tireurs et Partisans (FTP) to end class as well as foreign domination (p.77). His group is brushed aside by the tanks of Leclerc's IIème DB, with the victorious arrival, between the Hôtel de Ville and the Tuileries, of their bourgeois counterparts who include Daniel, to whom, David, in a gesture of submission and self-denial, offers the girl Sophie. The image of liberation 1944-style as represented by Daniel and Sophie together on the turret of the Sherman tank is subsequently revealed as false when a chance meeting years later shows that Daniel has lived a double life as respectable heterosexual and secret homosexual, but the narrator's immediate reflections are more eloquent:

Tubert l'avait bien dit. Ces jeunes gens qui s'avançaient sur les chars n'habitaient pas le quai de Javel, leurs pères n'étaient pas des contremaîtres chez Citroën... C'est vrai que la bourgeoisie, toujours elle, regagna en 1944, la guerre qu'elle avait perdue en 1940. C'est vrai que les classes restèrent inégales et séparées. Le principe de séparation, qui fut inscrit à nouveau dans la société française, détermina notre sort également. La Libération de Paris, qui ne libéra pas les plus faibles de la domination des plus forts, fut pour les minoritaires un échec, dont les conséquences ne tardèrent pas à retomber sur nous. (p.79)

There will be no revolutionary 'lendemains qui chantent' for the working class, while in the legal and moral domain (freedom for sexual minorities), the reestablished Republic, endorsing legislation of 1942 which changed the age of homosexual consent from sixteen (the same as for heterosexuality) to twenty-one, bodes to be as repressive as Vichy.[18]

Hence the importance of 1968, in which David meets his lover, the young Communist Alain, one of 'les enfants de mai' (p.53) to whom the novel is addressed (it opens, symbolically, with David eulogizing the sleeping Alain's traits) and which promises a private and collective fulfilment denied twenty years earlier. May, he claims, will definitively erase the sexual division introduced by history, and reverse the moral/existential divide symbolized by the day/night distinction. In a speech delivered to the student occupiers of the Odéon Theatre, he hears a woman *cégétiste* argue that '68 est l'inverse de 89, comme la nuit est l'inverse du jour, comme la prise réussie de l'Odéon est la revanche du peuple de Paris sur la prise manquée de la Bastille' (p.360). Reasserting the rights of night over day, of rest, sleep and dreams over work and exploitation, her peroration combines the eulogy of the night with images of a classically left-wing provenance:

> Il n'y a de liberté que nocturne, dans la continuité mystérieuse, sans interruptions, sans coupures, de la nuit une, indivisible, immense, scintillante, infinie. A bas le jour, vive la nuit! La Révolution en marche prend le ciel étoilé pour bannière. (p.360)

Alas, Tubert, now a hardened militant and forgetful of the humiliations of 1944, is intolerant of homosexuals and denounces Alain (pp.379–83), whose long hair has already earned him a beating from the CRS as a 'gauchiste' and 'une fille' (pp.365–6). The PCF has become a pillar of the political system and a guardian of the moral order. Denounced by the very Tubert who was once 'excluded' by bourgeois triumphalism, Alain ostentatiously tears up his Party card and accepts his homosexual identity. Real liberation, however, the narrator concludes, will have to wait; it remains in 1968 as incomplete and as false a dawn as the historico-mythic prototype of 1944.

L'Irrévolution is situated in a provincial technical school ninety miles north of Paris, and in the post-revolutionary period, a time/space distanciation which partly explains its nostalgic tone – 'Que c'est loin, le mois de mai, le joli mois de mai' (p.114) – and negative outcome.[19]

It explores the socio-cultural divide between a 'prof de philo' seeking to radicalize working-class students and the students themselves, whom he discovers to be docile and conformist. Insecure about his own motives and identity – 'Je ne sais pas au juste si je me hais à travers la bourgeoisie, ou si c'est à travers moi que je hais la bourgeoisie' (p.44) – the narrator defines the revolutionary impulse as 'le mal du siècle', effectively subordinating it to a visceral psychological state or a Romantic literary cliché. The fictional location – Sottenville – and the protagonist's sense of inauthenticity – he feels 'de trop', spends hours in his hotel room or the ironically-named 'brasserie de l'Univers', and has curiously detached sexual encounters with 'l'infirmière', the middle-class fiancée to whom he makes love before dinner, 'parce qu'après, elle sait que je ne vaux rien' (p.158) – are powerfully reminiscent of Roquentin and Bouville in Sartre's pre-War *La Nausée* (1938), a symptomatic though not necessarily conscious derivation.

L'Irrévolution is regressive in inspiration and in message, since it concludes on the fundamental impossibility of revolution and even of significant non-revolutionary change. But the regression is also structural and psychological. Successive descriptions of the hotel room in which the novel opens, and which, by their circularity, deny the 'absence of revolutions' in the title, all lead back to childhood. Musing on his nomadism – 'j'ai depuis longtemps l'habitude d'errer un peu à la surface des choses et des lieux' (p.13) – the narrator reveals that this began when they left the house of his birth, adding: 'depuis, *c'est l'exode*' (ibid; my italics). The reference to the civilian exodus of 1940 is confirmed and its contemporary echoes reinforced by the narrator's contemptuous though whinging dismissal of 'l'infirmière' and her bourgeois circle:

A les entendre à la lettre, il faudrait qu'on aille demain faire le coup de feu dans les rues, dresser des embuscades à la sortie de chez Hermès ou de chez Hédiard, qui sont un peu les *Lutetia* de la nouvelle occupation. C'est ça: on est en pleine occupation. Et moi, me demande-t-on, est-ce que je 'résiste' de la bonne manière à Sottenville? Ils me font rigoler. Je voudrais bien les voir, tiens, avec mes élèves, avec les collègues, avec le censeur; je voudrais bien les voir 'résister'! (p.106)

What or whom is being 'resisted' here? Logically, the call to resist must be directed against the new 'occupiers' of May '68, who are from a bourgeois point of view, the students. In identifying the latter with right-bank luxury symbols such as Hermès or Hédiard, is Lainé underlining the essentially middle-class nature of the student revolutionaries themselves? Alternatively, in identifying them with the symbols of German Occupation, is he indirectly exploiting the racism mediated by the May events (revolutionaries = Cohn-Bendit = German Jew)? Or is he attacking the conspicuously wealthy from whom 'l'infirmière' and her friends feel excluded, in which case they are the objective allies of the opponents of a consumer society whose repressive forces are caricatured as successors of the Nazis ('CRS–SS')? That each is possible and none entirely plausible is characteristic of *L'Irrévolution* as a whole, and, to some extent, of the polyvalence of May itself. But what emerges weakened from these pages is the very concept of resistance, and with it, its transcendent, iconic expression, liberation, the liberating moment, the exit from the night of occupation:

> On nous appela la 'pègre', je m'en souviens. Et pourtant rien ne m'a jamais paru plus pur que cette foule, dans la rue, qui ne grouillait plus, mais qui s'épanouissait en larges vagues éclatant au roc, au promontoire du continent obscur, de la nuit policière, des boucliers et des matraques [...] Et j'avais imaginé que la rue, fécondée par la foule étrange, par l'irréel, par ce rêve, par mon rêve des milliers de fois répété, crié, par d'autres que je découvrais mes semblables, peut-être, allait enfanter l'homme nouveau. (p.35)

The text voices an aspiration towards collectivity, solidarity, the promise of the dawn and renewal, yet the experience is also disturbing, marked by unreality ('irréel', 'étrange') and ambivalence, traits consistent with the regressive dynamics of a novel from which, on the one hand, parental figures have largely disappeared, and, on the other, there is hope of a providential saviour figure 'qui me sauverait de la ressemblance avec moi-même' (ibid.).

Like other novelists of May '68, Lainé uses the Oedipal myth, but since the narrator is the would-be revolutionary and his students the conformists hoping to 'do better' than their fathers inside the system, the roles are reversed: 'Et moi, ce qu'on me reproche, ce qu'on n'ose pas me reprocher, c'est de représenter Oreste ou bien Œdipe, sur mon estrade; c'est d'être de la race de ceux qui, dans un sens ou dans l'autre, font naître le désordre' (p.99). The periodicity of this passage – 'ce qu'on me reproche... ce qu'on n'ose pas me reprocher', 'Oreste ou bien Œdipe', 'dans un sens ou dans l'autre' – and the narrator's ambivalent assumption of the role of predestined harbinger of 'le désordre' are characteristic. But if the Oedipal reference subordinates the revolutionary impulse to personal difficulties and removes it from the political arena, the reference to Orestes, the problematic liberator of Argos as transmogrified into the Sartrian liberator of occupied Paris in *Les Mouches* (1943), is more profoundly subversive. It is emblematic of the final irrelevance of the Sartrian ethos of 'commitment', demonstrated in May–June 1968 and now reduced, like the Liberation itself, to safely intertextual expression.

Notes

Unless stated otherwise, the place of publication is Paris.

1. Pascal Ory, *L'Entre-Deux-Mai*. *Histoire culturelle de la France, Mai 1968–Mai 1981*, Seuil, 1983, p.12.
2. In *L'Enragé*, no.1 [n.d. May 1968], author's private collection.
3. Quoted in Olivier Todd, *Jacques Brel: Une vie*, Livre de Poche/ Laffont, 1984, p.320.
4. Jean-Louis Curtis, *L'Horizon dérobé*, Flammarion, 1978, p.299. Elsewhere, Patrick Combes found the CRS likened to 'statuaire grecque, hoplite, fantassins hittites, guerriers d'Arno Breker'. See *La littérature et le mouvement de mai '68: écriture, mythes, critiques, écrivains*, Seghers, 1984, p.157. Breker was 'official' sculptor of the Third Reich whose 'Aryan' aesthetics formed part of collaborationist propaganda for the 'New European Order'.
5. I am indebted to my colleague Alistair Blyth for a copy of this song, published in 1970 or 1971, but composed earlier.
6. See Roger Absalom, *France 1968: the May Events*, London, Longman, 1971, p.66.
7. Gaullist supporters sounded 'Algérie française' rhythms on car horns; there were shouts of 'Cohn-Bendit à Dachau' or 'Au four!' (Absalom, *France 1968*, pp.59–60). The concentration camp motif also figures in cartoons (e.g., Wolinski, *L'Enragé*, no.6, July 1968).
8. In *Choses et Autres*, Gallimard/Folio, 1972, pp.210–11.
9. The expression is Pierre Seghers's, in the poem 'Octobre 1941'.
10. Jean-Louis Curtis, *Les Forêts de la nuit*, Livre de Poche, 1947, pp.446–7.
11. Such imagery is of course an abiding characteristic of wartime writing: 'les années noires/sombres', 'la nuit de l'occupation/ Nacht und Nebel', 'la clandestinité', 'Les Editions de Minuit, l'aube, les lendemains qui chantent', etc.
12. See for example Alain Brossat's recent *Libération fête folle, 6 juin 44 – 8 mai 45: mythes et rites ou le grand théâtre des passions populaires*, Autrement, Série Mémoires, 1994.
13. Jean-Louis Curtis, *La Chine m'inquiète*, Grasset, 1972.
14. 'Et notre sang épris de qui va le saisir/ Coule pour tout l'essaim

éternel du desir.'

15. The director's own specifications bear repetition here: 'Dans cette campagne écrasée de soleil, sans aucune présence humaine [*sic*], on aura l'impression d'être hors du temps, de l'histoire (plus aucune allusion à la guerre)... Ce final, serein, mélancolique, sera comme un point d'orgue, comme une note prolongée' (Patrick Modiano and Louis Malle, *Lacombe Lucien*, Gallimard, 1974, p.139). The penultimate frame shows Lucien 'couché sur le dos... mâchant un brin d'herbe (ibid., p.144), soundtracked by flute-like pipes, the faun's instrument of predilection.

16. Dominique Fernandez, *L'Etoile rose*, Grasset et Fasquelle, 1978.

17. That the seducer was Jewish is not explicitly stated, but the episode is presented as a quasi-Biblical sacrifice (pp.83–5). Fernandez recalled that his father, notwithstanding his collaborationism, travelled 'dans le dernier wagon du métro' as a gesture of solidarity with the Jews (*Le Monde*, 15 June 1979).

18. See Antony Copley, *Sexual Moralities in France, 1780–1980*, London, Routledge, 1989, pp.203–4.

19. Pascal Lainé, *L'Irrévolution*, Gallimard, 1971.

23

Reflections on Life, Death and History:
Jeanne Champion's *Le Bunker*

John Flower

Au bout d'un certain nombre d'années nous acceptons une vérité que nous
pressentions mais que nous nous cachions à nous-même par insouciance
ou lâcheté: un frère, un double est mort à notre place à une date et dans
un lieu inconnus et son ombre finit par se confondre à nous.

These words which close Patrick Modiano's most recent novel *Chien
de Printemps*[1] are recalled by the narrator as having been the farewell
remark addressed to him by a mysterious Belgian photographer Francis
Jansen. Jansen has made his reputation with the publication of a book
of photographs *Neige et soleil*. The narrator tells how he has attempted
to track down the man behind these photographs but has failed; clues
which he thought he had uncovered have just as quickly slipped from
his grasp, melting indeed like snow in the sun.

By the end of *Chien de Printemps* Jansen's identity has in fact become
confused with that of someone bearing the same name who proves
now to be dead. All the familiar ingredients of a Modiano novel are
here – the uncertain time-frame, the confusion over identity
underlined in this case by the matter of accuracy and reliability of
photographic representation, the reluctance to come to terms with a
truth from the past whatever it may be, the lack of precise details
within the narration and which would give it a firm structure, the
sense that the narrator (nineteen years of age in 1964, like the author)
and Modiano have something in common. And overall is the
impression that just as photographs are somehow unreliable so too are
words; for all their apparent simplicity and limpidity they ultimately
fail to explain. As always, Modiano's writing is disturbing.

While Jeanne Champion recognizes that Modiano, her junior by
nearly twenty years, enjoys a high reputation, she no more admits to
having been influenced by his work – indeed she denies having read

much of it – than by that of any other writer. Her ten earlier novels[2] share a number of recurring preoccupations – the fusion of past and present, cyclical patterns in history, reincarnation, madness and hallucination, and death. Not infrequently the novels raise important social issues, question the reliability of language, eschew conventional narrative forms, generally challenge, and invite a number of readings. Clearly in some, if not indeed in much of this, there is a deal of common ground with Modiano's writing and it may be that there are similarities elsewhere with works by other authors from the same period. Though Alan Morris does not mention Champion and her work in his *Collaboration and Resistance Reviewed. Writers and the 'Mode Rétro' in Post-Gaullist France*,[3] he alludes to some of these other authors. He reminds us of how in Dominique Garnier's novel *Nice, pour mémoire*, for example, the protagonist Noémi Fogelmann visits Nice where her own mother (Sarah) had waited in vain early in the Occupation to be reunited with the grandmother who had in fact already been deported. Sarah's anguish and desperation are somehow later transmitted to Noémi across the years by the surroundings in which she finds herself and she is momentarily absorbed by them: '[T]out me rappelle que quelque chose s'est passé. Mais quoi? Moi, Noémi Fogelmann, sans souvenirs, je crois, je ne suis pas. Ce sont... [...] Ce sont les souvenirs d'une autre.'[4] Unlike this novel, and indeed unlike the works of the many authors Morris discusses, Champion's novels do not as a group warrant inclusion in the 'mode rétro' category,[5] but there is no doubt that *Le Bunker*, of which we find an uncanny echo and almost perfect summary in the closing words of Modiano's *Chien de printemps*, does.

Le Bunker recounts how Germain Viard, a Parisian architect, fascinated by *Bunker Archéologie* by Paul Virilio,[6] a study of the construction of the defensive bunkers on the Normandy coast, determines to visit them. But it is not simply out of archaeological or architectural interest. Already Viard has sensed the presence of, and has been haunted by, some kind of spectral figure described as 'un homme dont la beauté ne devait guère avoir plus de vingt-cinq ans. Vêtu d'un uniforme de couleur assez sombre, l'inconnu [...] lui avait adressé la parole puis donné des ordres dans une langue étrangère' (pp.18, 19).[7] Viard abandons his wife and children in Paris and drives to the Normandy coast where he rents a room in a hotel near Arromanches. He will stay for about three months. Here his impression of *déjà vu* increases. The spirits of Kurt Rieter, the German officer who was responsible for supervising the construction of the local bunker and of his younger brother Heinrich who died on the Russian front, slowly possess him. Viard meets figures who played key roles in the past – Roger Cartaret, a Resistance fighter and Marie Coutances, his former fiancée who became Rieter's lover. Gradually past (1944) and present (1984) merge.[8] Viard spends time in the bunker, discovers Rieter's diary and eventually falls (or leaps) to his death from the cliff-top.

Such is the relative complexity of the structure of *Le Bunker* that a word should be said about it at this early stage. There are nine sections of varying lengths. An opening one dated November 1984, by an omniscient narrator, offers a part summary of what is to come. Its five paragraphs with repetitions and modifications of the same text bear unmistakable echoes of the *nouveau roman* (and especially of Robbe-Grillet's *Dans le labyrinthe*) and they read almost as if the author were searching for an appropriate formulation for the beginning of the novel. This opening is followed by the translation of a poem by Hölderlin on love, separation and pain, which also contains an allusion to an ideal unity. The third, seven pages long and dated September 1980, begins the account of Viard's departure for Normandy. After this we have the largest section of the novel dealing with the next two to three months, 174 pages long and subdivided into twenty sections of varying lengths (on average about nine pages) each introduced by a quotation from the translation of another Hölderlin poem, his last ode, *Patmos*, about divine immanence and the spreading of God's word through the German language. The poem is gradually built up, each quotation, added to the previous one, triggering what happens in the following pages. This central part of the book is followed by the complete quotation from the poem with a further seven lines added which raise questions about the sense we are to make of our lives and about God's divine role. The sixth section dated November 1984, with textual echoes of the opening one, focuses on Cartaret's visit to the bunker, before it turns into a form of diary recording in brutal terms (Cartaret's or the narrator's?) the events of 6 June 1944 as seen from both sides. It ends with the description of Rieter's death and the recording of Germain's birth in Paris on the same day. The seventh section begins in the same way as the sixth, again with echoes, and has Cartaret reading Rieter's diary which Viard had discovered days before his death. The commentary and reflection which this diary makes on the long principal section of the novel are self-evident but significant. The eighth part repeats the Hölderlin poem (albeit with the last line now in French as well) and we return finally to the bunker and Roger Cartaret, again with textual echoes but now with the revelation as well that it is he – or possibly he – who, like Rieux at the end of *La Peste*, is the author of the novel we have just read.[9]

In a number of respects the accounts we have in *Le Bunker* of certain features of the last months of the German presence and of the Allied invasion conform to those found in many novels dealing with the Occupation and Resistance. Kurt Rieter is cultured, sympathetic, speaks excellent French and is uncertain about the values for which he is fighting; the normally taciturn Cartaret has a reputation as a Resistance fighter, though inwardly he is racked by anguish at having lost Marie and having been powerless to prevent her public humiliation at the Liberation (pp.185, 6); Marie Coutances, having gone mad after Rieter has been killed, is punished for her love for him by being publicly disgraced and having her head shaved. (Cartaret has continued since then to care for her.) We have villagers who were indifferent, others who collaborated. Why Champion should reproduce what amounts virtually to a series of stereotypes in this way is not clear. It may be, given that the principal concern in the novel is rather different, that she has recreated a context which would be easily recognizable and assimilable; but it seems more than possible that she wants her reader to realize precisely how easy it is to accept such a view unthinkingly, without reflection. Certainly her description of the invasion passes from a reference to 'les heures glorieuses de la Libération' (p.13), through the breathless Hollywood-style description of the German installation and eventual defeat given by the guide at the Arromanches museum (pp.52–7) and the matter of fact account offered by Le père Grimaud (pp.96–7), to a final authorial one (pp.203–12) which brings home the true lunatic nature and barbarity of the conflict. Nearly a third of the way through the novel Mme Lison, the owner of the second hotel where Viard stays, comments about the bunker: 'Si seulement il pouvait basculer dans la mer et le souvenir de la guerre avec lui!' (p.74). Champion's point appears to be that such an attitude, while understandable, is meaningless because impossible. The War was real, its divisive effect on the French population is ineradicable, and the tens of thousands of deaths during the hours of the Allied landings, evidenced today by the vast stretches of military cemeteries, remain a permanent scar. All that can be hoped is that the War – and indeed war – will be seen as the supreme human aberration and folly and that civilization must remain unstinting in its efforts to prevent its recurrence. At the same time, and it is here that the novel has clear affinities with the 'mode rétro', *Le Bunker* is a reminder that no single, unchallengeable view of events between 1940 and 1944 is necessarily the only possible or correct one.[10]

Within this broad perspective Champion's principal concern in the novel is the exploration of the spiritual relationship between the dead Nazi officer Kurt Rieter, his brother Heinrich and Germain Viard. At once the transparency of the architect's Christian name, meaning both German and close relative, strikes us, though Champion has claimed that the choice was quite unintentional: 'Quand j'ai commencé ce livre, Germain s'est imposé à moi. Je n'ai même pas fait le parallèle, ça m'a complètement échappé.'[11] In addition to this we learn that Germain was born the day Rieter dies, 6 June 1944 (pp.183, 212). The process of the gradual 'occupation' of Viard by one or both of the Germans, of a kind of reincarnation, procedes through several stages. Before he leaves for the Normandy coast Viard dreams about Rieter (p.18), hallucinates and imagines both that he sees the German's reflection in a mirror (p.21) and that he (Viard) is dead in an armchair; at breakfast the following morning – to his wife's horror – he recites a passage from Virilio's book in a strange voice (p.28). The owner of the first hotel where he spends a single night, Mme Osmanville, remarks 'il est évident que vous n'êtes pas français, mais allemand... vous en avez d'ailleurs l'allure et le type' (p.37). At the museum in Arromanches he hears himself speak with 'cette voix qu'il ne reconnaissait pas [...] cet accent guttural qui ne lui appartenait pas' (p.59). A facial description of him is virtually identical with the one of the figure he had seen in the mirror in Paris (pp.60, 19) and the museum guide makes the same assumption as Mme Osmanville (p.60). Germain recognizes the village where he will eventually stay (p.66) and when he books his room in Mme Lison's hotel he does so in the name of Germain von Bechmann (p.69). She is convinced he is German (p.75); Le père Grimaud will say to him directly: 'vous avez une tête d'Allemand' (p.97) and a voice within him recites German, a language he has never studied (pp.100, 104). From the moment of his arrival he is referred to almost exclusively by the narrator simply as 'Germain' and by other characters in the novel anonymously as 'l'homme', 'l'étranger', 'le client de Mme Lison' and simply as 'un Allemand'.[12] By now he can admit to himself: 'Quelqu'un me possède... un autre agit à mon place... il est lui et moi à la fois' (p.101).

Two incidents in particular illustrate this possession. The first is the account the young boy Gérard gives of his meeting Viard as the latter goes in search of Roger Cartaret and, more importantly, of the bunker. He overhears him speaking German to himself, has the impression that for a moment he physically alters ('le visage mobilisé par la haine était devenu irréconnaissable' [p.81]), and feels threatened by him. Later, in his hotel room, Germain recalls the same events. One gesture in particular is now different. Whereas on seeing Gérard he is described as having pointed at the boy (in the latter's words when he recounts the incident to his parents) – 'se servant de sa main comme on se sert d'un revolver' (p.81) – Germain's own recollection has a different ring to it: 'levant le bras *à la manière hitlérienne*, il fit signe à

l'enfant de disparaître immédiatement' (p.103). The second incident
occurs when he meets Marie Coutances for the first time. Her
opening words to him – 'ils l'ont enfermé à l'intérieur... dépêchez-
vous, je vous en supplie, allez vite le délivrer avant que l'autre
n'arrive!' (p.127) – trigger an hallucination, and Germain 'experiences'
Kurt's death both as it resulted from a hand-grenade attack and as
though he is executed by a military firing squad.[13]

From this moment on Germain is powerless to escape. Moreover
his presence and behaviour make him an increasingly disturbing figure.
Mme Lison has a vision of him lying dead in the bunker (p.138), she
too senses the presence of another spirit in the hotel (p.146) and
decides he must leave. When Viard's wife arrives in a desperate
attempt to persuade him to return to Paris, she is met with blunt
refusal: 'Je ne peux pas te parler [...] Germain Viard est mort Isabelle...
il est enterré non loin d'ici, dans le cimetière de La Cambe, à côté ou
à la place d'un type de vingt ans, un dénommé Kurt Rieter' (pp.147–
9). Marie comes to the hotel but flees before Viard can open the door;
he is left calling after her in German (p.161). Finally Germain meets
Cartaret to whom at one point in their many conversations he
comments: 'Je me suis éloigné de moi-même, de ma vie, de mon
histoire pour rejoindre celle d'un autre. Le seul lien qui me rattache
encore au monde, c'est ce bunker' (p.187). Within days he will be
discovered dead by Gérard on the rocks at the foot of the cliffs on
which the bunker is built. When his body is recovered his face is at
peace – 'paisible, presque souriant, ses yeux surtout, les yeux de
l'Allemand grand ouverts' (pp.213, 251).

While the bunker itself is the focal point of the action of the novel
and of Jeanne Champion's preoccupations, other features, notably
mirrors, windows and the omnipresent seagull, also have important
contributory roles to play. The first two are clearly linked and have
always been used by Champion in her work in a traditional way as
symbolizing points of communication with the world of the spirit. In
Paris Kurt appears to Germain in the mirror 'plus nettement encore
que dans le rêve', and the architect believes he hears 'à l'intérieur du
miroir [...] le bruit d'une respiration contrariée' (p.21). After he has
been accused by Le père Grimaud of having 'une tête d'Allemand',
he fails to recognize himself in the wardrobe mirror in his hotel room;
he appears to be afraid of his reflection (pp.100, 113). In a similar, but
this time imagined, mirror he sees the firing squad (pp.128, 9). Rieter
too records in his diary that in the same room in Mme Osmin's hotel
'il m'a semblé que de l'autre côté du miroir quelqu'un me faisait signe'
(p.226), and a day or two later that he has dreamed of someone with
'la blondeur de mon frère en même temps que mes traits' (p.228).

Whether in his Parisian apartment (p.11) or in his hotel room, the window is an invitation to be drawn outside but it remains closed, and Germain claims at one point, even though he is drunk, that 'he' is trying to get in.

If the intended significance of these two features is clear, that of the seagull is even more so. Again the technique is not unfamiliar in Champion's work; she often has recourse to animals or trees (notably in *X*) as reincarnations of individuals or of spiritual values. The gull makes its first appearance while Viard is in the museum and, as he watches it swoop and turn, his mind is suddenly flooded by images of war (p.58). Subsequently it will appear when he visits the bunker for the first time (p.106) and when later he is challenged by the police over the false name he had given to Mme Lison, rather like a reproach 'le cri d'un oiseau de mer vint mourir contre la façade de l'hôtel' (p.112). After he has fallen to his death, the bird spirals tirelessly above his corpse (p.194).

That the gull symbolises or is even the bearer of the spirit of Kurt Rieter is obvious; like mirrors and windows it provides another link between the world of the living and the world of the dead. But it also symbolizes escape from the 'folie meurtrière des hommes' (p.58) so amply illustrated by the permanency of the bunker, described by Virilio as 'le reflet de notre puissance de mort, celui de notre mode de destruction' (p.38).[14] In simple terms the bunker for the Nazis is part of a defensive system constructed to protect what they have conquered; for the French it is an emblem of oppression. In either case it resonates with death. Germain feels its 'pesanteur tombale' (p.106) when he first goes into it; Kurt writes in his diary that 'lorsqu'on pénètre à l'intérieur de cet édifice on a l'impression d'entrer dans un caveau ou dans une crypte... ce bâtiment évoque la mort' (p.225), and Gérard too 'senses' 'cet écrasement mortuaire' (p.197).[15]

During his conversations with Viard, Cartaret at one point describes the massive task of building the bunker which French and Polish prisoners of war had been forced to carry out:

Cette masse qui ne parvenait pas à se dégager du sol tant elle était lourde, cette masse les digérait. Et puis, peu à peu, ils avaient vu surgir le monstre. Le moment le plus extraordinaire dans cet horrible accouchement, c'est lorsqu'ils avaient fait sauter les coffrages de la façade ouest et qu'ils avaient libéré le regard, ce que les architectes appellent la fente de visée. Quand elle avait été complètement dégagée, Français et Polonais s'étaient précipités à l'intérieur, et là ils avaient découvert l'infini capté par l'œil d'un cyclope. (p.177)

The bunker is therefore born and is a womb itself.[16] But instead of generating new life it produces only death, a point made by Champion in an interview with the paper *Ouest-France*: 'Le bunker est une architecture fondamentalement féminine. C'est un utérus qui n'est pas là pour donner la vie, mais pour servir la mort.'[17]

While it is self-evidently significant for the role which the bunker itself plays, the image of enclosure is apparent in the novel elsewhere and, in addition is reflected by its overall structure. We learn that as a student Germain had enjoyed the seclusion of his 'chambre de bonne' (p.25). On his way to Arromanches he appreciates the comfort and warmth of his car: 'Germain se laissait bercer par le ronflement du moteur'. He is 'blotti dans la chaleur de cette voiture' (pp.25, 6). In Mme Osmanville's hotel he enjoys an untroubled night's sleep in a narrow bed 'fermé par de lourds montants de bois' (p.35). On arrival at Mme Lison's he instantly feels 'en sécurité' (p.66). Here too 'seul le lit lui [offre] un secours' (p.102) and, as we have noted, he prefers to leave his bedroom windows closed. Beyond the hotel 'les haies [...] bornaient l'horizon et servaient de barrières aux pâturages' (p.102). Nor should we neglect the fact that by the end of his stay five days of rain have virtually isolated them and that the bunker is at the end of 'une étroite langue de terre serrée entre un talus d'herbes sèches et le précipice' (p.105). In most if not all cases enclosure is protective and, with this in mind, the roles of the two hotel owners are important. Both are widows, both it seems are childless (in fact it is suggested that Mme Lison is barren) and both adopt maternal attitudes or make maternal gestures towards Germain. The former provides him with a simple meal on arrival and as he eats it 'avec une simplicité presque enfantine, était venue tricoter en face de lui' (p.34). Mme Lison reflects: 'Cet homme pourrait être le fils que je ne n'ai pas eu; pourquoi ne prendrais-je pas soin de lui pour un temps?' (p.66). This she does, becoming anxious about his health (p.98) and his evident preoccupations (p.71), and lying awake waiting for him to return (p.130).

Ultimately, of course, Mme Lison finds Germain's presence increasingly uncomfortable and makes it clear that she wishes him to leave. Reluctantly he agrees but his last words are: '[J]e suis ici et ne puis être ailleurs... et cela, vous ne pouvez le comprendre... soyez sans crainte, je libérai les lieux dès le début de la semaine prochaine... laissez-moi encore ce week-end!' (p.191). The following Saturday he visits the bunker, leaves Rieter's diary open at the entry where the German had recorded the news of his brother's death *three months before*, and falls to his own. The lapse of time is significant. Germain has also been in Normandy for three months and had he not, the night before he left Paris, had the hallucinatory experience of seeing his own corpse?[18] During this time therefore it is as though, having abandoned his family, his journey from Paris flat to open sea takes him more significantly back through adolescence and childhood in search of the moment of his birth, which is then realized as one of death. The bunker is indeed 'un utérus qui n'est pas là pour donner la vie, mais pour servir la mort.' But death is not an end; instead it is a release from what Kurt Rieter in his diary refers to as his 'exil éternel' (p.247). Through it he, Heinrich and Germain escape from the restraints imposed by corporeal existence by time and by history[19] and discover a realm of spiritual communion, a new beginning. And madness serves the same purpose. As Viard says to Marie: 'Non, Marie, vous n'êtes pas folle! Vous avez tout simplement cessé d'exister' (p.129). Abstracted in this way, the treatment of such themes sets *Le Bunker* squarely within Jeanne Champion's recurrent preoccupations, but its very specific frame of reference and the manner in which it is composed invites a slightly different – albeit related – meaning.

As we have already noted, each quotation from the Hölderlin poem in the main section of the novel acts as a kind of spur or dynamic for the pages which follow. The intratextual echoes and repetitions function in much the same way on a broader scale, and at the end the discovery of Carteret's true role (whether author or 'agent') inevitably forces the reader back to the beginning and invites a fresh consideration of the text he or she has just read. There is also the question of Rieter's diary. Whether we accept it simply as part of the fiction or rather in the eighteenth-century fictional convention as an 'authentic' document, its status is important in that it helps to explain and validate Viard's intuitions and behaviour.[20] Even so, at the end we are left with a novel that is about to begin again and may prove to be different, if only marginally so on the next writing/reading. Champion seems to be saying that to provide a single consistent and reliable interpretation of facts, particularly those of such a sensitive period as the one dealt with in *Le Bunker*, is not simply difficult but impossible and will remain so. Such a conclusion would also be supported by the novel's shifting narratorial voice and by Champion's authorial omniscience.[21] Her purpose is to widen her focus, not in any way to lose the sharpness of the events of early summer 1944 (or even of 1940–44), but rather to introduce issues of more general historical, spiritual and above all moral significance. The quotation already cited from Virilio's book underlines the human capacity for destructive acts; to look at the bunker itself is as 'contempler un miroir, le reflet de notre puissance de mort' (p.38).[22] This is, it seems, an irresistible temptation. Cartaret says to Germain at one point, while war in all its apocalyptic horror and 'lasse de visiter l'Europe est allée porter ses fruits ailleurs' (p.177), it is rarely far away. And wherever it is present, war dehumanizes, it separates people from each other, preventing their uniting in the 'single voice' of which the Hölderlin poem speaks.[23]

Just before he visits the museum in Arromanches, Germain telephones his family to say that he plans to return to Paris that evening. His wife's relief and affection are unmistakable but somehow he feels distant and as though some greater force creates a barrier between them: 'L'affection qu'on lui portait, détournée par une force mystérieuse, ne parvenait plus jusqu'à lui. A l'image du jumeau dont le frère est mort dans le ventre de la mère, Germain était venu au monde endeuillé par la perte d'un être cher' (p.50).

The image is significant and anticipates the end where union with his spiritual brothers will not be achieved in any form of rebirth but through death. History, war, the bunker cannot be forgotten or ignored but the warnings they offer can be heeded. At a time when the world seems to many to be bent on self-destruction, Champion's appeal through her novel is for us to reflect and remain vigilant. Already by the year of its publication (1985) – and here again there are similarities with Modiano's most recent works – Le Bunker may be said in broad terms to show signs of a growing fin de siècle unease, uncertainty as to how to read the past and anxiety about what the future may bring. But as an invitation to reflect on this dark period of recent French – and German – history and to ponder its lessons, it cannot and should not be ignored.

Notes

Unless stated otherwise, the place of publication is Paris.

1. Patrick Modiano, Chien de Printemps, Seuil, 1993, p.121.
2. Born in Lons-le-Saunier in the Jura in 1931, Jeanne Champion comes from a rural background and is very largely self-educated. Before turning to imaginative writing, she painted, producing works which are surrealist in inspiration. She is fascinated by the unconscious and the unusual. Several of her written works deal with a kind of dream world in which chronology is destroyed and gives way to a mixing between periods of history at will. She is concerned too by problems of justice, communication and the meaning of language. To date her novels are: Le Cri (1967); Les Miroirs jumeaux (1968); X (1969); Vautour en privilège (1973); Ma fille Marie-Hélène Charles-Quint (1974); Dans les jardins d'Esther (1975);

Les Gisants (1977); *Les Frères Montaurian* (1979); *La Passion selon Martial Montaurian* (1981); *L'Amour capital* (1982); *Le Bunker* (1985). Champion has also written two *biographies romancées*: *Suzanne Valadon* (1984) and *Le Hurlevent* (1987). The second of these received the Prix Goncourt for Biography. In 1989 she produced a series of reflections on the theme of exile, *Mémoires en exil*. She is currently working on a massive history of the world.

3. Alan Morris, *Collaboration and Resistance Reviewed. Writers and the 'Mode Rétro' in Post-Gaullist France*, Oxford and New York, Berg, 1992.

4. Ibid., p.99.

5. 'The widespread reassessment of the Occupation that took place from 1970 onwards', ibid., p.7. See, too, Colin Nettelbeck, 'Getting the Story Right: Narratives of World War II in Post 1968 France', *Journal of European Studies*, vol.58, no.15, June 1985, pp.77–116.

6. Paul Virilio, *Bunker Archéologie*; first published as the catalogue to an exhibition of Virilio's own photographs, organized by the Centre de Création industrielle at the Musée des Arts décoratifs in Paris, December 1975–February 1976. The catalogue was subsequently published as a book in 1991 in Les Editions du Demi-Cercle; references are to the latter.

7. Jeanne Champion, *Le Bunker*, Calmann-Lévy, 1985. References here are to this edition and are included in the text. The description of this figure contains features of the two brothers, as we learn subsequently.

8. These are in fact two 'presents': the time of the action (1980) and the time of composition (1984).

9. The text relies on the passive voice: 'Mais voici qu'il [Cartaret] se laisse gagner par l'hébétude; à l'intérieur d'une sorte de rêverie, une histoire au titre court *Le Bunker* est en train de s'écrire' (p.251). According to Champion the passive is deliberate. There is no precise author but each reading of the text brings to it a new dimension and interpretative possibility; the direction the book could take is, to use her word, 'imprévisible' (interview with the present writer, 20 April 1994).

10. See, too, p.179: 'le débarquement n'était guère pour les Français qu'un sujet de film ou de dramatique de télévision.'

11. Interview with Pierre Maury, *Le Soir*, 17 October 1985 – confirmed in conversation with the present writer, 28 February 1994.

12. Apart from one reference to the name he adopts when he signs in at Mme Lison's hotel, Germain von Bechmann (p.69), he

remains anonymous; see, in particular, between pp.62–97.

13. The execution is only explained subsequently (p.237) when we learn that Kurt Rieter knows he risks being shot should his diary be discovered. This kind of anticipation is also important as a means by which the text is pulled together and given an internal density.

14. Virilio, *Bunker Archéologie*, p.46.

15. One of Rieter's men, Wolf, comments: 'J'en ai assez de vivre dans ce tombeau' (pp.196, 239). Virilio makes much of this comparison (*Bunker Archéologie*, p.13) and also sees the bunker as a form of archetypal tomb from which new life will ultimately spring: 'S'il s'apparente ainsi à la crypte qui préfigure la résurrection, le bunker s'apparente également à l'arche qui sauve, au véhicule qui porte au-delà du danger, par la traversée des risques mortels' (p.46). This interpretation was obviously influential for Champion.

16. When it has been completed the German soldiers occupying it are described as 'accroupis' (p.57).

17. *Ouest-France*, 24 June 1986.

18. When he hallucinates and believes he sees his own body it is described as 'la tête basculée en arrière, sur le dossier recouvert de velours noir, son visage aux yeux clos allait et venait au rythme de la vague qui venait s'échouer sur un amas de rochers dressés au milieu du salon' (p.22). When he is eventually killed his eyes remain open. Kurt wonders whether Heinrich's eyes were open or closed at the moment of death (p.196).

19. The theme of exile generally is treated by Champion in *Mémoires en exil* (1989). The proceeds from the sales of this book were given to Amnesty International.

20. Kurt writes in his diary: 'J'ai peur de Temps, des lieux, de l'Histoire' (p.214).

21. The whole question of the reliability of language is again illustrated here. Gérard reads two paragraphs of the diary (pp.196, 7); when the diary as a whole is reproduced subsequently there are a number of differences between them (pp.239, 40).

22. A narrative voice representing three generations may be a deliberate ploy to show how each reacts. It also seems probable that together with the emphasis on cyclical patterns that Champion's fragmented narrative offers us a feminist perception of these events. I am grateful to Claire Gorrara for this suggestion.

23. Virilio, *Bunker Archéologie*, p.46.

- 24 -

Uranus: the History of Mediocrity

Ginette Vincendeau

From Book to Film

Uranus was written by Marcel Aymé (1902–67) and published in 1948 by Gallimard, four years after the Liberation and *épuration*. It was conceived as an anti-Resistance and anti-communist pamphlet and was partly motivated by the execution of Aymé's friend the fascist writer and film historian Robert Brasillach, on 6 February 1945. The book was a success. Aymé, often referred to as a 'right-wing anarchist', is a populist writer whose work is characterized by ideological ambivalence and has been frequently adapted to the cinema. For instance, while he kept publishing during the war in fascist and collaborationist papers such as *La Gerbe* and *Je suis partout* (though not explicitly 'fascist' articles, rather extracts from his books or general pieces), he also worked with the Communist director Louis Daquin. In the 1930s he worked with left-sympathizer Pierre Chenal, who shot Aymé's *La Rue sans nom* in 1933, the first film to receive the label of 'Poetic Realism.'[1]

Claude Berri (born 1934) directed *Uranus* in 1990; he also co-produced it through his company Renn-Productions. His previous films as director included, at the time, an autobiographical story about anti-Semitism, *Le Vieil homme et l'enfant* (1967), *Tchao Pantin* (1983), and the very successful pair of 'heritage films': *Jean de Florette/Manon des sources* (1986). Like Aymé, he could also be characterized as a populist, as his films, especially in the later period, were aimed at a wide audience. Berri has declared in interviews that he made *Uranus* because he thought the novel 'powerful', fielding criticism about Aymé's fascist-collaborationist involvements by pointing out the writer's ambivalence and work with Communists. He also argues that he had considerably toned down Aymé's anti-communism.

Uranus was an expensive French production, costing 80 million francs, roughly four times the average budget at the time. The expense was largely attributable to the cost of studio decors and costumes, and the actors' salaries (Gérard Depardieu and Philippe Noiret, the top two stars, were at the time respectively the first and fifth best-paid actors in France, with Depardieu receiving anything above 5 million francs, Noiret about 3 million francs. Others, such as Michel Blanc, Jean-Pierre Marielle and Fabrice Luchini were also prominent 'bankable' actors, receiving between one and two million francs per film[2]). By Berri's own admission, casting so many stars and *vedettes* of the French cinema was a 'producer's idea' designed to attract audiences; it was one that paid off: *Uranus* was the second most successful French film of the 1990–91 season, after *La Gloire de mon père* (the box-office that year was headed by *Dances with Wolves* and *Pretty Woman*).[3]

The publicity surrounding the release of *Uranus* made constant reference to the book, a tribute to Aymé's place as one of the best-known twentieth-century popular writers in France. The press book for the film contains a whole section on the novel and reviewers of the film, without exception, make reference to it (though until then it was not Aymé's most famous). It was reissued in paperback by Folio, with a version of the film poster on the cover. Such linking is part of common marketing practice and reflects, in the case of literary adaptations, the desire to add legitimacy to a particular product. Even so, the high level of attention devoted to the novel in the promotion of the film for French audiences makes the consideration of the process of adaptation relevant, though it is emphatically not my intention to provide a comparative value judgement. While my primary interest here is the film, it is important to recognize the novel as a very public intertext for it.

Uranus concerns characters and events in the small provincial town of Blémont in the spring of 1945, during the *épuration*, when Communists, Gaullists and ex-*résistants* pursue and punish known or suspected collaborators and fascists. Half of the town is in ruins due to an Allied bombardment. The Catholic bourgeois Archambauds (Jean-Pierre Marielle is Archambaud, Danièle Lebrun his wife, and Florence Darel their daughter Marie-Anne), who already house schoolteacher Watrin (Philippe Noiret), have to share their flat with the Communist Gaigneux (Michel Blanc) and his family. Their cohabitation is fraught. Unknown to the Gaigneux, they also hide Maxime Loin (Gérard Desarthe), a fascist on the run. Jourdan the schoolteacher (Fabrice Luchini), an 'intellectual' Communist, and Rochard (Daniel Prévost), a hard-line Communist railway worker, try to exact reprisals against ex-collaborators while Monglat (Michel Galabru), a black market profiteer, tries to salvage and hide away his fortune, with the reluctant help of his son Michel. Watrin is given to humanist poetic diatribes on nature, but is also haunted at night by nightmares about the planet Uranus (hence the title). The split between his daytime rosy views and his night-time horrific visions provides a metaphor for the divided nation. Finally, there is Léopold (Gérard Depardieu), a brutish, alcoholic café owner who discovers poetry while Watrin holds French literature classes in his café. Léopold is arrested on the suspicion that he is hiding Loin. On his release he drunkenly shouts confused accusations against the whole town, especially Monglat. Prisoners of war return. During the ceremony to welcome them back, Gallien, a renegade Communist among the returning men, is savagely beaten up. Marie-Anne Archambaud catches her mother and Maxime Loin having sex. Léopold is shot dead by the policemen who have come to arrest him, on the instigation of Monglat. While visiting Marie-Anne, whom he desires, Gaigneux discovers Loin in the Archambaud sitting-room, and takes him to the police station.

Uranus the film is largely faithful to the novel, following its narrative line, characters and locations, and reproducing entire passages of dialogue. There are also noticeable differences – some inevitable technically, others clearly the result of choice. The first concern narrative simplification. Though *Uranus* is not a particularly long novel, it is dense with characters and small incidents. Berri and co-writer Arlette Langmann (his sister) had to simplify. For instance, the scenes between Monglat and his son have been reduced to two; the scenes of Léopold in jail are dramatically reduced in narrative time. The second type of difference arises from the elimination of inner monologues. The characters' inner thoughts, developed in the novel, tend to be lost in passage from novel to film, with a few exceptions: Maxime Loin's brief moment of voice-over when he writes his diary, and Jourdan's reading aloud his letter to his mother as he is writing it; occasionally inner thoughts are transferred to film dialogue. This produces some inevitable shifts. For instance, the character of Marie-Anne ends up both less complex and morally 'purer'. In the book, though she is repelled by Monglat's son, she cannot bring herself to give him up. Thus while Marie-Anne in the novel partakes of the general quagmire of compromises and mediocrity, she is somehow abstracted from it in the film. One could see Berri's decision to change her piano tune from Edith Piaf to Mozart in the same light.

A third type of difference has to do with the toning down of Aymé's polemic *vis-à-vis* the Communist party. For example, while retaining his hard-line views, Gaigneux becomes a more sympathetic character, playing with, and looking after, his young children, which is not found in the book. In the scene of the prisoners' return, the extreme violence of the punishment inflicted on ex-Communist Gallien is considerably reduced. Generally, references to excessive violence committed by Communists (e.g. piercing someone's eyes in reprisal) are fleeting or toned down. Finally, Aymé's black humour, which characteristically mixes the grotesque and the vulgar with realist observation, psychology and wit, has been somewhat 'cleaned up'. It is left to Léopold to be the chief embodiment of excess, and even this is largely a function of Gérard Depardieu's star persona.

Historical Narratives

As a film made in 1990 based on a 1948 novel of events set in 1945, *Uranus* poses the question of its engagement with history. Like all historical fiction films, *Uranus* is made of three narratives: the 'empirical narrative' of the events in the public domain transmitted through learned and popular history and memory, the literary narrative (the events depicted in the book), and the filmic narrative. Beyond the differences between literary and filmic narratives mentioned above, there are discrepancies between these three narratives which point to different agendas on the part of Berri compared with Aymé and more generally of the late 1980s as opposed to the immediate post-War. There is first of all a collapse of chronology, already present in the book, but more emphatic in a film made (theoretically at least) with a great deal more historical hindsight. The return of prisoners did take place in May 1945, the time of the story. But by then the FFI had been incorporated in the regular army and thus vanished from the public scene; they could not have been visible as they are in both novel and film. The kind of patriots who punish Gallien would also no longer have been active in such a context.

The violence of the *épuration* is exaggerated by both book and film. The 'épuration sauvage' took place in the summer of 1944; by the spring of 1945 reprisals were largely in the hands of the courts of justice. Recent historians[4] emphasize how the punishments meted out at the Liberation have been exaggerated in history books and popular accounts of the early post-War period. For instance, contrary to rumours at the time and the accounts of subsequent historians such as Robert Aron, the victims of the *épuration* totalled probably 10,000, rather than the 30,000 or 40,000 often claimed. But whereas in 1948 Aymé may have plausibly believed the higher figures (and he was not averse to distortion, claiming a fanciful 100,000 in 1965[5]), by 1990 Berri had access to the necessary knowledge to redress the balance, which he chose not to use.

The relative power of the Communist party at the time of the book and at the time of the film is also relevant. Aymé may have written *Uranus* as a response to Brasillach's death, but between 1944–45 and 1948 other events intervened which can be assumed to have coloured his view of communism. Communism then enjoyed its highest level of representation in parliament (166 MPs in 1946), and the Communists had been active in the 1947 strikes, provoking also a virulent anti-communism in the international context of the beginning of the Cold War. By 1947, according to Jean-Pierre Rioux, already 'the spirit of the Liberation was disappearing'.[6] Berri had his personal agenda *vis-à-vis* anti-communism, and reportedly made the film as a nostalgic tribute to his father who had been a Communist. In this respect, we might speculate that the sympathetic characterization of Gaigneux played by Michel Blanc was developed with this in mind. But at the same time, the dramatic decline in power of the Communist party in late 1980s France made the making and success of *Uranus* in the France of 1990 a significant contribution to the attendant anti-communist backlash.

Berri has made the somewhat extravagant claim that 'My film is the fictional version of *Le Chagrin et la Pitié*.'[7] However, on the level of its form alone, *Uranus* cannot be like *Le Chagrin et la Pitié* precisely because it is fiction. Moreover, the films' modes of spectatorial address are very different too. There are in *Uranus* no heroes (as in Melville's *L'Armée des ombres*) or anti-heroes (as in *Lacombe Lucien*), but identification is still focalized through a collection of individuals, while *Le Chagrin et la Pitié* embeds its interviews with individuals in the wider context of politics and historical events. And, as Christopher Lloyd has remarked, Aymé's critique of parties is, in the film, also reduced to individual destiny.[8] Even though we are dealing with a group of individuals instead of one, political orientations of individual characters, for instance, are attributed to personal psychology: Monglat's collaborationist activities are explained by his disappointment in his son and Jourdan's intellectual communism to his lack of virility and over-dependence on his mother.

Collectively, the characters of *Uranus* form a microcosm which extrapolates into the nation, not the nation as a series of irreconcilable positions as in *Le Chagrin et la Pitié*, but as a coherent whole made of reconciled antinomies. This is emphasized several times in the dialogue, with remarks such as Archambaud's, 'The whole of France is hypocritical.' Collectively, the narrative operates on a principle of 'checks and balances'. It is a microcosm without outside threats or presences (such as the Germans or outsiders of any kinds, such as Jews). If there are divisions between the factions and characters and within them, these divisions are in turn carefully cancelled out by each other. The most prominent example of internal division is Watrin, with his planet Uranus metaphor ('Astre sombre et glacé qui pèse sur tous les points de mon être...'). The Archambauds (centre-right bourgeois) and Gaigneux (Communists) share the same flat, quarrel but ultimately manage to get on. Léopold's café is both café and school. Léopold and Loin are both imprisoned, and both die. The Monglat father/son conflict is echoed by the Archambaud father/son and mother/daughter conflicts. Gaigneux, Jourdan, and Rochard exemplify divisions within the Communist party, while Loin, Watrin, and Archambaud exemplify splits within the Right. Most pointedly, Gaigneux the Communist and Loin the fascist were friends before the war and eventually 'understand each other' when they have their final talk. They also both desire the same woman, called Marie-Anne (a homonym for Marianne, the allegorical representation of the French Republic). As identification shifts like a pendulum throughout the story, the 'attack' on one faction is neutralized by one on the other, producing again a sense of pervasive averageness, of mediocrity.

The film's microcosm is male, the function of women purely sexual or biological, as in Aymé. Marie-Anne, Mme Archambaud, and Watrin's widow are seen or talked about in relation to sexual liaison; Mme Gaigneux is simply a mother. When Leopold's wife is talked about at all, it is to ridicule her absence of sexuality. But while this could simply be put down to Aymé's customary misogyny, the all-male focus has a more interesting sexual slant which, while not the subject of this chapter, is worth briefly discussing. Aymé's novel is quite explicit in its anxieties about virility. Jourdan is ridiculed for his asexuality ('not liking women, not liking life'). Watrin's house is destroyed as he imagines his wife making love to her lover. Marie-Anne only feels repulsion for the two sexually active men, young Monglat (who makes love to her) and Loin (to her mother). The novel (unwittingly perhaps) ends up portraying a collective de-sexualization of the men of Blémont which is absent from the film. Berri even adds a scene in which Léopold has brutal intercourse with his wife on his return from prison. This shift from the novel could be first of all attributed to the need to offer more flattering portrayals of the male characters in line with the star personas of the main actors. But its effect is certainly another stripping of the historical inscription of the film. Feminist historians have offered convincing analyses of the blow dealt by the War to collective French masculinity, evoking it as the failure of the authority of the family and therefore the father, both collective (Pétain) and individual. Young women who lived through the War are quoted as saying that 'War was their [the men's] collective failure... it put in question a lot of their mighty principles; they could not give themselves as the absolute reference anymore.'[9] Berri's erasure of this dimension in the novel is another way in which its topicality is played down, but also a way in which his film is a narrative for the 1990s rather than for the 1940s.

The Performance of History

As part of the War and Occupation genre, *Uranus* is visually unemphatic compared with the 'retro nostalgia' films of the 1970s and 1980s (e.g. *Le Dernier métro*). Its iconography nevertheless carefully reproduces some of the icons associated with the period: dresses for women, sweaters for men, Black Citroen Traction cars (with FFI painted on), newspapers with pictures of de Gaulle, popular film magazines, and so on. It thus takes its place within this important sub-genre of French cinema.[10] Rather than focussing on the Liberation as sign of hope and renewal, *Uranus* focusses on its negative aftermath, symbolized by the ruins carefully displayed at the beginning of the film.

In this respect, a comparison with *Les Portes de la nuit* (1946), directed by Marcel Carné, based on a script by Jacques Prévert is useful. *Les Portes de la nuit* is set in Paris in 1945. Strongly driven by the aesthetic features of Poetic Realism, the film creates a visual universe which refers back to the pre-War period. However its narrative tries to come to terms with the aftermath of the War by evoking conflicts among the 'little people' of a popular area of Paris (the environs of the Canal Saint-Martin). As in Poetic Realist films of the 1930s, the film juxtaposes a couple of idealistic young lovers (Yves Montand and Nathalie Nattier) and the inhabitants of the area, played by such character actors as Saturnin Fabre and Carette. This is one way such films formulate the poetic/realist duality in Poetic Realism.

Les Portes de la nuit, made around the time of the writing of *Uranus*, is an interesting work to compare with *Uranus* from the perspective of how, forty-five years later, a fiction film for a popular audience tries to represent a community profoundly divided by the war experience, a community which in many ways is the audience itself. I will also draw some parallels with Henri-Georges Clouzot's *Le Corbeau* (1943), one of the few that can be seen to comment (however obliquely) on this issue. Clouzot, Carné and Aymé were all the target of anti-collaborationist criticism during the *épuration*, but it could also be argued that the uneasiness created by their films or writing related to their raising the then taboo issue of the 'Franco-French war'[11] created by the German Occupation and/or its aftermath.

The visual aspect of each film echoes the idea of an enclosed microcosm as defined by the narrative: *Uranus*, *Les Portes de la nuit* and *Le Corbeau*, all start with large-scale, aerial or high-angle views of the town, and then zoom in to a detail of the town – a square, a building, a métro station – to remain within the community for the rest of the film. They also end (with the exception of *Le Corbeau*, strictly speaking) with a reverse movement. Thus the visual construction of the town makes it a self-enclosed and distant world but, at the same time, it elevates it to universal status. In *Uranus* and *Le Corbeau*, this is reinforced by the anonymity of the town, while paradoxically in *Les Portes de la nuit* the same effect is achieved by the 'universalizing' iconic status of Paris. The first and last shots of *Uranus* take in a square with the war memorial, and end pointedly on a ceremony at this monument, which symbolizes death, but also evokes nostalgia for the heroes of the First World War when France had been heroic. (Aymé's novel ends in a low key fashion by comparison: characters are having a good gossip at a café while Gaigneux and Loin walk to the gendarmerie.)

A Return to the Tradition of Quality or a Heritage Movie?

Uranus, like Berri's earlier *Jean de Florette* and *Manon des sources*, has frequently been compared to the 'tradition of quality' of the classic French cinema, and especially the literary adaptations of the 1950s, because of the dimension of performance, smooth and virtuoso camera-work and its use of literary adaptation. Indeed *Uranus*, like *Les Portes de la nuit*, reflects high production values: its fluid camera movements are virtually always put to the service of the actors. The films also share a predominance of long takes combined with two- and three-shots rather than close-ups and rapid cross-cutting.

The classical French cinema, and particularly the 'tradition of quality', is a cinema highly involved in performance, especially by male actors, who tend to become implicated in definitions of national identity, as can be seen by the star personas of Jean Gabin and Gérard Depardieu. A comparison between *Uranus* and *Les Portes de la nuit* shows continuities which confer the label of tradition of quality on *Uranus*, as well as differences, which are indicative of important shifts in recent French cinema, both in generic terms and in terms of its modes of historical representation. *Les Portes de la nuit* used for its depiction of its 'little world' a number of the so-called 'eccentrics'[12] of French cinema, namely actors who were ever-present, who were associated with a particular social type, and who rarely had leading parts but were very popular and thus constituted another type of stardom. Saturnin Fabre, Carette and Raymond Bussières in *Les Portes de la nuit* can be considered such 'eccentrics'. Philippe Noiret, Fabrice Luchini, Michel Blanc, Jean-Pierre Marielle can be seen as later examples of the phenomenon. In this respect, *Uranus* continues this tradition of classical French cinema. Another particular feature uncannily links the two films: *Les Portes de la nuit* and *Uranus* portray a father and a son who were both collaborators during the Occupation; in both cases the son tried to become an eleventh-hour *résistant*. Both films have a scene in which father and son exchange a traumatic double accusation, with, in each case, the failure of the father matched by the hopelessness of the son. This proposes a symbolic discourse on the effect of the War on the social fabric of France, in which, interestingly, both generations are equally guilty.

These thematic similarities, however, must be contrasted with other differences which point in the direction of a loss of historicity in the more recent film. The lovers of *Les Portes de la nuit* are romantic dreamers rather than agents of change, but are nevertheless animated by a desire to escape their surroundings, even though, as is typical of the pessimistic Carné-Prévert universe, this desire is 'doomed'. In *Uranus*, this desire itself has disappeared, levelling all characters to the same position. This is also true of performance. In films of the classical period, performance types were more obviously related to social types in a cinema which was trying to recreate a cinematic social universe, however stylized. Thus, though *Les Portes de la nuit* shows similar divisions, pettiness and mediocrity in its community as *Uranus* does, these divisions are subsumed by a dominant narrative discourse connected to the fate of the lovers who embody absolute goodness. The male hero (here Montand in a part written for Gabin) is meant to be an incarnation of the community with its contradictions, and to offer identification by reconciling these. In *Uranus*, none of the male characters, including Léopold (Depardieu), can be said to condense the world of the film. The performances of the 'eccentrics' in classical cinema existed in a hierarchical relation to that of the stars. In *Uranus*, despite Depardieu's star status, there is no such hierarchy. In the same way as no single character embodies a dominant discourse, performances are juxtaposed to each other; each actor does a 'number'. This is in line with the 'checks and balances' narrative structure discussed above, but it points to something else.

In *Uranus*, history is seen neither 'from above' – from an ideal hero's point of view – nor 'from below' – from the level of the quotidian.

It occupies a middle, truly 'mediocre' space. But *Uranus* is a film of its time in generic terms too. The representation of this cowardly, mediocre 'France profonde'[13] has moved from the accusatory mode of *Le Chagrin et la Pitié* and the popular exposé of the rétro movies such as *Lacombe Lucien*, to the celebratory mode of many heritage films. *Uranus* is a pleasurable, comfortable film, and was received as such in France. Apart from reviews in *L'Humanité*, *Libération* and *Le Monde diplomatique*, reactions to *Uranus* were positive, provoking very little debate compared to the earlier exposé films. As Serge Daney put it: '[P]aradoxically, it is this non-event which was the event "of the film".'[14] By December 1990, the trauma of the War in terms of the resistance–collaboration conflict can be said to be finally 'over', as far as its popular representations are concerned. If Aymé's novel documented – in a fictional form – the 'mediocrity' of the *France profonde* environment of most of the war experience, Berri's celebrates it. This is due to Berri's use of the generic features of the film, the heritage film often presenting a beautiful, but sanitized and non-conflictual picture of its depicted historical events.[15] It is a feature uncannily anticipated by Aymé himself, who puts in Watrin's lips, at the end of the novel, a tirade on his state of mind (and that of France), which could serve as a comment on the aesthetic 'façade' of Berri's film, and is worth reproducing in full:

> I often enjoy looking inside myself. It looks like a beautiful, spacious shop, incredibly opulent and full of dazzling treasures. But order is far from perfect. Despite plenty of cupboards, endless drawers and keen assistants, it often looks messy. One thing however is always perfectly tidy and polished, and that is the shop window. This is because its point is to please passers-by, to attract them without humiliating or antagonizing them. In short, the shop window must be what passers-by want it to be. [...] Right now, they are not brilliant, but it won't last forever. Just wait a little. Just wait fifty years...[16]

Another aspect of Berri's *Uranus* turns Aymé's vitriolic pamphlet into a less contentious and more celebratory portrait of the Liberation and *épuration* period, and that is its relation to communism. While, as I have said, Berri's film tones down the anti-communism of Aymé's novel, it nevertheless retains its condemnation of the Communists' dogmatic and violent behaviour while mostly exonerating collaborationists. As such, *Uranus* (the film) is part of the backlash against communism and left ideologies characteristic of 1980s/1990s France. But there is something else. The choice of this particular book for a 1990 film, under its apparently polemical surface, was an eminently safe one as the novel rehearses now well-known events and traumas, and ignores the really traumatic Second World War topic which resurfaced throughout the 1980s, namely the Vichy government and the French population's involvement in anti-Semitic policies. If this seems surprising on a personal level, considering Berri's Jewishness, it is on the other hand typical of the heritage film's resistance to tackling deeply divisive issues. As in Aymé's prophetic 'shop window' quoted above, fifty years after the writing of the book, anti-communism acts as a screen to attract spectators, without 'humiliating or antagonizing' them.

Notes

Unless stated otherwise, the place of publication is Paris.

1. Michel Goret, 'La Rue sans nom', *Cinémonde*, October 1993, quoted in Pierrette Matalon, Claude Guiguet, and Jacques Pinturault (eds), *Pierre Chenal*, Editions Dujarric, 1987, p.56
2. *Studio magazine*, November 1992.
3. *L'Année du cinéma*, 1991.
4. Jean-Pierre Rioux, *La France de la Quatrième République: l'ardeur et la nécessité 1944–1952*, Seuil, 1980.
5. Christopher Lloyd, *Uranus, La Tête des autres*, Glasgow, University of Glasgow French & German Publications, 1994, p.15.
6. Rioux, *La France de la Quatrième République*, p.186.
7. *Le Quotidien de Paris*, 12 December 1990.
8. Lloyd, *Uranus, La Tête des Autres*, p.67.
9. Brigitte Friang, quoted in Hélène Eck, 'Les Françaises sous Vichy', in Georges Duby and Michelle Perrot (eds), *Histoire des femmes, Le XXᵉ siècle*, Plon, 1992, p.197.
10. Cf. Henry Rousso, *The Vichy Syndrome, History and Memory in France since 1944*, London, Harvard University Press, 1991, and Jean-Pierre Jeancolas, 'Fonction du témoignage (les années 1939–1945 dans le cinéma de l'après guerre'), *Positif*, June 1975, pp.45–60.
11. Cf. Rousso, *The Vichy Syndrome*.
12. Cf. Raymond Chirat and Olivier Barrot, *Les Excentriques du cinéma français*, Henri Veyrier, 1983.
13. Claude Berri, interview, *Le Parisien*, 12 December 1990.
14. *Libération*, 12 December 1990.
15. Cf. Andrew Higson, 'Re-presenting the National Past: Nostalgia and Pastiche in the Heritage Film', in Lester Friedman (ed.),

British Cinema and Thatcherism, Minneapolis, University of Minnesota Press, 1993.

16. Marcel Aymé, *Uranus*, Gallimard, 1948, Folio edition, pp.376–7.

Notes on Contributors

Karen Adler's doctoral research at the University of Sussex is on women and Jews in France after the Liberation. Her publications include 'Responses to the 50th Anniversaries of Liberation', *Modern and Contemporary France*, 1995, and reports on the convent at Auschwitz and on the French far Right, *IJA Research Reports*, 1989 and 1990.

Nicholas Atkin, Lecturer in History at the University of Reading, is author of *Church and Schools in Vichy France, 1940–1944* (New York, Garland, 1991), and co-editor of *Religion, Society and Politics in France since 1789*, (London, Hambledon, 1991).

Richard D.E. Burton, Reader in French in the School of African and Asian Studies at the University of Sussex, has published widely on Baudelaire and the French West Indies. He is the author of *La Famille coloniale. La Martinique et la Mère-Patrie, 1789–1992* (Paris, L'Harmattan, 1994).

Tony Chafer, Principal Lecturer in French Studies at the University of Portsmouth, has published articles on French relations with sub-Saharan Africa. He is currently writing a book on decolonization in French West Africa. He is co-editor of *Modern and Contemporary France*.

Martyn Cornick, of the Department of European Studies at Loughborough University, is an editor of *Modern and Contemporary France*. He has published widely on French intellectual history and Anglo-French relations.

Hanna Diamond, Lecturer in French History at Bath University, has published articles on French women's experiences during and after the Second World War, the subject of her doctoral thesis. She also works on oral history.

Philip Dine, Lecturer in French at Loughborough University, is the author of *Images of the Algerian War: French Fiction and Film, 1954–1992* (Oxford, Clarendon Press, 1994). In addition to decolonization, his research interests include sport and popular culture in France.

Martin Evans, Lecturer in French Studies at the University of Portsmouth, has recently completed his doctorate at Sussex University on the French Résistance to the Algerian war. Currently he is part of a research team at Portsmouth University exploring the impact of colonialism on French national identity.

Hilary Footitt, Head of Languages at the University of Westminster, has published on the politics of Liberation (1943–45), on the home front in the Second World War, and on women in the Resistance.

John Flower, Professor of French at the University of Exeter, has published extensively on authors as varied as Mauriac, Bernanos and Vailland. He is also author of *Writers and Politics in France* and *Literature of the Left*. His study, *Pierre Courtade: the making of a party scribe* is to be published in 1995. He is general editor of *The Journal of European Studies*.

Claire Gorrara, Lecturer in French at the University of Wales College of Cardiff, has recently completed her doctoral thesis at Oxford University, entitled 'A Woman's Occupation: French Women Writers and Representations of the Occupation in Post-1968 France'.

Nicholas Hewitt, Professor of French at the University of Nottingham, has published extensively on authors such as Céline, Malraux and Troyat, as well as on literary and cultural history. His book on the literature of the French post-War Right is to be published by Berg in 1995.

Norman Ingram, Assistant Professor of History at Concordia University in Montreal, is author of *The Politics of Dissent: Pacifism in France, 1919–1939* (Oxford, Clarendon Press, 1991), and several articles on French Pacifism.

H.R. Kedward, Professor of History at the University of Sussex is author of *Resistance in Vichy France* (Oxford, Oxford University Press, 1978); *Occupied France* (Oxford, Blackwell, 1985); *In Search of the Maquis* (Oxford, Oxford University Press, 1993), and many articles on French Resistance.

Michael Kelly, Professor of French at the University of Southampton, has published widely on French cultural studies and intellectual history, including books on the Catholic philosopher Emmanuel Mounier, French Marxist philosophy, and the reception of Hegel in France. His book *French Cultural Studies: an introduction*, edited with Jill Forbes, will shortly be published by Oxford University Press.

William Kidd, Senior Lecturer in French at the University of Stirling, has published extensively on twentieth-century French literature and ideology, war and memory, and psychocriticism.

Notes on Contributors

Simon Kitson's doctoral research at the University of Sussex concerns the Police in Marseille from the Popular Front to the Liberation. His publications include 'La Reconstitution de la police marseillaise (août 1944 à février 1945)', *Provence Historique*, January 1995.

Corran Laurens, doctoral research student at the University of Southampton, is researching the cultural history of the Liberation period, particularly the representation of women from 1944–49.

Martin O'Shaughnessy, Lecturer in French and European Studies at the Nottingham Trent University, has published widely in the areas of French cinema, literature and ideology, political discourse and racism and education.

Judith K. Proud, Principal Lecturer and Subject Leader in French at the University of Plymouth, has recently published a book on propaganda fiction for children in Vichy France, and is author of a number of articles on French publishing history.

J.C. Simmonds, Assistant Dean in the School of European and International Studies at the University of Derby, has researched and written on France in the Second World War, and published with Hilary Footitt, *The Politics of Liberation: France 1943–1945*. He also works on political history in the post-War period.

Jill Sturdee, Course Tutor in French at the Open University, is currently completing her doctoral thesis at the University of Sussex on the effects of the Nazi Occupation on the children of Caen.

Carrie Tarr, Principal Lecturer in French and Media Studies at Thames Valley University, has published articles on gender and ethnicity in French and British cinema.

Ginette Vincendeau, Professor in Film Studies at the University of Warwick, is co-author of *Jean Gabin, Anatomie d'un mythe* (1993) and co-editor of *French Film: Texts and Contexts*. She is currently editing the *BFI/Cassell Encyclopedia of European Cinema*.

Nancy Wood, Lecturer in Media Studies in the School of European Studies at the University of Sussex, is co-editor of *In Search of Central Europe* (Cambridge, Polity, 1989). She teaches and writes on media and collective memory in post-War Europe.

Index

Index

Bernard-Derosne, Jean 205
Berri, Claude 347–58 *passim*
Bertin, Célia 95, 96, 175
Bertin-Maghit, Jean-Pierre 23, 104
Bertrand, Emile 36
Bidault, Georges 50, 271, 278
Binet, René 287
Blanc, Michel 348, 351, 355
Blanzat, Jean 183, 185
Blondin, Antoine 290, 292, 294
Blum, Léon 130, 257, 259
Bohec, Jeanne 145
Boico, Christine 35
Boisset, Yves 273
Boisson, Governor-General 242
Bonnard, Abel 185
Bouchard, Pierre 306
Boudiaf, Mohammed 264
Boulenger, Jacques 185
Boulogne 277
Bourdet, Claude 185–6, 273
Bourget, Paul 291
Boutang, Pierre 192, 294
Boyer, Pierre 3
Brasillach, Robert 8, 190, 285, 347, 351
Brassens, Georges 175
Braun, Madeleine 136–7
Brazzaville 242, 243, 246, 250, 262
Brédiger, Mme 300
Brel, Jacques 323
Breslau 305
Britain 70, 211, 243
Britton, Celia 277
Brive, Marie-France 78, 91
Brosman, Catherine 276
Brossat, Alain x, 6, 176, 309, 311, 314–17
Bruckberger, Père 158
Bruller, Jean (Vercors) 190, 274, 288
Brunellière, Mgr Varin de la 227
Burlingham, Dorothy 301
Bussières, Raymond 355

Caen 297–308
Calvados 217
Calvo 63–9
Cambridge 328
Camus, Albert 120, 269, 288
Cannes 16, 309
Capa, Robert 174
Capelle, Jean 245
Capy, Marcelle 210, 212
Carette 353, 355
Caribbean 227, 228, 232, 234

Carné, Marcel 104, 353–4, 355
Carovis, Monsieur 96
Caruth, Cathy 318
Cassou, Jean 185, 190–1, 192
Catroux, Governor-General 261
Cazou, Madame 95
Ceadel, Martin 210
Céline, Louis-Ferdinand 288, 294
Chaban-Delmas, Jacques 48
Chack, Paul 190
Chagrin et la Pitié Le 273, 351, 356
Challaye, Félicien 210–11, 213, 214, 215, 219
Chalon-sur-Saône 19, 21
Chambon, Charles 52
Champion, Jeanne 335–46
Chamson, André 290
Chantilly 106
Chardonne, Jacques 290, 293
Charlemagne 286
Charpentier, Armand 210
Chartres 156, 169, 174
Château-Jobert 271
Châteaubriant, Alphonse de 185
Chenal, Pierre 347
Cherbourg 166, 302
Chiappe, Jean 47
Choltitz, Dietrich von 49, 203–4
Christian-Jaque 103,109
Churchill, Winston 67, 70, 261
Clarence, Nicole 77
Clavel, Bernard 275
Clay, Philippe 324
Clemenceau, Georges 236
Clément, René 15, 23, 25, 104
Clerempuy, René 231
Clermont-Ferrand 1
Clouzot, Henri-Georges 353
Cocteau, Jean 289, 291
Cogniot, Georges 50
Cohn-Bendit, Daniel 324, 332
Colette 106
Colin, Lucien and Marcel 304
Colin, Paul 117–18
Collin, Claude 33
Compiègne 215
Constantinois 262, 263
Contat, Michel 276
Corbasson, Lieut-Col Gaston 304; Jean-Paul 298, 299, 301, 302, 304
Corrèze 2
Corsica 2, 3
Côte d'Ivoire 243, 245
Coudert, Marie-Louise 77

Index

Index

Index

Index